PHalarope Books

PHalarope books are designed specifically for the amateur naturalist. These volumes represent excellence in natural history publishing. Each book in the PHalarope series is based on a nature course or program at the college or adult education level or is sponsored by a museum or nature center. Each PHalarope book reflects the author's teaching ability as well as writing ability.

Exploring Tropical
Isles and Seas

Exploring Tropical Isles and Seas

An Introduction for the Traveler and Amateur Naturalist

Frederic Martini

A Spectrum Book

Prentice-Hall, Inc., Englewood Cliffs, New Jersey 07632

Library of Congress Cataloging in Publication Data

Martini, Frederic.
    Exploring tropical isles and seas.

    (PHalarope books)
    "A Spectrum Book."
    Bibliography: p.
    Includes index.
    1. Tropics—Description and travel.   2. Natural
history—Tropics.   I. Title.
G905.M37 1984   910'.0913   83-27244
ISBN 0-13-295949-6
ISBN 0-13-295931-3 (pbk.)

10   9   8   7   6   5   4   3   2   1

Production/editing supervision: Marlys Lehmann
Book design: Alice R. Mauro
Cover design: Hal Siegel
Manufacturing buyer: Doreen Cavallo

This book is available at a special discount
when ordered in bulk quantities. Contact Prentice-Hall, Inc.,
General Publishing Division, Special Sales,
Englewood Cliffs, N.J. 07632.

Prentice-Hall International, Inc., *London*
Prentice-Hall of Australia Pty. Limited, *Sydney*
Prentice-Hall Canada Inc., *Toronto*
Prentice-Hall of India Private Limited, *New Delhi*
Prentice-Hall of Japan, Inc., *Tokyo*
Prentice-Hall of Southeast Asia Pte., Ltd., *Singapore*
Whitehall Books Limited, *Wellington, New Zealand*
Editora Prentice-Hall do Brasil Ltda., *Rio de Janeiro*

ISBN 0-13-295949-6

ISBN 0-13-295931-3 {PBK.}

This book is dedicated
to all who dream of tropical isles,
but especially to those who follow their dreams.

Contents

Preface   xi

Acknowledgments   xiii

Introduction   xv

PART ONE   THE LIFE IN TROPICAL SEAS

Chapter One
The Tropical Environment   3

Chapter Two
Coral Reefs and Islands   24

Chapter Three
The Marine Fishes   48

Chapter Four
The Infamous Sharks   77

Chapter Five
Marine Reptiles and Mammals   93

Chapter Six
The Reef Environment   136

PART TWO   ISLANDS IN PARADISE   169

Chapter Seven
The Life of an Island   111

Chapter Eight
Island Arcs and Chains   195

Chapter Nine
A Review of Tropical Island Groups   223
   The Tropical Pacific Islands   230
   The Tropical Atlantic Islands   285

Appendix: Advice Concerning Tropical Hazards   342

Glossary   386

Additional Readings   394

Credits   398

Index   401

Preface

The traveler interested in natural history will find that the tropics provide an ideal setting for becoming acquainted with the basic principles of biology, geology, and climatology. Any tropical island provides innumerable illustrations and examples, and this book will introduce you to them, using practical terms. No formal training in the physical or biological sciences is required, and all you need is an active imagination and an appreciation for crystalline waters and unusual scenery.

Part I talks about the tropical climate and the life found in tropical waters. We explore the reef environment and become familiar with the diverse plants and animals that can be found using a mask and snorkel. We also discuss the whales and sea cows that spend part or all of their lives relaxing in the tropics. Throughout this portion of the book you will be introduced to patterns of form and behavior, and in the closing chapter these are interwoven to produce a three-dimensional picture of life around tropical islands.

Part II relates the varied appearance of an individual island to the natural forces that are creating, shaping, and destroying islands and entire island groups. With this information at hand you will be able to make accurate predictions about the structure and climate of any island you might visit, and this will enable you to plan your itinerary appropriately. Specific information about most of the inhabited islands of the tropical Atlantic and Pacific is provided in condensed form, and an appendix presents advice concerning health and safety while traveling through these areas.

This book will also answer your questions as your trip progresses. Are you worried about sharks? Read Chapter 4 and get a better perspective. Are you amazed at the colors of reef fishes? Zero in on Chapter 3 for some explanations. Do you marvel at spectacular waterfalls? Check Chapter 7 and find out how they form and age. Did a mild tremor jar your morning coffee? Review Chapter 8 and see what's happening. And if you wonder about the local drinking water, regional medical services, or whether or not you can fly/sail/cruise to a nearby island, you will find the answers in the closing portions of the book. The intention is to inform and entertain and in the process make your travels safer and more rewarding.

Acknowledgments

Dr. Kathleen Welch provided invaluable assistance with the overall editing and with the organization of the appendix dealing with medically related topics. Dr. Joseph N. Schneider, Jr. provided data concerning medical facilities in the tropical Atlantic, and Continental Travel of Bradenton, Florida, assisted with the location of air and ship facilities. Fred Martini and Betty Martini, my parents, were also helpful during the design and editing stages. Various illustrations throughout the volume are the work of Dennis Strasser, whose efforts are deeply appreciated. Special thanks are due to Russell M. Nilson, president, and the staff of Marine Environmental Research (MER) with whom many of my research and teaching programs were conducted. Finally, I would like to thank Mary Kennan and the staff of the General Publishing Division for their expertise and assistance with the preparation of this book.

Photographic Credits

By the author: Figs. 2–4 (c); 2–5 (b); 2–6 (c); 4–4; 7–3 (c); 7–5 (b); 7–13 (c)(d)(e); Plates I; IIIb, c, d, VI, IX, X (left), XI

By the author and R. Mitchell Nilson: Figs. 5–2 (upper and lower left); 7–2 (lower); Plates IIIa, IV, V

By MER staff, including the author, R.M. Nilson, Ronald Harelstad, Betty Martini, and William Norfleet: Figs. 2–6 (a)(b); 7–2 (upper and middle); 7–3 (b); 7–5 (a); 7–6 (b)(d); 7–7 (b)

By Claude Tellef: Figs. 2–5 (a)(d); Plates II, VII (right), VIII, X (right)

By Wayne D. Lord: Fig. 5–2 (upper and lower right)

Introduction

This book focuses attention on islands in the Atlantic and Pacific oceans found between the Tropic of Cancer and the Tropic of Capricorn. Most of the world's islands lie within these boundaries, yet altogether their dry land approximates only that of the state of California and is scattered across oceans that cover almost 60 percent of the earth's surface at these latitudes.

Organized scientific exploration of these oceans did not begin until the nineteenth century. The *Beagle* expedition (1831–1836) only scratched the surface, yet provided a wealth of biological and geological information. The far more substantive and analytical efforts of the *Challenger* expedition (1872–1876) represented the first oceanographic research cruise. This period of exploration continues to the present day and will not end in the foreseeable future.

The basic problem is one of sheer size. All the dry land areas of the world combined would amount to only 57 percent of the areas covered by the Atlantic and Pacific oceans. Our basic geographical knowledge is still incomplete, even with the help of satellite photos. Several of the nautical charts now used in the southwestern Pacific are reproductions of Captain Bligh's original survey reports, and many more recent charts leave even the coastlines of several islands without form. Our mapping of the ocean floor is even further from completion, with only a negligible percentage charted in topographic detail. These limitations are all too familiar to modern sailors, who must face chart notations such as "Incorrectly Charted," "Island Not in Charted Position," "Existence Doubtful," or even "Not Intended for Use in Navigation" on dark and stormy nights.

Other basic discoveries await us in the biological sciences. With an average depth of 12,000 feet, the oceans are not only enormous in expanse but also in volume. Totally new and unexpected creatures, such as the giant megamouth shark accidentally snagged in a Navy sea-anchor, will continue to appear to the delight of specialists and those who long for a real sea monster.

Although there is still much to be learned, recent decades have seen an information explosion in the fields of biology and geology. Over this same period, tourism in the tropics has been increasing, and even the more remote islands are now accessible to the adventurous traveler. Relaxing in the warm waters or hiking around the island, the visitor is surrounded by beauty that represents the animate and inanimate expression of underlying principles. The chapters that follow consider a number of these in detail, but before we begin, some perspective on the volume as a whole will prove useful.

Part I: Because of the enormous surface area, the tropical oceans play a key role in determining the physical and biological conditions found on the entire plant. The surface waters trap and store solar energy in the form of heat, which may be transported by surface currents to other areas or more widely distributed by radiation or evaporation into the atmosphere. The transfer of energy to the overlying air masses powers the global wind machines that modify regional climates and establish global weather patterns. Friction between the moving air and the surface waters produces waves, which eventually cause a slow movement of the underlying waters. It is these oceanic currents that distribute warmth, nutrients, dissolved gases, and the forms of life that these support across the oceans of the world. The interrelationships between temperature, winds, and currents are considered in Chapter 1, because they provide a backdrop for the discussions of both the first and second parts of the book.

As is the case on land, plant life forms the basis for life in the sea. But unlike the situation ashore, the most important marine plants may be the most difficult to spot. As you might predict, plants are restricted to the sunlit upper portions of the ocean. The most conventional-appearing marine plants, the seaweeds, are usually limited to shallow areas that provide stable platforms for attachment. In the open ocean, suitable habitats are few and far between. The most important marine plants are microscopic in size, floating in the moving surface waters. They are members of the *plankton*, a collection of small plants and animals that drift wherever the currents may take them.

While the surface waters of the tropical ocean are capturing solar energy, powering wind machines, establishing weather patterns, and transporting animate and inanimate materials, the plants of the plankton are using sunlight for photosynthesis. This helps to replenish the oceanic and atmospheric oxygen required by animals. As these tiny plants grow and reproduce, they are packaging solar energy in a form that can support all the more familiar forms of marine life, from the tiniest anchovies to the largest whales.

Even on the shallow, sunlit platforms around tropical islands, it is the microscopic plants that are of primary importance. Coral reefs, despite their superficial resemblance to forests, are produced by colonies of small animals. One of the keys to the success of these reef builders is their curious partnership with microscopic plants that grow and reproduce within the tissues of their coral hosts. The plants get a nicely protected environment with fringe benefits, and the corals gain an assortment of nutrients and oxygen. Because of their dependence on this partnership, reef-building corals are restricted to clear, sunlit surface waters—darker, deeper waters let too little light reach the plants. Turbid waters can cause problems as well. Corals do not rely solely on their plant associates, for they also capture food from the surrounding water. Because a coral colony can't simply pick up and leave when local conditions change, nor can it easily dust itself off, a thick coating of debris, mud, or sand will not only block out light but will also make feeding impossible.

Coral reefs similar to those we find today first appeared around 200 million years ago and spread with varying success throughout tropical seas. Corals have fairly straightforward requirements for survival, which can be summarized as warm, clear waters and a shallow but solid foundation on which to build a reef capable of withstanding the impact of ocean waves. If these criteria are met and remain stable, colonies of coral animals can produce massive reef complexes that endure for tens of millions of years, even after the island that originally supported them has disappeared. The biology of the reef-building corals, their physical structure, and their overall success are the topics of Chapter 2.

The branching limbs, massive blocks, and delicate plates of the reef provide a complex environment for a variety of other animals that have adapted to these surroundings. When first snorkeling over a shallow coral reef you will probably be astounded by the number and variety of marine fishes. Fishes are by far the most successful of humanity's vertebrate relatives, and they live in an environment that is very different from our own. At first glance, and often at second, it can be rather difficult to sort out the different sizes, shapes, and colors into recognizable patterns. Some advertise their presence with bizarre shapes and brilliant colors, whereas others may be indistinguishable from the rocks among which they live. They may be as large as a refrigerator, or as small as a pearl; round as a soccerball or sleek as a torpedo. Yet each is faced with the same basic problems: finding food, avoiding enemies, and producing little fishes.

Most fish, like most people, move around in their environment and they must breathe, eat, grow, compete, and reproduce to be considered successful. But fish live within the constraints imposed by a medium that is very different from "thin air." Because water is relatively dense, movement through the water is more difficult, and streamlining is more important than is the case for terrestrial animals such as ourselves. Moving *water* is also more difficult than moving air, and because the oxygen content of water is relatively low most fish use a lot of energy just managing to breathe. Over 20,000 species have evolved unique physical, physiological, and/or behavioral strategies in response to these limitations. No one aspect of any animal's life can be examined in isolation, and Chapter 3 examines the interaction of strategies for locomotion, feeding, self-defense, and reproduction in the marine fishes.

Many visitors arrive with an almost overwhelming paranoia about sharks. Although sharks are certainly worthy of respect, it is reassuring to note that far more people are struck by lightning, sucked into tornadoes, or attacked by killer bees each year than are killed by sharks in a decade. Nevertheless, sharks are fascinating creatures, once thought to be primitive and now seen as being among the most highly advanced and specialized fishes. Understanding more about them and the sensory systems they possess should help to ease cases of tropical "fin-phobia," so the biology, physiology, and behavior of sharks are the topic of Chapter 4.

We have other relatives, somewhat less distant, in tropical waters. Marine reptiles such as the sea turtles and marine mammals, including whales, seals, and sea cows, may be found around reefs either as occasional visitors or permanent residents. Although you might not encounter these animals while snorkeling, they are often seen from boats or from vantage points ashore. With the probable exception of the sea snakes, humans have had an even greater effect on these animals than on the reefs themselves, and in most areas marine reptile and mammal populations are retreating or declining. Some aspects of the biology of these beasts and a discussion of their current prospects for survival are presented in Chapter 5.

We are members of a motley assemblage of larger-than-average animals collectively known as *vertebrates*. Vertebrates include the fishes, amphibians, reptiles, birds, and mammals—all animals no doubt familiar to you. Being large animals ourselves, we tend to notice other large animals first. On the reefs we spot the fishes, and in the forests we watch for the occasional deer or bear. But despite our naturally "vertebrat-o-centric" outlook, these are not the most important and successful creatures on the planet. If you were to count heads (or oral surfaces, front ends, or whatever is appropriate) you would find that 95 percent of the one million animal species are "others."

This relatively silent majority is rather arrogantly grouped by us as *invertebrates*. These legions may be sorted out into more than thirty major evolutionary lines, called *phyla* (plural of *phylum*), each containing a variety of different body forms and lifestyles, and each as distinct from other phyla as fishes and frogs are from corals and jellyfish. Several phyla of invertebrates will be seen by the novice on an afternoon's snorkel, and because these are rather diverse we will examine them with an eye toward their functional roles in the reef community.

Any biological system, even an entire coral reef, operates on a fixed budget. A certain amount of solar energy is available to the plants, and only a percentage of that amount is subsequently available to the animals of the community. Thus a coral reef can be viewed as a biological system whose plant and animal members interact to maximize the use of solar energy. This energy is trapped and converted to biological materials by the plants, and the animals may feed either on the plants or on one another. The bodies of the dead and the waste products of the living provide an alternative, recycled source of energy. Over hundreds of millions of years the varied inhabitants of the reef have specialized to increase their chances of obtaining a portion of the available energy. How their different feeding and foraging techniques interact to produce a balanced and healthy reef system is an interesting study in ecology and evolution, and Chapter 6 considers these topics in detail. In doing so it synthesizes information presented in earlier chapters and completes the first part of this book.

Part II: To the nonspecialist all coral reefs look pretty much alike, and you will still see parrotfish, butterflyfishes, and wrasses whether you are snorkeling in Hawaii or Grand Cayman. This is because all tropical reefs are united by the basic living requirements of the coral animals. Since the appearance of their islands above the water is of little consequence to the corals, the islands on which reefs are built may look very different. The low, ring-shaped islets of the northern Tuamotus, the volcanic peaks of Hawaii, the sandy bars and banks of the southern Bahamas, the verdant slopes of Samoa, Fiji, or Jamaica— each island has a distinctive character of its own. For hundreds of years geologists and biologists have sought a coherent theory that could predict the similarities and explain the differences between the varied tropical islands. With the acceptance of the theory of continental drift, more properly called *plate tectonics*, we have begun to understand some of the principles involved. The realization that continents are not eternally fixed in position, but that they are more often moving, growing, fragmenting, combining, colliding, or sliding past one another has profoundly altered our basic assumptions about geology, geography, and evolution. Islands are now seen as extremely dynamic structures uplifted by the collision of massive plates or born of volcanic activities deep beneath the ocean floor.

Although it may suddenly appear above the surface of the sea, it takes quite some time to make a pile of lava extending 12,000 to 14,000 feet above the ocean floor. While this lava is accumulating, or if volcanic activity ceases before the embryonic island reaches the surface, the volcanic slopes may be detected by an oceanographic survey ship and recorded as a submerged seamount. Virtually as soon as the volcano reaches the surface it begins to be destroyed by erosion, from above by rain and wind and from below by the pounding of waves along the shoreline. Over time the island may settle slowly into the sea, exposing new portions of its flanks to the waves and drowning the river valleys that drain its upper slopes. If the erosional and subsiding processes continue unabated, the island will eventually disappear beneath the surface once more. The seas then march across the peak of the island, leveling it and producing a seamount with a distinctly flattened top.

Variations on this basic theme of emergence, erosions, and subsidence are common. In tropical waters modifications often result from the activities of coral animals. Assuming that the favorable conditions of temperature, water clarity, and so forth, persist, once a coral reef has established itself along the shores of an island it will continue to grow toward the surface as the island settles. Even when the island itself has disappeared beneath the waves, the surf along the reef will remain to mark its former location. As the reef continues to become more massive, storm-tossed debris and sand may accumulate on its upper surface to form a reef island or *atoll* that shows no traces of its volcanic foundations.

There are several less predictable sources of variation. Fluctuations in sea level have been relatively common. Each time glaciers form sea level falls hundreds of feet, air-drying coral reefs and exposing new portions of the slopes to the waves. At the same time, the lowered water temperatures may discourage the reestablishment of coral reefs until the climate warms and sea level rises once again. At any time during the life of an island renewed volcanic activity can create a larger island alongside of or on top of an older island, and more dramatic movements of the ocean floor may lift an island or drop it thousands of feet in a (geologically) short time. Any and all of these events interact in a complex fashion to produce the characteristic structure of an individual island. Chapter 7 examines the life of an island and considers a number of case studies in island history.

Typical midocean volcanoes form over localized hotspots, which are areas of intense activity in the molten mantle layers beneath the ocean floor. Probably the most accessible and best-known of the midocean volcanoes are those of the Hawaiian Archipelago. Conveniently enough, these islands have clearly recorded the effects of the forces that are creating, shaping, and destroying them. The Hawaiian islands formed over a stationary hotspot, but although the hotspot stands still most of the Pacific ocean floor is being driven to the northwest. The net result is a string of islands in a line that reflects the direction of movement of the ocean floor. In traveling from the erupting volcano of Kilauea on the island of Hawaii to the submerged seamounts at the other end of the chain one can span roughly 4,000 miles and 70+ million years of geological and biological history. Hotspots can occur in other locations and produce island or seamount chains like those at Easter Island, Ascension Island, or St. Paul's Rocks, but their histories and fates are comparable.

Island groups such as Tonga, the Marianas, and the Greater Antilles formed in a very different manner. These island arcs are characteristic of zones of compression, where continental and/or oceanic plates are colliding and oceanic crustal materials are being recycled. The lava released differs in chemical nature from that found over hotspots, and as a result island arcs and chains are structurally distinct. Chapter 8 takes a close look at the modern interpretation of plate tectonics, and shows what these concepts can tell us about the geological history of tropical island groups.

The modern island societies were shaped as immigration, emigration, and/or conquest incorporated the technology, religions, and standards of European societies into cultural frameworks established long before. The opening portions of Chapter 9 provide a brief history of the tropical Pacific and Atlantic islands before moving on to a detailed examination of individual island groups. There is information on island size, height, formation, climate, reef structure, weather, politics, language, accessibility, and much more of interest to the traveler and naturalist armed with the insights gained in earlier chapters.

These two parts share a unifying theme: All things change. A species evolves through interactions with an environment that includes other organisms as well as its physical surroundings. None of these relationships is fixed and immutable, because there is a continual interchange between the animate and inanimate components. A change in one species affects an entire community, and communities influence the gradual reshaping of the physical environment by natural forces. Nowhere is this interdependence more apparent than on tropical isles and in tropical seas.

Part One

The Life
in Tropical Seas

Chapter One

The Tropical Environment

In Part I you will become acquainted with some basic concepts in marine biology. Many are straightforward, others a trifle more devious, but all reflect the underlying truth that life is shaped by interactions with its surroundings. Although an environment has both living and nonliving components, it is really the physical characteristics that set the basic ground rules within which the living members of a community are free to develop. Because most of the important aspects of the tropical marine environment are beyond the influence of living creatures, at least in the open ocean, we need to examine these aspects before going on to more animated subjects.

Let's start with a basic fact about tropical life: the presence of abundant sunlight. From this given we will follow the increasingly intricate connections that set the stage for life in the tropics. Even in the tropics, sunlight is not evenly distributed. Because the earth's axis is not vertical with respect to the path of its orbit around the sun, each hemisphere experiences seasons, periods in which the sun appears to move north or south across the skies. The apparent direction of this solar movement reverses each year on 22 June, when the sun is over the Tropic of Cancer (latitude 23½°N) and on 22 December, when it reaches the Tropic of Capricorn (latitude 23½°S). These limits mark the approximate boundaries of the tropics, a region where the seasonal variations are slight and that receives a large and relatively constant share of the solar energy reaching the planet.

Because they cover 71 percent of its surface, most solar radiation strikes the oceans of the world rather than the continents, and this has a tremendous influence on the overall conditions of the planet. Dirt is an excellent insulator (i.e., a poor conductor of heat), so the surface of a continent heats and cools rapidly. There are deserts where temperatures reach 140°F by day, yet fall below freezing at night. By comparison sea water is an efficient conductor, and the oceans serve as a hot water bottle for the world. This stored heat is lost only gradually, and it has been estimated that if solar energy were to be completely cut off for an entire day the temperature of the surface waters would change by only about 0.1°.

Almost three-quarters of the surface of the globe between the tropical latitudes is covered by oceans. Because solar energy is ultimately
the basis for all life, how this energy is distributed is quite an important
question. For the moment we will ignore the seasonal meanderings of
the sun and consider the "average" condition, with the sun suspended
over the equator. We will also ignore the disturbances caused by the
continents and consider sunlight striking a planet covered entirely by
ocean. Now that we have eliminated most of the variables, let's switch
on the sun and see what happens on our model planet.

Out of the energy reaching it, fully 60 percent will be reflected into
space, primarily by clouds in the atmosphere. Most of the energy that
reaches the ocean surface is stored as heat, and the surface waters
gradually warm up. Because light only penetrates a few hundred yards
into even the clearest ocean waters, this warming is limited to the
upper portions of the ocean. Because of a quirk in the behavior of
fluids, it is here that this energy will remain; as is the case with air,
warm water is lighter, less dense than cold water, and the warm surface
waters float over the deeper waters with little interchange between the
two. The sharp temperature change that marks the density interface is
called a *thermocline*, but the separation actually has effects far beyond
simply temperature. The transfer of oxygen, nutrients, and other materials is greatly retarded as well, and in several respects the tropical
surface waters come to form a discrete subdivision of the world's
oceans. Figure 1–1 presents a few of the important results of this isolation, which will be examined in greater detail later in the chapter.

The solar heating of our model ocean will continue until the
amount of energy received by the surface waters is just balanced by the
amount lost by reradiation into the atmosphere. With a little time, and
a tractable computer, you could calculate what the surface temperatures should be at equilibrium as a function of latitude. The results are
not very satisfactory, for the calculated surface temperatures and the
real, measurable surface temperatures are quite different. The predicted equatorial temperature is warmer than the actual (91°F vs. 79°F),
whereas the polar temperature is far colder (−43°F vs. −9°F). It is clear
that much of the energy reaching the tropics is somehow winding up in
other regions. How is this accomplished?

On our model planet, energy transfer to the atmosphere should be
maximal near the equator, where surface temperatures are greatest,
and minimal at the poles, where temperatures should be lowest. The
air over the equatorial ocean is warmed by radiation from the sea
surface, and because warm air is lighter it rises. As it does so, it draws
cooler air along the surface from higher latitudes. A simple circulation

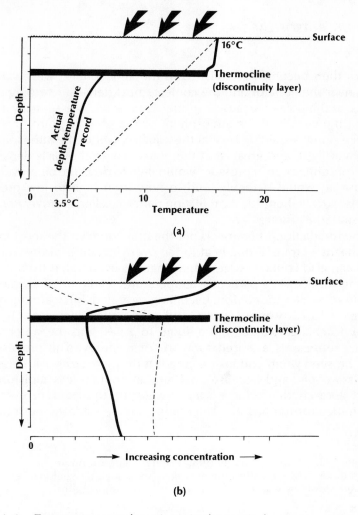

Figure 1–1. Temperatures and nutrients in the tropical ocean
(a) The formation of a discontinuity layer or thermocline in the sea. With the water surface warmed to 16°C in summer and the bottom water at 3.5°C, a simple temperature gradient might be expected to follow the broken line. In fact, the actual depth-temperature record shows the existence of a thermocline, or a limited discontinuity layer in which the temperature decreases rapidly with depth. The upper layers of warmed and less dense water are separated from the deeper layers of cold, denser water by the thermocline. Provided that heating from the surface continues, a thermocline will persist and become more marked as a discontinuity; and little or no exchange of water or solutes takes place through an established thermocline. (b) The effects of an established thermocline on the exchange of biologically important materials between surface and deep water masses. (The solid line represents oxygen and materials produced by plant activity; this line could also be taken as indicative of the total amount of plant and animal life in the water column. The dashed line represents the concentration of nutients required by plants during photosynthesis, such as nitrates or phosphates.)

pattern then becomes established in the atmosphere, with warm air rising near the equator and the coolest, most dense air settling to the surface at the poles. Because barometric pressure is essentially a measure of the weight of the atmosphere over a specific point, the pressure measured would be least at the equator, where the atmosphere is warm and light, and greatest at the poles, where the air is dense and cold. This difference in pressure would help to drive the air movement, because air would naturally tend to flow from high to low pressure regions. Such a theoretical circulation pattern, called an *advection cell*, is illustrated in Figure 1–2.

The reradiation of energy is not the only, or even the most important, means of transferring heat to the overlying atmosphere. Air over the ocean also contains water vapor that has evaporated from the underlying surface. At a particular temperature, a volume of air can only contain so much vapor before becoming saturated. But warming the air enables it to carry more vapor, and evaporation increases. It takes energy to change water from a liquid to a gas, and the water vapor actually represents a stored form of solar energy. The process can easily be seen when you take a mug out of the freezer. Air closest to the glass cools, and because cool air can contain less moisture the water vapor condenses as a layer of water on the glass, or even as a mist in the surrounding air. The energy released during the return to

Figure 1–2. A simple model of atmospheric circulation
First model system, with sunlight striking the equatorial region of a world covered only by water, but with an earthlike atmosphere.

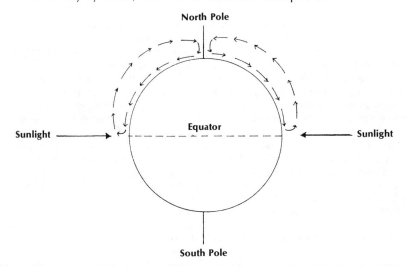

liquid form warms both the glass and the air. In the atmosphere, as warm moist air rises it cools, but as the water vapor condenses, forming clouds, additional heat is released. This provides more energy to help drive the atmospheric circulation.

Thus our initial projection has allowed us to see how solar energy, stored as heat in the surface waters of the tropics, can help drive a simple wind machine with surface winds traveling from the poles to the equator. Before considering how this would affect temperatures on the planet, let's make our model resemble reality a little more closely.

The first adjustment is required because the earth is actually rotating on its axis. Although it may seem to us to be stationary, any object on or over the surface of the planet is actually rotating right along with it. The speed at which a particular object is spinning varies depending on its location, specifically its latitude, as shown in Figure 1-3. The earth spins completely around its axis once every twenty-four hours,

Figure 1-3. Rotational speeds at the earth's surface.

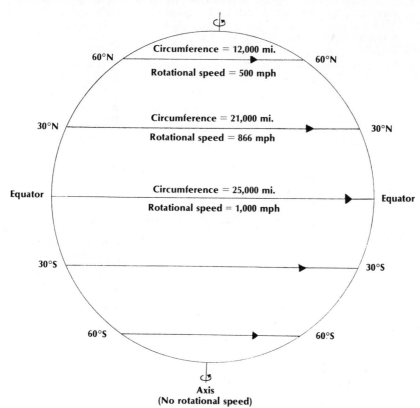

yet in one revolution an object at the equator travels at least 25,000 miles . . . while an object at the north pole merely turns in place. So the speed of rotation, which is west to east (because that's the way the world turns) is greatest at the equator and least at the poles.

Now picture a giant standing at the equator, throwing a baseball at a target located at the north pole. As he winds up to throw, the ball, like the giant, is already moving from west to east at about 1,000 mph. Although he may aim the ball right at the target, as soon as it leaves the equator it will begin traveling east more rapidly than the objects along its intended path. At 30°N, for example, it would be heading east 144 mph faster than other objects at that latitude. As it turns farther ahead, it will appear to the giant that his ball is curving strongly to the right, as shown in Figure 1–4.

Figure 1–4. Playing giant baseball
See the text for a detailed explanation. The dotted line represents the intended path of ball; the arrows indicate the observed flight path.
  Parts (a) and (c) give the view of an observer on the surface of the earth, and (b) and (d) that of an observer located in space. The relative positions of the giant, baseball, and target are indicated at Time 1, Time 2, and Time 3.

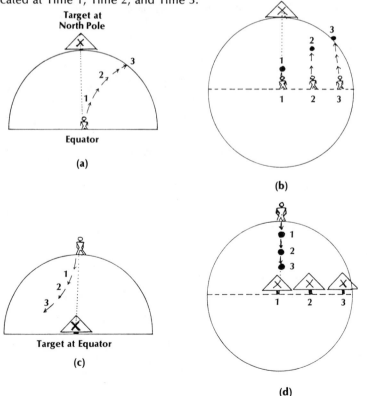

Now let's reverse the picture and put the giant at the north pole with the target at the equator. This time as soon as the ball leaves the pole it enters latitudes where everything is heading east much more rapidly, and so the ball lags farther and farther behind the target. Conveniently enough for our illustrator, it once again will appear to the giant that his pitch is curving to the right as the earth turns ahead of the ball. If we were to perform the same mental experiments in the southern hemisphere, we would find that the balls thrown there would always curve to the *left*, toward the east when traveling south from the equator and to the west when traveling away from the southern pole.

These predictable deflections of objects moving north or south in either hemisphere, caused by differing speeds of rotation, are one important part of the *Coriolis effect*. Although it is sometimes called a force, it is not a force like gravity, but simply the result of moving across the surface of a spinning globe. There are many aspects to the Coriolis effect that are important in technical oceanography and meteorology, and the interested reader is referred to the Additional Readings at the end of the book.

In addition to making giant baseball extremely frustrating, the Coriolis effect has a profound influence on our atmospheric model. As in our initial advection cell, air heated near the equator does become less dense and rises to form an area of lower-than-normal barometric pressure. In the real world this region is called the *intertropical convergence*, or ITC, which is known to sailors past and present as the "doldrums." Here the dominant wind movement is vertical, surface winds are light and variable, and because of condensation in the atmosphere above, showers are frequent. As this rising air is displaced toward the poles, the Coriolis effect results in an apparent turn to the right in the northern hemisphere and to the left in the southern hemisphere—in either case, toward the east. These moving upper air masses continue to turn, and as they do so the air becomes cooler, drier, and more dense. At roughly 25°N/S latitudes the dry, dense air settles to the surface in a zone of relatively high barometric pressure. Because the predominant air movement is vertical here as well, the surface winds are often light, but because the descending air is cool and dry there are few clouds and the sky is usually clear and bright. These regions are known as the *subtropical convergences*, or STCs, alias the "horse latitudes."

There is some disagreement over how they got this name. One theory holds that the Spanish ships became becalmed in these regions and their horses died of thirst; a second interpretation is that the sailors were dying of thirst, so the horses were driven overboard to conserve water; and a third states that the horses were served as en-trées when everything else edible had been polished off by the starving crew.

The air flowing along the surface from the STC to the equator completes the tropical circulation in one of the most regular and im-pressive meteorological displays you are likely to see. Turning toward the west, this surface wind system forms the famous tradewinds, which opened much of the tropical world to European sailing vessels on their voyages of discovery in the fifteenth, sixteenth, seventeenth, and eighteenth centuries. The same pattern is found on both sides of the equator, producing the northeast and southeast tradewinds.

Having gone this far, we may as well fill in the rest of the global wind patterns for the higher latitudes. In each hemisphere there are

Figure 1–5. A more complex model of atmospheric circulation
This is as close as we will try to come to the real wind patterns of the world.

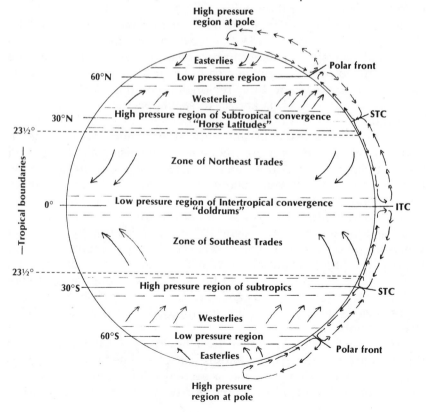

related wind cells that participate in the distribution of solar energy, and on the surface these are responsible for the westerlies and the polar easterlies. In the northern hemisphere these wind cells are strongly influenced by the continental land masses (see Figure 1–5), but in the southern hemisphere these wind cells are free from such disruptive effects, and they behave much as our model would predict. Sailors, who are rather in awe of the surface winds found at high southern latitudes, speak of the Roaring Forties and the Screaming Fifties when they mean 40 and 50°S.

We will consider only two other sources of variation between our model and the real world. First, we should look at the effects of the earth's axial tilt, which we have been able to ignore until now. During the course of the year the sun appears to move north and south between the Tropics at 23½° latitude, and it should be easy to imagine that the maximum amount of solar energy at any given moment will arrive at the latitude corresponding to the sun's apparent position. For this reason the ITC moves in the course of the year, shifting north or south appropriately.

The second major source of variation from our model is the presence of continents. The effects of continents on atmospheric flow can easily be seen in miniature when visiting tropical islands, so let's begin with a "typical" island, discuss the local effects, and then work from there.

You will recall that earth is a poor conductor of heat; actually it gains and loses heat about five times faster than sea water. Because of this, during the day the land heats up much more rapidly and to a much higher temperature than does the surrounding ocean. Early in the morning the moist oceanic air over the island begins to be heated from below and starts to rise. As it ascends the air cools and tall clouds form that are noticeably different from the typical puffball tradewind clouds. An experienced navigator can locate even a small, lowlying island simply by looking for the characteristic land clouds. In *very* still air these clouds may even duplicate the outline of the island, complete with bays and harbors!

As you might expect, the rising air is replaced by relatively cool air from offshore, and a comfortable onshore or sea breeze develops that may last throughout the day. This is essentially a small, localized advection cell, as shown in Figure 1–6, and there is often enough moisture in the rising air that showers may occur over inland regions.

At night the situation reverses rapidly. The land quickly loses heat, cooling below the surface temperature of the surrounding ocean. Now the cool overlying air descends, moving out to sea as the evening offshore or land breeze. This air mass, usually laden with the heavy scent of island vegetation, may also be used by navigators, and it is said that the blossoms of Tahiti may be appreciated up to twenty-five miles away.

On most islands the climatic conditions vary, sometimes greatly, from one portion of the island to another due to differential rainfall. The orientation of the island to the prevailing winds can play a major part in determining the nature of these variations. Islands have *windward* (facing the prevailing winds) and *leeward* (facing the opposite direction) sides. If the island has a mountainous peak or series of peaks it will present an obstacle to the tradewinds. As air is forced up the slopes, like water over a rock in a stream, clouds condense and moisture is released in rains that may be almost continuous. The basic process is illustrated in Figure 1–6.

The overall effect depends on a complex relationship between island size, height, and shape. In general, if the mountain is less than 6,000 feet high, the greatest rainfall occurs near or at the summit. On higher mountains the ascending air masses on the windward slopes

Figure 1–6. The effects of land masses on local winds
(a) sketch of Borabora and its morning clouds, looking north.
(b) Factors that produce such clouds are diagrammed for the same island scene.

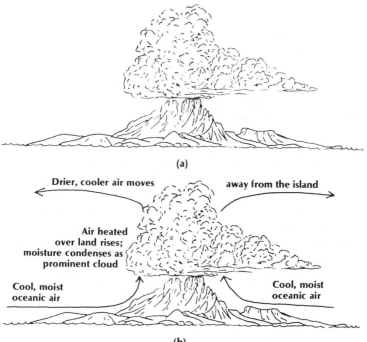

(a)

Drier, cooler air moves   away from the island

Air heated over land rises; moisture condenses as prominent cloud

Cool, moist oceanic air   Cool, moist oceanic air

(b)

lose most of their moisture at 2,000 to 6,000 feet, and the upper slopes are relatively dry. When that dry, cool air flows down the leeward slopes "rainshadow" desert conditions can be produced. Large scale rainshadow deserts are found in the western half of the United States for similar reasons. Oceanic air brought by the prevailing westerlies loses moisture as it ascends once in crossing the Cascade/Sierra Nevada range, and again in crossing the Rockies. The air which descends and warms on the leeward side of these mountains is extremely dry, and in the shadow of the windward rainfall you find leeward deserts. Such conditions are encountered on several continents where the prevailing oceanic winds strike mountain ranges oriented along a north/south axis. The island of Maui, second largest of the Hawaiian islands, is particularly useful as an illustration because of its compound nature. Geologically the island consists of two separate volcanoes joined by a narrow isthmus. The easternmost peak, Haleakala, is over 10,000 feet high and roughly one million years old. The smaller shield to the west is just over 5,000 feet high and about 500,000 years older. Take a good look at Figure 1–7 which summarizes rainfall patterns on both mountains, and you will see why the terms windward and leeward may often be swapped for wet and dry respectively. Sometimes the change from wet, windward conditions to dry, leeward slopes occurs over a very short distance, as Plate 1 documents.

Yet even though the leeward side of an island is often drier than the windward side, all islands cannot be divided into rain forest or desert on that basis. On Tutuila Island, American Samoa, there is a low mountainous spine, and much of the island is very narrow (less than two miles across). Showers develop at the ridge line, but drench both sides of the island, and there is little difference between windward and leeward coasts. On very large islands, such as the island of Hawaii, local heating of the leeward slopes during the day may produce showers in the afternoon that offset the rainshadow effect.

Each of these factors, the difference in heat storage and release rates between land and water, and the presentation of obstacles to the prevailing winds, can be seen on a much larger scale over the continents. In the northern hemisphere, which is about 50 percent land and 50 percent water, the net effect is to introduce fluctuations or eddies into the atmospheric circulatory pattern. This is especially noticeable in the relatively narrow, landlocked North Atlantic. In the southern hemisphere, which is over 90 percent ocean, the observed wind conditions are reasonably close to those predicted by Figure 1–5. The only significant alteration results from the size of the frozen expanse of Antarctica. This continent is so large and cold that the southern polar air mass is

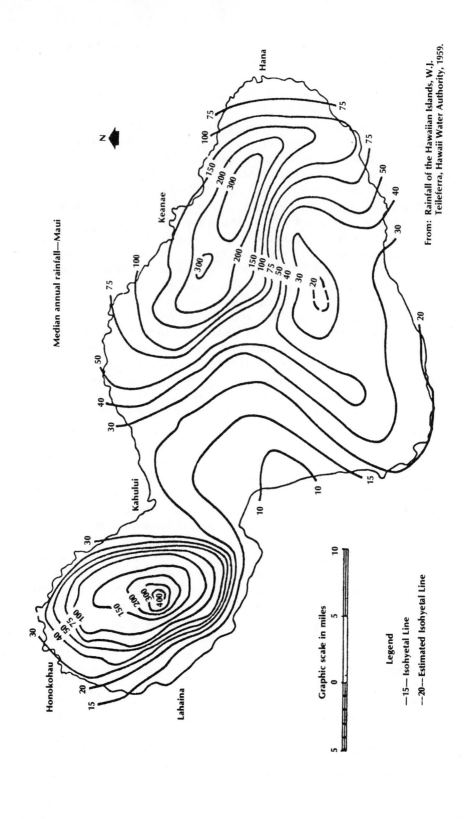

Median annual rainfall—Maui

Honokohau

Lahaina

Kahului

Keanae

Hana

N

From: Rainfall of the Hawaiian Islands, W.J.
Teileferra, Hawaii Water Authority, 1959.

Graphic scale in miles

5   0   5   10

Legend

—15— Isohyetal Line

--20-- Estimated Isohyetal Line

much more massive than its northern counterpart. This essentially shifts all of the wind cells to the north. As a result, the ITC is seldom found south of the equator, even at the height of the southern summer, whereas it may wander as far as 15°N when the sun is over the Tropic of Cancer.

Having noted these few variations, we will not seek a closer approximation of reality, and I will close this portion of the chapter with some information concerning weather and climate in the tropics. We are dealing with generalities, for local weather reflects an interaction among the effects of latitude, island height, surface area, orientation to the prevailing winds, and so on, but because this topic may have special importance to the traveler, even the generalities may prove useful. More specific information on individual island groups will be presented in Chapter 9.

In the Central Pacific, the rainy season extends from November to April. At these times the tradewinds may be variable in intensity or even intermittent. As you travel to the eastern or western limits of the tropical Pacific, this pattern changes and the wet season may extend to June or July at Easter Island (eastern South Pacific) or the Marshall Islands (western North Pacific). Cyclones, also known as hurricanes or typhoons, form during the summer months near the boundaries of the ITC. Along its northern border these fierce storms develop from July to October. Cyclones form along the southern border of the ITC from November to March. Once again the pattern shifts as you leave the central Pacific, and in general cyclones are more frequent to the west. In the western North Pacific they may occur throughout the year, although peak months are still from July to October. To the east the frequency of storms decreases, and cyclones are seldom encountered as far east as the Marquesas Islands.

The Hawaiian Islands have a unique climate because of their proximity to the high pressure zone of the STC. Seasonal changes in temperature are slight, and "typical" weather is clear and sunny, with northeast tradewinds. The rainy season, such as it is, extends from November to March or April. Low pressure centers may form in the vicinity of the islands and move towards the east, as the tradewinds are weak or absent around them. The rainy weather that these lows bring to the islands is accompanied by southerly to southwesterly winds. As these strike the normally sheltered leeward coasts they have earned a

Figure 1–7 (opposite page). Yearly precipitation on Maui
Notice the pronounced difference in rainfall amounts and patterns on the slopes of the East and West Maui mountains as a result of differing heights and orientation to the prevailing winds, which arrive from the northeast.

special name, and since the leeward side of an island is the "kona" side these are called kona storms. While the winds are cyclonal, and may reach hurricane force, they form *outside* of the tropics and move *eastward*. Tropical cyclones form to the southeast of the islands from July to October or November, and they move to the *west*. Fortunately, because of the location of the islands, neither of these storms arrives with any regularity. Kona rainstorms may occur once or twice a year, on the average, and fewer than half a dozen cyclones have seriously affected island weather in the last thirty years. It is not an accident that none of the local television stations employs a weatherman.

In the tropical North Atlantic the tradewinds blow with regularity throughout the year. Many of the islands are without a definitive rainy season, but for the larger, northern islands there is a tendency for maximum rainfall to occur from May to November. Hurricane season peaks between July and September, with occasional storms forming a month earlier or later.

You should carefully review seasonal weather patterns when planning a visit to the tropics, for arriving at the height of the local rainy season can best be described as an experience in frustration and mildew. You should also give some thought to local variations in climate when visiting the larger islands. In general, the leeward side is a more pleasant spot for active vacationing, because it tends to be less humid and to receive more sunshine during the dry season. Because of the light winds and low rainfall, the surrounding waters usually offer better visibility for swimming and diving. On the other hand, the weather side is usually cooler, breezier, and more spectacular. The high rainfall often produces waterfalls, a more eroded and wild coastline, and more abundant greenery. (The interactions of these features will be considered in Chapter 7.)

This discussion on atmospheric circulation began with an observation that the actual climate on the planet is far more hospitable than simple solar energy incidence would predict. If you were to take our now-revised model, fiddle with it a bit, and do the necessary calculations, you would find that roughly 70 percent of the difference between the predicted and actual temperatures can be accounted for by the processes of radiation, evaporation, and redistribution by the tropical atmosphere. How do we account for the missing 30 percent?

The answer lies in the physical movement of warm tropical surface waters by ocean currents. Figure 1–8 summarizes the surface wind patterns that we derived earlier in the chapter, and compares them with the major surface currents. The similarities are not coincidental. Friction between the moving air and the water surface produces waves

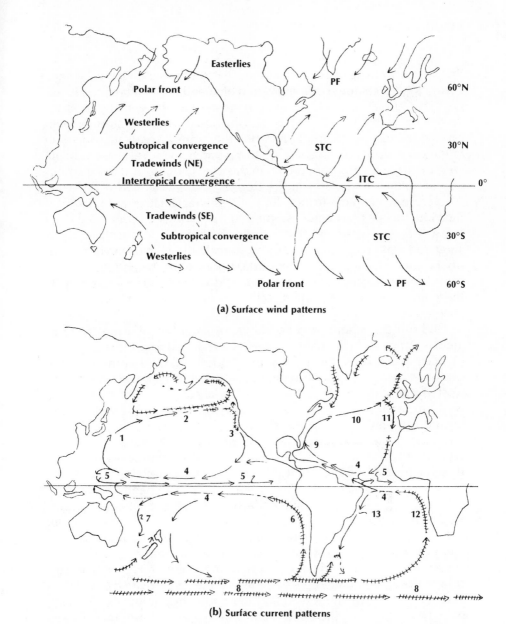

(a) Surface wind patterns

(b) Surface current patterns

Figure 1–8. A comparison of surface wind patterns and surface current of the Atlantic and Pacific Oceans (a) surface winds; (b) surface currents: (1) Kuroshio Current; (2) North Pacific Current; (3) California Current; (4) North and South Equatorial Currents; (5) Equatorial Countercurrent; (6) Peru or Humboldt Current; (7) East Australia Current; (8) West Wind Drift; (9) Gulf Stream; (10) North Atlantic Current; (11) Canaries Current; (12) Benguela Current; (13) Brazil Current. Solid lines represent warm current; hatched lines represent cool/cold current.

that in turn create a slow movement of the surface waters. Ocean currents have seldom been measured at speeds over fifteen miles per day. They are also highly variable. If westerly storm winds persist for several days, the normal east to west currents may slow, stop, or even reverse themselves temporarily, while the same currents may increase in force and volume if pushed by strong tradewinds. Yet these variable currents have a significant effect on the quality of life and the distribution of animals and plants in the tropics.

Before we go any further, let's face the fact that an abundance of individual names has been assigned to the various current systems of the world. Is it essential that you know them? No, it isn't and you shouldn't wear yourself down trying to make them stick in your memory on the first reading. The important points are the *patterns* found, especially as regards the warm and cold currents. The reasons why these are especially important will be brought out a little later in the chapter.

In both the Atlantic and Pacific Oceans the basic current patterns are the same—only the names have been changed to protect the sanity of oceanographers. Pushed by the tradewinds and turned by the Coriolis effect, the currents on either side of the ITC travel from east to west as the northern or southern equatorial currents. On reaching the western limits of the ocean basin, most of the moving waters turn toward the poles, away from the ITC, and carry warm tropical water into cool latitudes. A variable amount of water is deflected toward the ITC, whereupon it reverses direction and moves from west to east as the equatorial countercurrent. This erratic and unreliable current follows the ITC, because in this region of predominantly vertical air movement there are no strong tradewinds to oppose an easterly flow. Sailors often watch for these currents, for if you are heading east under sail anywhere else in the tropics you are bucking westbound currents, and you will feel like a salmon swimming upstream.

As the warm currents move away from the equator, they gradually turn to the east, and after passing the STC they are driven east with the assistance of the westerlies. As they continue, they gradually lose heat, but when they strike the eastern limits of the ocean basin they are still markedly warmer than waters would otherwise be at these latitudes. Most of this current then turns toward the equator, completing the circuit and bringing relatively cool waters into the tropics.

Let us consider how these persistent currents affect life in the tropical Atlantic and Pacific. In the northwest Pacific the warm Kuroshio Current takes tropical waters north along the Japanese coast before turning east. Coral reefs, normally limited to tropical latitudes, are found off the coast of Japan, roughly 750 miles north of the Tropic of Cancer, at the same latitude as San Luis Obispo, California. Even after cooling in its passage across the Pacific this current has an effect on North America. Southeastern Alaska is warmer than one might expect, and the cool waters flowing south along the California coast mean that temperatures between southeastern Alaska and San Diego differ by only 10 to 20°F year-round. In the northwestern Atlantic the Gulf Stream has a similar effect on the climate of northern Europe, and en route the warm waters permit the growth of coral reefs around Bermuda, approximately 550 miles north of the Tropic and at a latitude close to that of Charleston, South Carolina. As the current loop closes, and cool waters flow south along the European coast, coral growth is inhibited, even in tropical latitudes.

This points out the fact that cold currents may have just as significant an effect as warm ones. The Galapagos Islands are small volcanic islands roughly 600 miles west of the Ecuadorian coast of South America. Although these islands are scattered right around the equator, the cool waters of the Peru Current produce mild conditions along coastal regions even when there are extensive deserts inland. Animals such as penguins and fur seals, which normally are found only in more temperate latitudes, are present in abundance. Even after reaching the Marquesas Islands, 2,500 miles away, the current may still have noticeable effects. Despite the proximity of these islands to the equator at 8 to 11°S, the isles show little coral reef development, and this suggests that the Peru Current occasionally lowers water temperatures below levels that support healthy coral growth (other possible factors, such as isolation, will be discussed in later chapters). In the southeastern Atlantic, the cold Benguela Current has a similar effect, and modern coral reefs are not found along the African coast or around the tropical islands off the coast. Even Ascension Island, in the mid-Atlantic, is without reefs.

The long-term reliability of surface currents is also extremely important in the reproduction and geographic distribution of many reef animals. Even for relatively active animals such as the reef fishes, the open ocean between islands is inhospitable, with little to eat, nowhere to hide, and a long way to swim. Colonization of remote areas is usually accomplished by riding the surface currents not as adults, which would take effort that could be devoted to eating and reproducing, but as tiny floating eggs and larvae which drift effortlessly for weeks or even months.

Finally, you should realize that we have so far considered only the existence and importance of the wind-driven surface currents. Such currents extend to depths of 600 to 1,000 feet. With an average depth of 12,000 feet, there must surely be deeper currents that circulate materials from the surface to the depths. These deep water currents seem to be as important to the overall ecology of the tropics as are the surface currents, but of course they are much more difficult to study.

The tropical surface waters are relatively isolated from the underlying water masses, as noted in our earlier discussion of thermoclines, and this isolation places restrictions on the activity of plants and animals found in these waters. As in the terrestrial environment, most life in the sea ultimately depends on the plants which convert solar energy into biological materials which can be consumed by animals. Marine and terrestrial plants require more than just sunlight to grow and reproduce. They need nutrients such as nitrates and phosphates like those found in garden fertilizers. Without an adequate supply of nutrients, plant activity comes to a grinding halt. Phosphates and nitrates are produced by bacteria that convert chemical compounds often, but not exclusively, obtained during the decomposition of organic materials. Where do such materials wind up in the open ocean?

They sink, of course. The lightest, low density materials, like the earthly remains of planktonic plants and animals, may remain suspended for a time at the thermocline. Analysis of the bacterial count in this region shows a large bacterial population, and as the suspended materials are broken down, the bacterial action provides a small but steady supply of recycled nutrients to the surface waters. But it is the bacteria found on the ocean floor that decompose most of the organic debris, fecal products, and carcasses which rain down from the waters above. At the cool temperatures and high pressures of the depths, this process proceeds slowly but inexorably. The nitrates and phosphates released by this bacterial action are then dissolved, enriching the cool dark depths. Because they *are* cool and dark, there are no plants around to benefit from this nutritional bonanza, so here we have a real problem. Most of the nutrients are near the bottom, where there is no light, whereas the surface waters have all the sunlight a plant could ask for, but they are separated from the nutrients by the thermocline.

In actual fact, there is no easy solution to this problem, and the plants within the tropical surface waters are present in abundance only where the thermocline is either distorted or absent altogether. Near the eastern shores of both oceans the prevailing winds, aided by the Coriolis effect, drive cool coastal currents offshore. As these waters move out into the open ocean, cold, nutrient-rich waters are drawn from the depths to replace them. Called *upwellings*, these are sites of fantastic productivity, because nutrients are continually flowing into a zone of intense sunlight. The most famous upwelling occurs off the coast of Peru, where the Peru Current swings offshore, but others are found off the Californian and African coasts. Figure 1–9 details the mechanics of an upwelling.

Bacterial action at the thermocline and regional upwellings are two important sources of nutrients for tropical waters. There are other, less consistent sources worth mentioning. In coastal regions nutrients can be washed from the land by rains and carried by streams and rivers which eventually reach the sea. The enriched coastal waters are later carried into the open ocean as the currents swing offshore, in the case of continents, or swing past, in the case of islands. Another route is via currents from more temperate regions, where nutrient entry from deeper waters occurs on a seasonal basis.

At temperate and polar latitudes the approach of winter is accompanied by a reduction in sunlight. The surface waters cool, become more dense, and eventually the thermocline vanishes. Surface and deeper waters are then intermixed through diffusion and the turbulence caused by waves and currents. Despite this influx of nutrients there is no great population explosion in the plankton, for now it is sunlight that is in short supply. Most of the nitrates and phosphates will remain in the surface waters until they are either transported by currents into tropical regions or springtime arrives. This seasonal recharging of the surface waters makes temperate and polar latitudes far more productive than tropical waters. Each spring, when sunlight reaches acceptable levels, life in the plankton explodes. Plant and animal populations soar. This planktonic revelry does not last throughout the sum-

Figure 1–9. Diagram of an upwelling.

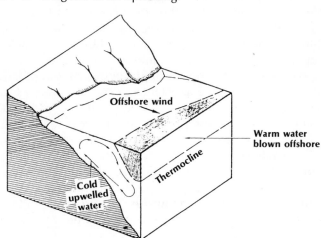

mer, however, for as the season progresses a thermocline begins to form. The vastly increased number of plants quickly removes phosphates and nitrates from circulation; the plant population then declines, as animals consume plants that are no longer reproducing. The summer months are quiet, with the same limitations faced by tropical surface waters all year long. Then in the fall, the breakdown of the thermocline permits a brief flurry of planktonic activity before the winter sets in. These population explosions of planktonic plants, invariably accompanied by increases in the number of planktonic animals, are called *plankton blooms*, and are characteristic of temperate and polar latitudes. Seasonal plankton blooms of this kind are unheard of in the tropics, and the relatively localized areas of upwellings are only roughly comparable. In fact, the picture formed of life in tropical seas is surprisingly somber. Because nutrients are always in short supply, tropical surface waters in the open ocean support only meager populations of plankton. "Productivity" is an estimation of the amount of new organic materials assembled by plants, and it therefore represents the potential energy available for animal populations. Figure 1–10 illustrates the contrasts between temperate and tropical waters. Compare it with Figure 1–8 and Figure 1–9 to visualize the effects of currents and upwellings. Few people realize that the crystalline clarity of tropical waters is a result of their rather inhospitable and unproductive nature.

With such an unenthusiastic description of the productive potential of tropical waters, how can we explain the staggering variety of marine life encountered around tropical islands? Recent studies suggest that modern coral reefs have a number of features that effectively trap nutrients and prevent them from being lost into deep water or swept downstream by currents. Coral reefs are restricted to the sunlit surface waters, and thus they are always found above the thermocline. Because things that die on the reef tend to remain trapped within the interstices, bacterial activity liberates organic materials and nutrients into the local environment for immediate recycling. This is a key point because the return of nutrients lost into deeper waters takes a lot of time barring the assistance of seasons and/or local upwellings.

There is no single mass of water extending from 600 feet to the bottom, and oceanographers can identify several different intermediate water masses on the basis of temperature and salinity characteristics. Each has a different history, but it is the deepest, known as the bottom water, into which bacterial action liberates nutrients. Because each of these stacked water masses is separated from the overlying one by a thermocline, diffusion towards the surface is limited, but there is a physical circulation of the bottom water rather reminiscent of our first

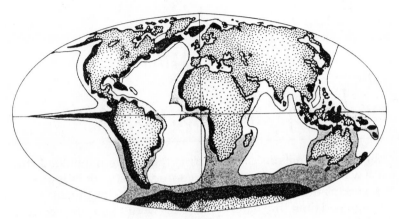

Figure 1–10. Productivity of the oceans
Relative productivity of the open ocean is indicated by shading from
low (white) to high (darkest). Compare this figure with Figure 1–8
(surface winds and currents) and Figure 1–9 (vertical circulation at
upwellings).

advection cell model. Cold, dense water settles to the bottom near the
poles and travels along the ocean floor toward the equator. Eventually
these deep waters mix into the overlying intermediate water masses
that surface at upwellings. In the Atlantic the voyage from the surface
to the bottom and back may take 750 years, whereas in the Pacific the
journey may last twice as long.

The remainder of Part I will focus on tropical biology, particularly
the biology of coral reefs. We have set the stage in this chapter by
considering some of the important physical conditions that directly
affect life in the tropics. We have, in passing, discussed the essential
role of tropical surface waters in establishing wind systems, global
climatic and weather patterns, and providing a mechanism for the
overall recycling of materials in the oceans. It is sobering to realize that
despite these functional roles the actual amount of water involved is
but a thin slice off the top, perhaps a few hundred feet out of an
average depth of over two miles. Because the circulation time is
around 1,000 years, any damage done to the surface waters by pollutants will be both long-lasting and have far-reaching consequences.

Chapter Two
Coral Reefs and Islands

For hundreds of millions of years coral reefs have dominated shallow tropical waters. Until the eighteenth century most people assumed that corals were plants, but in the early 1700s the French naturalist Peyssonnel recognized their true nature. His ideas were so poorly received that he had to find another line of work. Truth has a way of surfacing, fortunately, and less than fifty years later there was a reversal of opinion and a general agreement that corals were indeed animals. Despite the research that has been conducted over the intervening years, few people who visit the tropics today know any more about these unusual creatures. This is a shame, for there is no single aspect of the region that is at once as spectacular, distinctive, and accessible as its reefs. Visitors to the tropics often splash around in the warm waters within hours of their arrival, jet lag or no jet lag. Living corals in the form of clusters or entire reefs are only an Australian crawl away, and less adventurous souls can always find areas where they can wade along with mask in hand. This chapter will introduce you to corals and the reefs they produce in the hope that you will use every opportunity to explore them first hand.

The phylum that includes the corals and their relations is an extremely ancient one. Its members are known as *coelenterates*, a term that refers to their simple digestive system (*coel*, "cavity"; *enteron*, "gut"). Fossil coelenterates have been found in rocks over 500 million years old, and there are about 9,000 living species. The group that includes the corals, the sea anemones, and related forms is the largest branch of the coelenterate family tree, with around 6,000 species.

We can divide the corals into two major groups on the basis of the kind of skeleton that the animals produce. In the soft corals, this skeleton is constructed from organic materials and is relatively flexible. Soft corals vary in form and habitat, and they can be found over an extensive range of depths, and from the tropics to the polar seas. In this chapter we will discuss only those tropical forms that occasionally compete for space with their more robust relations, the hard corals.

Hard, alias "stony," corals secrete skeletons that are composed of

99+ percent minerals. Hard corals may be subdivided into those that produce reefs and those that don't. We will ignore the latter entirely—their average depth of occurrence is over 1,500 feet, and because they thrive in darkness and in frigid polar waters you will probably have no occasion to encounter them.

The reef-building corals are restricted to waters warmer than 72°F, as are most tropical adventurers. Most species are quickly killed by exposure to extremely high temperatures or fresh water because they are unable to prevent overheating and have little ability to regulate the composition of their body fluids. In general, all coral animals resemble the sea anemones, despite a considerable difference in average size. Figure 2–1 presents several aspects of an individual coral animal or *polyp*.

Each coral polyp is shaped like a tube with one end firmly attached to a solid foundation. At the free end there is a single opening that handles materials both inbound and outbound, to and from the central body cavity. The region around this opening is called the *oral disc*, and around the outer edges of the disc are arrayed a number of small tentacles. Both the oral disc and the tentacles are covered with cells bearing small projections or *cilia* that beat in a coordinated fashion toward or away from the mouth as needed.

The reef-building corals are all carnivorous, as are the sea anemones. They capture their prey with the aid of elaborate stinging cells called *nematocysts* that are distributed over the surface of each tentacle. Despite their small size these are formidable weapons, and when a drifting planktonic animal contacts the trigger an hydraulically operated harpoon system injects a poison into the hapless victim. Mucus, which is secreted by other cells on the tentacles, oral disc, and even the general body surface, then entangles the catch. The mucus is moved by the coordinated beating of the cilia across the oral disc, through the mouth, and into the digestive cavity. It is useful to remember that there are several other stimuli that will result in the firing of nematocysts. The armament is also used as a defense, either against predatory starfish, competing corals, or swimmers who occasionally crash into them. (The latter eventuality will be considered in more detail in the Appendix.)

The lining of the digestive cavity is thrown into pleats and folds that are covered with cells specialized to secrete digestive enzymes, absorb organic substances, and move materials toward or away from the dual-purpose mouth. By having such a convoluted lining, the number of cells exposed to the contents is increased, for there is far more surface area than there would be if the lining were simple and unruf-

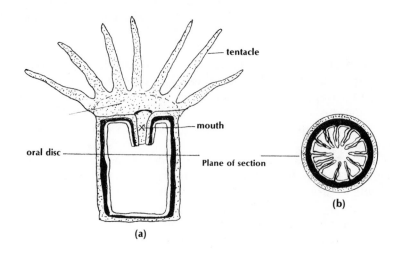

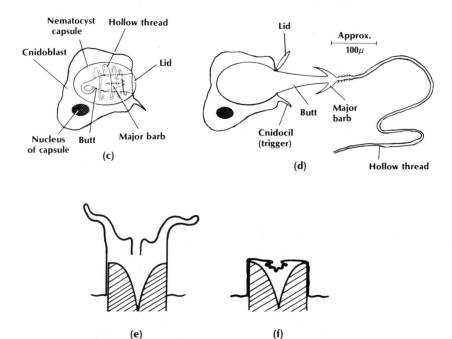

Figure 2–1. Anatomy of a coral polyp
(a) and (b): view of a single coral polyp in section through the long axis of the body (a) and across the body (b) note the prominent folds of the lining of the gut. (Stipple lines represent the ectoderm, black lines, the acellular middle layer, and white areas, the endoderm.) (c) and (d): Details of a single stinging cell or nematocyst found on the surface of a tentacle. (e) and (f): Section showing the structure of the protective theca produced by the polyp, and the retreat of the polyp when threatened. (Hatched areas indicate calcium carbonate.)

fled. This feature is quite common in the digestive tracts of higher forms of life, up to and including human beings.

The lining cells of this interior chamber are called *gastrodermis* (*gastro*, "gut"; *dermis*, "skin") or *endodermis* (*endo*, "inside"). The outer skin of the polyp is called either the *epidermis* (*epi*, "over") or *ectodermis* (*ecto*, "outside"). These two layers are separated to a variable degree by a noncellular middle zone, across which pass wandering cells shuffling materials from place to place and between the cellular layers. There is often coordinated activity between the gastrodermis and epidermis, as when digestion is completed. At that time the general ciliary beat of the gut and oral disc is reversed, and the waste matter is passed out the mouth, across the oral disc, and "over the side."

Most polyps feed actively at night, retiring by day into pockets or *thecae* that surround the bases of the individual polyps. The epidermis at the base and sides of each polyp and the undersurface of the cellular connections between adjacent polyps secrete the thecae and the surrounding portions of the coral skeleton. A single coral head represents the combined activity of countless tiny individual polyps, with the colony forming a thin surface layer, sort of a living carpet, over the massive inert skeleton that supports them all.

These massive colonies begin with but a single polyp that reproduces itself by *budding*, a process of in-house cloning that results in an ever-increasing number of polyps all in contact with one another. Each individual polyp produces its own theca, and with time more minerals are deposited beneath the attached base, adding to the thickness of the skeleton. Meanwhile the colony as a whole is growing, as more and more polyps build and elaborate on more and more thecae. What shape the colony will assume depends on several factors that affect the pattern of budding and the speed at which it occurs in various portions of the colony. Because each species differs in genetic programming, and each colony can be influenced to some degree by particular local conditions, the shape of a coral head is extremely variable. Some species even have the ability to alter the shape of a colony in response to changes in the surrounding environment, as illustrated in Figure 2–2. Fortunately for biologists, who would like to decide whether colonies (a) and (b) are the same or different species, the shapes of the individual thecae do not vary, but remain constant within a species. This records for posterity the characteristic pleats and folds of the digestive cavity, and if you have a chance to examine a piece of coral skeleton with a hand lens you will begin to see how many interesting variations might be possible. At the moment there are between 200 and 800 species recognized by specialists, and the large range is an indica-

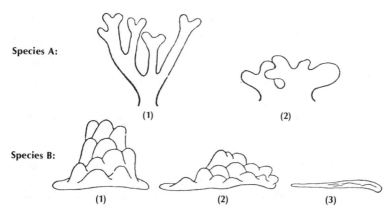

Species A:

(1)   (2)

Species B:

(1)   (2)   (3)

Figure 2–2. Variations in the shape of coral colonies formed under differing environmental conditions: (1) growth form in quiet waters; (2) growth form in shallow, rough waters; and (3) growth form in shallow, very rough waters (only Species B can tolerate these conditions).

tion of just how much confidence everyone has in their identifications. Plate 2 shows the thecal shapes characteristic of two different species.

Coral reefs of modern form first appeared about 200 million years ago, and later spread throughout tropical seas. As these animals are hardly equipped to stroll from place to place you might wonder how new and relatively remote areas are colonized. The original polyp, whose successful budding may form such a variety of colony shapes, is itself the result of sexual reproduction of the polyps of mature colonies. Eggs and/or sperm are produced within the body walls of these polyps and are released into the surrounding waters either before or after fertilization, depending on the species. The larval stages of the polyps are called *planulae*, and these are carried within the plankton wherever the currents may take them. The planulae may drift for weeks before finally answering some unknown call to settle to the bottom and begin developing into young polyps. Once attached to potentially secure foundations, budding begins and new colonies are in the making.

Thus the appearance of a particular species in a new environment depends on a series of random interactions: the currents must flow in the right direction, the right cues must be given to the planulae, and the polyps must find a suitable place to attach where they will not be removed by waves, buried in silt, exposed by the tides, or otherwise discomfited. The further away a potential reef site is from other colonies, the lower the odds that it will quickly be colonized, and the fewer the species that will eventually manage to reach it.

The greatest diversity of reef-building corals is found in the waters around Indonesia and the Philippines. Whether you travel east or west from this region the number of species declines, but the effect is more pronounced in the tropical Pacific. This is because the prevailing equatorial currents proceed from east to west, and the planktonic larvae can go "against the grain" only when transported in the intermittent countercurrent, or when there are temporary alterations in current patterns. Figure 2–3 indicates the number of coral species found in different portions of the tropical Pacific; similar distribution patterns are found among other life forms that rely on currents for transport from west to east. (We will discuss the distribution of marine fishes in Chapter 3.) In most areas of the tropical Pacific, the novice will be unable to detect the subtle differences in detail that result from the presence or absence of particular coral species. The differences do become apparent as you approach the northern and eastern limits of the tropics.

The waters around the islands of Hawaii and the Marquesas are close to the minimal acceptable temperatures for healthy coral growth, at least during a portion of the year, and their reefs today are relatively poor in coral species, and limited in extent. In the case of Hawaii, this is probably a function of latitude and water temperature, exaggerated by the physical isolation from the central and western Pacific. In the Marquesas, several factors may interact to limit the growth of reefs in addition to isolation by distance and currents. The coral larvae must attach to dense, smooth lava slopes, siltation from rainfall and wave action is heavy, and cool waters from the Peru Current may arrive from time to time. Well-defined reefs are not found, and coral colonies survive as patch reefs or narrow fringing bands in shallow waters. These are most often encountered along the northern coasts of the islands that are sheltered from the prevailing seas and warmed by the sun.

Drifting into the Indian Ocean would seem far easier, but how did corals arrive in the tropical Atlantic? We will examine the matter further in Chapter 8, so for the moment I will simply report that they did so by spreading through the Mediterranean (and to a lesser extent across the eastern Pacific) at times when these oceans were not isolated from one another. The distances were still great, however, and the number of coral species in the tropical Atlantic is relatively low—only 10 percent of the number found in the western Pacific. Yet you should not get the impression that Atlantic reefs are dull and drab, for this is not the case at all. Because each species can assume a variety of colony forms depending on local conditions, the low diversity is not evident. In addition, soft corals and sea fans are much more common than in the Pacific, lending a beautiful impression of flow and motion to the reefs.

Conditions suitable for coral reef growth are less widespread in the

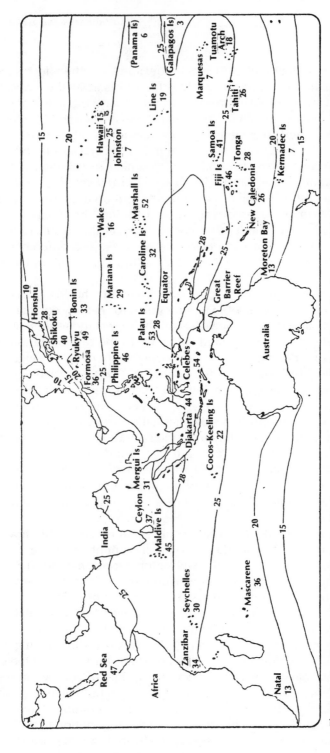

Figure 2-3. Distribution of Indo-Pacific hermatypic coral genera based on the faunas of thirty-two areas. Isotherms are given in degrees centigrade. Numbers linked to areas indicate the number of genera known to occur there.

tropical Atlantic than in the tropical Pacific. Because of the cold Benguela Current flowing north along the west coast of Africa, and the cool upwellings that occur where this current swings offshore, there are no modern, substantial reef communities in the eastern tropical Atlantic. Along the eastern coast of the Americas coral reefs are rare south of 5°N, mainly due to the effects of siltation and runoff from numerous rivers and estuaries centered around the Amazon. So when we are comparing Pacific and Atlantic coral reefs and coral islands, we are essentially considering the tropical Pacific and the Caribbean Sea. For our purposes, the two regions may be dealt with simultaneously 99 percent of the time.

One of the major mysteries facing biologists earlier in this century was how to account for the intense biological activity around reefs while accepting the fact that the surrounding ocean is relatively barren. Preliminary studies showed that too little plankton arrived at most reefs to support their measured growth and development. Later work indicated that coral reefs actually *produce* more biological materials than they consume. You might expect this in a forest community, where plants dominate the scenery, but a quick look at a coral reef is enough to show that large, bona fide plants are a rarity. Are they hiding somewhere, or was the research in error?

The problem was resolved with the realization that the reef-building corals have evolved an unusual cooperative arrangement with a group of microscopic algae called *zooxanthellae*. Each gastrodermal cell of a polyp can contain one to three of these unicellular algae, which measure around 1/2500 of an inch in diameter. How they get there in the first place, and whether or not each species of coral has the same species of algae are still subjects for research.

During the day these captive plants behave much like their relatives in the plankton, using the solar energy that reaches them through the translucent body of their host-polyp. Unlike their free-living cousins, they have a much more reliable environment because they are hidden from herbivores and are in no danger of drifting below the sunlit surface waters. They also have far more delicate and permeable cell walls, which is useful because they are surrounded by animal tissues that produce CO_2 and the very organic compounds that are in such critically short supply in the tropical ocean. So the plants get protection, carbon dioxide, and nutrients. But what's in it for the polyps?

First of all, the coral polyps have a ready disposal site for waste products such as CO_2, phosphates, and ammonia. In addition, the polyps get plenty of oxygen while photosynthesis is underway, and a variety of organic byproducts such as amino acids that diffuse through the thin walls of the zooxanthellae and into the gastrodermal cells of the polyps. This kind of mutual interdependence and collaboration between unrelated lifeforms is called *symbiosis*, and in this instance it appears to be responsible for the overall success of the reef-building corals.

Not all colonies rely to the same degree on plankton capture versus zooxanthellae production for their actual survival. In areas with an abundance of plankton the nutrient contribution of the algae may be relatively minor. But it has been shown that these captive algae are somehow essential for the proper growth and maintenance of the colonial skeleton. A coral colony grows at least ten times faster in light than in dark, and if the zooxanthellae are removed the presence of light has no beneficial effects. In the lab, a colony kept in darkness survives as long as there is planktonic food available, but in real life it would probably fail to outpace the destructive effects of predators, disease, and other natural forces. In short, the production and maintenance of a massive stony skeleton appears to be a complex, delicate, and energetically expensive undertaking, and there are no reef-building corals that thrive in the absence of either planktonic prey *or* light.

Such limitations are not apparent in the soft corals, which may also have captive algae. Some species appear to farm their algae, and they rely solely on the nutrients obtained from them. These species lack nematocysts entirely and have no need of plankton. Other species rely wholly on plankton capture, and can develop quite happily in total darkness or at great depths. These variations enable the soft corals to dominate habitats that are inaccessible to their stonier brethren.

As any engineer or sailor knows, it never hurts to have backup systems if they don't require a lot of energy to maintain. Hard corals show this principle as well. The mucus that is essential for the transport of planktonic prey is also used for snaring bacteria that abound in and around the bottom sediments, and the epidermal cells of each polyp can absorb organic materials directly from the surrounding sea water, much as the endodermal cells remove nutrients from the digestive cavity. This flexibility in feeding tactics no doubt aids the colonies in coping with seasonal, regional, and local variations in the reef environment.

Each colony works out a balance between hunting plankton, trading with algae, and snaring bacteria or passing nutrients. Its ultimate success or failure may be determined by the site of attachment chosen by the original polyp, so we should take a look at an "ideal" habitat. With their dependence on the activity of zooxanthellae, reef-building corals are restricted to the surface waters. In the tropics this usually means no deeper than about 180 feet, and in turbid waters this range is greatly reduced. Coastal waters that are extremely murky because of local shoreline or stream erosion will not support reef-building corals for several reasons. The sand, mud, or silt that settles to the bottom covers any firm substrate that would attract the attention of planulae. If the siltation occurs after attachment and growth is underway, a small amount will be tolerated by the colony; the mucus flow over the surface of each polyp is increased, and the ciliary beat reversed to sweep the oral disc clean from time to time. More significant amounts of debris eventually exceed the cleaning abilities of the polyps, and as the feeding tentacles are coated, plankton capture ceases. At the same time the darkening waters are absorbing light that is required by the zooxanthellae. Coral reefs cannot survive, let alone flourish, under these conditions.

Soft corals may have an edge at such times, and as the hard corals die off they may come to dominate the area. A dusting of debris is more easily tolerated by soft corals, and a colony may actually flex from side to side, shaking off a layer of sediment.

A concept that I hope you will accept as we wander through this portion of the book is that any form of life is a compromise between the conflicting opportunities and restrictions that confront it. The compromises are worked out over long periods of time through natural selection, which is a simple but effective process. These individuals who can make the most of the opportunities around them simply out-reproduce the competition. (We will examine the process of natural selection further in Chapter 3.) Yet no animal, like no automobile, is perfectly adapted for any single function. The fastest car wouldn't waste any space or permit the dead weight of a driver; the most comfortable might be the size of a house and too expensive to fuel; and the safest would be inherently unable to leave its parking place.

You can see this principle in action when you look at the varied shapes of coral colonies. No single species does well under all environmental conditions, and no single colony shape is ideal. A colony in the form of a thin, flat plate parallel to the surface can grow rapidly, spread horizontally past the shadows of shallower colonies, and expose the maximum number of member polyps to sunlight. But the polyps may easily be smothered by silt, and the colony is relatively fragile and easily damaged by waves. An upright, branching form grows toward the surface rapidly, is difficult to smother, and presents a maximum number of polyps to the plankton carried by passing currents. Yet this form is also fragile, and many of the polyps are likely to be shaded by adjacent branches. A solid, lumpish colony is the ultimate in wave resistance, but such colonies grow slowly because of their enormous volume, and all portions of the colony are not equally exposed to light and food. Colonies with this shape are subject to overgrowth and shading by more expansion-oriented species.

The seaward slopes of a reef form a complex environment, with variations in lighting, wave surge, current, and siltation rates. A reef is a dynamic structure, continually responding to the slightest environmental alterations, even though our life spans may be too short to see many of the responses. Only by comparing the appearance and distribution of coral colonies in a variety of different locations can you begin to understand the ways in which coral colonies interact, and how they respond to environmental changes. We will begin with a relatively small, isolated, and undisturbed reef complex and proceed from there.

Atolls are ideal subjects for discussion because they support extensive reefs but are small and (usually) sparsely populated. Atolls owe their very existence to the activity of coral polyps, for the inhabitable portions of these islands consist of sands capping a massive reef structure. The formation and development of atolls will be discussed in Chapter 7, but the basic features of an individual atoll are illustrated in Figure 2–4. There are about 300 atolls in the tropical Pacific, and ten in the tropical Atlantic. Plate 3 gives a visual impression of atolls.

Let us begin a tour on the outer edge of the atoll along its windward coast. Often the seaward edge of the exposed reef is broken by surge channels that dissipate the forces of the prevailing seas. These channels are usually continued along the outer slopes of the reef as submarine canyons that are the preferred pathways for the retreating waters. Corals within these channels are either small and sturdy or massive and encrusting, for only these forms are able to resist the strong currents that scour the bottom with transported sand and debris.

Between these channels there are long ridges of coral that give the reef a "groove and spur" appearance. Along these ridges there is a marked segregation of species into distinct regions or zones. These zones represent a biological response to changes in local environment with increasing depth and decreasing exposure to waves. A verbal description follows, while representative photographs are presented in Figure 2–5.

Zone 1. Just beneath the surface the sunlight is intense, oxygen and plankton abound, but the seas are often fearsome. The most common colony form here is a massive irregular, encrusting type.

Zone 2. As you descend further you enter an area where wave surge is less pronounced. Here there are branching colonies that present maximum area to local currents.

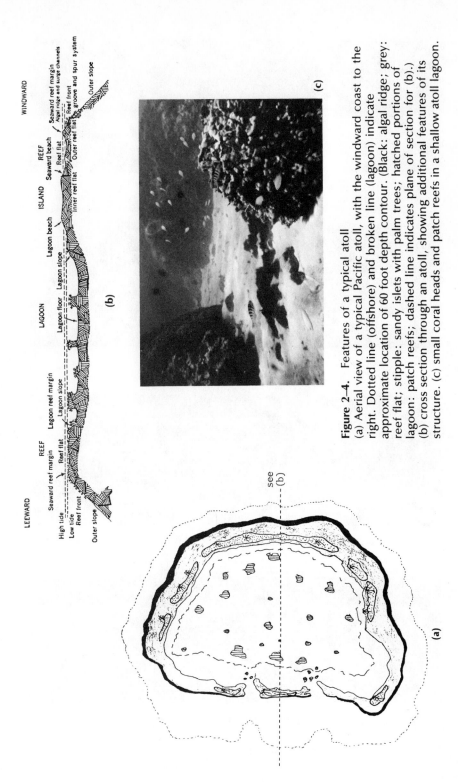

Figure 2-4. Features of a typical atoll
(a) Aerial view of a typical Pacific atoll, with the windward coast to the right. Dotted line (offshore) and broken line (lagoon) indicate approximate location of 60 foot depth contour. (Black: algal ridge; grey: reef flat; stipple: sandy islets with palm trees; hatched portions of lagoon: patch reefs; dashed line indicates plane of section for (b).) (b) cross section through an atoll, showing additional features of its structure. (c) small coral heads and patch reefs in a shallow atoll lagoon.

(a) Zone 1: shallow waters subjected to heavy surge

(b) Zone 2: slope dominated by branching colonies

(c) Zone 2/3 boundary: mixture of branching and platelike colony forms

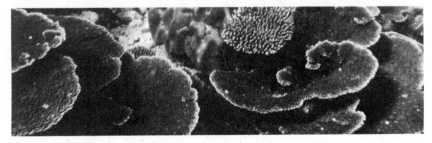

(d) Zone 3: slope dominated by platelike colonies

Figure 2–5. Zones of the seaward slopes

Zone 3.   Deeper still is a region where current and wave action are almost negligible. Coral colonies are large and platelike, a shape that presents maximum surface area to the sunlight and plankton that descend from the waters above. Whereas a firm foundation is essential within the shallower zones, corals in the deeper portion of the reef may grow on loose debris or even on top of one another.

Zone 4.   Finally you reach a depth where the nutrient supply is no longer sufficient to support healthy reef-building corals. You have entered a twilight zone, where light is dim and the world around you consists of blacks and blues. Zooxanthellae are inefficient under these conditions, and at this level reef-building corals fail to compete with other forms of marine life such as sponges or soft corals.

As you become more familiar with the entire range of coral shapes and sizes along the slope, you will begin to notice variations within these zones. Along the sides of the grooves, near the surface, the encrusting forms may grow in overlapping layers like poured fudge, shedding sand and gaining a slight angle from the vertical, which increases exposure to light. Among the branching corals of Zone 2 there may be colonies that are short and squat near the shallower portions of the zone, taller and more delicate in deeper waters. Some platelike colonies in Zone 3 may produce vertical finger-shaped projections across their surface, whereas in areas where sand drifts over them the plates may angle noticeably toward or away from the reef face, enlisting the aid of gravity in removing debris. After still more time, you will begin to see variations that are clearly the result of localized, small-scale differences in conditions, such as delicate colonies growing in the shelter provided by more massive forms.

Zones are established not by rule but by dynamic interactions. Planulae settlement occurs primarily at random, and weeding out is done through competition with other colonies and the mechanical forces of the seas and currents. Although the life of a coral along the submarine slopes may seem rather tranquil and laid back, it is actually a life and death struggle fought in slow motion. During a calm season a branching colony rises amid more massive forms, shading and killing many of their polyps. It grows larger, becomes unable to resist the resurgent waves, and is hurled up onto the reef flat or blown down the reef face to shatter more delicate colonies below. Encrusting colonies grow over one another. Platelike colonies grow away from the slopes, shading and killing portions of deeper plates. The dead areas are fair game for boring organisms, algae, and collection sites for debris until the skeleton fractures. The entire colony may then lose its grip on the slope and slip off into the depths.

No single colony lasts forever, and only the most massive and encrusting forms survive for a thousand years. Most colonies succumb to competition, waves, boring organisms, predators, or disease. You can always find dead colonies covered with threads of algae and partially broken down, even on the healthiest of reefs. Scattered fragments of past generations lie wedged in the interstices between living colonies. Yet this is how reefs really grow, for the living colonies are as small a layer over the surface of the reef as the living polyps are above the surfaces of their colonial skeletons. As soon as a fragment of a coral skeleton reaches the bottom it is secured in place by algae and bacteria that produce a mineral-rich cement. In the process they are enlarging the base of the reef and creating a new site for the attachment of planulae.

Because of the abundance of living colonies along the outer reef face, such activities may be difficult to spot. Instead of digging about between the colonies, let us return to the relative calm of the reef flat, where we can more easily see reef growth in progress. Near its seaward edge you will encounter an area completely covered by encrusting or "coralline" algae. This algal ridge is sometimes brightly colored, and it is here that their action can easily be examined in the absence of coral colonies, which have difficulty handling the temperatures, wave action, and tidal exposure of this portion of the reef. The algae are really partners in the formation of the reef complex, cementing the debris and skeletal remains of the corals. (In a few cases, notably in Hawaii, the Bahamas, and Rocas Island off Brazil, algal action has been responsible for the formation of sizable reefs in the absence of large coral communities, but these are special cases that we will generally ignore.)

Now we will proceed across the flat, upper surface of the reef toward the enclosed lagoon. The windward reef flat is often quite extensive, 500 yards or more in width, and the algal ridge is present only along its seaward margin. Immediately inside the ridge the reef flat is still not particularly hospitable. It is usually very shallow and even exposed to the air at low tides. This region is usually covered with bits of debris, broken fragments of colonies hurled there by the seas. At high tides wave action churns these pieces and produces large quantities of sand that may be swept back over the ridge or carried over the inner portions of the reef flat.

Farther from the sea there may be an area of shallow depressions or pools. Corals will survive here despite the daily temperature fluctuations and the occasional deluge of fresh water that accompanies the storms of the rainy season. Some of these colonies arrived as planulae, but most are surviving fragments of deeper colonies that were battered and thrown onto the reef flat by waves. Because of this you may find quite a variety of different species in the deeper pockets. Some representative views of reef flats are shown in Figure 2–6.

At its inner edge the reef flat often supports a sandy islet. Whatever survives there must be able to tolerate salt spray, abrasive windborne sands, and the occasional prolonged droughts of the dry season. Although the number of species able to handle such conditions is limited, each may be present in abundance and veritable jungles are found on atolls with unusually heavy rainfall, such as Fanning or Palmyra Islands (Line Islands). The appearance of a more typical islet is shown in Plate 3. Whether or not islets occur there is often a layer of beach rock just short of the lagoon. This gently sloping platform is clearly different from the outer reef flat, but its actual mode of formation is still debated. Most likely it is the result of fresh waters dissolving the outer surface of the reef flat, and the materials precipitating near its inner margin.

The lagoon is an enclosed body of water that may communicate with the open sea through one or more reef breaks or "passes." The depth of the lagoon varies. In the Pacific, atoll lagoons are 150 to 200 feet deep; in the Atlantic they seldom reach 50 feet. In either event, conditions in the lagoon are rather different from those along the outer reef slopes. Lagoon waters are relatively shallow and confined, so they warm beyond the surrounding sea temperatures. The resulting updrafts, clouds, and showers may lower the salt content of the lagoon waters from time to time. Sand is continually being carried into the lagoon by waves, more sand carpets the floor of the lagoon, and so visibility in lagoon waters is lower than that of the open ocean. Despite these qualifications, the sheltered confines of the lagoon contain abundant marine life.

The nature of the inner reef flat/lagoon boundary varies, but often the lagoon nearby will be relatively shallow with a gradual slope to the depths of the central lagoon. Massive reef development similar to that seen along the windward slopes is uncommon. Even when the waves wash regularly across the entire reef flat the presence of large quantities of sand and the decreased impact of the waves changes the local zonation and species structure. More often, coral colonies are found in scattered clusters or *patch reefs*. In shallow waters these may consist of many colonies of a single species, such as the branching staghorn corals. These colonies are tall, slender, highly branched, and the fastest growing colony form. The ability to grow rapidly toward the surface prevents these colonies from being buried by shifting sands and the vertical branches shed sand with the aid of gravity. The polyps, of

Figure 2–6. The reef flat
The reef flats of islands bordered by fringing reefs can be explored relatively easily. Over most of the coast of Tutuila, American Samoa, the reef flat is shallow and extensive. (a) aerial view of reef flat, southeast coast of Tutuila (b) warm, shallow waters over the reef flat support small colonies of corals and coral debris hurled over the reef front by large waves (Tutuila) (c) beach rock can be seen here at the inner edge of the reef flat (Rarotonga)

course, have a good exposure to whatever plankton the lagoon currents may bear, and wave action is very light. Thickets of staghorn corals may be scattered over a wide area.

Other patch reefs are more massive, involving many species. These formations can be found in deeper lagoon waters as well. Large patch reefs, and even table reefs a mile across, are steep-sided, rising like towers from the floor of the lagoon. All the lagoon-bound corals subsist on the sunlight and plankton that arrive either over the windward reef flat, through the passes, or within the lagoon itself. Circulatory patterns around an atoll and within its lagoon are complex, as illustrated in Figure 2–7. Patch reefs often occur in lines, responding to variations in current and wave action that are as yet poorly understood.

The broad blue expanse of the lagoon is dotted with swatches of color that mark the location of the patch reefs. Navigation under these conditions would be virtually impossible were it not for the fact that you can quickly learn to use the color of the water as an index of depth, from deep blue (80+ feet) through intermediate shades to aquamarine (30 feet or so), yellow (dangerously shallow), and red-brown (awash at low tide). Raroia Atoll alone contains approximately 2,000 patch reefs in its lagoon. Guiding a vessel through such a maze is a nerve-wracking experience.

The leeward reef flat is usually narrower than its windward counterpart because reef growth is slower. (The windward coast receives the plankton brought to the island by the prevailing currents.) It is here that you will find passes leading from the lagoon to the open ocean in a

Figure 2–7. Currents around an atoll
Hypothetical circulation around an atoll, showing the formation of counterrotating eddies in the lee of an island, and strong currents inshore over the shallow (ten fathom) terrace. Within the lagoon the surface currents flow from east to west, in response to the push of the tradewinds; deeper currents flow west to east along the floor of the lagoon, upwelling at the eastern lagoon boundary

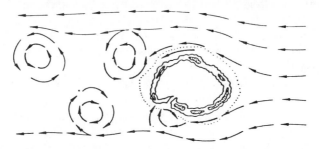

typical Pacific atoll. Caribbean atolls have very poorly developed lee-ward reefs, and the lagoons are in broad confluence with the ocean. When a pass is present, the entrance on the lagoon side is often guarded by a concentration of especially robust patch reefs that benefit from the plankton contained in the waters that enter and exit via the nearby channel.

Passes are usually shallower than the lagoon as a whole. Several factors may have been responsible for their formation. They may be relics of earlier stages of atoll formation, as discussed in Chapter 7, but they may also indicate areas where severe westerly storm seas have breached what is normally a sheltered portion of the atoll's reefs. In addition, over the past two million years sea level has risen and fallen repeatedly. When sea level was at its lowest, atolls and lagoons were exposed to the elements. The more narrow, delicate leeward reefs suffered most from erosion, and the rising seas that later struck them encountered relatively less resistance. In any event, once formed, such passes tend to remain for a time before filling in.

Each pass has a particular character all its own. When currents are swift the central portion of a pass may be devoid of corals, either because of the scouring action of transported sands, periodic smother-ing by large amounts of sand, or some combination of the two. Even when corals are present within a pass, if the waters flowing by are less salty, warmer, or more turbid than would be considered ideal, coral growth may be restricted. But at other islands the inner walls and floors of the passes may resemble the slopes of the leeward reef.

The leeward slopes are less spectacular than those along the wind-ward side of the atoll. Near the passes the corals may be periodically exposed to turbid lagoon waters, and the oceanic waters that reach them traveling along the coast may be low in plankton after passing among the colonies upstream. In addition, the swift currents moving offshore through a pass may produce a localized upwelling of cooler waters that may further inhibit reef growth. Even away from the pass-(es) the marked zonation that was apparent on the windward slopes is less obvious. Sheltered from the prevailing winds and seas, the more delicate but faster-growing species thrive closer to the surface. These areas may be swept clean when severe westerly storms arrive, and a cycle of growth, destruction, and recovery is the general rule along the leeward coast.

We have now considered two extremes, the windward and leeward reef faces. There are many intergrades between the two, and the ap-pearance of the reef will vary in a more or less predictable manner as you travel along the coast. Each portion of the reef should be examined in terms of its relative exposure to the seas produced by the regular tradewinds or the occasional but more severe westerly storms. As exposure to the prevailing seas decreases, the coral zones move toward the surface as the more rugged massive species are replaced by more delicate forms. Completely sheltered areas that receive neither prevailing winds nor storm seas will be totally dominated by large and delicate forms. Such total protection is uncommon on atolls, and usually either broad, upwardly displaced zones comparable to those of windward slopes or a stage in the destruction/recovery cycle typical of leeward reefs are found.

The general structure of a barrier reef or fringing reef is much the same. A barrier reef looks like an atoll encircling one or more volcanic islands. The major differences are that the lagoon is often shallower than that of an atoll, and there may be reefs developed along the coast of the enclosed island(s) as well. There are few barrier reefs in the Atlantic, but innumerable examples are found in the tropical Pacific. Fringing reefs resemble atolls with the entire lagoon filled up by the island, leaving only the reef flat and the seaward slopes. Fringing reefs show the greatest differences between leeward and windward reef structure, for there are often portions of the leeward coast that are totally sheltered from seas of any kind. Under these conditions large, platelike colonies may even be found growing over the surface of the reef flat.

A little experience should enable you to pick out these variations, and you will find that looking for such details will keep your snorkeling trips from ever becoming boring. Whenever you explore a tropical reef you will encounter variations in colony size, shape, and depth distribution that reflect differences in exposure to waves, sunlight, and plankton.

Before concluding this chapter I should mention some practical applications for this information. Figure 2–8 summarizes several details, and although the illustration depicts an atoll the overall pattern would be equally valid for fringing or barrier reef formations. I will make two additional observations that are directed at readers who might find themselves aboard a vessel approaching an island that bears coral reefs. Rule Number One is to regard your charts with suspicion. Look at the date of the survey, not the printing, and if it wasn't done yesterday, or better still today, it is bound to be inaccurate. Just how fast coral reefs grow and change is a complex question, but experimental results indicate that an average value of 8 feet per 1,000 years for the reef as a whole is probably close to the mark. However you must not make the mistake of assuming from this that your charts will only vary by 0.09 inch per year, for the growth rate of individual coral colonies may be much higher than that of the reef as a whole. Branching corals can grow toward the surface at over 3 inches per year, sands can drift into passes overnight, and massive coral blocks may be tossed in any direction by storms. Figure 2–9 compares the published and actual conditions found near the pass at Christmas Island, an atoll in the Line Islands. Because of its military potential as an airfield, this island was surveyed relatively recently (1949–1951), which makes it current compared to those on which many other Pacific charts are based. With changes as radical as these after only thirty years, it is clear that you should not make any assumptions from charts prepared in the mid-nineteenth century. If your eyes and your charts disagree, the eyes have it!

Figure 2–8. Useful information concerning a typical atoll

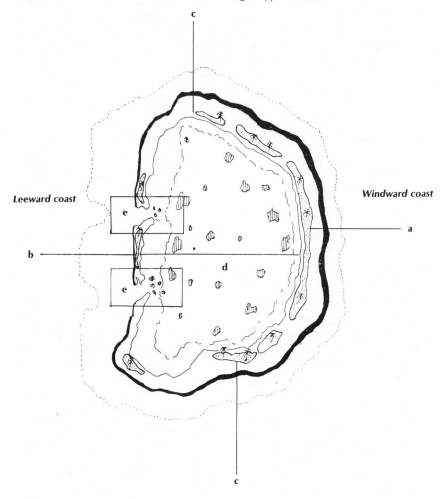

Site	Reef Flat	Snorkeling	Reef Slope	Diving	Fishing
a	broad; may have pools near islet; good beachcombing; shelling in deep pools inshore	possible if pools exist; beware of strong currents because wave-driven waters return over algal ridge; stay inshore	steep; heavy and dangerous surge; coral depth limited due to surface turbulence reducing incident light	excellent; enter from tended boat and approach below surge level; watch for strong currents to the island making return to boat strenuous	good trolling in deep water close to the reef
b	narrow; poor shelling and beachcombing; pools may be absent	possible and safe if pools exist	gradual slope; calm; corals to greater depth than (a)	good to excellent; entry over reef table or by boat; watch for offshore currents associated with passes	good bottom fishing along reef slope
c	intermediate width; good shelling and beachcombing	usually excellent; watch for currents near surge channels	slope varies; often calm; interesting zonation	excellent; entry over reef table or boat depending on conditions; watch for currents running parallel to coast, away from entry point	superb bottom fishing in and among patch reefs
d	may be extensive; calm, excellent shelling	excellent around patch reefs; good shelling on sandy bottom	gradual slope; calm waters; less diversity of species in general	good; entry anywhere; visibility less than outer reefs	
e	variable	DANGEROUS due to currents	variable	DANGEROUS but possible with experienced divers and boat tender	

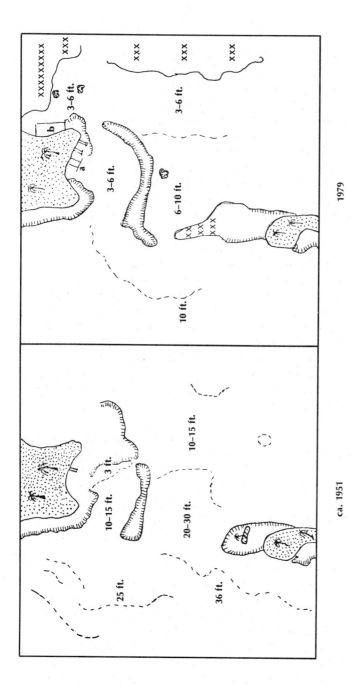

ca. 1951

(a)

1979

(b)

Figure 2–9. Changes in the reef at Christmas Island
(a) details of the lagoon entrance taken from a British Admiralty chart, based on New Zealand government surveys of 1938–1941 with corrections through 1950 (b) details of the lagoon entrance as of 1979; note the changes in structure and depth within the confines of the pass (stipple: sandy islet; hatched line: reef (awash); hatched circles: patch reefs; XXX: under 3 feet depth; a: functional pier with adjacent ruins; b: copra loading wharf with floating dock/barge).

In Chapter 1 you may have noted that I neglected to mention the effects of tidal cycles on tropical seas. Tidal ranges in the tropics are relatively small, approximately 2 to 3 feet, and have few significant effects on coastal marine life. But near passes through the leeward reef, tidal effects may merit more serious attention. Rule Number Two states that approaching vessels must always arrive at the proper tide, and whenever possible the lagoon should be entered with the sun behind so that variations in depth can be more easily seen.

The size and structure of an atoll, as well as the number of passes into the lagoon, should be considered in planning your approach. On atolls with a substantial beach on the windward reef, there is a periodic ebb and flow with the tides. The larger the island, the more water must be moved through the pass(es). Even with a small tidal range we are talking about removing or replacing the top 2 to 3 feet of a lagoon, which probably covers several square miles. At full bore, the current flowing through the relatively narrow passes will be fierce, and currents in excess of 10 mph are not uncommon. This velocity exceeds the speed limits of most yachts and some larger vessels. Caught in a full incoming tide, careening through a narrow pass in the grip of such a current toward a seemingly unbroken wall of patch reefs—this is an experience to avoid. So is attempting to enter against a building tide and finding yourself unable to make further headway—or turn around—as darkness falls. Under these conditions the ideal time to enter or leave is during the brief slack period following a high tide, preferably in the late afternoon (entering) or early morning (leaving) so that the sun will be behind you.

On atolls without protecting sand islets to weather, or on larger barrier reef systems, the prevailing seas may cross into the lagoon on a regular basis. The continual influx of water will then result in a one-way flow through the leeward passes regardless of the state of the tide. When tide and wave work together currents may approach 15 mph, and huge whirlpools may form along the outer portions of the pass. Passage into the lagoon may be virtually impossible for small vessels except on an incoming tide, preferably early in the morning before the tradewinds increase in intensity.

In this chapter you have become acquainted with the basic features of coral reefs and learned a bit about the biology of the animals responsible for them. The reef-building corals are only one part of an integrated community that also includes plants, bacteria, and many other animals. For the duration of this part of the book we will gradually expand our discussion to include some other important members of the community. We will begin with the colorful marine fishes.

Chapter Three

The Marine Fishes

What exactly *is* a fish? As I noted briefly in the Introduction, fish are vertebrates, members of a diverse phylum known as the *chordates*. At some point in their lives most vertebrates share features that reflect their common ancestry, notably the presence of gill slits, vertebrae, and a braincase or cranium.

The vertebrate herd can be subdivided into separate classes whose members share additional characters because they are even more closely related. Two different classes have members that satisfy a broad definition of "fish"—they rely on gills for respiration, have characteristic paired fins for propulsion and steerage, and possess internal and external features that restrict them to life in the water. In other respects these two groups are quite different. The smaller class encompasses the sharks, skates, rays, and rabbitfishes, collectively termed *cartilaginous fishes*. This is the Class *Chondrichthyes* (*chondros*, "cartilage"; *ichthys*, "fish"), a relatively homogeneous assemblage of around 600 species. Several of these will be discussed in Chapter 4, so we will disregard them for the moment.

The other class of fishes is far more formidable. The Class *Osteichthyes* (*osteo*, "bone") has representatives in fresh and salt waters, from the equator to the poles, and from the bottoms of the deepest trenches to the tops of mountains. No one knows exactly how many different kinds of bony fishes exist, but estimates run as high as 40,000 species, only half of which have been described to date. Their possible forms, sizes, and life styles are far too diverse to be considered in the course of a single chapter, or even a single book, so please forgive me if I pick and choose.

First let us examine the appearance and importance of some physical characteristics of bony fishes. Many people think of them as unsophisticated creatures, but actually they have changed greatly since their ancestors swam in the seas more than 400 million years ago. Extremely primitive fishes were protected by a dense bony armor that ensheathed their entire bodies, including their fins. This armor was particularly massive over the head, usually breaking into numerous smaller elements farther aft. Such a covering is useful as a defense against predators and as a mineral storehouse. It is also heavy, and therefore expensive, because it takes a lot of energy just to carry it around all the time. Because the fossil record is rather sketchy, we know very little about the lives of these animals, and even their exact relationship to modern bony fishes has yet to be agreed upon.

Bony fishes clearly related to modern forms appear around 100 million years later. They were still rather well defended, with large, thick scales and stout spines, but they were probably faster and more maneuverable. They were still heavy. To keep themselves from settling to the bottom, these fishes had to produce an upward force to overcome the pull of gravity. This lift was provided by the combined actions of the asymmetrical tail and the broad, low-set pectoral fins that functioned like airplane wings. The other fins of the body acted to control progress through the water, keeping the animal from rocking and rolling. With this arrangement a fish could stay off the bottom as

Figure 3–1. Primitive fishes (a) typical representative of a group of fishes common in the seas roughly 400 million years ago (b) primitive bony fish from fossils approximately 280 million years old. (See text for discussion.)

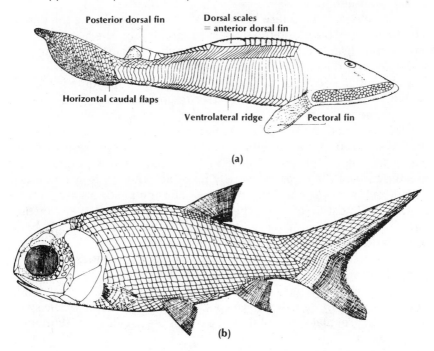

Posterior dorsal fin   Dorsal scales = anterior dorsal fin

Horizontal caudal flaps

Ventrolateral ridge   Pectoral fin

(a)

(b)

long as it was moving, but as soon as it stopped, gravity would take over. The possible habits of such fishes were therefore restricted, for without the ability to control their position above the bottom while at rest these fishes could chase things or filter plankton from the water, but would hardly succeed in quietly browsing over the bottom or maneuvering gracefully in tight quarters.

Between 300 and 200 million years ago there were more progressive developments. Many of the changes were ramifications of a single development that was internal, not external, in origin. Over this period shallow water fishes appeared that had blind pockets branching from their throats. The walls of these pouches were lined with blood vessels, and by gulping air and forcing it into these chambers these fish could obtain additional oxygen from the air. These lunglike structures conveyed an additional, extremely important benefit to the fish that possessed them. Air is buoyant, and the air contained in these chambers lowered the underwater weight of the fish just as the air in a diving vest lowers the underwater weight of a scuba diver. Lighter fishes were more maneuverable and faster, and less energy was required to produce lift. With more speed, armor could be reduced, because more predators could be outrun. The fossil record shows how successful these fishes were, and how this "small" development snowballed in subsequent generations.

Take a look at a modern bony fish (Figure 3–2) and note the generally streamlined body and the placement of the fins. The ancient armor has all but disappeared, reduced to a series of thin bony plates, or scales, which develop just beneath the epidermis. These scales are flexible, and they overlap to permit a wide range of movement and still provide some protection from predators and parasites. The massive bony elements protecting the head, sense organs, and gills have been similarly reduced to a number of larger scales. Narrow, modified scales or "rays" support the membranous fins. By moving these rays the useful area of the fin can be altered to a precise degree, permitting far greater control than was previously possible. The tail is symmetrical, putting all its power into forward thrust, and the pectorals are high on the sides, almost in line with the axis of the body. Here they function most effectively in braking and turning, rather than acting as bowplanes and wings, which are now unnecessary.

The "swim bladder" of modern fishes has also changed from the primitive lungs of ancestral forms. Usually it is single, not paired, and it is partially or completely cut off from the throat. Instead of swallowing or belching air, these fishes have special glands in the wall of the swim bladder that regulate the volume of gas to a precise degree. With most

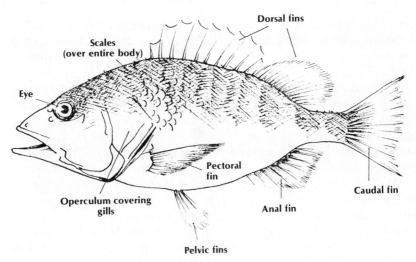

Figure 3–2. Appearance of a modern bony fish
Note the placement of the fins and the general contours of the body.
(See text for additional details.)

of the armor eliminated, by carefully regulating the volume of the swim bladder at about 5 percent of the total volume of its body a marine fish can be neutrally buoyant. This means that the fish can hover motionless in the water without expending any energy in the process.

When this capability first appeared it was the key to a variety of new behaviors, feeding strategies, and life styles. Precise control of position became ever more important, and fin placement and body shape altered accordingly. Most significant of all, for our purposes, was that just as armor was fading out and neutral buoyancy was becoming a possibility, the modern three-dimensional coral reefs were evolving. In short, while a new and complex habitat was appearing, fishes were developing an ability that would enable them to explore its every nook and cranny.

Simply to list all the various species of reef fish would accomplish very little. The list would be very long, very dry, and would bore all of us. Instead I would like to help you to understand a limited number of patterns that link the general appearance of a fish with its behavior and life style. In this way you will become able to make educated guesses about any reef fish you are likely to meet. These patterns exist because diversity does not just happen. The fantastic diversity of reef fishes developed over time in response to a basic fact of life: If you don't eat, you won't survive. Different fishes show the same general patterns of appearance and behavior because they have independently reached a solution to the same basic problems of competition and survival. If you know how fishes compete for food, and how competition has led to the diversity of modern species, then you will be able to recognize important patterns when the fishes swim by.

We have already discussed how corals compete on the reef face, so let's begin on familiar ground. Zonation exists because the species of corals differ in the shape of their mature colonies. Which species dominates the reef at a particular site is determined by competition with adjacent colonies and the general character of the physical environment, notably light, currents, and wave action. You could say that a species is "selected" to survive by its responses to its animate and inanimate surroundings. The term *natural selection* can be used to describe the weeding out that occurs as a result of these interactions. Yet all too often it is treated as if it were a law of physics, like gravity. It is hardly so predictable. Natural selection is underway all along the reef slope, yet the species selected differ from place to place. Natural selection is simply a convenient phrase to describe the *process* of selection through interactions with the living and nonliving environment.

Natural selection along the reef face has affected the survival of one species versus another and has created zones. But when you stop and think about it you realize that it is not the *species* that has been selected, only a few individual members of the species. These *individuals* are the ones that have managed to survive and compete against members of other species *and members of the same species as well.* This subtle distinction would hardly be worth mentioning but for the fact that all members of a particular species are not identical. Because they differ, the process of natural selection can be held accountable not only for the changes in species that occur over time, but also for the appearance of new species.

You might wonder how we manage to characterize a species, let alone tell if it is changing, if all the individuals differ to some degree. The most convenient method is to describe an "average" member. For example, people come in all sizes and shapes, but we still can speak of the height and weight of the average human being.

The members of a species live, reproduce, and die. New variations are continually appearing for a number of reasons, and sexual reproduction shuffles these to produce different combinations in later generations. Natural selection judges the success of each variation as it appears, and in the eyes of natural selection most variations are insignificant, like the different colors of roses—they neither help nor hinder the individuals as they struggle to survive. Many other variations reduce the individual's chances for survival, like roses without thorns, which are quickly eaten by grazing animals. Only a very few of the many possible variations give the individuals a competitive advantage. These fortunate individuals will do much better than average, and as their numbers increase in subsequent generations the "average" qualities of the species will gradually change as a result. This, then, is how we may define change in a species: The average characteristics of future generations are different from those of the present generation.

Now we will use some imagination to predict what kinds of variations would be advantageous if they appeared in a nondescript group of fish. We can make such predictions because fish, unlike most governments, operate on a fixed budget. Better still, fish lack the ability to function forever in the red. The ground rules are simple. Each fish is competing to get energy "income" in the form of food, which it then spends on activities essential for its survival. How can we measure the relative success of an individual fish?

We simply audit the energy accounts. Average fish will manage to meet their expenses and have sufficient surplus left over to provide the energy for reproduction. This insures that there will be roughly the same number of similar fish in the next generation. The effects of an unfavorable variation are immediately apparent, for a fish that fails to obtain enough food to perform all its essential functions will die, or if you prefer, it will be "eliminated by natural selection." The rare and favorable variation will wind up with a larger-than-average surplus, and hence with more energy to devote to reproduction. This will mean that the number of similar individuals in subsequent generations will increase, because its progeny will share the favorable character, whatever it is. But what might it be?

Basically it will have to be responsible for either increasing the amount of food obtained or decreasing the amount of energy that must be spent on essential activities. Obviously, before we can be more specific we must identify these expenses in greater detail. The energy obtained in food will be called E_f, and this energy must be spent in the following ways:

1. Future meals must be broken down before they can be absorbed in the intestine, and we can call this expense D, for digestion.

2. Even if the fish moves nary a muscle, the cells of its body will require some energy to stay alive, and we can call this basal metabolism, Bm.

3. All animal cells require oxygen, so a fish will have to spend some energy on the physical act of breathing, B.

4. Because no process involving energy is very efficient, a lot of

potentially useful energy will wind up being lost as heat or returned to the environment in the fecal wastes or urine. We can call this regrettable evidence of inefficiency *L*, for lost.

Therefore, if a fish wastes no effort at all, and never does anything but sit, breathe, and digest, the energy in its food must at least equal these basic expenses, and

$$E_f = D + Bm + B + L$$

if the fish is to survive. This is much too simplified, even for us, because there are other unavoidable expenses involved in operating a fish. Unless food walks into its mouth unassisted there must be some energy expended in chasing prey or seizing suitable plants *(C)*, and for carnivores an additional expense exists in chasing prey that later escapes *(O* for oops!). If the fish moves between meals it must expend some energy in swimming *(S)*, and probably some in avoiding predators *(A)*, and some in any one of a number of activities that have no direct involvement with finding food or avoiding enemies, such as defending a territory *(M* for miscellaneous). Therefore, a more realistic energy budget must be along the lines of:

$$E_f = D + Bm + B + L + C + O + S + A + M$$

With its budget in the black, whatever surplus is left over can be diverted into growth and/or reproduction. These don't really compete, for fish with a reliable surplus of energy both grow more and reproduce more. Periods of growth alternate with the reproductive seasons, and larger fish produce more (not larger) eggs or sperm.

Now the ways in which a fish may differ from others can be examined more closely. For our purposes the cost of digesting food *(D)*, keeping cells alive *(Bm)*, and losses due to biological inefficiency *(L)* are very difficult to fiddle with. The other major expenses can be adjusted, but many of them are interrelated. Let's look at each one.

B: A fish that swims all the time can just open its mouth and let water flow over the gills, and this reduces *B*. It also increases *S*, of course, and swimming is not cheap.

C: Increasing your capture efficiency can be accomplished via several routes. You could propose a change in mouth structure, which might influence *B*, or you could make the fish more difficult to see by changing its color, which could incidentally lower *O* and *A* as well.

O: This could be reduced by increasing camouflage, which would also reduce *A*; moving stealthily and slowly, which would reduce *S* but increase *B*; moving swiftly, which would increase *S*; or changing mouth structure or feeding techniques which might also affect *C* or *B*.

S: You could either increase streamlining, and hence increase speed, decrease *S*, and probably lower *B*, or stop swimming altogether, which would eliminate *S* but drastically increase *B*.

M: Most of the above changes would have their effects on this, as on *Ef*, so it is difficult to address *M* as an isolated phenomenon. But you could follow several lines of reasoning, such as decreasing territorial defense, courtship displays, and so on.

Now we can begin to see the basis for general patterns of form and behavior. You might experiment for a moment and create several complex patterns for yourself to see how the relationships work out: decrease *S* by not swimming, decrease *O*, *C*, and *A* by camouflage, and you have a basic description that applies to a scorpionfish; decrease *S* by streamlining, decrease *B* and *O* by swimming fast, decrease *O* and *A* by changes in coloration, and you are designing a fish rather like a mackerel.

This kind of mental exercise can give you a feel for the kinds of patterns that might exist, and how these patterns solve the overall energy equation in different ways. Yet it does not explain how *many* complex patterns could arise from what were presumably rather primitive average fishes. Our discussion of natural selection and energy budgets thus far has enabled us to describe the advantages of changes, and how a particular species may change, but not how new and different species appear. Because these two processes are closely related, and each has been partially responsible for the diversity of modern reef fishes, we need to sort them out a little more carefully.

We can do this pretty easily now that the groundwork has been established. First I will summarize the mechanism for producing changes within a species by setting up another simplified model. This time it will be a model fish species. We are dealing with a species with only 100 members, and each member is slightly different from the others. These fish live only one year, and they reproduce asexually, which means solo, and each of the progeny is identical with the adult parent. The entire population spawns on 24 December and dies on 1 January, and each adult fish produces around 100 little fishes. Ninety-nine percent of these die before reaching maturity, falling to predators or simply bad luck in finding enough to eat, because the local reef will support only 100 adult fish of this kind.

We are interested in following the fate of one particular fish, and just about the time we first visit the reef our fish has matured. It so happened that as a result of a passing cosmic ray that struck the fertilized egg, this fish is slightly different from its parent. It is not much of a difference, just a different color pattern, but because of this variation our fish has been very successful. With its unusual coloration the fish is more difficult to spot against the backdrop of the reef, so it has a lower A expense; it also has better luck sneaking up on potential prey, so O is down and Ef is up. As a result this fish has an exceptional surplus of energy all its life and is larger than other fish in the population at maturity. Because larger fish of a given species make more (not larger) eggs, on 24 December this fish releases into the world 120 fertilized eggs instead of the usual 100. Ho-hum, you might say, a few more little fish, but in fact these are important little fish because they all will share the color pattern of the parent. They will easily out-compete the other young fish for the limited food supply, fewer will starve, and although predators may take a few the mortality rate is bound to drop, perhaps to 95 percent instead of 99 percent.

This means that when the breeding season arrives the following year the population will consist of ninety-four "average" fish and six of the new color. When we return the next year we find *thirty-six* of the new shade, and the year after that the "normal"-type fish will have been completely replaced, and the species average will have our new coloration. The variation in color has provided our fish with a selective advantage and as a result the character of the entire population has changed over time.

In the real world such changes in entire species do occur, but the process is much slower. For one thing, most fishes reproduce sexually, which means that not all of its offsprings might show the favorable character. Large populations also complicate the picture. The number of individuals is often so great that a new variation, no matter how favorable, cannot possibly reproduce enough to eliminate other forms in a few generations. In addition, while *one* favorable variation may be gaining ground, *others* might appear, in which case the results become very difficult to predict.

So the lesson to be learned here is that the characteristics of a species are most likely to change quickly and completely if the population is relatively small. This hardly seems relevant, for most species of fish contain an enormous number of individuals. But suppose a population became split into several isolated groups. Let's take our original fish population and divide it into two groups, I and II, with Group II containing our original "new" fish. In the latter group the progeny of the unusually colored animal come to dominate the population even more rapidly than before because the population is only half the size. But variations appear at random, and in Group I a *different* variation appears in the form of a fish with a slightly different shape of mouth which makes it able to grab unwary shrimp just a little faster and hold them more firmly. This individual would then possess a selective advantage compared with the average fish of its population, because it would have lower O expenses and higher Ef as a result. Therefore, its offspring would soon dominate Group I.

Now let's go a little further. Individual variations continue to appear in Groups I and II, but most of these are without beneficial effect. But let us suppose for the sake of argument that exactly the same variation were to appear in each population. The different fish in each group has a rather bizarre fleshy tab or flap hanging off its snout. In Group I this might have no effect, or perhaps the flap waves about in the water while the fish is trying to stalk its prey, thus scaring off the shrimp. Obviously this fish would find itself with no selective advantage, and perhaps a serious liability. Meanwhile in Group II small fishes that fail to spot the camouflaged fish swim up to investigate what appears to be a worm and get swallowed for their trouble. The "new" fish in Group II, therefore, has a great selective advantage, because O and C have almost been eliminated. This is a good, if simple, example of how one random variation may affect the selective advantage conveyed by later variations: The fleshy tab was of no particular use unless the fish were already difficult to see.

In this way complex chains of events may occur, rather like falling dominoes. These changes could potentially accumulate until the two groups, originally members of the same species, are so different that they must be considered as separate species. In our model populations we would have to make a judgment call based on general habits and appearance, but in nature we can use more discrete criteria. In animals that reproduce sexually, if isolation breaks down and the two populations interbreed successfully, the obvious differences between the two will decrease in future generations, and the two populations did not represent distinct species. All dogs are members of the same species, despite the fact that chihuahuas and mastiffs are quite distinctive in appearance. Regardless of the physical differences between them, the two animals can and will interbreed (given the opportunity) to produce puppies that are not representative of either variety. In essence these will be closer to average for the species as a whole.

But if isolation continues, and changes continue to accumulate, the odds are pretty good that sooner or later some of these cumulative variations will affect their abilities to interbreed with members of the parent species. If the barriers are removed and the two populations intermingle without crossbreeding, then we are dealing with distinct species.

Populations of fishes have very short generation times, and a new species can evolve in only 5,000 to 10,000 years. Because bony fishes have been hanging around coral reefs for 200 *million* years, there has certainly been enough time for a large number of species to appear. The only question is how they became isolated from one another. We have already commented on the immense size of the tropical oceans. Most reef fishes rely on surface currents for the transport of floating eggs and/or larvae, and the appearance of a particular species at one location or another depends on their transport in the right direction at the right time, just as we saw in the case of reef-building corals. The farther two islands or reefs are apart, the greater the degree of isolation between them. One may be relatively more isolated than another because of the direction of the prevailing currents.

Because arrival at a relatively isolated area is primarily a matter of luck, such a reef may only be colonized by a few individuals of one species, despite the fact that they may be common elsewhere. With a small resident population, any variations that appear will accumulate rapidly, perhaps changing the average characteristics of the group to the point that they constitute a distinct and unique species. At first this species will be found only at that particular isolated reef system. Such species are called *endemics*. There are no laws to restrict the distribution of their progeny, however, and if the isolation was due to contrary currents transport downstream may be relatively easy. Endemic species have appeared and later extended their ranges repeatedly, adding to the crowding of modern reefs.

We have cited Hawaii as having a relatively isolated reef system, so let's take a closer look. Johnston Island is a small atoll located between the Hawaiian island chain and the reefs of the central Pacific. At Johnston Island, 72 percent of the species collected in a field survey were found both in the central Pacific and the reefs of Hawaii.[1] An additional 12 percent had managed to reach Johnston but had not appeared in Hawaii. Fourteen percent of the Johnston Island collection consisted of species found in Hawaii but *not* in the central Pacific, and about 2 percent of the collection consisted of endemics known only from the local reefs.

[1] William A. Gosline, "The Inshore Fish Fauna of Johnston Island, a Central Pacific Atoll," in *A Natural History of the Hawaiian Islands—Selected Readings*, ed. E. Alison Kay (Honolulu, HI: University Press of Hawaii, 1972), pp. 456–97.

It might seem that this kind of intermingling would result in more and more competition between species for limited resources, and that the less successful species would be eliminated. Instead an abundance of different species are found, but relatively few individuals in each. Why should this occur?

A reef is an extremely complex environment, extending over a range of depths and in four dimensions. Competition between species can be reduced and a selective advantage gained by specializing in some way. Often this involves becoming more efficient at obtaining a particular food supply, or by selecting a specific depth, bottom type, coral species, or time of day. Specialization implies that the individual members of the species can maximize their personal E_f by avoiding competition and probably reducing C and O, which further increases their energy surplus. Yet it does limit the species by restricting the total population of fish to a smaller segment of the total resources of the reef. This means that the potential number of individuals supported by the reef will be smaller.

Increasing specialization has been possible because seasonal changes on the reef are minimal, and life on the reef is much the same day to day, month to month, and century after century. Why should this be important? Look at a specialized species, such as a butterfly fish that feeds almost exclusively on certain species of coral polyps. It plucks these from the surface of the reef with the aid of an elaborate tubular snout, and with its slender body it can penetrate narrow crevices to browse in peace. The selective advantages are clear: better E_f, lower C, O, A, S, and so forth, and the species as a group obtains a reliable share of the reef's resources. You can probably imagine some chain of events that could result in such a specialization: an isolated population feeding on small animals; an individual with a slightly longer snout appears that can reach into pockets a bit better; then a longer snouted form; then an individual that finds its long snout enables it to pluck unsuspecting polyps from the surface of certain coral colonies, and so on, domino style. Such evolutionary fine tuning has its disadvantages, for if something happens to alter the environment, the specialist is out of luck. Imagine what would happen if suddenly all corals began shedding their polyps every fall, like leaves before the first snowfall. Any fish with a specialized snout would find itself with a tremendous liability because its curious muzzle would be poorly suited for obtaining any other kind of food.

The specializations seen on and over the reefs take a variety of forms, but their appearance is the result of natural selection favoring variations that occurred in a relatively small number of unspecialized populations. Our original model fish was successful at camouflage. When we examined Groups I and II we saw how the variations accumulated to favor the retention of a fleshy lure in Group II but not in Group I. If you now split Group II into two parts, a member of IIa might tend to stay motionless and wave its lure around, whereas in IIb the trend might be to develop massive spines for defense, or perhaps additional tabs and lures. After years of further subdivision, variation, and natural selection there might be hundreds of different species, but we could still identify them as descendants of our original noncamouflaged species. When sorting through the various types of some later date we would include all these related species in a single family and all the members would share common characteristics, such as shapes, colors, or habits to some extent as a reflection of their common ancestry.

By looking for these similarities, the living bony fishes can be sorted out into about 300 families. This is certainly a marked improvement over 20,000 to 40,000 species but it still exceeds my attention span. Fortunately we can restrict our attention to those families whose members you will encounter while snorkeling or diving in the tropics. Several of these families can themselves be grouped according to their general pattern of life style, body form, or habits. Does this mean that they are closely related? Not necessarily—for example, a variation in color could appear in any population of fish, and if it conveyed a selective advantage it would be retained and spread through the population. This alteration would in turn affect the value of later variations through the domino effect discussed above. The appearance of similar patterns in unrelated groups as a result of natural selection and the domino effect is called *convergence*.

In the following pages I will discuss the common patterns found in each group of families and follow up with some brief remarks about the distinctive characteristics of the individual families. These will be generalizations, but because we are looking for trends this is not a particular problem. In addition to these bits of information each family will be represented by a typical silhouette. Once you have become familiar with these outlines you will find fish watching more enjoyable, and anyone who wishes to pursue the identification of individual species will find this ability invaluable when it is time to face the trials and tribulations of field guides.

THE GENERALISTS

We begin with a group of families that I will typify as *Generalists*. These are relatively large predators, and intense specialization has been discouraged. Although we will return to these fishes in a later chapter, for

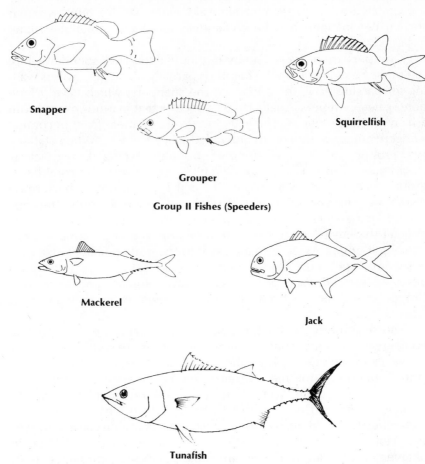

Group I Fishes (Generalists)

Snapper

Squirrelfish

Grouper

Group II Fishes (Speeders)

Mackerel

Jack

Tunafish

Figure 3–3. Fishes of Groups I and II

the moment you might choose to think of the ability to pursue and capture a variety of prey as a specialty of sorts, one that insures sufficient E_f through versatility.

Generalists are not highly specialized in their physical appearance. They are not excessively streamlined nor blindingly fast, but they are quick over short distances. They are not perfectly camouflaged, but they may be difficult to spot; they are not bristling with spines and shields, but their speed and size make them less subject to predation. In short they can pursue or surprise many different kinds of prey, and in enough volume that they can grow to considerable size.

Snappers capture their prey with short, swift bursts of speed, but they may hover or cruise slowly over the reef for most of the day. Large individuals are usually seen traveling alone or in small groups, whereas the smaller snappers may be brilliantly colored and sometimes found in large schools.

Groupers are more sedentary in their habits. They spend much of their time nestled among the corals or partially hidden in caverns waiting for passing prey. In contrast to the snappers, which have prominent scales, groupers usually have fine scales that may be covered with a heavy layer of mucus. This may help to keep them from becoming wedged, stuck, or otherwise entangled while hunting. When stalking prey groupers often sneak along the bottom, rushing at their victims from below. They can be very difficult to see against the coral background because of their coloration, which can properly be termed disruptive. The collection of large colored blotches, spots, freckles, and odd patterns tend to break up the outline of the animal, making it difficult to detect. You will occasionally swim right up to one without noticing it until it scoots into a crevice in the reef virtually under your nose. Small specimens may be quite gregarious, but larger individuals up to several hundred pounds are usually solitary and territorial. Groupers feed most actively at dusk and dawn, when they are even more difficult to see.

The squirrelfish, in contrast, feed at night and are the principal predators of the night shift (as far as bony fishes are concerned). They do not grow as large as either the groupers or snappers, but they are more common on the reef. Because few beginners enjoy snorkeling over the reef at night, you will have to look under things and into pockets in the reef if you want to have a close look at one. Their preference for life in the dark is suggested by their unusually large eyes and their deep reddish tones (the latter will be discussed further in Chapter 6). The squirrelfishes are muscular beasts, protected from larger predators by an array of prominent spiny rays on their fins and by sharp edges on their gill covers and elsewhere on their heads.

THE SPEEDERS

Now compare the Generalists with the *Speeders*. Speeders are always moving, usually at considerable speed, and although they may feed over the reef they do not actually make use of its living space. Because these fishes are among the most highly specialized types we will look at them closely in terms of their adaptations.

Water is about 850 times as dense as air; swimming, therefore, requires a lot of energy—roughly one third of the total E_f for a Generalist fish. Clearly, streamlining should carry a high selective advantage for a fish swimming all the time. In fact, the body of a Speeder is quite distinctive, and more than any other feature demonstrates how specialized they have become. The ideal streamlined form consists of a smoothly tapered spindle, with its maximum diameter located one third of the way along its length. This form disturbs the water least as it moves along, and less disturbance or drag means less resistance to movement, hence higher speeds at lower energy cost.

Mackerel and tuna have body forms very close to this ideal shape. Their scales are small and set so deep below the skin that their bodies appear completely smooth and slick. The bony shield at the head remains, but the sutures are almost invisible, and there are none of the usual bumps, ridges, or ornaments that might disturb the smooth flow of water over the front of the fish. Even the eyes have their edges tapered into the contour of the head so that the general bullet shape is unbroken. There are few other structures on the body that would increase drag, and even the fins fold away into contoured pockets in the body wall. The pectorals are set low on the body, where they steer and generate lift at low speeds, and they retreat like the retractable wings of jet fighters as the fish accelerates to high speeds.

This location of the pectorals is reminiscent of that of primitive fishes, those lacking swim bladders and the capability to achieve neutral buoyancy. For a fish that charges around all the time to have a swim bladder imposes several disadvantages and limitations. Gases expand and contract with increasing and decreasing pressure, and in water the pressure increases rapidly with depth. A fish that changes its depth on the reef has to reset its swim bladder by increasing or decreasing its volume to keep it close to the magic 5 percent figure if it is to remain neutrally buoyant. When depth changes occur suddenly, as when a grouper is yanked to the surface by a bottom fisherman, the swim bladder expands out of control, disturbing nearby organs and creating an enormous bulge that extends into the mouth. Speeders tend to have reduced, nonfunctional swim bladders, and they are able to zoom from one depth to another without difficulty.

The tail of a Speeder is narrow, stiff, and forked. This shape is not very effective at low speeds, and it would hardly do for quick bursts from a standing start because of its small surface area. For that you would expect a broad tail like that of a Generalist. But unlike the massive tails of the latter the forked tail can be whipped back and forth very quickly. Because the speed at which a fish moves through the water is a function of the number of tail beats per minute, a narrow, forked tail is essential if a fish is to reach speeds of 50 mph or more.

At such high speeds even a perfectly streamlined shape would only be efficient if it were rigid—squashing, flexing, or otherwise deforming under pressure would produce a lot of drag and waste energy. These fishes are highly muscular, and when swimming at top speeds their bodies appear almost immobile, with motion restricted to their tails, which are driven back and forth by tendons originating in the compact body mass.

Catching prey on the run is not easy, and these fishes have large eyes and excellent vision. They prey on smaller fish, squids, and/or various planktonic animals. Their speed is an excellent defense against predation, but in addition their elaborate coloration helps to hide them from predators and potential prey alike. This countershading is typical of open water fishes: They are dark blue or green above, silvery along the flanks, and white along the belly. From above you see the color of the deep sea, from below the light of the sky, and from alongside you see reflected light that masks them completely. So effective is this countershading that you might fail to notice a Speeder until it cruises right up to you. Their lives hinge on the need to keep on the go. Most will actually suffocate if they stop swimming, for they are unable to pump water over their gills, relying instead on the continual free movement of water past them.

Look at these features in terms of energy and you will begin to see how closely integrated these modifications are. Think about how you could start the entire domino chain with a simple change in streamlining.

Mackerel are common over reefs, and even the larger tuna swim through from time to time, particularly over the deeper portions of the outer reef. The jacks are the Speeders most often seen by snorkelers inside a lagoon. Although these fish are less highly modified than the mackerel and tuna, their general appearance, streamlining, and tail shape should enable you to identify them. To make things easier, jacks are very curious about strangers, and they will sometimes stay with a swimmer for quite a while, circling around almost within arm's reach.

THE MANEUVERERS

Maneuverers could hardly be considered sleek and racy; indeed, they have specialized in the opposite direction. These are small fishes seen in and around the corals of the reef, flitting in and out of narrow,

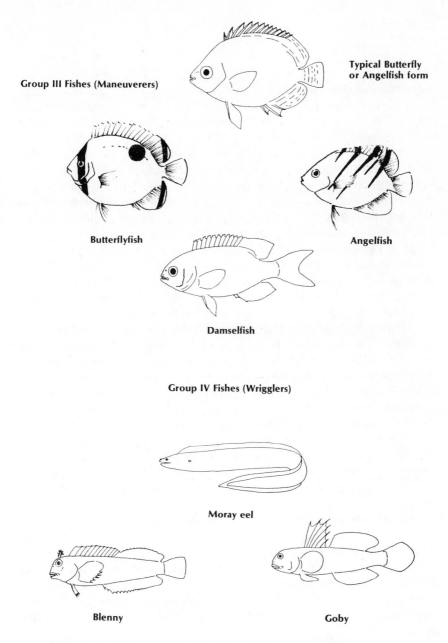

Group III Fishes (Maneuverers)

Typical Butterfly or Angelfish form

Butterflyfish

Angelfish

Damselfish

Group IV Fishes (Wrigglers)

Moray eel

Blenny

Goby

Figure 3–4. Fishes of Groups III and IV

confining spaces or hovering motionless nearby. These fishes feed by plucking small invertebrates from the water or the bottom, or by scraping algae off the surface of the reef. Precise control of position is their trademark, and they can feed quite delicately even amid the surge, currents, and disturbances around them. This kind of slow and deliberate life style leaves them open to attack by more aggressive predators, but they are easily startled and seldom stray far from a potential hiding place.

Maneuverers are disc-shaped and slender, with the pectoral fins set high on the sides near the center of the body. Here they serve for turning, braking, and making fine adjustments. Turning underwater encounters resistance—just try putting a long board in the water and spinning it around. For a fish of a given weight, the shorter and deeper it is the faster it will be able to turn to either side.

Look closely at one of the butterfly fishes. Notice that the caudal fin is unremarkable, almost continuous with the rest of the fins and body. Being short, deep, and slender, the entire body can act like a tail. Because their bodies offer little resistance to forward movement, they can glide well and their usual motion is a graceful snap-and-slide. Butterfly fishes can't move at high speeds, for they are not streamlined and swimming with the whole body uses a lot of energy. But they can turn on a dime and dart to safety, and once inside a slender space they will erect their spiny fins and wedge themselves in tight, beyond the reach of any but the most dedicated aquarium owner. In addition to the ability to flash to safety, several species also have prominent eyespots near their tails. Because these fishes are almost symmetrical front to back, an approaching predator will often react to this mark as if it were an eye, and attack with the intention of heading off a forward rush to safety. In the split second before the predator realizes its mistake the butterfly fish zips into the protective reef, apparently in full-speed reverse.

The Maneuverers are among the most colorful of the reef inhabitants, and often have brilliant stripes, bands, or bars of color that may act to break up their outlines and/or send courting signals or territorial information to other members of the species. Butterfly fish are seldom seen in schools, and are usually found alone or in small groups of from two to four individuals. There are so many different species, though, that seeing more than a dozen types on a single snorkeling trip is not unusual.

The angelfishes look much like the butterflies, but many have a more obvious tail, and a few grow to over a foot in length. The angelfishes have a stout spine on their cheeks, which the butterfly fishes lack, and angels feed on algae and small invertebrates. Both of these families stay close to home, and you may see the same fish day after day, flitting around the same coralheads.

The damselfishes, the last of the Maneuverers to be discussed, are present in large numbers on shallow reefs. Small damsels may be brilliantly colored, schooling in clouds that swarm around coral colonies like bees around a hive. Larger ones may be more drab and sedate, preferring to stay close to pockets in the reef, but with hundreds of individuals spread over a relatively small section of the bottom. Damselfishes feed on invertebrates, although some are quite fearless and will swim right into your mask or tug at your hair.

THE WRIGGLERS

Wrigglers are even more highly modified for life within the meandering passageways of the reef. Their habits and life styles are very different from those of the previous group, and precise control is relatively unimportant to them. These fishes inhabit the really tight quarters in narrow caves and deep within the conglomerated body of the reef.

The eels are the largest and most highly modified members of this collection. There are several different families of eels, but they are distinct enough from all other forms that only one is figured in silhouette. Eels and other Wrigglers are elongate and often slightly compressed; swimming involves the entire length of the body, which is thrown into a series of waves that move from head to tail or tail to head, depending on which direction the animal intends to travel. The fins are small and far apart, and precise control of position is lacking. This poses little problem because most of their feeding activities consist of brief darts from concealment to grasp an unwary victim.

Often the entire body fails to leave the protective confines of the reef during the day, even when seizing a meal, and most of the eels are nocturnal explorers of the reef if they travel at all. The skin is slick, scales are reduced or absent, and the surface layers produce a heavy mucus that coats the entire animal. Even over the head there are no large scales or bony plates, for these animals are protected from other predators by the reef itself, and any spines, scales, bumps, or other inflexible features would probably get stuck fast in some narrow passage.

Eels seldom rush about, so they must pump respiratory water over their gills, and this gulping of water makes them look as if they are continually gnashing their teeth.

Many of these adaptations are shared to some extent by numerous small blennies and gobies. Some of these miniature inhabitants of the reef spend their entire lives on a single coralhead. A close look at most

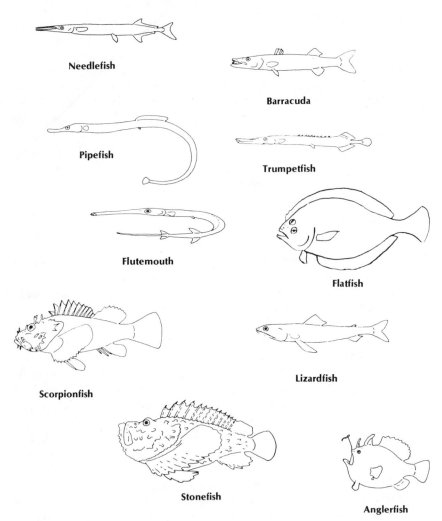

Needlefish

Barracuda

Pipefish

Trumpetfish

Flutemouth

Flatfish

Scorpionfish

Lizardfish

Stonefish

Anglerfish

Figure 3–5. Fishes of Group V (Commandos)

shallow sections of the reef will allow you to spot one, and most of them show characteristic adaptations for getting along in tight quarters. Their bodies are elongate and their skins are smooth; they are mucus coated, and spines or head ornamentation are very rare. Because these animals spend much of the day on top of the reef, except when hiding from snorkelers, some species are rather colorfully decorated and difficult to see against the colorful backdrop of the reef. One species of blenny is common among rocky tidepools and elevated portions of the reef flat. These carnivorous "skippers" travel from pool to pool by bouncing over the damp rocks. Chasing them can keep children entertained for hours.

THE COMMANDOS

Commandos are usually found in plain sight, but they are experts at escaping attention, whether they live on or above the bottom. Those staying on the bottom are usually poor swimmers, relying instead on surprising their victims at close range. These fishes do not swim often or very far; therefore, they usually have reduced swim bladders and gravity helps them to stay motionless on the bottom. Fishes with this life style are always exposed to predators, but their camouflage makes them difficult to detect. They are often as difficult to handle as they are to see; most are armed with spines, and the bony plates of the head are elaborate structures covered with sharp edges and points. Molesting them is hardly a good idea, as several species possess poison glands to reinforce their already formidable arsenal of spines.

Lizardfishes are probably the easiest to spot. They are usually found on sandy patches where their mottled browns, tans, and whites disrupt their outlines. These are small but voracious predators on smaller fishes and crustaceans, darting from rest with their mouths open wide to grasp their prey. Once you find one you can examine it at leisure, for they seem to feel that their camouflage is so effective that they will remain in place unless actively threatened.

Scorpionfishes, and their close relatives the stonefish, are found right in among the corals of the reef. They are so well disguised that even when they are fully exposed they will usually be overlooked by the casual snorkeler. These fishes, like the crafty anglerfish, are decorated with fleshy tabs, warts, and lumps, and they are a nondescript mottled brown and tan color. Not one of these three families is particularly attractive (to our eyes anyway). The stonefish and other members of the scorpionfish assemblage have poison glands associated with their spines, and these will be discussed further in the Appendix.

The anglerfish are the perfect commandos of the bottom, with fleshy tabs drooping from their movable, retractable dorsal fins. These are used to lure smaller fishes to disaster. The flatfishes, such as the flounders found over sandy areas, can be just as difficult to spot. These animals lie on their sides on the bottom, sometimes beneath a light dusting of sand. The upper side of each of these animals has pigment cells whose activity is under nervous control, and this enables the fish to blend in with its surroundings. Flatfishes lie either left or right side up. They cannot change sides, for during larval development their skulls have twisted to place both eyes on the *up* side.

Commando tactics are also used by fishes living above the bottom; such fishes are usually elongate, cigar-shaped forms. Pipefish, trumpetfish, and flutefish are predators on small invertebrates. Some do their best to resemble reeds or sticks floating above the bottom. The tubular snouts of these fishes are an important part of their feeding success, for with them they can quickly suck up unsuspecting prey at a distance, rather like a diver's slurp gun or a big straw. Pipefish are the smallest of these families, and they are related to the seahorses. Like the latter group, pipefish have reduced or lost the caudal fin. Swimming is accomplished with the body held rigid, and propulsion is provided by rapid fluttering of other fins, notably the dorsal and anal fins. This is not a very rapid way to get around, and these fishes seldom stray far from a suitable haven.

Trumpetfish are larger, and they too hunt by drifting along with their bodies held immobile. But trumpetfish have retained their caudal fins, which they use to cruise longer distances over the reef—and for quick escapes.

Needlefish or barracuda are sometimes seen floating motionless near the surface like floating bits of debris. Notice that the stabilizing fins are located well back along the body, where they act like the feathers on an arrow. The narrow, tapered body can accelerate rapidly, and with a powerful stroke of the tail the fish darts forward to seize its prey, usually smaller fishes. The long, narrow beak of the needlefish is studded with teeth, and because it is so narrow it can be swung quickly to either side should its intended victim attempt to flee at the last moment. Further discussion of the barracuda may be found in the Appendix.

THE GRAZERS

The *Grazer* tag is used here as a catchall for fishes usually seen in large groups wandering en masse over the surface of the reef. They vary widely in appearance, but are the most easily seen and approached of any group other than the Advertisers, the next group to be considered. Grazers are always exposed to predators while feeding, and when threatened they will either seek shelter in the reef or tighten up the school and move away rapidly. Schooling has several advantages if a fish is not a large predator nor highly specialized. Predators can be confused or intimidated by large groups, and in any case the odds of a single individual being eaten are probably reduced.

The wrasses and parrotfish are closely related families and contain more species than any other families of tropical marine fishes. Many are brilliantly colored, several change colors as they mature, and some

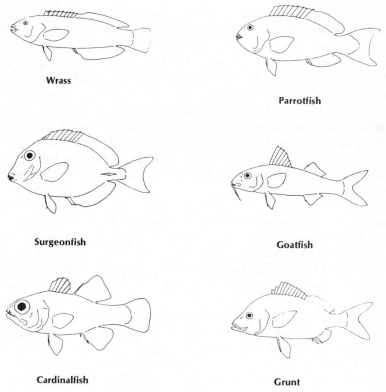

Wrass

Parrotfish

Surgeonfish

Goatfish

Cardinalfish

Grunt

Figure 3–6. Fishes of Group VI (Grazers)

have different color patterns in males and females of the same species. Even more confusing, some species members can change their sex and/or coloration. As a result there is still a great deal of uncertainty over the exact number and definition of species in these two families. Telling the *families* apart is not too difficult if you can get close enough to see the individual clearly. Parrotfish have large, heavy scales and a prominent bony beak that is used to crop and crunch coral skeletons. The polyps are digested and the skeletal minerals are eliminated as fine sand. They have no trouble finding food wherever they go on the reef, and members of some species may grow to several hundred pounds.

The wrasses are smaller, with finer scales. They have numerous individual teeth, which they use to feed on algae, plankton, or small invertebrates on the bottom. Neither the parrotfish nor the wrasses are highly streamlined, and they are not strong swimmers. Often they will be seen "rowing" their way along with their large pectoral fins.

The surgeonfish are also common on tropical reefs and they also may form large schools. Surgeons are primarily herbivores who nibble or crop the algae that coats dead corals or grows on bare patches or litter along the bottom. Surgeonfish bear their name because of a single or double bladelike spine that lies just forward of the caudal fin on either side. This can be used as a weapon with great effectiveness, as many an overconfident spearfisherman has discovered. Potential predators are warned of its presence in several species that have these areas brightly marked in contrasting colors. Although if pursued diligently they will seek shelter in the reef, most schools will pay little attention to a snorkeler, who can accompany them as they browse their way over the reef.

The goatfish are less colorful and much more streamlined than the surgeonfish. Their mouths are directed downward, and they have distinctive barbels that droop from their snouts like Fu Manchu moustaches. These odd structures are covered with taste buds and the goatfish schools prowl around sandy patches in and about the reef, tasting away along the surface or just beneath as they search for small invertebrates.

The little cardinalfish and several of the carnivorous grunts will seldom be seen out on the reef by day, but by looking under coralheads and in dimly lit caves you may spy a few sharing their daytime havens with the squirrelfish. The cardinalfish, as Grazers of the night shift, feed on plankton above the reef while the grunts seek out nocturnal invertebrates along the bottom.

THE ADVERTISERS

The last of the family collections, the *Advertisers*, consists of another mixed assortment. They make no attempt to head for cover unless they are actively pursued, even though most of them are brightly colored. Why advertise yourself?

First, because you *want* to be seen. The young of several different families, particularly the wrasses, are often seen swimming over coralheads in plain view, apparently ignored by local predators. These are likely to be "cleaner fishes," and they survive by removing the parasites from the skin of other, larger fishes. For this invaluable service they appear to be immune to predation. Cleaning stations are scattered over the slopes of a reef, usually near large coral colonies or hummocks, where fishes gather to be groomed. Sometimes you will find several large fishes waiting patiently in line like cars during a gas crunch.

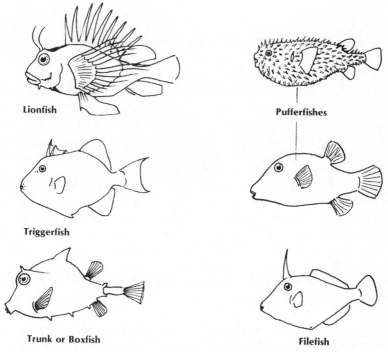

Lionfish

Pufferfishes

Triggerfish

Trunk or Boxfish

Filefish

Figure 3–7. Fishes of Group VII (Advertisers)

The second reason to advertise is to be *remembered*. Recall the marks on the tail of the surgeonfish? There is a small blenny that lives over reefs in the central and western Pacific. A brilliant purple and gold animal, it seems to be completely fearless and will swim right up to your mask and zip around your body without the slightest signs of concern. These little fish have large fangs in their lower jaws and glands that produce a mild but apparently memorable toxin. Experiments have shown that when one is placed in a tank with a predatory fish that has never seen one before, the predator will gulp it right down. On its way through the throat the resourceful little blenny bites at the sensitive walls near the gills—and the stunned predator promptly spits it out. So effective is the poison, and so unpleasant is the experience, that one encounter is usually enough to insure that never again will the predator attack anything that even resembles the brightly colored blenny.

The prickly and inflatable porcupine fish is another brightly colored reef inhabitant. These fish are so sure of their immunity that a swimmer can often grab one by the tail and steer it around. In addition to their prickly spines, their flesh is extremely poisonous.

The ornate lionfish, a relative of the stonefish, has a fearsome array of poisonous spines and a wild color pattern that makes it difficult to mistake for anything else. In addition to warning potential predators, the lionfish uses its colorful quills to back smaller fishes into corners where it can pounce on them. With all those tassled spines it cannot swim very fast, but if a predator is foolish enough to threaten it the lionfish will rush forward aggressively and attempt to strike the intruder with its spines.

The filefish and triggerfish have extremely tough hides and prominent dorsal spines. When the latter are erected they make quite a mouthful. Filefish have a single spine and the triggerfish have two, one of which locks the larger, primary spine in the erect position. These are very solid fish, and instead of flexing their bodies from side to side they usually flap their way through the water using their winglike dorsal and anal fins. These fish move rather slowly, but very gracefully, and they are beautiful to watch. Large specimens are often seen flapping quietly over the reef, and they will not be too disturbed by your approach. In addition to their tough spines and hides, several species have toxic flesh.

The clumsy boxfish swim in a similar fashion. They have little choice, because their entire body except for the fins is encased in a rigid bony armor. In addition to the armor, these fish can exude a poison from glands in their skin that is quite effective in discouraging predators.

After several trips to the reef you will begin to become familiar with many, if not most, of these family groups. If you are especially interested, you might consider carrying along a piece of plexiglass and a grease pencil to mark down notes or copy a quick silhouette that you find unfamiliar. Fish watching is pleasant and requires less dogged determination than I have found necessary when spying into the private lives of more intellectual creatures such as birds or bears. Nevertheless you will soon see that each species and each individual fish has its own particular range of activities and its own trials and tribulations. Although we have not examined every species, nor even every family, you have caught a glimpse of the principal characteristics and how these interact to form patterns.

Before moving on to other subjects, take a moment to consider Figures 3–8 and 3–9. Figure 3–8 presents a slightly different perspective on the relationship among form, habitat selection, and behavior; it is particularly interesting because it is based on direct experimental re-

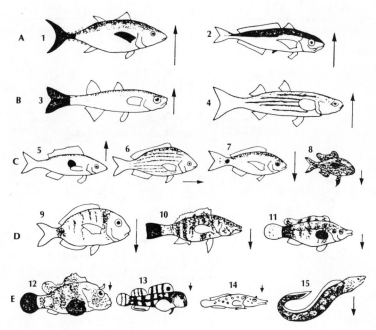

Figure 3–8. Relationship between body form and degree of association with the bottom in fishes

Row A: 1, *Thynnus*; 2, *Trachurus*; in the open sea pelagial

Rows B and C: 3, *Atherina*; 4, *Mugil*; 5, *Spicara*; 6, *Boops*; 7, *Oblada*; 8, *Chromis*; in the coastal pelagial

Row D: 9, *Diplodus*; 10, *Serranus*; 11, *Crenilabrus*; near the bottom

Row E: 12, *Scorpaena*; 13, *Blennius*; 14, *Lepadogaster*; 15, *Muraena*; living on the bottom

Note the shape of the body, tail, and pectoral fins; coloration; characteristic markings (completely black in some forms); the arrows denote direction of flight, their length the flight distance; No. 6 takes flight along the bottom. (A: speeders; B: other fishes living in open coastal waters, not on the reef; C: grazers; D—9, 11: grazers, 10: generalist; E—12: commando, 13–15: wrigglers.)

sults. Figure 3–9 summarizes several aspects of the chapter by illustrating how the various groups of families share time and space on the reef.

Bony fishes are not the only predators found on or around tropical reefs, and many visitors to the tropics arrive with a marked uncertainty about sharks and how much of a threat they pose. We will consider these cartilaginous fishes in Chapter 4.

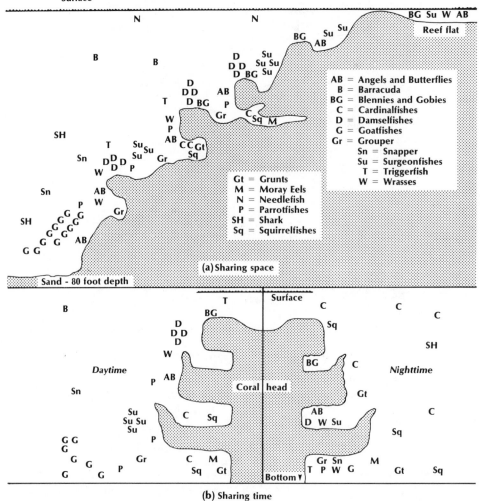

Figure 3–9. Sharing time and space on the reef
(a) Location of various fishes along the slopes of a reef during the daylight hours, from the surface to a sand bottom at 80 feet *(not to scale)*. (b) Fish populations around a typical portion of the reef illustrating the time sharing that occurs as diurnal and nocturnal fishes dominate the environment in turn.

Chapter Four

The Infamous Sharks

Each spring it seems that the theatres subject us to a series of "fin-flicks," piscine horror stories with imaginative blends of *Lassie*, *Creature from the Black Lagoon*, and *Perils of Pauline*, with just enough sex to hold our attention while the monster is off camera. Although movies dealing with other sea creatures are mercifully forgotten by summer, those dealing with sharks manage to stir up questions and apprehensions that invariably reappear whenever those around us are changing into their bathing suits. These accumulated doubts, fears, and hesitations are usually carted along by the visitor to the tropics, who views the tropical ocean as the Realm of the Great Shark. In extreme cases of "fin-phobia," sharks are seen lurking behind every low-tide line, waiting for the unwary tourist to provide an aquatic entrée. This is certainly not the case, for attacks worldwide number fewer than 100 a year, and your chances of meeting an untimely end through bee stings or lightning bolts are far greater.

But other visitors adopt an equally unfounded attitude that sharks are no trouble at all, creatures to be ignored, ridden, teased, or even speared with impunity. Unfortunately these are precisely the actions that will invite an attack, more appropriately termed self-defense. A more common variation on the no-problem theme is that sharks are potentially dangerous and that attacks do sometimes occur—but always someplace else. The precise location of the nearest danger zone will vary depending on the local authority consulted and whether or not there is a tourist industry nearby. In any event, a complacent attitude, coupled with misinformation, can lead to careless swimming or diving activities that increase the risks of attack.

There are few regions between 45°N and 45°S latitudes where shark attacks have not occurred at one time or another, and even in the statistically safe locations it is safer to assume some problems in data collection or a dearth of bathers than to assume that there are no sharks in the area. But with a worldwide tally of 50 to 100 incidents each year, the odds are astronomically low—so low that it makes driving to work seem like a daredevil stunt. Nonetheless there are certain do's and don'ts to either activity. I wouldn't drive to work blindfolded, nor would I attract sharks and then jump in with bleeding fish tied around my neck. A proper sense of perspective is required, and this chapter will present some basic information about sharks and a few common-sense rules that should minimize the already low chances for your finding a future as a statistical oddity.

Sharks have been around for about as long as the bony fishes considered in Chapter 3. How closely these two classes of fishes are related has yet to be worked out. The best guess is that neither gave rise to the other, but that both evolved independently from primitive armored fishes along the lines of Figure 3–1a (page 49). Sharks are often called *cartilaginous fishes* to differentiate them from the bony fishes. Unfortunately this creates the impression that these animals are somehow rather insubstantial, soft, mushy fishes that flex their way through the water without firm skeletal supports. This is hardly the case, for although cartilage is structurally different from bone it is not necessarily inferior, and may contain large amounts of calcium and phosphate, which are the basic mineral components of bone. Cartilage does have one disadvantage for biologists, however, because it doesn't fossilize as well as bone, and as a result we may never find out how the bony and cartilaginous fishes are related. Yet if you compare a typical bony fish, such as one of the snappers, with a typical shark you can see just how different the modern representatives have become.

At the business end you will notice that the openings for the gills are separate and distinct slits, or clefts, in the shark whereas the snapper has a large, bony plate covering its gill region. The basic shark pattern of fins and fin placement resembles that of the snapper, for reasons of control and balance considered earlier. The shark has its pectoral fins set low on the body, and the tail is asymmetrical with a large upper lobe. In these respects the shark resembles the more primitive bony fishes.

There are functional reasons for this resemblance. In our discussion of the success of the bony fishes it was pointed out that the development of the swim bladder was to a large extent responsible for the great diversity of sizes and shapes found among bony fishes on the reefs today. Neither the sharks nor their ancestors seem to have possessed either lungs or swim bladders, and their method of buoyancy control was evolved independently. If you were to weigh a 900 pound shark underwater, assuming that it would permit such goings on, you would discover that it weighs only about 10 pounds. This is because the shark stores its energy surplus in the form of large quantities of light-weight oils. These are concentrated in the liver, a massive organ that

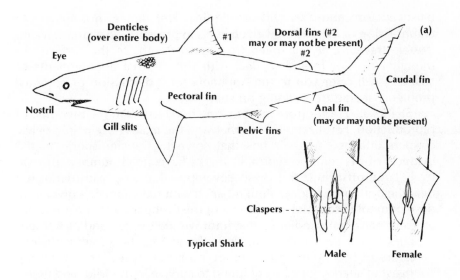

Eye

Nostril

Gill slits

Denticles
(over entire body)

#1

Pectoral fin

Pelvic fins

Dorsal fins (#2
may or may not be present)
#2

Caudal fin

Anal fin
(may or may not be present)

(a)

Claspers

Typical Shark

Male

Female

Typical Bony Fish

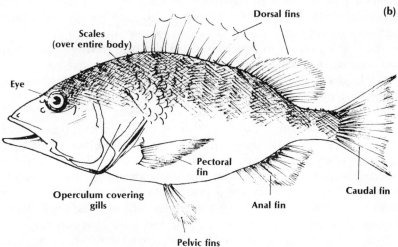

Scales
(over entire body)

Dorsal fins

(b)

Eye

Pectoral
fin

Operculum covering
gills

Anal fin

Caudal fin

Pelvic fins

Figure 4–1. Comparison of sharks and bony fishes (See also Figure 3-2)
(a) typical shark (b) typical bony fish

dominates the entire abdominal cavity. It performs the same function
as the swim bladder of bony fishes, and it is found in the same general
location (near the center of the body, so the animal's weight is evenly

balanced fore and aft). Oils are liquids, and hence, not subject to compression or expansion with changes in pressure, so sharks have no trouble traveling at full speed from great depths to the surface. Although I do not intend to deal with the internal appointments of sharks, I will refer you to the Appendix for a discussion of potential problems arising from dining on shark livers.

Sharks also differ from most marine bony fishes in their method of reproduction. Fertilization is internal, and the males have paired pelvic claspers attached to their fins that serve to transfer sperm to the oviducts of the female. Typically, sharks have small numbers of relatively large offspring, and these develop within egg cases deposited near the bottom or (more often) retained within the female's body until development is completed. In some of the livebearing sharks there are efficient placental conditions that improve the oxygen and/or nutrient supplies to the embryos. In all cases the young shark is essentially a miniature of the adult, and there are no larval stages. Thus even the youngest of sharks must be equipped to survive in the wild, and therefore, they also deserve a little respect.

You will notice that the scales that are so distinct on the snapper are lacking on the skin of the shark. Instead the dark skin feels hard and smooth when stroked from head to tail, and rough and scratchy when you reverse directions. On close examination you can see that the shark is sheathed in a mozaic of small, interlocking plates, but a hand lens or dissecting scope is needed to make sense of the finer details. Figure 4–2 will do just as well, and there you will see that each interlocking plate is actually part of a complex structure, with a sturdy base buried well beneath the surface of the skin.

The individual unit is called a *denticle*, each of which bears characteristic ridges along its outer surface, and usually has a prominent spine that is directed toward the tail of the animal. These spines are responsible for the rough texture that is felt when you "rub a shark the wrong way" (obviously never a good idea). The denticles on some sharks are so fine and the rough texture so delicate, that until recently sections of shark skin were dried, cut, and sold to woodworkers as *shagreen*, an exceptionally durable sandpaper for finish work. Other sharks, like the basking shark, have denticles that are so large and sharp that they will tear up a wetsuit with ease.

If a shark encounters an unfamiliar but interesting object, it may bump it with its snout. This bump actually represents a quick, hard rub, with the snout passing backward across the surface of the object. If the item in question is tender and delicious, the denticles will scrape and tear its surface, releasing odors that convey such information.

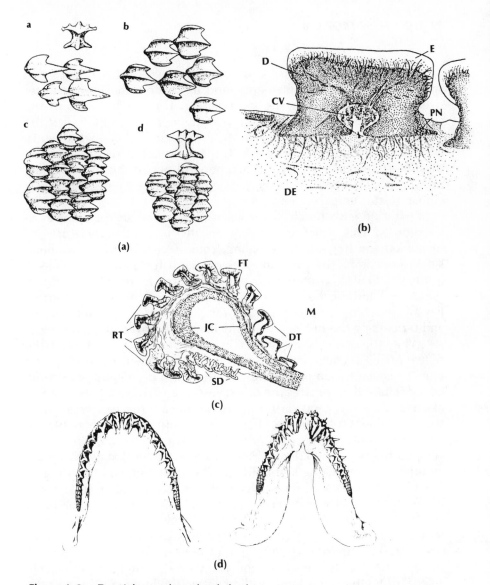

Figure 4–2. Denticles and teeth of sharks
(a) denticles from several different species, showing different shapes and methods of interlocking; in *a* and *d* a single denticle is shown in its entirety, including the lower portion normally buried in the skin (b) cross-section through a denticle (PN: base plate; DE: deep layer of skin; D: dentine layer; E: enamel layer; CV: central chamber containing blood vessels and the nervous supply); (c) ground thin-section through a cross-row of functional and replacement teeth of the lower jaw and through adjacent denticles (M: mouth cavity; JC: cartilage of jaw; DT: developing teeth; FT: functional teeth; RT: replaced teeth; SD: denticles of the skin); (d) upper *(left)* and lower *(right)* jaws of a shark showing the replacement teeth normally concealed by the oral lining.

The shark has other uses for these denticles. The grooves and spines of the individual elements tend to channel the flow of water over the skin, improving the streamlining. Unlike the scales of the snapper, the denticles of the shark continue uninterrupted over the surfaces of the fins, which are far more substantial in appearance. In addition to their streamlining effect, these durable structures protect the fins from damage that might otherwise be caused by struggling prey or other sharks. They may also be used to test interesting objects with a quick bump.

Sharkskin is so tough that it will dull even the sharpest knives in short order. This is one reason why despite the fact that there are lots of sharks, and they are good eating, commercial fisheries have been slow to develop. The wear and tear on the fish-cleaning machines is just too difficult to contend with and still clear a reasonable profit. On the other hand, leather goods made from sharkskin are almost unbelievably durable, and there is a minor fishery that focuses on obtaining and processing the hides. (The denticles are removed along the way.)

While still on the shark, sharkskin is an effective armor because the outer surface of each denticle is covered with enamel. The body of the denticle is composed of dentine, and there is a prominent pulp cavity near the base that receives the blood vessels and nerves. If this sounds like a tooth, it is not too surprising, for as one approaches the angle of the jaw the denticles enlarge, change shape, and begin to resemble the teeth even more closely. It is pretty clear that the teeth of sharks developed from modified denticles that formed in the skin overlying the mouth to aid in seizing and holding prey. Although you can roughly identify a shark by the shape of its denticles, identification is far easier when representative teeth are available, in some cases even allowing you to say whether the shark was male or female. Teeth are very important to sharks for obvious reasons, and different species have specialized in the form and function of their teeth.

By cutting away the soft connective tissue of the gums a veritable arsenal of teeth can be seen nestling within the inner curvature of the jaws. These extra teeth are one of several keys to the success of sharks as predators. A tooth anywhere in the mouth actually is in use for only a brief period (about two weeks in those species studied) after which it becomes loose, falls off, and is replaced by one of the innumerable spares that are produced throughout the life of the animal. The advantages of this arrangement are quite striking. If there were but a single set of teeth, they would quickly become dull, broken, or lost to struggling prey. This would put the shark in an increasingly awkward position. With a single tooth in use for only a short time, there are no such troubles, for a new, razor-sharp tooth fresh from the factory will re-place any dull, damaged, or lost elements in, at most, two weeks.

Another factor in the success of modern sharks is the array of special senses that they utilize to detect, track, and close with their prey. No other predator shows such a well-orchestrated complex of sensory systems. To understand sharks, at least enough to avoid tempt-ing fate, you should know a bit about how sharks view the outside world.

Scattered across the head and flanks of a shark are a number of distinct pockets that are bordered by large, unusually sharp denticles. These pit organs will serve to introduce one of the primary sensory elements used by sharks.

Under a microscope, or in Figure 4–3, you can see that a pit organ consists of a depression in the skin that houses specialized cells or-ganized into a functional unit called a *neuromast*. Each of the neuromast cells has a cilium projecting from its outer surface, and these are oriented in a precise manner with respect to the rest of the shark's body. The tips of these cilia are embedded in a mass of jellylike material, and disturbances in the water nearby distort, move, or vibrate this jelly cap. The movement stimulates the cells of the neuromast to pass this information along to neighboring nerve cells. In this way the shark becomes aware of small, localized disturbances in the surround-ing water, changes in the water flow over its skin, and perhaps other bits of information that we have yet to understand.

The lateral line system is one of the most important sensory sys-tems of all fishes, but it is basically just an elaboration of the pit organ. The location of the lateral line is seen as a light line passing along the side of a shark forward from the tail, and near the head it divides to form several distinct bands that surround the snout, the jaws, and the eyes. The visible line marks the path of a shallow, sunken canal that communicates with the surface of the skin through a series of small pores. These can be seen most clearly on the lower surface of the head and on the snout of a freshly caught animal.

The functional unit of the lateral line is a neuromast equipped with a jelly cup large enough to block the canal. At least one neuromast lies between each pair of pores, and when something moves in the water, pressure waves are created that reach the surface of the skin and are conducted through the pores and into the canals. If the activity is closer to one end of the canal than the other, pressure at that end will be greater and the jelly cups all along the canal will be displaced away from the disturbance. When the pressure wave passes, the cups return to their normal positions. If the disturbance is intermittent, the jelly

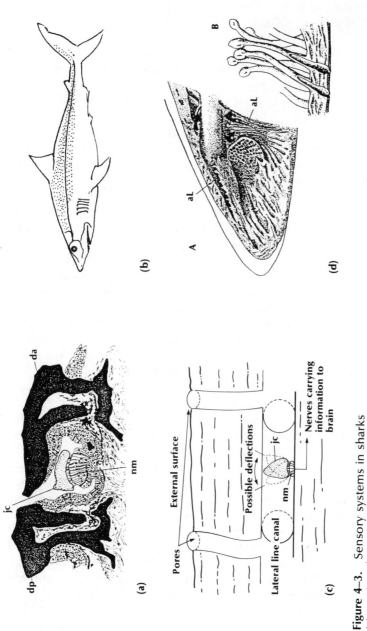

Figure 4-3. Sensory systems in sharks

(a) section through the skin at a pit organ (da: anterior (forward) denticle; dp: posterior (aft) denticle; jc: jelly cup; nm: neuromast; (b) typical shark, showing the pattern of distribution of the lateral line, with stippling indicating the location of pit organs (c) simplified diagram showing the structure of the lateral line canal when cut along its length (d) ampullary organ, with A showing the exposed snout of a shark with some of the skin cut away, and B indicating the structure of individual ampullae. The neuromasts are located at the swollen ends of the tubes

cups will oscillate back and forth in time with the stimulus. As long as the frequency is low, such as the disturbance produced by the tailbeats of a struggling fish, this system works superbly. Sensitivity to high frequencies is poor, because the canals are narrow and fluid-filled, and there is a lot of resistance to rapid changes in the direction of movement of the jelly cups.

Not all portions of the lateral line system are oriented in the same way. If the commotion is directly in front of the shark, the portion of the lateral line along the flanks may hardly be affected, whereas several branches on the snout will be at right angles to the incoming pressure waves and highly stimulated. The shark is probably swimming toward the source of the disturbance, so the signals reaching the brain from different branches of the lateral line will constantly change as its body moves and the angles between these branches and the source increase and decrease. At a given moment signals arrive from the entire system, including portions of the lateral line that are in line with, at right angles to, and over a range of intermediate angles relative to the source. When all this information is processed the shark can come up with a good idea of where and how far away some underwater activity is occurring. It works equally well day or night, and it is extremely sensitive. Sharks can detect underwater detonation at around ten miles, and the struggling of a hooked or speared fish over at least one quarter to one half of a mile.

A shark's sense of smell is another useful long-range receptor. The nostrils do not communicate with the mouth, but are simple pockets guarded by incurrent and excurrent flaps (see Figure 4–4). The sensory lining of the nostrils responds to the presence of substances dissolved in the water, and a shark can detect and track a stream of blood or tunafish juice for one-quarter of a mile.

Although rumors persist that sharks are almost blind, vision is actually very important over intermediate distances, say inside of 50 feet, when underwater visibility is good. The original misconception arose because most sharks have eyes that are good at detecting contrast and movement, but not fine detail. Precise and accurate vision is important to us, as to most diurnal animals. Incoming light is focused by the lens of the eye and directed to a specific point on the retina where it stimulates light-sensitive cells. Once the light passes through the receptor layer it is absorbed by a pigment layer behind the retina. If the pigment layer were missing, the light would presumably reflect back through the retina, where it would stimulate a different set of visual receptors and spoil the clarity of the visual picture received by the brain.

Perhaps because a shark has so many other senses available to it that can give precise information at close range, their visual systems

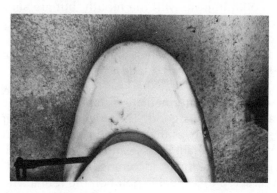

Figure 4–4. Shark anatomy
Top: a freshly caught animal—note the beautiful streamlining and countershading. The lateral line can be seen as a light line passing along the side just below the dorsal fin—(compare with Figure 4–3(b) *middle and bottom:* side and underview of the head—note the slitlike nostrils, gill clefts, large eyes, and individual pores of the lateral line in the middle photography; in the bottom photograph note the scattered pores of the ampullary system.

seem to have specialized not toward accurate vision but toward increased sensitivity to contrast and motion. Most sharks possess a reflecting layer behind the retina, which in dim conditions reflects light back into the receptor cells, giving them a second chance to notice it. Even though the reflecting plates are precisely oriented, and even the amount of reflecting plate exposed at a given time can be controlled, the same visual receptor is unlikely to be hit when a light ray passes on its way back through the retina, so fine details of shape are lost. But the increased sensitivity to contrast and motion under twilight conditions more than make up for any loss in precision, and sharks are able to perform their intended functions in light so dim that it would probably escape our notice.

You will recall from the last chapter that there are actually two populations of bony fishes on a reef, one active during the day and the other at night. At dusk and dawn the shifts change, and at such times all of these fishes are at a disadvantage. At dawn nocturnal fishes linger for a last snack, and find themselves in abnormally bright surroundings. After they have retired from the scene the diurnal fishes appear in the hopes of finding breakfast before the rush, and although they are difficult to surprise in the full light of day, they are vulnerable in such dim light. So it is at these times that sharks (and other predatory fishes) feed most successfully. It is interesting to note that similar conditions prevail during dark and overcast days.

At very close range a shark has yet another sensory system to rely on. The snout of a freshly caught shark has a number of large pores on it, pores unrelated to the branches of the lateral line canals. If the region around a pore is depressed, a quantity of jellylike material is exuded, and when the skin overlying the snout is removed and its underside examined you find that each of the pores connects with a long, jelly-filled tube. Different views of this system are presented in Figures 4–3 and 4–4. Each tube has a slightly enlarged pocket or *ampulla* at its end, and the functional element of the ampullary system is once again the neuromast. But this system performs a very different function from that of the lateral line, apparently because of the unusual composition of the jelly. Experiments have demonstrated that these ampullae can sense electrical fields in the surrounding water. They are so sensitive that they can detect the tiny electrical events that accompany the contraction of muscles, even when the muscles are very small and buried in the sand more than a foot away. This is the guidance system that enables sharks to close with their prey even in darkness or zero visibility water.

All these highly sophisticated detection systems can be used simultaneously or in sequence while a shark is tracking, approaching, and attacking its prey. With such a variety of senses available there is probably no *single* system of overwhelming importance. If something smells or sounds good, it may not matter if it looks strange and is electrically silent.

Sharks are famous for attacking and sometimes consuming a bizarre variety of items. An amorphous plastic bag may be attacked if it is brightly colored, and when drawn by a tantalizing odor a shark may attack an electrical wire buried in the sand nearby. Everyone has heard of shark stomachs that contained license plates, bricks, tarpaper rolls, old boots, and other unusual and indigestible items. Although your first impression was probably that any animal so stupid and indiscriminate in its feeding habits must be primitive and unsophisticated you should now have cause to reconsider. This form of feeding really shows that they are so good at finding potentially edible items that they can afford to feed on a percentage basis: If they eat it now, and identify it in detail later, anything succulent will neither escape nor be lost to another shark, whereas anything that might have seemed attractive for one reason or another, but which was actually useless (old boots and license plates included), can always be rejected later.

Out of the 250+ species of sharks, only around twenty-five are considered to be dangerous to humans. Although the rest may not be innocuous, they are either too small, found too far offshore, or swim too deep to pose a threat to the average bather. There would be little to gain from a discussion of each of the 250 species, or even each of the dangerous types, for all share the basic characteristics discussed above, whether you look at the tiny Midwater shark, which matures at six to eight inches, or the giant Whale shark, which is the largest of fishes and may reach 60 feet in length. Although the largest sharks are microcarnivores, all are carnivorous, and I will limit the discussion of individual species to a few of the more infamous representatives.

Among the dangerous varieties, the Great White shark, alias the White Shark, White Death, and so on, has the worst reputation and the statistics to back it up. White sharks are large, powerful, and highly streamlined. They prey on sizable animals, many of them predators in their own right, such as other sharks, billfishes, tuna, and marine mammals. White sharks are known to reach 25 feet in length, and they may grow considerably larger than that. Fossilized teeth have been found that are virtually identical with those of the modern Great White except for their size, which indicates an animal 40 to 45 feet long. Because there have been unconfirmed reports of White sharks 35 feet in length, and the largest individuals are found at great depths, a really large specimen may yet appear. For all practical purposes, however,

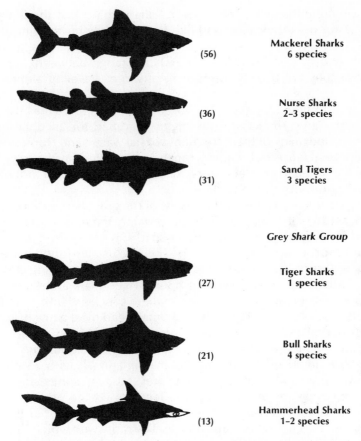

	Mackerel Sharks
(56)	6 species
	Nurse Sharks
(36)	2–3 species
	Sand Tigers
(31)	3 species
	Grey Shark Group
	Tiger Sharks
(27)	1 species
	Bull Sharks
(21)	4 species
	Hammerhead Sharks
(13)	1–2 species

Figure 4–5. Statistics and silhouettes for the most dangerous families of sharks
The number in parentheses denotes number of attacks out of 257 in which attacking sharks could be identified; exact species identification was not always possible. The remainder of attacks were due to many species, primarily in the grey shark group, with 1 to 3 attacks per species.

the difference between 25, 35, and 45 feet is purely academic, for I would not care to meet any of them—even tiny ten footers—in the water. White sharks are not common sights in tropical waters, which is fine with me, and they seem to prefer the cooler waters of the depths or of temperate latitudes.

White sharks share a number of characteristics with two other dangerous sharks, the Mako and the Porbeagle, and together they are often known as the mackerel sharks. In the process of adapting to their free-swimming life style, the mackerel sharks have lost the ability to pump water over their gills, and like the tuna they must swim to survive. They are very fast swimmers, and cover great distances in search of their equally fast prey. Mackerel sharks range between 46°N and 46°S, but they are usually found well offshore, traveling alone or in pairs.

A second, much larger collection of species is known as the grey sharks. The grey sharks are less highly modified for an open-ocean existence, and many of them frequent coastal waters and tropical reefs. They are generalized predators, capable of preying on the variety of animal life found in coastal waters. Most are able to remain motionless on the bottom from time to time.

The Tiger shark is one of the largest of the grey shark group, reaching at least 18 feet in length. They are certainly the most unpleasant of the lot, feeding on bony fishes, other sharks, birds, marine mammals, and turtles on an opportunistic basis. They are usually found patrolling coastal waters or the outer reef faces during the day, coming closer to shore during twilight and evening hours. Tiger shark attacks account for around 10 percent of those attacks where species identification was possible, but like most sharks these animals feed most actively at dusk and dawn, on heavily overcast days, or in dark and murky waters—and few divers or snorkelers are splashing under these conditions.

To sum things up, sharks are fascinating animals with a variety of senses to locate and analyze potential prey. Human beings are around the same size as the average shark (6 feet), so we are probably more often considered a curiosity than a potential meal by all but the very largest and most aggressive individuals. The rarity with which these are encountered can be deduced from the attack statistics: fewer than 100 attacks per year, with a fatality rate of 35 percent or less. Nevertheless, propriety dictates that you take precautions to reduce the already small odds of an unfortunate incident. Although I would never worry about sharks spoiling my snorkeling or diving vacation, I would certainly refrain from doing anything to *invite* an attack or increase the odds. The details of a recent nonfatal attack in Hawaii will give you some idea of what I mean.

In early August a young man was boogie boarding just outside the reef break on Maui's western coast. It was 6:00 P.M. (almost dusk) on a cloudy and rainy day (even darker than normal for that hour) and the underwater visibility was less than a yard because of the rain. The area is locally known as "Shark Pits," and sharks had been seen and ignored earlier in the day. Just prior to the attack, fishermen had cleaned their catch nearby. The victim was wearing bright international orange swimming trunks and riding an international orange boogie board.

Luckily enough, in the course of the attack the boogie board was mortally wounded, and the young man got away with several dozen stitches and a gray hair or two. The point of the story is not the attack, but the fact that a little knowledge about sharks and their behavior would have warned him that his actions at that particular time and place were ill-advised. In fact, other than tying himself to a wounded fish I am uncertain about what other more effective attractant stimuli could have been presented to the shark.

To close this chapter I will summarize the most important rules you should remember while swimming, snorkeling, and diving in the tropics.

1. *Don't leap without looking* when swimming from a boat or raft. Unusual objects attract curious fishes, and you wouldn't want to land on a fish.

2. *Don't tow someone behind a slow moving boat*, because the individual is quite defenseless. Sharks have been known to follow boats for days feeding on edible tidbits lost or discarded overboard.

3. *Don't swim alone, and keep your eyes open*. A little knowledge about your surroundings can be quite useful.

4. *Remain calm and leave the water as quickly and quietly as possible* after seeing a shark. Experienced divers who can identify the species involved may elect to remain in the water, with an eye on the animal, but for the novice discretion is advised. Splashing, yelling, or making intimidating gestures may discourage some sharks and encourage others. Remember that the shark doesn't know what you are, and you don't want to give it the wrong impression. Some attacks— perhaps a majority—seem to be territorial defense actions on the part of the shark who sees a large, possibly threatening intruder. You lack the proper physique to respond in whatever manner befits a submissive, noncompetitive shark, so you had best move out of the territory, and better yet out of the water.

5. *Don't swim at night or in murky waters.*

6. *Divers are not immune; if you are spearfishing get your catch out of the water at once, and do the same with yourself after seeing a shark.* Spearfishing puts a variety of strongly attractive signals into the water, with the struggling movements of the speared fish, blood in the water, and your own rapid, perhaps jerky movements. A shark entering your area will be understandably curious and perhaps excited.

7. *Don't festoon yourself with international orange or otherwise gaudy bathing suits, wet suits, vest, and so on.* International orange is known as "yum-yum yellow" to shark researchers.

8. *NEVER mess with a "harmless" shark.* Experienced divers may

choose not to leave the water after seeing one, but if it begins to act erratically or aggressively, it should be treated like any other shark. You will notice from Figure 4–5 that nurse sharks are frequently involved in attacks despite their benign reputation, and most of these incidents would be ruled as self-defense in a court of law.

9. *Don't try to bring a large but apparently subdued shark aboard a boat.* Cut the line instead. Large sharks have severely damaged boats when they were boarded prematurely.

10. *If you catch a small shark for food, don't eat the liver.* The flesh, however, is usually quite tasty.

11. *Don't put faith in the myth about sharks being absent or intimidated by dolphins.* To be blunt, field observations and lab research have shown that there is no "natural animosity" between sharks and dolphins, despite isolated instances that have been widely publicized. There have been a few accounts of dolphins attacking sharks, and many more accounts of sharks harrying pods of dolphins. There have even been shark attacks while pods of dolphins were nearby. If I were to wager on a bout between a fast, relatively bright, soft, and naked skinned mammal and an equally fast, insensate, armored underwater eating specialist it would be very difficult not to back the shark.

Several questions concerning shark attacks remain unanswered. Statistically men are ten times more likely to be victims than are women, even after adjusting the data for exposure, position in groups, and the like. Is this due to fluidity of motion, kick patterns, or some unknown chemical substance released into the water? Sharks sense tiny electrical fields. Can these senses be reliably overloaded or scrambled on demand? Some marine organisms are free from predation by sharks in particular areas. Will their characteristics (odor, color, gland secretions, and so on) repel *all* species at *all* times? Until research on such subjects makes precautions obsolete, a discrete departure will remain the safest course of action.

Fishes, bony or cartilaginous, are not the only vertebrates found around tropical reefs, and for many people the marine reptiles and mammals are equally exciting. These relatively rare animals are seen less often, but the encounters are memorable and occasionally electrifying. Because you are already passingly familiar with the basics of evolution, convergence, and natural selection, and you have looked at the varying adaptations of two groups of fishes, you should be ready to move on to these higher vertebrates and gain new insights about life in the tropical oceans.

Chapter Five

Marine Reptiles and Mammals

You have seen some of the ways in which fishes have adapted to life within the complex reef environment. This kind of explosion in diversity is to be expected whenever you consider a varied and complex habitat, a reliable physical environment, and small (or isolated) initial populations. The adaptations of fishes to coral reefs was not the first such event in the history of vertebrates. Almost 150 million years earlier a different, even more complex environment became available to the fishes of the day, and the results were spectacular to say the least.

The vertebrate colonization of dry land depended on the previous pioneer settlement of other forms of life. Roughly 50 million years earlier, primitive land plants had made their appearance. These were probably relatives of the modern green algae. As they spread over the land and adapted further, several groups of invertebrates, notably the insects, emerged from the water to feed on plants or one another. By 350 million years ago primitive tropical fresh water fishes had developed lungs, and there were abundant food supplies and negligible competition just a crawl away.

A fish that could make use of even a portion of this new habitat possessed a tremendous selective advantage, and forms ancestral to modern amphibians developed rapidly. In a relatively short time reptilian characters appeared in some isolated populations of amphibians, and as the reptiles spread and diversified primitive mammals were evolving. In less than 100 million years, all three classes were inhabiting dry land.

Life on land is very different, and in several ways more rigorous, than life in the water. These differences resulted in major changes in the energy accounts of primitive fishes, which were suddenly faced with a new series of problems. Each of the three classes of more terrestrial vertebrates that later evolved responded to these problems in different ways. By comparing their distinctive solutions to the problems of life on land, we can not only learn more about this new environment, but we can also build reasonably clear definitions for each class.

How was life different for the first, unspecialized visitors to the land? Let's say that you are one of the first fishes to leave the water part-time, perhaps to escape predators or to snack on some tasty insects along the shore. There will be six major obstacles that confront you, and all of them will increase your energy expenses.

You are likely to overheat in the sun (Bm goes up); you could easily dry out at the same time (M must go up to avoid this); you can't swim very well on land (S is high and inefficient to boot); your underwater senses are not very useful ashore (C is up; O is up); your gills are liabilities (B is up, as your swim bladder/lungs are not very efficient); and whatever do you do with your eggs?

Presumably the opportunities to increase Ef and lower A were sufficient to offset these additional expenditures, but as you see there are certainly many different ways in which natural selection could produce improvements in overall efficiency. Let's look at these problems one at a time and see how the amphibians, reptiles, and mammals differ in their general adaptations for life on land.

PROBLEM 1: REGULATING BODY TEMPERATURE

Living things depend on chemical events that are supervised by proteins called enzymes. A particular enzyme works best over a narrow range of temperatures, and in general they are most efficient when they are kept close to the warm end of the scale. Almost all fishes have body temperatures equal to that of the surrounding water, but their body temperatures are fairly constant because the day to day temperature changes in water are very small. Throughout their entire lives most fish are exposed to temperature changes of only a few degrees, which is especially true for tropical species.

By comparison, temperatures on land are very unstable. Even in the tropics the air temperature varies 10 to 15°F over a twenty-four-hour period, and in temperate latitudes the changes are even more extreme. Such fluctuations in body temperature are very undesirable, and amphibians, reptiles, and mammals all control their body temperatures to within relatively narrow limits, at least while they are up and about.

Amphibians and reptiles rely on an external source of heat to bring their body temperatures up to specs, and because of this they are called ectotherms (ecto, "outside"; therm, "heat"). Once an ectotherm is warm enough it relies on behavioral tricks, such as popping in and out of the shade, or changing exposure to the sun, to fine-tune its body temperature.

A mammal maintains a constant body temperature by retaining heat that is lost during the breakdown and subsequent utilization of food *(L)*. Fine adjustment is possible by varying internal activities as well as changing behavior, and most mammals show more precise regulation of their body temperatures than do most reptiles. Mammals are known as *endotherms* (*endo*, "inside"), and one important requirement for this strategy is that the animal must be able to keep from wasting energy by losing heat to its surroundings. Compared to water, air is a poor conductor of heat. A covering of fur is an excellent insulator because it traps dead air spaces close to the warm surface of the body, rather like thermopane windows on a house.

Ectotherms are sometimes called cold-blooded, but the term is very misleading. Most amphibians, like the salamanders and frogs, have soft, moist, and naked skins, and they will dry out if they remain in the sun for too long. In addition they spend much of their time around the water, which absorbs heat twenty-seven times faster than air. Nonetheless, they maintain their body temperatures at around 68°F throughout the day.

Reptiles are more fully terrestrial, and actually have body temperatures comparable to those of mammals. Most lizards, for example, regulate their body temperatures to somewhere around 95°F, and several species prefer higher temperatures.

The idea that producing and regulating your body temperature is somehow vastly superior to making use of solar energy is true only in a very restricted sense. The cost of making your own heat is high, for being warm-blooded actually requires that you *increase* and control *(L)*. Mammals spend nearly 90 percent of their food energy just in maintaining a constant temperature, leaving only 10 percent for all other essential activities, including reproduction. Reptiles and amphibians, on the other hand, do not have such a massive drain on their E_f, and they normally end up with a 30 percent *surplus* to devote to growth and reproduction. So what are the relative advantages of endothermy that can offset the obvious disadvantages? Why are there so many diverse mammals in the world today, and so few large reptiles?

These questions do not have simple answers. For a long time (almost 65 million years) ancestral mammals were small, and large modern forms appeared only after the dinosaurs had disappeared. If endothermy were inherently superior, you would expect that larger mammals would have evolved sooner and replaced the large reptiles. If ectothermy were markedly more efficient, why did the small mammals survive for so long in the same environment with all those small reptiles? We need to look more closely at the relationships between these animals and their physical environments.

The body of a small ectotherm heats up quickly in the morning sunlight, but it will also cool almost as rapidly when evening rolls around. Heat is stored in the body mass, but lost across the body surface, and a small animal has a relatively large surface area. This relationship is a familiar one, although you might not recognize it per se. Blowing on a bowl of hot soup is less effective than blowing on a spoonful, and a cup of coffee cools more rapidly than the pot it came from. The net result is that small ectotherms are most active during the day, when their body temperatures are up. As long as there is intense sunlight they can survive even as far north as the Arctic Circle. Nocturnal activity is limited to extremely warm, summery nights, and at other times these creatures are forced to retire as their body temperatures decline in the evening.

In the world of the small, the night shift belonged to small endotherms. The small ancestors of modern mammals survived on a time share basis with the more diverse reptilian forms. Why didn't large mammals appear to time share with the large reptiles? Because the same rules do not apply on a larger scale.

It took a long time to warm the enormous bulk of a giant reptile like one of the bigger dinosaurs. But like the tropical surface waters, this stored heat could only be lost gradually to the surrounding environment. In this case we are dealing with a large volume and a relatively small surface area. The body temperature of such a large ectotherm would only lower by around a degree, even during a cool night, and there was no energy expended in the process. This made large ectotherms extremely efficient, giving them an enviable surplus to devote to reproduction. The idea that all dinosaurs were warm-blooded, which has been suggested, would seem very unlikely just for this reason alone (and there are other reasons as well). The reptiles of the day were very diverse, and several groups of smaller dinosaurs probably did evolve endothermy, but large endotherms would hardly have gained a selective advantage relative to large ectotherms if their only difference was that they spent nine times as much energy to achieve the same result.

The real hang-up with being a large ectotherm is that you are depending on your environment remaining stable on a day to day basis. Once your body begins losing more heat at night than you gain during the following day, you are caught in a temperature tailspin. This means that large ectotherms are poorly suited to survive seasonal fluctuations in temperature, such as those experienced in temperate latitudes. It now seems likely that a general lowering of the world's thermostat combined with some geological changes underway 65 to 70 million

years ago to make the general climate more variable. When this occurred, the large ectotherms were doomed.

Their departure left many vacancies in the terrestrial ecosystem. In
the absence of reptilian competition, natural selection worked on
populations of primitive mammals, and the ancestors of modern
mammalian groups were soon to appear. It is interesting to speculate
that if the temperature had remained warm and constant, the large
reptiles would probably still be around, and mammals might still be the
size of rats, running around in the dark.

PROBLEM 2: RETAINING BODY FLUIDS

Amphibians today have rather moist and naked skins that offer little
resistance to drying. Because of this, they are primarily restricted to
tropical or temperate regions where there is an abundance of water.
Reptiles have a dense scaly skin that develops not from bony plates,
like the scales of a fish, but from the outer epidermal layers. These scales
are made of a protein called *keratin*. Keratin is familiar to you as the
basic ingredient of hair, fingernails, cowhorns, and calluses. It is quite
a versatile biological material. Keratin is flexible, waterproof, and can
be produced in a hurry. Better still, it is nonliving, so it can be scuffed,
bumped, scraped, or bashed without damaging anything important.

In mammals, hair aids in water conservation as well as temperature
regulation. Moisture evaporation from the skin saturates only the air
trapped in the spaces between the hairs, and little is lost to the surrounding atmosphere.

PROBLEM 3: LOCOMOTION

Salamanders, which are good representative amphibians, use much
the same wriggling motion that typified their piscine ancestors. This is
neither particularly efficient nor very rapid. The entire body must be
thrown from side to side, and the limbs serve merely as props. When
the animal is really in a hurry, the limbs are forgotten and the animal
wriggles along on its belly.

In addition to the side-to-side thrusts of the body, reptiles tend to
rely on the movements of muscular limbs to provide the "oomph" for
locomotion over land.

Mammals generally keep the body rigid, with no side-to-side
movement at all. They rely solely on the limb musculature for propulsion, although the vertebral column may bend slightly, inchworm
style, to increase the length of the stride.

PROBLEM 4: FINDING ENOUGH FOOD

Underwater sensors such as the lateral line system are useless to animals on land, but smell, hearing, and vision can be used in either environment. In amphibians and reptiles, vision and the chemical senses of smell and/or taste became increasingly important, whereas sound production and hearing were used for social communications.

Probably because of their time-sharing role, the most primitive nocturnal mammals concentrated on hearing and an acute sense of smell to locate their food. After the Great Reptilian Disaster occurred many mammals became diurnal and developed an increasing dependence on vision.

PROBLEM 5: BREATHING THE AIR

Amphibians and some reptiles gulp air, which is then swallowed and forced into the lungs. More advanced reptiles use the body musculature to expand their body cavities and suck air into the lungs like a bellows pump. In mammals, respiration is accomplished by movement of a muscular diaphragm that may be accompanied by movements of the ribs to further increase or decrease the volume of the lungs. The respiratory lining of the lungs changes as well. Amphibian lungs are relatively simple sacs with a vascular lining. Increased metabolic rates require increased oxygen supplies, and the lungs of reptiles are increasingly complex in structure. In mammals, the lungs contain hundreds of millions of alveoli, tiny air sacs surrounded by blood vessels, where gas exchange takes place.

PROBLEM 6: REPRODUCTION

Typical amphibians spawn with their eggs developing in fresh water. Usually there are larval stages that remain in the water for some time before developing into the more or less terrestrial adult forms. All this time the eggs and larvae are exposed to predation by fishes and other amphibians. With the odds stacked against them, the females use their 30 percent surplus of energy to produce prodigious numbers of eggs, few of which will survive to maturity.

Reptiles rely on internal fertilization, and most produce a shelled egg that can be hidden on land. The females produce fewer eggs, but may expend energy guarding the nest sites or even the hatchlings, and there are no larval stages. All these factors tend to lower the mortality rate.

Mammals also reproduce by internal fertilization, and the young are retained and nurtured within the body of the female, usually until they are miniature models of the adult. The newborn mammal is totally dependent for some time thereafter, while it feeds upon the milk secreted by special mammary glands of the mother. Parental attention helps to keep predation to a minimum until the young animal is ready to fend for itself. All in all, a lot of energy is devoted to supporting and nurturing each individual, and relatively few young are born at one time.

This brief discussion has highlighted some of the variations that appeared in the process of adapting to a primarily terrestrial existence from ancestral populations of fresh water fishes. The information is further summarized in Table 5–1.

Table 5–1. Comparison Between Terrestrial Amphibians, Reptiles, and Mammals

Problem	Amphibians	Reptiles	Mammals
excessive cooling	Sunbask on land	Sunbask on land or surface of warm waters	Increase metabolic activity; sunbask; fur insulation
overheating	Change exposure to sun; enter shade or water	Change exposure to sun; enter shade or water	Change exposure to sun; fur insulation
water loss	Stay near water or high humidity areas; restrict basking	Thick, keratinous hide or scales	Fur insulation
gain fresh water	Absorb through skin; drink liquid	Drink water; obtain from food	Drink water; obtain from food
locomotion	Modified swimming with limbs as props (salamanders)	Reduced swimming with limb muscles assisting	Limb muscles with no swimming motion
locate prey	Vision primary, smell secondary, hearing/vibration minor importance	Vision primary, smell secondary, hearing/vibration minor importance	Smell, vision, and/or hearing all important depending on the animal
respiration	Oxygen absorbed through moist skin; air swallowed into simple lungs	Lungs filled and emptied with bellows-pump system	Lungs filled and emptied with diaphragm and/or bellows pump
reproduction	Fertilization external; eggs deposited in fresh water or wet areas; larval stages	Fertilization internal; eggs deposited on land; no larval stages	Fertilization internal; embryo retained by female; no larval stages

The amphibians, tied to water by their permeable skins, never competed successfully with reptiles or mammals for the control of the land. Neither could they exploit the resources of the seas, for their general physiology and reproductive patterns depend on *fresh* waters.

The reptiles were not so limited. As competition increased ashore, and bony fishes multiplied in the tropical seas, several families of reptiles turned to the ocean. One hundred million years ago there were many different kinds of marine reptiles swimming about, but most of them disappeared along with their terrestrial brethren. Only four major types of marine reptiles survive today in the tropical oceans: the marine iguanas, the salt water (alias estuarine) crocodiles, the sea turtles, and the sea snakes.

Shortly after the disappearance of the reptilian multitudes the ancestors of three separate groups of modern mammals began adapting to life in the ocean. Their descendants are known as the sea lions/seals, the sea cows, and the whales.

In adapting to a marine environment, these reptiles and mammals could not simply regress to the forms of their finny ancestors, reacquiring scales, fins with rays, gills, and so on. Animals can't de-evolve any more than a rock can de-fall after being dropped. Evolution is a one-way street, and in adapting to life at sea these animals had to address the same basic problems that faced the first explorers of the land, only this time in the opposite direction. They must strive to (1) maintain an acceptably high and constant body temperature; (2) find a way to get fresh water in a salt-water habitat; (3) swim efficiently; (4) locate their food even when smell, and often vision, is useless; (5) get enough oxygen to keep operating while submerged; and (6) reproduce successfully in very different surroundings. Each modern group has solved these problems in its own fashion, by its own distinctive domino-chain of modifications. As we consider these animals you should try to think in terms of adaptation, specialization, and convergence, because you will not see more beautiful examples of these principles anywhere.

There is only one tropical marine lizard, and it is found only along the shores of the Galapagos Islands. The marine iguana is an herbivore that feeds on marine algae which it scrapes or gnaws off the rocky bottom at depths of up to 35 feet. Its slender body cools rapidly in the chilly waters of the Peru Current, and upon its return to the shore the iguana indulges itself in a prolonged warmup before it is willing to consider rushing back into the water, even if pursued by curious photographers. Most of its waking hours are spent sunning on the black lava rocks, with occasional trips to the submerged feeding grounds. Plate 4 shows them relaxing at home.

The skin of the iguana is dry and tough, with small scales and a series of fierce-looking spines along the crest of the head. Marine iguanas drink seawater, and excrete the excess salts through a special gland in the nose. If you watch one for long you will see it snort or sneeze, and as it does so it sprays salt crystals in all directions.

When diving, the iguana swims with a powerful sculling motion of the tail and with the limbs folded tightly against the body. This is not a particulary rapid swimming style, and the animal moves along at the speed of a leisurely stroll. When submerged the iguana's metabolism is lowered dramatically, and its heart-rate slows even to the point of stopping for brief periods. In this way the iguana lengthens its stay underwater by reducing the demand for oxygen.

Eggs are deposited ashore, and there are elaborate social interactions. As you approach an iguana, it may rise up on its front legs and bob up and down as if doing pushups. This is a threatening display, which apparently works reasonably well with other iguanas. Although they do reach 4 to 5 feet in length, marine iguanas are dedicated herbivores and are completely innocuous. Some long-term residents of the islands have tamed them, and they are exceedingly fond of apples. The practice is heartily discouraged by the authorities, however, and the species is rigorously protected from contact with human beings.

Marine iguanas are not in any immediate danger of extinction, although they were not always so fortunate. They are gregarious creatures, usually found sunning in large numbers. Because they are also reported to be tasty, and are undeniably slow moving on land, early visitors to the islands hunted them for food. Unfortunately, the occasional discovery of campfires surrounded by iguana and flamingo bones indicates that today there are still people who enjoy experimental dining.

The marine iguana is related to the terrestrial iguanas that inhabit the temperate and tropical portions of South America. In our consideration of the bony fishes of the reef, we made models to show how isolation could lead to specialization and speciation, and these islands are excellent terrestrial examples of this principle. The Galapagos chain lies roughly 600 miles off the coast of Ecuador, squarely in the path of the Peru Current as it swings offshore. Colonization of such an isolated location is very slow, and return to the mainland is almost impossible, assuming that the animal under discussion is unable to fly. The marine iguanas are terrestrial endemics, and their ancestors presumably drifted across from the mainland. Once the marine iguanas evolved, they were prevented from spreading to other Pacific islands by the 2,600 mile gulf that separates them from their nearest downstream neighbors, the Marquesas Islands.

Crocodiles are the only surviving reptilian descendants of the dinosaurs. All crocodiles are extremely formidable creatures, and marine crocodiles are the largest of the lot, reaching lengths of 20 feet and weights of over a ton. Marine crocodiles are found throughout the tropical Indian Ocean, but penetrate the tropical Pacific only along its western boundaries. They are known (and respected) in the Malaysian/Indonesian region and along the northern coast of Australia. They have been reported from the Solomon Islands, and more rarely from the New Herbides, Fiji, and western Micronesian islands. In the Caribbean there is a different species, but just as large and worthy of respect.

Like the marine iguanas, marine crocodiles sun themselves on land to raise their body temperatures, but because they are restricted to warm tropical waters these periods of basking can be less intensive and frequent. Marine crocodiles drink seawater, and the excess salts are removed not by a gland in the nose, but by a similar organ that lies beneath the tongue. The thick keratinous hide of the crocodile overlies a number of bony plates that give the animal a tough, flexible, and waterproof armor.

A crocodile swims by throwing its body into a series of curves, relying mainly on its broad, flattened tail for propulsion. The limbs are very muscular, enabling the animal to hunt along the shoreline as well as at sea. Prey is found visually, and crocodiles feed on fishes, other reptiles, birds, and mammals—whatever the occasion permits. When submerged, crocodiles lower their metabolism and heart rates and are known to remain submerged for up to five hours at a time. It seems likely that they have some accessory mechanisms for extracting oxygen from the surrounding waters, as do the sea turtles and sea snakes considered below.

The female croc builds a large nest on land from leaves and other plant debris, and buries twenty to forty eggs inside. The heat produced by the decomposition of the plants warms the eggs while the female stands guard nearby. Those who have reared marine crocodile hatchlings report them to be fierce, aggressive little beasts, and the adults have much the same reputation with the native populations wherever they occur. The sight of a 20 foot crocodile approaching at full gallop must be rather intimidating to say the least.

The sea turtles are probably the most familiar and "lovable" of the marine reptiles, and they are found throughout tropical seas. The typical turtle shell consists of a series of bony plates that have fused with the vertebrae, ribs, portions of the shoulder, and pelvis. The entire structure is sheathed in a set of keratinous scales that are characteristically ornamented and/or colored in different species. Contrary to what

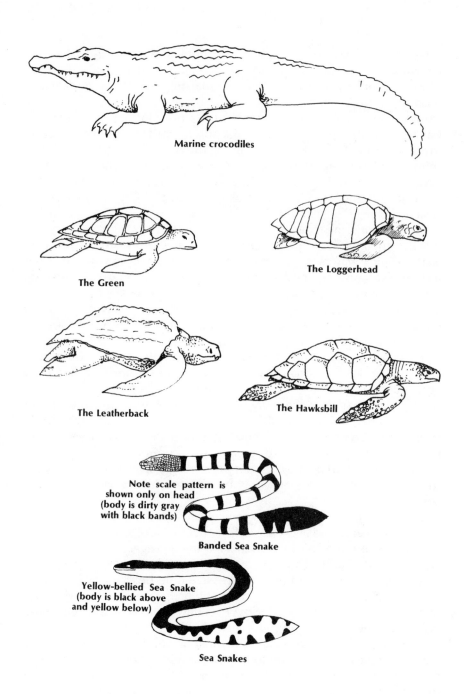

Marine crocodiles

The Green

The Loggerhead

The Leatherback

The Hawksbill

Note scale pattern is shown only on head (body is dirty gray with black bands)

Banded Sea Snake

Yellow-bellied Sea Snake (body is black above and yellow below)

Sea Snakes

Figure 5–1. The marine reptiles

you might expect, a turtle shell is still quite sensitive to touch and temperature. The upper portion of the shell is relatively thin, perhaps allowing the animal to bask effectively while floating at the surface. With such a rigid body covering, no side-to-side flexing of the body is possible, and the sea turtles use their flipper-like forelimbs to flap their way through the water. Because their shells are smooth and relatively streamlined, these are the fastest of marine reptiles. As in other diving animals, marine turtles lower their heart rate and general demand for oxygen when submerged. Their diving time is extended by their ability to extract oxygen from the water via highly vascularized regions of the nasal passages, and they can remain submerged for hours at a time.

Both carnivorous and herbivorous sea turtles rely on vision to locate their food. Although modern turtles lack teeth they possess bony beaks with sharp edges, backed up by strong jaw muscles. Marine turtles drink seawater, like the marine crocs and iguanas, but they have yet another gland for excreting the salts, this time located in the orbit of the eye. This gland is responsible for the heavy "tears" seen when the animals are out of the water.

All marine turtles seem to use their own special sites for breeding and egg laying. Only the female turtles come ashore, and they remain just long enough to dig a shallow burrow in the sand, deposit their eggs, and cover them up. Hatching, finding the ocean, and surviving are the responsibility of each little turtle, because the female has no further interest in them. The native populations of the area are hardly so aloof, and turtle eggs are considered excellent fare—a fact that has not helped the turtle populations very much.

The Green turtle feeds on long grasses that grow in shallow lagoons and reef flats. The turtle clips off the plants with its sharp beak. Green turtles are highly prized for their flesh, and they are still hunted actively in many parts of the world despite the fact that they are protected almost everywhere. Green turtles are the largest of the common island turtles, and mature individuals will reach as much as 1,000 pounds if given the opportunity.

The Hawksbill turtles seldom enter lagoons, but they may be encountered over the outer reef slope, where they feed on molluscs and crustaceans. Hawksbills reach a length of around 3 feet and weights of nearly 300 pounds. They are distinctively colored, and the keratin of the shell is extremely thick. This translucent tortoise shell has been so sought after for jewelry that the species has been hunted to extinction in many portions of its range. In some areas the hapless creatures are taken from the water and doused with boiling water to remove the keratin, after which the poor beasts are returned to the water to (supposedly) "grow another shell."

Loggerhead turtles are about the same size as Hawksbills, but they have huge heads nearly twice the size of those other turtles. They can be further distinguished from the Hawksbills by their dull brown coloration and the shape of the shell. Loggerheads feed on a variety of other animals, including small fishes, sea urchins, starfish, and even jellyfish.

The enormous Leatherback turtles reach weights of almost a ton, and they are the most specialized of the marine turtles. The shell has been reduced to a series of small bones buried beneath a leathery hide. These are open ocean animals, so you are unlikely to encounter one while snorkeling or diving.

The sea snakes are truly marine reptiles, for they never leave the ocean at all. Basking, if any, is done while floating on the surface, and these animals may be found miles from the nearest land, drifting with the currents. They are able to float with ease because one of their lungs is very long, extending the entire length of the elongate body cavity. There are also large masses of fats within the body, which further reduces their underwater weight.

Sea snakes are usually found closer to shore, around coral reefs, pilings, or other debris where they can find the fishes on which they feed. Sea snakes are related to cobras, and their sharp fangs, strong jaws, and poisonous venom enable them to penetrate the scales and immobilize their prey quickly. In general, sea snakes are most common at the eastern and western extremes of the Pacific, and they are not found in the tropical Atlantic at all. Sea snakes are occasionally seen in the Marquesas, Hawaii, the Society, Samoan, and Tongan islands, but they become more common along the reefs of Fiji and areas farther west. Large numbers of animals, presumed to be breeding, have been seen off the Pacific coasts of Panama and Colombia, and in Malaysian waters. By "large" I mean LARGE, with one congregation reported to have been 10 feet wide and 60 miles long. The fertilized eggs are retained within the body of the mother, and the young snakes are born alive and swimming. The significant numbers of sea snakes found off the western coast of Central America is one cause for concern should a sea level canal ever be built.

A sea snake swims with an expanded, blade-like tail and can move quickly when hunting or being pursued—an activity not recommended for the average diver. Sea snakes can remain submerged for several hours, in part because of the large volume of air in their lungs. In addition, they are able to absorb oxygen from the water across thin patches of skin between adjacent scales. Sea snakes are taken accidentally in fishing nets, particularly in the Philippines, and there is some commercial use for the skins. In general, these species are in no danger of extinction at the moment, and they are one of the few groups of marine reptiles or mammals to be so fortunate. Being poisonous does have its advantages!

Many snorkelers or divers are unduly startled by the appearance of small eels, and invariably the question arises "How do you tell the difference?" Initially I would say that if the animal is chasing you, don't stop to worry about such matters, because even an eel can give a nasty bite. But if you see one nearby, perhaps above the surface of the reef, there are several quick ways to spot it as a reptile and not a fish. The scales are present in a mozaic pattern, not overlapping as in most fishes, nor reduced or absent as in the eels. At a slightly greater distance you should be able to see that a sea snake has no gill openings and no fins at all. Even the swimming tail is clearly an expanded portion of the body itself, and not "finny." The two most common species are illustrated in Figure 5–1 on page 104.

Before continuing with a discussion of the marine mammals, let's look for trends or patterns among the marine reptiles. Basking in the sun is obviously important, and this can be accomplished either ashore or at sea. Because water absorbs heat so readily, only those animals that bask ashore at least part of the time have been able to reside year-round in areas where the waters are relatively cool (marine iguanas and some crocodiles). The rest of the marine reptiles stay in relatively warm surface waters, either remaining in the tropics (sea snakes) or wandering to more productive temperate latitudes only during the summer months (sea turtles). The giant Leatherback has a special characteristic, in that its large size and tough, oily skin enables it to retain some of its metabolic heat, and thus remain warm even in cool northern waters.

In general, it seems that the four-legged stride of terrestrial reptiles did not translate into an efficient swimming stroke, and one particular region or structure predominates. Side-to-side flexing is typical of most marine reptiles, and the usual swimming technique involves a long tail, with the limbs, if present, held close to the body. Turtles, which cannot flex their bodies at all, use their forelimbs or pectorals to fly through the water. This is a distinct change from the swimming styles of more landlocked species, such as the snapping turtles or painted turtles of the United States, and the advantages of flying versus dog-paddling must be significant.

When diving, a reptile permits a decline in its body temperature, which is accompanied by a reduction in heart rate and an overall decrease in the demand for oxygen. Sea turtles and sea snakes, at least, have auxiliary mechanisms for absorbing oxygen through specialized portions of the skin. Despite the ability to remain submerged for long periods, they are not deep-diving animals, and they find their food by using their eyes in shallow, sunlit waters.

The degree of specialization for a marine existence seems to be related to how important a role the dry land plays in the life history of each group of marine reptiles. Marine iguanas and marine crocs are essentially representatives of terrestrial (iguanas) or fresh water (crocodiles) groups versatile enough to survive in the ocean. Both spend a lot of time ashore, and both depend on the land for temperature control, social interactions, and reproduction.

Only female turtles leave the water at all, and then just for a brief "layover," and the sea turtles have specialized to a point where getting around on land is extremely difficult. It is unlikely that any further reductions in the limbs would carry any advantages, because this would either reduce swimming efficiency or make terrestrial locomotion and nest building even more difficult. Different modifications for streamlining, food types, and coloration do characterize the various species, and one (the Leatherback) has reduced the bony shell that has been the hallmark of the turtle clan for more than 200 million years.

The terrestrial snakes that were the ancestors of today's sea snakes were already very specialized, having elongate bodies and no limbs. Because animals can't devolve, we should expect only elaborations on this basic "snakish" theme. Yet sea snakes, like several other snakes, bear their young alive, so they never need to leave the water. In adapting to their environment they have diverged greatly from other snakes in scale pattern, body form, and respiration, and they are quite helpless when placed on terra firma.

So our conclusion might be that extreme physical adaptation to life at sea is found in concert with a reduction in the importance of the land in *all* aspects of the life history of the animal. With this in the back of our minds we can proceed with our discussion of the three groups of tropical marine mammals.

The modern sea lions, seals, and walruses are collectively known as *pinnipeds* (*pinna*, "fin"; *ped*, "foot"). All pinnipeds have several features in common. They retain hair over the surface of their bodies, but this may or may not overlie a layer of fat or blubber just beneath the skin. There is often a considerable size difference between the sexes, with the males being much larger than the females. Their bodies are streamlined, and they are strong swimmers with excellent diving abilities. When diving, air is kept out of the nostrils by a muscular flap that is closed in the relaxed position and closed even more securely when pressure is applied from the outside. Pinnipeds feed on fishes, squid, and other invertebrates including shellfish. They are extremely supple and can bend or turn quickly while pursuing agile prey. A variable portion of the year is spent ashore in rookery areas, where the young are born and nursed. The young pinnipeds grow rapidly, thanks to a diet of milk that is extremely rich in fats.

Sea lions and seals look very much alike, but they differ in several important details. The sea lions are the popular stars of stage and screen, famous for tooting horns and applauding themselves by slapping their front flippers together. These hairless flippers are very modified forelimbs and provide the propulsion for swimming much like the marine turtles. From the muscular chest the body tapers smoothly both fore and aft, and the streamlining is very noticeable. There are few parts of the body that disturb the smooth flow of water over the animal. The external ears are reduced to tiny flaps only an inch or so in length, and the male sexual organs and the nipples of the female are contoured in pockets hidden beneath the fur that covers the entire body with the exception of the flippers and feet. The legs are tapered into the general body contour, with only the ankles and feet sticking out into the world. These are used for steering while swimming, and out of the water they can be turned under the body to help with locomotion on land, even to the point of climbing ladders with beachballs balanced on their snouts. In the wild their terrestrial talents enable them to establish rookeries on extremely rocky and even cliffed coasts. In many species the males move ashore first, to establish and hold a territory. Females arrive later, and large harems form within the territory of a successful male.

A sea lion's fur is its primary source of insulation against the ocean's chill. If the insulating properties of the fur are destroyed by heavy oil spills or other pollutants, the animal may die from heat loss (hypothermia). Because of the importance of its air-trapping abilities, good grooming is essential, and glands at the bases of the hairs produce secretions that help lubricate and waterproof the coat. Sea lions out of the water are usually fluffing their coats by shaking themselves as they dry in the sun. When basking, or when swimming rapidly, there may actually be a problem with getting rid of excess heat, which is accomplished through the naked surfaces of the flippers and feet. The blood supply to the surface of the skin in these regions is closely monitored, and they can serve as radiators when required. On land they will also be found rolling in damp sand until they are completely dusted with white. The light color of the sand, and perhaps its coolness as well, helps reduce the heating of the body.

Sea lions are able to dive for thirty minutes at a time, and they can descend to 500 feet below the surface. At this depth the water pressure would be sufficient to squash the lungs and airways of most mammals, but those of the sea lions and other deep-diving mammals are reinforced by blocks of cartilage. Their diving time is increased because their lungs are large, and their blood can carry and release a large amount of oxygen. In addition, the heart rate slows and the circulatory pattern changes to insure that any oxygen removed from the lungs is distributed only to essential organs, primarily the heart and brain.

It is rather dark 500 feet down, and although sea lions rely on vision for locating their prey in clear surface waters, they can also echolocate. Echolocation is basically biological sonar, in which the animal makes a series of sounds and then listens for the echoes. A fast, loud echo means that the object is close; a faint, delayed echo means the object is farther away. By rapidly scanning around, the animal builds up a precise picture of its surroundings without using vision at all.

Sea lions are found throughout subarctic and temperate waters, and they extend into the tropics where there are cool or cold currents. Fur "seals" are actually sea lions with a dense layer of short underfur beneath the outer coat, and they are found in many of these same areas. Both the California sea lion and the fur seal are found along the coasts of the Galapagos Islands, often sunning themselves in the company of the marine iguanas.

Seals are even more highly modified for streamlining. There are no external ears, and most of the feet are contained within the body mass, with just the outer portions of the soles exposed and facing one another. Swimming in these seals involves a side-to-side motion, with the feet providing the propulsion. The forelimbs are covered with fur and often have claws. With most of the skeleton of the foot enclosed within the body mass, seals are unable to use their feet when traveling overland, so they must either slide or inch-worm their way along. This makes them rather easy to catch, a feature that has not helped them greatly in their dealings with humanity.

The fur of a seal is actually pretty lightweight, although some species are commercially valuable. Insulation in these animals depends on a layer of fat just beneath the skin. In some species the blubber may account for 25 percent of the weight of the animal! Fat is an excellent insulating agent, for fats do not conduct heat nearly as rapidly as other tissues. In addition, it requires few blood vessels to keep the fat cells alive. The fur, skin, and outer portions of the blubber layer are allowed to drop in temperature to just above or at the temperature of the surrounding water, but the inner body mass is kept comfortably warm. When overheating threatens, cooling is accomplished across the

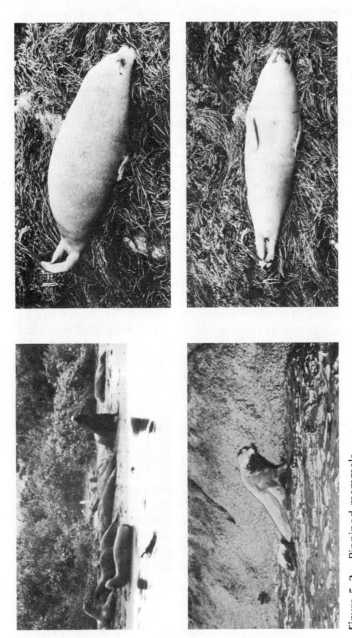

Figure 5–2. Pinniped mammals
upper left: a large male sea lion stands at the ready while his harem snoozes in the tropical sun; notice the erect, four-footed posture, the large, hairless flippers, and the relatively large size as compared to the surrounding females; *lower left*: a female sea lion and her pup; note the sleek body form and the small but distinctive external ear flaps; *upper right*: a small seal for comparison; notice the lack of external ears, the furred flippers that retain visible digits, and the way the feet are largely concealed within the tapered body mass. Examine these features from another angle in the lower right photograph.

naked surfaces of the hind feet, and the sight of a seal waving its feet in the breeze while sitting in the sun is quite engaging. Seal hunters, who seek either the blubbler for oil or the pelts for clothing, are seldom so amused. The yearly killing of harp seal pups in northern Canada points out a particular limitation of this form of insulation. The young seals are born ashore and are unable to enter the cold northern waters until they have accumulated enough of an insulating blanket of fat that they are protected from freezing. The white fur coats that they possess over this critical period help protect them from the predators of the region while the blubber layer builds, thanks to the fatty milk of the mother. Once the blubber layer is substantial, the attractive white coat is shed and the young seal can take to the water.

Seals are excellent divers. Indeed, one species is able to reach depths of almost 2,000 feet. This is markedly deeper than any of the sea lions, and it may be due to the fact that whereas fur is an effective insulator, its efficiency decreases with depth, for increasing pressure squeezes the air from beneath the hairs.

Like the sea lions, seals prefer islands or ice flows for social activities, but unlike the average sea lion most seals are monogamous. There are many more species of seals than other pinnipeds, and three species have adapted to tropical waters. Unfortunately, man's use of these same areas has led to their gradual destruction. The Hawaiian Monk Seal prefers the shallow waters around coral reefs. Until they were protected, hunting reduced their numbers drastically, and there are probably fewer than 2,000 individuals left. Now that the species is completely protected it is hoped that they will become increasingly familiar sights to both residents and visitors to the Pacific as their population and range increases. The Caribbean Monk Seal does not seem to have received similar clemency, and it probably became extinct in the last twenty years. (The Mediterranean Monk Seal didn't last as long.)

The other pinniped group, the walruses, are restricted to northern polar and high temperate latitudes, so you are unlikely to meet any in the tropics. I will simply note that they combine features of both the sea lions and seals with some unique developments of their own.

The sea cows or *sirenians* arose independently, and their closest living relatives are the elephants. The two share a number of characteristics: The bones of sirenians are large and massive, like those of elephants, and the teeth are broad, flat, and distinctively ornamented in both groups. Elephants and sea cows alike have unusual muscular snouts that are used to obtain their food, which consists of either terrestrial or aquatic vegetation. But the similarities are mainly internal, and externally sea cows are quite distinctive in appearance. The head seems to blend into the body without a clearly defined neck. The eyes are small and weak, and the entire face is dominated by an elaborate muzzle that looks and acts like an abbreviated trunk. There are no external ears, and with the exception of the muzzle the body is covered with a thick, naked hide. Tiny sensory hairs like fine whiskers may be scattered over the surface an inch or so apart, and the muzzle is covered with heavy bristles. These are the only remnants of the fur coats of their terrestrial mammalian ancestors. There are no external indications of any hindlimbs, and internally there are only vestiges of the pelvic bones. The forelimbs are also highly modified.

Two different types of sea cows have managed to survive to the present day. *Manatees* are found in fresh-water tributaries of the tropical and subtropical Atlantic and congregate during the winters in the interior waterways of Florida, where they are perhaps the most intensively studied. Manatees were once found in fresh waters of the Caribbean islands as well as along the tropical Atlantic coasts of Central and South America, but today they are almost unknown in the Caribbean, with only occasional reports from Puerto Rico. Along the entire Atlantic coast of the Americas the total population is probably under 15,000, and with the exception of the region around Guyana the numbers seem to be declining dangerously. Manatees are primarily fresh-water inhabitants, although they are sometimes found in estuaries and even along the adjacent coast.

If you should catch a glimpse of one you will be unlikely to mistake it for anything else. The skin is rough and creased, and the tail, which provides the propulsion, is pancake-shaped. Manatees are not strong swimmers, and they seem most content to graze slowly through beds of grasses or water lilies. Their forelimbs are short, but traces of fingers can still be seen, complete with fingernails, and the "hands" are used to manipulate bundles of vegetation that are stuffed into the muscular muzzle. They are lethargic, nonaggressive creatures whose most serious enemies seem to be hungry humans and, in areas of high technology like Florida, outboard propellors.

The other living sea cow is the *dugong*, which is more highly specialized and completely marine in habits. Dugongs are found in the tropical Indo-Pacific, ranging from Micronesia and Melanesia to the East African coast. The body form is much more streamlined than that of a manatee, and the skin is slick and rubbery, rather like the surface of a swim fin. The forelimbs look and act like steering paddles, and propulsion is provided by the large caudal flukes, which are broad and horizontally expanded. The body is quite stiff and muscular, and the head is not moved independently. When feeding, a dugong props itself on its flippers, with its bristly muzzle contacting the bottom. As it shuffles along it tears marine plants, primarily eel grasses, from the loose sand of the lagoon floor. No meticulous cleaning and sifting is done, although the movements of the muzzle and the array of stiff bristles will assist in removing debris, and bits of shellfish, sand, and small invertebrates are often found in the stomach.

Male dugongs have short tusks that protrude from the upper gums. All their uses are not clear, but natives of the western Pacific claim that they are used during courtship and in fights with other males. These reports appear to be supported by the long, parallel scars seen along the backs of male dugongs. Whatever their courtship rituals might be, dugongs are born in the water and remain with their mothers for at least a year. Because the mammary glands are located on the chest, close to the point where the flippers join the body, it is believed that the sight of a young dugong suckling may have led to the legend of mermaids. I can only say that the sailor who first thought of *that* had been at sea for a long, long time.

Groups of dugongs can sometimes be seen waiting near passes in the reef for the tide to rise, whereupon they spread out over the inner lagoon. When undisturbed they may be seen near the same location each day, but heavy boat traffic sends them in search of more tranquil surroundings. Near Noumea, New Caledonia, dugongs can be seen during the week within a mile of the city, but during the weekend invasion of pleasure craft they find peace and quiet elsewhere along the coast. It is a shame that the manatees do not show such discretion. As our utilization of their feeding grounds increases there will be an ever greater need for the establishment of preserves that are off-limits to power boats, but unfortunately in some areas the dugongs are not protected at all, even from hunters.

Dugongs were once hunted by Melanesian natives who built wooden platforms over the reef flat. Through trapdoors in these structures they hung large balls of eelgrass, and when a dugong found the conveniently packaged snack a native would grab a weapon and jump down on top of the animal. The risk factor was high on both sides, and neither combatant was in danger of eliminating the opponent species. The arrival of outboard motors, rifles, and iron spears changed the situation drastically, and today the dugong is threatened throughout its entire range. Reasonable populations persist in extremely isolated areas, as along the northern coast of Australia, but they are still speared on sight in many other portions of the Pacific, and even where they are protected there is considerable poaching. The problem seems to be that the natives hold the flesh in high regard, ranked with the world's great delicacies, and temptation is difficult to resist when the government is located two islands away.

The whales and their relations are called *cetaceans* (*cetus*, "whale"), and in this group we find the greatest degree of specialization for life on the high seas. They are streamlined, lacking external ears, hindlimbs, or any exposed sexual organs. Their bodies are naked, smooth, and firm, without hairs except in a few species that retain sensory hairs on the head or along the edges of the flippers. Beneath the skin there is a thick layer of blubber that insulates the animal from the relatively cool ocean water. There is no visible neck and the body is rather stiffly held, flexing up and down as the laterally expanded flukes provide propulsion. The flippers steer and brake, and are ill-suited for any other functions. The head is distinctive, with the nostrils located near the top of the head. These are closed in the relaxed position, and it takes conscious effort to open them for breathing.

Take a moment to compare the basic body forms of the cetaceans and sirenians shown in Figure 5–3. There are many external similarities, yet the two groups are not related to one another. There is general agreement that the ancestors of the modern cetaceans and those of the modern grazers—the cows and their relations—were one and the same. Both modern groups share physical and behavioral characteristics. The young are born alert, well formed, and ready to move around on their own. Cetaceans travel in large herds or "pods," and when startled they may move en masse in a stampede, which results in a group stranding if there is a coastline or shoal in their path. A comparison of eyes, male reproductive organs, and digestive tracts show many other similarities, and both cows and whales are subject to some of the same diseases—illnesses that do not affect other mammals. So how do we explain the apparent similarities between the sirenians and cetaceans? Each group has been modified through natural selection operating in a very demanding environment, and in each case the ancestral population consisted of furry, four-legged, terrestrial mammals. Strongly advantageous adaptations, such as streamlining, reduction of hindlimbs, and so on, were favored in both lines, and the descendants came to resemble one another as they reached similar solutions to common problems. Thus their similarities represent a particularly striking example of convergence. Although sirenians and cetaceans have converged in their general body form, their detailed anatomies, general life styles, and physiological responses are still quite divergent.

Young cetaceans are born in the water, fully able to swim on their own. They are usually born in warm waters, or at least during the local summer, as their insulation blanket is only partially complete. The

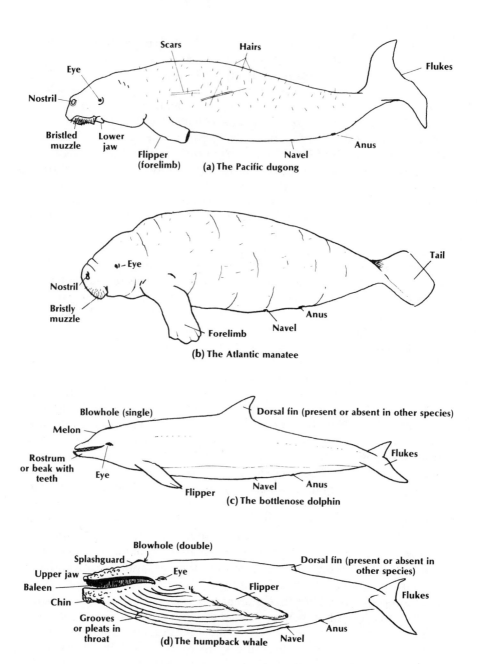

Figure 5–3. The basic body forms of sirenians and cetaceans.

blubber layer grows quickly, and efficient nursing at sea is made possible by special muscles around the mammary glands that enable the mother to provide a pressurized stream of milk to her calf. As in other marine mammals, this milk is high in fats, and the young calves, consuming prodigious quantities of the stuff, grow at a remarkable speed. They are relatively large at birth, and a single calf is the general rule, although twins are seen on rare occasions.

When in the open ocean, cetaceans sleep at the surface, either swimming slowly or lying motionless. This habit makes them subjects to attack or collision with boats, with unfortunate results for both parties.

Living cetaceans can be divided into two categories, those with teeth and those without. The toothed whales are called *odontocetes* (*odonto*, "tooth"). Odontocetes are active carnivores, primarily feeding on fish and squid of one size or another. Their eyes are relatively small but they have an excellent echolocation system, far more refined than that of the sea lions mentioned earlier. Toothed whales have a pronounced, dome-shaped forehead that houses a special, oil-filled structure called a *melon*. The skull is actually concave in front, rather like a spoon, to accommodate this organ, and in some of the toothed whales, like the killer whale or sperm whale, the melon may project all the way to the tip of the upper jaw. In others, like the bottlenose dolphin or the beaked whales, the melon extends only partway along the upper jaw, and a beak or *rostrum* is exposed. In any event, oils work on sound the way the lens of your eye works on light, that is, they can focus sound energy. The toothed whales produce high-frequency sounds in pockets off the nasal passages leading to the blowhole, and these sound waves are focused by the melon and beamed out in front of the animal. Most of the important sounds are too high-pitched for us to hear, for odontocetes can detect sounds of frequencies up to 200,000 cycles per second (Hz) as compared with our upper threshold of roughly 18,000 Hz. The ability to find your prey and spot your enemies is obviously quite important, and echolocation makes this possible even in turbid coastal waters or at great depths where vision is useless. The odontocetes are the more "brainy" whales, possibly because they are actively carnivorous. Carnivores that pursue large, mobile prey must be quick to respond to evasive tactics, and if the intended victim escapes it helps to remember where the chase went awry.

The bottlenose dolphin was responsible for the rising American concern for cetaceans and other marine mammals. They are easy to capture, they adjust to captivity readily, and their ability to learn and remember a variety of amusing tricks has made them the main attraction at marine shows all around the world. These engaging animals reach 10 to 12 feet in length and weights of almost half a ton. They are usually grey along their backs and sides, and either white or rose-colored along their bellies. The prominent beak contains numerous small, pointed teeth that are primarily used to seize small fish or squid. Bottlenose dolphins are extremely well streamlined, and although their cruising speed is only around 6 mph they can sprint to over 20 mph for brief periods.

Bottlenose dolphins, otherwise known as bottlenose porpoises (and a variety of television aliases) are common visitors to most tropical reefs and islands. Offshore these animals may travel in pods of a thousand or more individuals, but along a coast or over a shallow reef smaller pods are the rule. There is a definite social order to the pods, usually led by a dominant male or female. The members interact socially in complex ways. Other members of the pod may help an injured individual to the surface to let it breathe, a behavior that has saved more than one potential drowning victim. Bottlenose dolphins make a variety of social sounds in addition to their echolocation broadcasts, and some of these alert other members of the pod to some unusual event or strong emotion. It seems likely that they must live for twenty-five years or more in the wild, for captive animals have been held without problems for as long as twenty-one years.

Another group of dolphins includes the slender spotted dolphins, found in the Atlantic and Pacific tropical latitudes, and the spinners, residents of the Pacific. They are not commonly seen in captivity, and they seem less hardy than the bottlenose. The spotted dolphins will occasionally approach a boat to ride the bow wave, especially if it is a small vessel, and their distinctive mottling of pale blotches on a grey background makes them difficult to mistake. Pacific spinners are smaller, more slender, and have longer and narrower snouts than the bottlenose dolphins, but their most obvious distinguishing characteristic is their spinning behavior. Most dolphins and many other cetaceans leap out of the water from time to time, but when a spinner jumps it often twirls around in the air, sometimes completing seven or eight spins before hitting the water. Only the spinners know what they are trying to accomplish by this. Spinners are often seen in the open Pacific, but they are also common around islands, especially around the Marquesas, Hawaii, and the southern Line Islands.

Spinners and spotted dolphins are two cetaceans threatened with extinction not because of any commercial value, but because they provide useful markers for fishermen. Large offshore pods are frequently found swimming above large schools of tuna, and it is much easier to spot an air-breathing dolphin at the surface than to guess at the location of a school of fish far below. Fast boats with seine nets encircle the pod *and* the fish, with predictable results. Many of the dolphins panic when the net boats are seen, or they may blunder into the netting because the meshwork is invisible on their sonar. In either case they face the danger of becoming helplessly entangled and drowned.

Over the past ten years, United States regulations have greatly reduced, if not completely eliminated, the mortality attributed to the American fishing fleet. It is not at all certain, however, that populations of these species are recovering, and it remains to be seen whether this is due to some natural interactions with the environment, caused by the original decline in populations, or the continued take of foreign flag vessels, which can fish any way they choose.

Killer whales are the wolves of the cetacean clan. Male killer whales reach 30 feet in length, and females approach an average of 20 feet. These animals are strikingly colored with patches of white on a black background. The males have a prominent hooked dorsal fin that may be 6 feet tall; like the flukes, the fin has no skeletal support but is made of fibrous connective tissue. Killer whale pods usually contain fewer than eighty animals, and each group has a clearly defined social structure. Killer whales are large and hungry, feeding on squid, fish, seals, penguins, sea birds, turtles, and smaller marine mammals. Their teeth are conical and pointed, about one inch in diameter, and the teeth of the upper and lower jaws interlock in a decisive fashion. There are many stories and a few films that demonstrate their agility and cunning while hunting in packs. Other marine mammals will avoid them whenever possible, and the tape-recorded cries of killer whales have been used to keep dolphins and sea lions from ravaging the nets in commercial squidding operations. Although there are no clearcut reports of intentional feeding on humans, there have been several instances where individuals or groups of killer whales have attacked sailing yachts, some of which promptly sank. These incidents have been most common in the open ocean within a circle whose center lies midway between the Galapagos and Marquesas Islands. In accounts of these events, the people were not molested by the whales, although obviously if they had been there would have been no account filed. Killer whales are seldom taken by whaling vessels, probably because they are too clever and too fast to make the effort worthwhile.

The largest of the toothed whales are the sperm whales. Males of

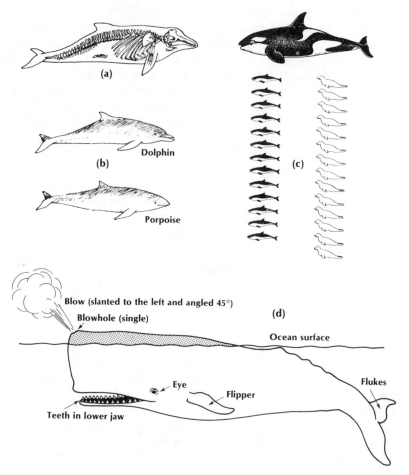

Figure 5–4. The ondontocete whales
(a) the skeleton of a small odontocete; compare with Figure 5–5(a). (b) typical profiles of a porpoise and a dolphin; notice the difference in the relative size of the melon. (c) killer whales can be quite voracious. The belly of one 24-foot animal contained 13 porpoises and 14 seals. (d) view of a sperm whale as soon in or out of the water.

this species reach 50 to 60 feet in length, whereas females are somewhat more petite, normally less than 35 feet or so. Almost one third of the length of a sperm whale consists of its head, and unlike other cetaceans the blowhole is located near the tip of the snout and angled to one side. This produces an unusual slanted blow which makes identification at sea quite simple. The melon of a sperm whale is enormous, and contains a very fine oil called *spermaceti*. In the heyday of American whaling, this oil was prized for smokeless lamps, as well as for supposed medicinal purposes. An unfortunate whaler was lowered into the exposed melon with a bucket, where he would bail out the entire chamber. It was not unknown for an *extremely* unfortunate whaler to lose his footing, slide out of sight, and drown in the whale's head. Today the oil is collected in a less dangerous manner, but it is still in demand as a lubricant for satellite and missile components in the Soviet Union.

The enormous melon and the unique air passageways of the head interact to make sperm whales the most powerful echolocaters of all the odontocetes. The complex forms a sound-laser that produces intense pulses of sound energy. This is presumably used to locate their prey at great depths and distances. Sperm whales have become entangled in undersea cables as deep as 3,600 feet beneath the surface, and their dives may last an hour and a half. They feed on squid of all sizes, and much of our knowledge of the large, deep-sea squids has come from the bellies of slaughtered sperm whales.

Squids are not tough and bony, so they are difficult to seize and hold. A sperm whale has large, conical teeth in the lower jaw that fit into sockets in the upper jaw. The lower jaw is slender, so it can be moved rapidly, and although there are no exposed teeth in the upper jaw it is tough and lined with heavy keratin.

Females and calves travel in small groups; sometimes the groups may be collected into pods of fifty or more animals, with the larger males scattered among their respective harems. Although the males may migrate to the polar seas each year, females and young are restricted to the area between 40°N and 40°S latitudes. Sperm whales in the northern hemisphere breed in April/May, whereas those in the southern latitudes get together in November/December. Some pod members from the Galapagos are shown in Plate 5. The gestation period is sixteen months, and the calf is about 13 feet long at birth. Left alone, a sperm whale will live for seventy-five years, although today such venerable individuals are rare.

American sperm whaling first peaked around 1845. Several factors led to its subsequent decline. The manufacture of kerosene in petroleum refineries ashore gradually eroded the market for spermaceti, and during the Civil War the whaling fleet suffered heavy losses as returning ships ignorant of the conflict were seized at southern ports. Over this same period, as the sperm whales declined in numbers and profitability, steam engines and harpoon guns were making the capture of the larger baleen whales much more attractive. Sperm whale meat was canned for domestic sale during World War I, but it was not warmly received by the American consumer. Sperm whales didn't come under heavy whaling pressures again, therefore, until the more valuable species of baleen whales had been hunted almost to extinction. Now there are probably fewer than 150,000 sperm whales left, and they are still the primary targets of the modern whaling fleet because they so far outnumber the other large species of cetaceans. A total ban on sperm whaling has been proposed, but whether or not it will be effective is anybody's guess. They are valuable for their meat, for their oil, for their teeth (scrimshaw artwork), and for leather. In addition, the digestive system of sperm whales is the source of *ambergris*, a waxy substance used in the preparation of expensive perfumes. Ambergris is produced through some unusual reaction between the beaks of certain squids and the whale's intestinal lining, and at one time it was literally worth its weight in gold. The principal sperm whaling grounds are off the Peruvian and Chilean coasts, where the cold Peru Current follows the shoreline. Large groups of animals are common sights around the Galapagos Islands, and sperm whales have been sighted from time to time all across the tropical Pacific. The Atlantic populations, naturally enough, were the first to be decimated when organized commercial whaling got off the ground. Sperm whales are very rare in the Caribbean, and are more common on the eastern side of the Atlantic both north and south of the equator. Large pods assemble off the Azores, which once supported a land-based whaling industry.

There are fewer than 100 species of cetaceans, and all but ten are odontocetes. The remaining whales differ from them in several important respects. While the baleen whales are carnivorous, they feed on much smaller prey, primarily animals of the plankton. Their favorite food consists of the small, shrimplike krill, which appear in great numbers in polar and high-temperature latitudes during the spring and summer plankton blooms. These animals are filtered from the water with giant screens called baleen plates.

Baleen is made of keratin, which is produced by the outer portions of the gums of the upper jaw. Each plate is composed of innumerable fine, hairlike filaments cemented together into a flexible sheet. In stiffness and texture a baleen sheet would remind you of your thumbnail. With time and general wear and tear, the outer cementing portions of the baleen plate disintegrate, leaving a meshwork of fine, stiff filaments. There may be hundreds of these plates within the mouth of a single whale. Together they make an efficient strainer. So many plates can fit within the closed mouth because they are quite thin, and they

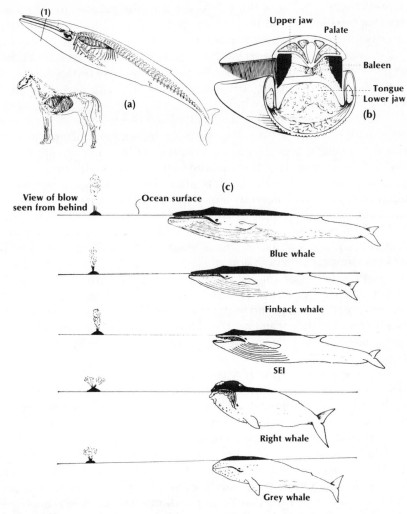

Figure 5–5. The mysticete whales
(a) skeletal features and position of the lungs in a horse and a blue whale; notice in the whale: the elongate head, reduced neck, modified forelimbs and digits, reduced pelvic bones, and the absence of hind-limbs. You will also note that the dorsal fin and flukes are without skeletal supports. The lungs are longer in the whale; this arrangement causes the animal to float roughly parallel to the surface, permitting more efficient breathing and locomotion. (b) this section was taken at point (1) marked in (a); notice the arrangement of the baleen plates produced by the gums of the upper jaw. (c) the relative size and appearance of five species of baleen whales, and the typical blow seen from behind the animal.

can also be long because the sheets are flexible and able to snap back into shape when the mouth is reopened. Baleen is the key to feeding success in these whales, for they lack teeth altogether and most species would be unable to swallow anything larger than a small fish, even if something larger entered the mouth, because the throat is only a foot or so in diameter. If it was a whale that swallowed Jonah, it certainly wasn't a baleen whale!

The baleen whales are also called *mysticetes* (*mystax*, "moustache"). They time their arrival at the polar feeding grounds to coincide with the springtime population explosion of life in the plankton. The whales have only to swim through the surface waters with their mouths agape to obtain their food. Yet there are different strategies used by the different species of baleen whales. Figure 5–5 presents silhouettes of several species. The "right whales" have enormous baleen plates that might be 10 feet long, and they strain krill or other slow-moving prey from the surface waters. If you've ever tried towing a small net or bucket from a moving boat you will recall that if you move faster than 1 to 2 mph you no longer have water movement through the net or bucket. At faster speeds you are pulling a lump of water along. So right whales, which swim around with their mouths open, swim very slowly. They are not highly streamlined, and their slow cruising made them the right whales to pursue if you were a whaler with only sail-power at your disposal.

Other species of baleen whales have diversified a bit. The Pacific grey whale is notable not because it is a regular visitor to the tropics, but because of its unusual life style and the fact that it has made a comeback from the edge of extinction. Greys feed by straining mud scooped from the bottom in coastal waters. The diving animal rolls to the side and takes a mouthful of material that is then filtered through the baleen plates. Small invertebrates, especially marine worms, are then swallowed. Once there were grey whales in both the Atlantic and Pacific oceans, but the Atlantic populations had probably been destroyed even before Europeans arrived (remains have been found in Indian middens). In the Pacific, grey whales were driven almost to extinction before protective measures were enacted. In the eastern Pacific the population has probably returned to prewhaling levels, but in the western Pacific their numbers have not rebounded. Greys have a very specialized technique for feeding, and there is only one species.

The most successful baleen whales are the *rorquals* such as the finback, blue, sei, and humpback whales. They are more streamlined, faster swimming, and able to pursue and capture more mobile prey like anchovies or herring which can swim considerably faster than 1 to

2 mph. Because of the abundance of food available, and the lack of gravitational limitations that plague large animals on land, these whales reach tremendous size if allowed to live out their lives without inter-ference. The blue whale, largest of the baleen whales (and hence the largest animal that has ever lived) reaches over 100 feet in length. Several other rorquals exceed 60 feet as adults. Yet their feeding time is limited, for they feed in polar seas, where summer thermoclines do not limit productivity. However, light is in critically short supply for six to seven months of the year. So for five months these animals are feeding almost continually, storing the surplus energy as a thick blanket of blubber. When the harsh winter approaches these whales seek warmer climes, where they can use the energy stores of the blubber to carry them through the rest of the year. (After all, polar insulation is hardly needed in the tropics!) Their actual guidance system while on migra-tion is unknown, for baleen whales lack a melon and appear to be incapable of producing high-frequency sounds similar to those of the odontocetes. As far as has been determined, the sounds they do pro-duce are used purely for social communications.

In traveling through the tropics visitors will most often see humpback whales, if they see any baleen whales at all. The life history of the humpback is fairly representative of rorquals in general, so the details will not be wasted even if you should be fortunate enough to catch a glimpse of a passing finback.

Humpback whales grow to around 50 feet in length and they weigh slightly less than one ton per foot. They can easily be distinguished from other baleen whales by their long, winglike flippers, and their peculiar humped silhouette when starting to dive. Humpbacks have roughly 800 baleen plates within their mouths, each of which is from one to two feet in length. The undersurface of the throat and upper chest is thrown into a number of parallel folds or pleats, which are also characteristic of the other rorquals. When these animals are feeding, the mouth can be filled with water and the pleats permit the expansion of a tremendous chamber formed as the tongue slides back beneath them. Even if the animal is lying motionless at the surface, this water mass can then be filtered when the surrounding muscles contract. Think about what this means for the whale. With such a distensible throat, a rorqual can swim into a mass of krill—or a moving school of fishes—at cruising speed. When the mouth is opened, a large ball of water can be taken in almost at once, and when the water has been strained through the baleen plates the whale is left with a mouth full of prey.

In the northern hemisphere, humpbacks feed from May to October. In the north Pacific they are found along the Alaskan coast, through the Aleutians and the Bering Sea, and off the shores of the Soviet Union. In the north Atlantic, sizable populations are found between Newfoundland and Cape Cod, and between Greenland and northern Europe into the Arctic waters. In the southern hemisphere, whales congregate in the waters around Antarctica from November to March. As fall approaches in either hemisphere, the feeding assemblages break up, and the whales follow the coastlines or prevailing currents to reach wintering grounds closer to the equator. It appears that most animals are making the same circuit year after year, returning to the same wintering grounds. Humpbacks from the north Pacific winter in tropical waters off Mexico, Japan, or among the Hawaiian Islands, and humpbacks from the northwestern Atlantic move to the waters off Puerto Rico or the Dominican Republic.

The arrival of the humpbacks in Hawaii is especially interesting because of the clear, calm waters and the large visitor population that migrates to the islands at around the same time. This gives many people a chance to get a good look (and some excellent photographs) at one of the large cetaceans. The first humpbacks arrive in late November or early December, and their numbers increase until February or March. At the peak of the season there may be 1,000 whales sporting around the islands, and if you are on West Maui, for example, it is a rare day on which you cannot spot a whale from the beach. During their stay in the tropics, which lasts until April or May at the latest, the humpbacks do not feed at all. (After all, they are in the relatively barren tropics.) So for that five- or six-month period they devote their attention to all the other activities that make mammalian life worthwhile. In the calm, clear waters they court and mate, bear and nurse their young, and occasionally play with passing boatloads of whale watchers. The gestation period is ten to twelve months, and the calves are about 14 feet long at birth. As is the rule with marine mammals, the mother's milk is extremely rich in calories, and the calf grows rapidly. In roughly ten and a half months the young whale gains 12 feet in length, or around half an inch daily.

While engaging in their social diversions, humpbacks produce a variety of haunting sounds or "songs." These have been studied intensively over the past decade, but their real meaning and significance is still rather uncertain. It seems that the males are singing, and that the songs play a role in courtship. But even more curious than the sounds themselves is the fact that all humpbacks in the northern Pacific seem to sing the same songs while wintering in the tropics, but the songs change from year to year, and the whales do not sing while on the

Figure 5–6. The appearance of a humpback whale, and the shape of a typical blow.

feeding grounds. How and why they change the same portions of their songs despite the fact that they may be thousands of miles apart is not known. It is to be hoped that we will have a chance to find the answer before all of the living subjects have been flensed and canned. Humpbacks are a protected species, but their numbers have not re-bounded as the greys' did under similar protection. There may only be 10,000 to 15,000 animals scattered across the oceans of the world today.

Cetaceans are fascinating animals, and before leaving them I would like to devote some space to answering the ten most common questions that surface whenever any of the whale clan are being discussed.

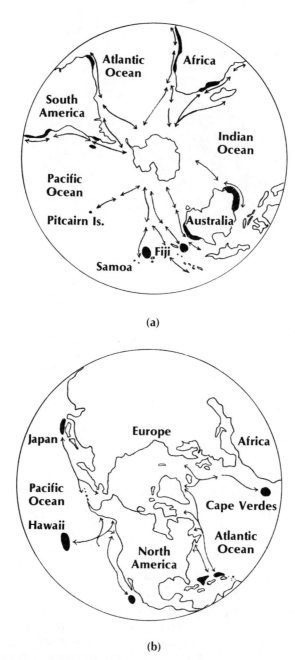

Figure 5–7. The humpback whale
(a) distribution and migrations of the humpback whale in the southern hemisphere. (b) distribution and migrations of the humpback whale in the northern hemisphere.

QUESTION 1: "WHY DO THEY LEAP?"

Cetaceans may jump, or breach, partially or entirely clear of the water for several reasons. Dolphins will leap repeatedly to free themselves from remoras, fishes that attach themselves to large marine animals in the hopes of guaranteeing a free ride and occasional table scraps. It has been suggested that larger whales may jump to crush barnacles or dislodge parasites that are bothering them. Humpbacks have been seen coming partway out of the water to land on another whale, in a pretty clear display of aggression. They also come partly out of the water while mating. Finally it can't be denied that some animals could be jumping just for the fun of it.

QUESTION 2: "HOW FAST CAN THEY SWIM?"

Cruising speed seems to be 4 to 6 mph for most cetaceans. The top speed for a baleen whale is around 30 mph for finbacks. Bottlenose dolphins can approach 25 mph, and although a few species may go a bit faster than this, the majority of cetaceans, large and small, peak out at slower speeds.

QUESTION 3: "HOW FAST DO THE NEWBORN WHALES GROW?"

The milk provided to the calf is rich in fats and thus calories. In seven months a young blue whale goes from 24 feet to 52.5 feet in length. This is impressive enough, but you should note that when the length doubles the volume must be at least cubed. Over this seven-month period the baby whale grows in length almost 2 inches per day, but its weight increases from about 2 tons at birth to *23 tons* at weaning.

QUESTION 4: "HOW LONG DO WHALES LIVE?"

Whales are long-lived, even for mammals. A blue whale may live ninety-five years, sperm whales seventy-five years, and the smaller porpoises and dolphins at least twenty-five years.

QUESTION 5: "WHAT IS THE DIFFERENCE BETWEEN PORPOISES AND DOLPHINS?"

For your purposes, there is very little difference, and you can call them whatever you like. Once upon a time the term *porpoise* was reserved for small odontocetes that had no breaks and spade-shaped (not conical) teeth. These were members of a very distinct, very small family. The term *dolphin* was used to describe most of the common odontocetes with beaks and conical teeth that were too small to be considered whales. I am not too certain about how the fuzziness in terminology began, but my personal favorite guess involves the inevitable public confusion over the difference between the dolphin/fish, an offshore gamefish that is quite tasty, and the dolphin/mammal. Restaurant managers as well as biologists dislike having to explain that the specialty of the day is not broiled fillet-of-Flipper, and the term *porpoise* became more widely used. Even in the scientific literature it has now become acceptable to call any small-toothed cetacean a porpoise or a dolphin, so you can't go wrong—as long as you don't call it a fish!

QUESTION 6: "HOW GOOD IS THEIR SONAR SYSTEM?"

Almost too good to be true. A bottlenose dolphin can tell the difference between a 2.125-inch and a 2.500-inch sphere while blindfolded, and it can also distinguish, without peeking, between one made of copper and another of aluminum.

QUESTION 7: "HOW DO WHALES AND SHARKS GET ALONG?"

It seems to depend on the time and place. Sharks and dolphins have been seen feeding on the same school of fish, and large sharks have been seen swimming through a pod of dolphins without either species paying much attention. Killer and sperm whales occasionally eat smaller sharks, and large sharks, such as the tiger or great white, may attack baleen whales. In aquaria groups of dolphins have been observed killing sharks by ramming them with their snouts, but it should be recognized that sharks in captivity are often "not themselves." Such incidents are rarely reported in the field and it is very difficult to train a dolphin to approach a shark on command, even under lab conditions. Certainly there is no natural animosity between the two groups, nor even mutual avoidance, and there have been shark attacks on humans while dolphins were in the water nearby.

QUESTION 8: "HOW INTELLIGENT ARE THE WHALES?"

This has turned out to be a very difficult question to approach, primarily because the world of the whale is so very different from our own. In my answer I will use the bottlenose dolphin as an example, because they are generally held to be among the brighter of cetaceans, and after years of television dramatizations they are often held to be at least as intelligent as many elected officials. (I will not attempt to address that question, however.)

Think for a moment about the dolphin's view of the world. Its single most important sensory system uses high-frequency sounds to identify objects. The sounds are produced over a range of frequencies that are accessible to us only through sophisticated electronic devices, and the animals are sensitive to subtle differences in shape and consistency that are virtually undetectable to the eye. Vision is a poor second sense for a dolphin, and a sense of smell is of no consequence. Yet the dolphin tends to react *to*, not change, its surroundings. Inanimate objects may be grasped or pushed, but not manipulated precisely; this is no great disadvantage, for the ocean world is not full of inanimate objects waiting to be put to good use. Most of its horizon consists of other dolphins, potential dolphin food, or dolphin enemies. Like other predators traveling in groups, learning and cooperation are essential if the pod is to obtain enough food. Social interactions and organization within the pod are also important to its success.

Thus the general life history of the bottlenose dolphin indicates a very sophisticated ability to process information gathered by the sonar system, a good memory and learning abilities, and intense social interactions. Do any of these characteristics require a blinding intellect? No. Bats have superb sonar, the visual tapestry of a bird is extremely rich and detailed, and bloodhounds can detect subtleties of smell that defy our imaginations. None of these animals is especially noted for its intelligence, and memory, learning, and social interactions are the general rule for higher vertebrates. There are no real indications that the social structure of a dolphin pod resembles a bridge club more than a dog pack.

But don't they have unusually large brains? Yes, but they have unusually large bodies to go with them. Brain size by itself means very little. Neanderthal man had a bigger brain than modern man, and the smallest modern human brain is only around one third the size of the largest, with no predictable difference in the intellectual abilities of the owners.

Don't they have a language? Current research indicates that they do not, although like many other mammals they do have social calls indicating distress, aggression, arousal, food, and so on, which are understood by other pod members. Attempts to give them a sound-sign language, with key sounds linked to objects or behaviors, are now underway. It has been slow to develop, and certainly the rumors that dolphins can be taught to speak and understand English (speeded up a lot) are purest fantasy. Basically on a scale ranging from "Go left 45° for a mullet dinner" to "Food," the natural dolphin language is closer to the latter.

Before I find my mailbox stuffed with hostile letters let me point out that dolphins, killer whales, and several other cetaceans are certainly more intelligent than the average dog in terms of their learning abilities. Yet there is no indication that they use, need, have, or even had any intellectual powers comparable to our own, or even those of the brighter apes.

QUESTION 9: "HOW DO YOU TRAIN A DOLPHIN?"

Different trainers use different techniques, but the basic pattern is similar. Once the animal has become familiar with its surroundings and accepted food from the trainer, real training will begin when the dolphin discovers that doing something will get it a reward—ultimately this means more food. Once this key hurdle has been passed, it is a matter of leading the animal through a series of small steps. For instance, you throw a ball into the tank. At first the result may be a very spooked dolphin, which might even go off its feeding schedule for a time while it becomes used to the new object. Once things have settled down, you watch and wait until one morning the animal accidentally bumps into the floating ball. You reward it at once. Later it will bump the ball on purpose, with the same result. Next you ignore any contact with the ball that knocks it further away and reward the animal only when the ball is pushed toward you, then only when struck twice, and so on. Pretty soon you have a "fetch-the-ball" routine. Suppose you then want to move to a "fetch-the-stick" act. Well, when you throw in the stick, you might wind up with a spooked animal again, but as the dolphin continues to work with you it settles down faster and learns what you want sooner. Then one day the dolphin may start doing unusual things like jumping or tail walking, and training then becomes a matter of selection and refinement. This kind of experimental behavior by the dolphin occurs when it is trying to discover a new action that will bring a reward, thereby indicating one way in which these animals show more intelligence than most dogs. But training has its confusing aspects as well. If you train your animal to a cue out of the water, where it relies on vision, and then put the cue in the water, where sonar can be used, the training may break down. If you train a dolphin in a small tank, and then move it to a large tank, your training may also break down. Teaching animals to work in the open ocean, which the Navy has done successfully, is a long-term expensive project, because the animal must be gradually acclimated to larger tanks, pens, pens with boats, and finally, outside with boats. The idea of parachuting commando dolphins into enemy harbors would not be practical, despite the ruckus raised by various papers late in the Vietnam era. Why then should the Navy be interested? Primarily because dolphins have been useful as diving companions who can carry equipment and/or messages to and from the surface, even at depths of 750 feet, and who can be trained to locate or retrieve objects or perform other useful tasks while submerged.

QUESTION 10: "ARE ALL CETACEANS LOVABLE AND FRIENDLY?"

No, not at all, and some are downright ornery. I have been knocked head over heels by a set of flukes for not rewarding a particular behavior, and one famous dolphin, Tuffy, was first called Tuff-Guy because it was rather hard on its trainers. Sperm whales have been credited with the sinking of several small whaling vessels, and at least one large ship, the *Essex*, which inspired Melville to write *Moby Dick*. Killer whales have been responsible for the loss of several yachts, and as the number of yachts increases we will probably hear of other incidents. Among the baleen whales, most of the reported incidents have been cases of accidental collision, presumably while the whales were feeding or sleeping at the surface. The sole exception seems to be incidents involving female whales with calves, when the whales may be reacting to a large, potentially threatening intruder. For those of you traveling by yacht, I would remind you that it is both unwise and illegal to approach or harass a whale. If your vessel is the object of attention for an odontocete, changing the color of your bottom paint would be less helpful than turning on your depth sounder, which broadcasts on a frequency they can hear. Starting your engine or triggering an air horn or siren may also be effective. Under no circumstances should you set off fireworks on top of the animals, or worse yet, shoot at them. For one thing they might get hurt, and for another, they might not take kindly to it. When cruising around baleen whales, you are the one with the best view of the situation, and it will probably be up to you to take evasive action.

Now let's look back over the marine mammals. The most highly specialized are those that do not need to come ashore to breed or bask. The ancestors of marine mammals were already livebearing endotherms, so the primary limiting factor was the efficient insulation required for avoiding hypothermia. In general the sequence of "hair—hair with underfur/hair with blubber beneath—sparse or no hair and thick blubber" seems to be in order of increasing efficiency. Only in sirenians and cetaceans, which have the latter form of insulation, do we find animals able to remain in the water throughout their lives. With gravitational limitations on size and body form eliminated, there has been a tendency for these animals to reach large size, whether they are predators or grazers.

Arching of the back, rather than side-to-side movement was characteristic of the ancestral mammals, and is most typical of modern forms. Because of the effect on streamlining, possessing a rigid body with caudal propulsion is most efficient, and the development of expanded, horizontal flukes occurred independently in both cetaceans and sirenians. The importance of maneuverability on land *and* water has encouraged very flexible vertebrae in the pinnipeds, and in the seals a form of side-to-side flexing is seen, with the exposed foot/tail combination acting like a caudal fin. The sea lions, like the marine turtles, use their flipperlike forelimbs, but they are still masters at supple bending and turning.

Diving times in marine mammals are increased by slowing the heart, increasing the oxygen storage capacity of the blood and tissues, and often by altering the circulatory pattern as well. Auxiliary techniques for obtaining oxygen from the water have not developed, for any region of the skin thin enough to permit substantial gas exchange would dump enormous amounts of body heat into the chilly environment. In those animals hunting in deep or murky waters, vision is sometimes complemented by echolocation systems.

On the whole, there is more social interaction, more variability in behavior, and more of an intensity to the lives of the marine mammals than we saw in the marine reptiles. What can be said about the future of these marine vertebrates? Among the marine reptiles, only the sea snakes are holding their own. A few species of sea lions are hanging on, but the fur seals and true seals are in trouble. The tropical monk seals are on the very edge of extinction in the Pacific, and are probably already over the edge in the Atlantic and Meditteranean tropics. The dugong is becoming increasingly rare throughout its range, but it is doing better than the manatee. *Both* are doing better than the third member of the sirenian group, a polar giant that was hunted to extinction within twenty-five years of its discovery. All the large, commercially valuable species of baleen whales are endangered, and the sperm whale has become increasingly pressured as the stocks of baleen whales have declined. The killer whale will survive for the moment, as will most of the smaller porpoises and dolphins, at least until the economic needs of the whaling fleets make processing such diminutive creatures profitable. That day might not be far off, as already the whalers are harvesting the smallest of the baleen whales, the Minke, which matures at under 25 feet. Perhaps the proposed ban on all whaling will end the hunting, yet even without the whaling fleets we will eventually be faced with some difficult decisions. Today there are fishermen in California, Hawaii, Florida, Israel, Russia, Japan, and elsewhere who are at war with dolphins or sea lions over commercially valuable fishes or squids. Problems of this kind are bound to continue and spread as we increase our dependence on the sea as a protein source. We are rapidly building ourselves an overpopulated, protein poor planet, and allocating a portion of what is clearly a limited resource to other carnivores is bound to become increasingly unpopular. To avoid such confrontations we will need to broaden our search to include less familiar but more efficient protein sources. What these sources are, and how we can improve our efficiency at obtaining food energy from the sea, will become apparent as we examine the dynamics of energy exchange in our discussion of the reef environment in Chapter 6.

Chapter Six
The Reef Environment

All living things operate on a fixed budget, with energy gained and spent. Each species represents a particular approach to achieving a workable balance among the essential energy accounts. Yet within a relatively isolated area, like a coral reef, the various species of plants and animals do not exist as separate populations, but as integrated components of a living community. Competition within a community is fierce because the number of possible energy sources is limited. In an earlier chapter we looked at the families of bony fishes and discussed how competition leads to differing strategies for survival. In the same way that competition and natural selection has been occurring within the class of bony fishes, it has occurred among the classes of vertebrates and between the vertebrates and the invertebrates of the reef. In essence, all animals on the reef are competing for a share of the profits generated by plant activity, for only plants can be considered producers rather than consumers. The producers rely on solar energy for their survival.

The sun doesn't just pour energy into space like a running faucet, but in tiny individual packets. All packets aren't created equal; some contain a lot of energy, others are comparatively weak. Solar energy packets are released with varied energy contents, but only a restricted range manages to reach the surface of the earth. Very high energy packets are potentially damaging to living things, but fortunately most of these are absorbed by ozone layers in the upper atmosphere. Very low energy packets are so weak that they are likely to be absorbed by water vapor in the lower levels of the atmosphere. Most of what perseveres to reach the surface of the planet can be detected by your eyes, and we simply call it light. The spectrum of visible solar energy ranges from deep violet, which carries the most energy, to deep red, which carries the least. When a particular energy packet strikes an object it might be deflected or it might transfer its energy to that object, and the outcome depends on what is struck and how much energy the packet contains.

White light contains a mixture of all the different energy packets of the visible spectrum. When white light strikes an object, some of the energy packets may be absorbed, whereas others may be reflected away. If all the energy is reflected, we see the object as white; if all the energy is absorbed, the object appears black. If *most* of the energy is absorbed, but a particular set of energy packets are reflected, then we see color in the object. For example, suppose white light strikes an object that absorbs all energy packets except those in the blue portion of the spectrum. The reflected packets enter our eyes, where they strike pigments contained within special cells of the retinae. Many of these pigments will *only* absorb blue light, and when blue light reaches them the energy is trapped and used to pass along information (blue light arriving at location X) to nearby nerve cells and thence to the brain. In this way our eyes rely on special pigments to trap specific packets of light energy, and the energy is used to begin a complex series of events.

Plants also rely on special pigments to trap solar energy. The typical pigment is chlorophyll, which is found in terrestrial and marine plants alike. Chlorophyll looks green to us because it traps some of the higher energy packets of the visual spectrum, and either reflects or transmits (that is, lets pass through) the rest in a mixture we perceive as green. When the right energy packet strikes a chlorophyll molecule it is absorbed, and the energy obtained is then passed along to other molecules under controlled conditions. Through this process of photosynthesis the plant can use the energy to manufacture sugars, absorbing carbon dioxide and nutrients from its surroundings and releasing oxygen. The sugars can then be used by the plant to build cell walls, or they might be converted to other organic materials or broken down to provide energy at some later date.

Because of the physical properties of water, a single photosynthetic pigment will not work well at all depths. As soon as light enters sea water it begins to travel among water molecules that are far closer together than those of the relatively transparent atmosphere. If an energy packet strikes a water molecule, it may stop right there, transferring energy that heats the water. This is particularly likely if the light is low in energy, near the red end of the visible spectrum. More energetic light packets, such as green and especially blue, are more often reflected or scattered. The highest energy components of the visible spectrum are also likely to be absorbed, not by water molecules alone, but also by larger organic molecules that are dissolved in the sea water. What does all this mean for the plants in the ocean?

For one thing it means that the deeper you go, the more likely it is that the light on its way to you will have been absorbed or scattered before it reaches you. Thus it gets darker as you descend. Light does not penetrate farther than 1,000 yards even in the most crystalline offshore waters, and you would need some sophisticated equipment to detect it at such depths. Light penetration is considerably reduced when there are suspended particles or debris or when the water surface is disturbed by waves, surf, or other turbulence. The visible colors also will change with depth. A particular color is seen because light of a certain portion of the spectrum is reaching our eyes. By the time you descend 10 feet below the surface you will notice that the red colors around you, perhaps on a bathing suit or a snorkel tip, are becoming muted, and before you reach 50 feet they will no longer seem red to you at all. The low-energy portion of the visible spectrum has been absorbed through collisions with water molecules at lesser depths. Other colors fade in a predictable sequence, and orange and yellow are gradually lost as you leave the surface waters. Meanwhile, at the other end of the spectrum, the higher energy light packets, the deep indigo and violet shades, begin to disappear as they encounter organic substances dissolved in the water. At 70 feet you are swimming in a world of blues and greens, and before a depth of 100 feet is reached, only varied shades of blue and black may be seen.

Once you have become familiar with these color shifts you can begin to use visible colors to estimate depth with surprising accuracy, a trick that can be useful even at the surface, as I mentioned in the discussion of atolls and lagoons in Chapter 2.

With these alterations in intensity and color, you can see why green chlorophyll will only be useful for plants at or near the surface of the ocean. Very few terrestrial plants have been able to reinvade the ocean, because the colonization of the land required a number of specializations. The mangroves and the eel grasses are two important exceptions. Mangroves dominate coastal regions of the tropics that are reminiscent of the salt marshes or swamps of more temperate shores: shallow waters overlying sediments rich in organic matter. The mangrove community grows as the plants extend a network of prop roots that trap additional sediments, and in effect the mangroves are extending the shoreline. The prop roots are coated with small marine animals such as oysters or barnacles, and the entire region serves as a nursery ground for many other animals that spend their adult lives out on the coral reefs. Mangroves are found throughout the tropical Atlantic and Pacific islands; the swamps are especially extensive in the western Pacific and Caribbean. In the Pacific the mangrove communities may be found in delta-headed embayments or along a coast sheltered by a barrier reef. In the Caribbean, where atolls and barrier reefs are in short supply, mangroves are often seen along the leeward shores, which are less precipitous than their windward counterparts. Seaward of the mangroves, over more sandy bottoms, there may be extensive beds of eel grasses, which look like large blades of grass growing from a vinelike runner. These provide food for a variety of marine animals, notably the marine turtles and sea cows.

The most important marine plants evolved and remained in the ocean. For those relying on green chlorophyll, the problem is how to remain in the surface waters, for the portions of the spectrum that this pigment absorbs fail to reach the depths. The phytoplankton are aided by their small size. To something only 10 to 20/25,000 inch in diameter, water seems very dense indeed, and even a solid object this size would sink very slowly. Many members of the *phytoplankton* (*phyto*, "plant") have wings, spines, and projections that help them resist sinking, and in addition, many store surplus energy as oil droplets, and of course oils float quite nicely.

In shallow coastal waters, where suitable attachment sites are available, large multicellular green algae may be found. These seaweeds are usually delicate or filamentous, and any wave or surge action is enough to keep the segments separate and exposed to sunlight. Some species secrete gas into special chambers to further protect them from being plastered in clumps along the bottom in calm waters. Others may be supported by small calcium carbonate plates, which may eventually contribute to the local sediments and the growth of the reef. But if they are to survive at greater depths, plants must cope with the reduction in intensity and the changes in color composition in the available light. Two different evolutionary strategies may be seen on the reefs today. In each group the absorbing qualities of chlorophyll have been altered, and some additional pigments added. The brown algae have extended their absorption range to include green light, whereas the red algae have a broad absorption range that extends from yellow through blue. As you might surmise, the red algae are more common in deeper waters. When you find them, it will be difficult to tell that they are red because they are absorbing almost all the light energy reaching them. They will therefore look black and will only take on their true ruddy colors as they are brought closer to the surface, to depths where red light penetrates.

Over intermediate depths the two groups of algae intermingle and presumably compete for space, although throughout the tropics the reds far outnumber the browns. Probably the most important of the red algae, for our purposes, are the coralline algae that may be found at any depth. These may take the form of small clumps with brittle tufts, thin and brittle sheets, or dense cementing crusts. The latter are particularly important in the preservation and growth of the reef (see Chapter 2). Because these algae are tough, low, and encrusting they are able to grow in areas subjected to heavy pounding by the surf, such as the algal ridge of the reef flat, areas that are generally unavailable to other algae or even corals.

The third major collection of marine plants found on the reef is actually found *within* the reef. The single-celled algae living within the gastrodermal cells of the coral polyps were mentioned earlier. There are also other species of algae that burrow into exposed portions of the coral skeletons.

In summary, sunlight, as it arrives at the reef, is captured by plants that use any one of three strategies. They either float within the plankton, attach themselves to the bottom, or are contained within the mass of the reef itself. Regardless of their location, all these plants require certain portions of the visible spectrum, carbon dioxide, and nutrients to proceed with photosynthesis, and photosynthesis produces new organic materials and releases oxygen into the surrounding waters. This all sounds very efficient, but actually most of the solar energy trapped by a plant is lost as heat or used by the plant during the following night. The 17 percent that survives as new material is all that remains to support all the animal members of the reef community. Just how this energy is distributed is an interesting question, but before we can discuss it, we had better take a look at who these dependent consumers might be. You may recall from the Introduction that there are over one million species of animals, out of which fewer than 50,000 are assigned to the phylum that includes the vertebrates. The invertebrate multitudes can be collected into about thirty phyla, but there are only six that we will consider. Most of the rest are either absent from the reef or are unlikely to come to the attention of the casual snorkeler or diver. Nevertheless they are a diverse lot, and quite numerous.

The sponges, members of the phylum *Porifera* (*porus*, "pore") are among the most primitive of all animals. We know that they were common in the ocean 600 million years ago, and the group was probably venerable even then. There are roughly 5,000 species, most of which are found at great depths, and all of which require a firm surface to support them.

Sponges are simple creatures. They consist of outer and inner cell layers separated by an amorphous noncellular middle zone. The epidermis is fairly tough, and the cells can contract slightly to change the shape of the sponge or close the pores that lead to the chamber(s) within. The middle layer contains cells that produce the supporting

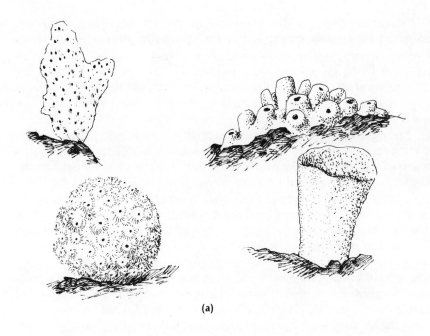

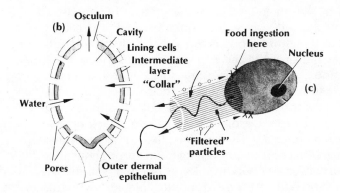

Figure 6–1. Sponges
(a) various shapes of tropical sponges. (b) section through a typical sponge, showing the basic structure (arrows indicate the flow of water through the animal). (c) a single lining cell of the inner chamber; a cilium pushes water past while the collar strains organic particles from the passing stream (from Russell-Hunter, 1969).

and stiffening network that gives the sponge its shape and keeps the pores and channels open. A commercial bath sponge of the non-synthetic variety will give you some idea of what this network looks like after the living cells have been removed. Water moves through the channels and into or out of the sponge, driven by long cilia on the cells of the inner layer. Around the cilia these cells have a series of extensions that trap and absorb any organic particles that strike them.

Sponges are most often seen growing in low, encrusting masses that have obvious pores, a spongy texture, and occasionally bright colors. Over the shallow portions of the reef they will sometimes be found in dark caves and corners where coral or algal growth is inhibited. There are other species that provide secure homes for themselves by boring into the skeletons of coral colonies. This does nothing very good for the corals concerned, and they may eventually weaken and destroy the affected colony. Sponges with more massive forms become more common with increasing depth, and once past the point where light is sufficient for coral growth sponges may cover a significant percentage of the submarine slopes. Some of the deep-water species are luminescent, producing an eerie blue/violet glow. The benefits of this are uncertain, but perhaps the light attracts zooplankton that have drifted to these depths.

We have already discussed the corals and sea anemones that are members of the phylum *Coelenterata*. This phylum also includes the hydrozoans and jellyfishes, and contains roughly 11,000 species. A key character of the entire group is the radial body plan, that is, they seem to have no left or right and can only be described in terms of oral/non-oral ends, and inner or outer surfaces. Most members are carnivorous, and rely on stinging nematocysts to capture their prey.

The typical hydrozoan looks like a colony of tiny coral polyps that lack a stony skeleton. Despite their small size, their life histories make them worth mentioning. Hydrozoans, like corals, are carnivorous, and most remain attached to something solid throughout their lives. Colony growth occurs by budding. Reproduction also involves budding, but the polyps bud to produce mobile, planktonic *medusae* that resemble miniature jellyfish. Medusae reproduce sexually, and their larvae settle to the bottom, attach, and develop into mature colonial hydrozoans. The true jellyfishes show no indications of an attached polyp stage during their adult lives, yet during one stage of their larval development they closely resemble a polyp. Meanwhile, the corals and sea anemones appear to have taken the other tack, and reduced the medusa portion of the life cycle, remaining attached throughout their lives. These interesting variations have taken time to evolve, and we

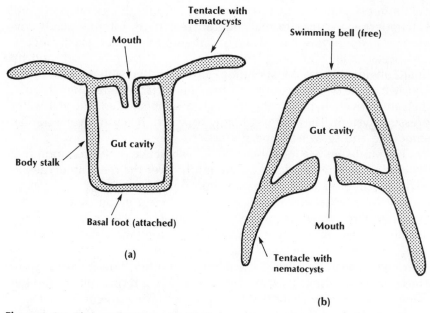

Figure 6–2. The coelenterate body plan
(a) polyp (sea anemone, coral, hydrozoan, etc.). (b) medusa (jellyfishes; see text for additional details).

may never figure out which came first (if either), polyp or medusa. Perhaps the medusa stage evolved as a method of dispersing the progeny of the sessile polyp forms, or perhaps the polyp stage appeared as a larval stage of the jellyfish took advantage of a particularly advantageous food supply or habitat. In any event, fossilized impressions of coelenterates have been found in rocks as old as 450 million years, but modern reef-building corals did not evolve until more than 200 million years later.

At first glance the members of the phylum *Echinodermata* (*echino*, "spiny"; *derma*, "skin") also appear to be built around a radial plan. This similarity is merely superficial, for a close look will reveal that they are actually built around a five-part plan. It is difficult to divide five into two equal parts without using a knife, and although it is difficult for us to distinguish from the outside it seems that one of these segments takes the lead when feeding, exploring, or escaping over the reef. This means that there must actually be right and left sides, although in practice it is still easiest to restrict distinctions to oral (where the mouth is) and aboral (where it isn't) surfaces. This phylum contains about 6,000 species, and includes the starfishes, sea urchins, brittle stars, sea cucumbers, and crinoids that reside among the coral reefs. All echinoderms are alike in that they possess hard, internal plates covered by an epidermis that may be ornamented by spines, small pincers, and occasionally, poison glands. There is no obvious head, and no brain, obvious or not. Most of these animals move with the aid of tube feet, which lie within grooves on the oral surface of the animal. Tube feet are moved hydraulically through a sophisticated internal water pressure system. They are fascinating to watch. Just turn over a starfish sometime and see what I mean.

The starfishes are the most colorful and active of the common reef echinoderms. They are found at all depths over the reef and occasionally are scattered over the sandy portions of the inner reef flat or lagoon floor. Most starfish are predators that prey on other invertebrates. A starfish feeds by extruding its stomach and wrapping it around its intended victim, so digestion and absorption take place outside the body proper. Many of the smaller species on the reef specialize in opening shellfish like clams or scallops, but other food will do as well. The large pin-cushion starfish, which looks like a throw-pillow, and the spiny crown-of-thorns starfish both prefer to dine on coral polyps.

In the tropical Pacific, young crown-of-thorns may be found most often along the surf zone inside the algal ridge or on the inner margins of the reef flat. Larger individuals are more common in and around the coral colonies farther down the seaward slopes of the reef. Under normal conditions they feed at night and show a preference for particular species of corals. If you are looking to find one, you must search for bare patches of coral, white areas indicating a region where portions of the skeleton have been exposed. If you look under rocks and peer into caves in the area you will probably find the starfish responsible. (If you do not succeed, you can stay dry and look at Plate 7.) For as yet undetermined causes, during the last twenty-five years large numbers of crown-of-thorns starfish, sometimes in the millions, have suddenly appeared and swept across Pacific reefs. At such times the starfish feed around the clock, and consume many if not most of the coral polyps in the area. Although many Pacific reefs have been affected, no obvious pattern has presented itself. As living corals become increasingly rare, these starfish show their opportunistic nature by feeding on anemones, soft corals, and one another if they are stacked deeply enough. When the group has moved on, the dead and algal-coated skeletons of the corals are broken down by the surf or the action of boring organisms, and the beauty and variety of the reef is largely destroyed. All is not lost, however, for it is only the living veneer of the reef that has been affected, and recovery will be slow but certain as new polyp settlement occurs. After five to ten years the reefs will be back in good shape, although replacing some of the larger, more venerable coral colonies takes more time. Although attempts to control these herds have been made, no satisfactory solution has been found, and no one yet knows why they appear in the first place. Only time will tell if this is a natural event that was overlooked in the past, or whether it is linked to some environmental changes produced by human activities. Curiously enough, another group of echinoderms has been causing similar problems by decimating the kelp beds off California and New England in recent years. Although they have not been noted for causing similar problems in the tropics, you will most assuredly see plenty of sea urchins as you roam across the reefs of the Atlantic or Pacific oceans.

During the day, many sea urchins will be found nestled securely within pockets or caves in the reef, with only their prominent spines visible. Urchins are herbivores and have complex scraping elements that protrude from their mouths as they move over the bottom. They graze slowly, removing the algal covering, and feed at night when potential predators like the thick-skinned triggerfish are sleeping. Sea urchins display a variety of different sizes, shapes, spines, and colors. Most of them should be avoided, or at least approached with caution, because the spines may be sharp, brittle, and sometimes associated with poison glands. Many people do enjoy eating some species of urchins, cracking them like eggs and eating the insides with a spoon. It is an acquired taste, but if you like caviar you will probably like urchin roe as well.

Brittle stars lie under chunks of coral or loose rubble on the bottom, either over the outer reef slope or in the littered sections of the inner reef flat. Their slender form makes it possible for brittle stars to hide easily and move around below the surface. If seized, the brittle limbs break easily, and because the broken appendage continues to wriggle a predator is likely to be momentarily distracted. The regenerative powers of all the echinoderms are quite good, and a new arm appears quickly. The brittle stars feed on bits of organic matter scattered over bottom, and these are passed to the mouth with the aid of slender, specialized tube feet.

The sea cucumbers are perhaps the least attractive members of the phylum. They are found in a variety of colors, and some grow to the size of a football. They are most easily seen over sandy patches inside a lagoon or over the reef flat, but there are species that inhabit the outer slopes as well. Sea cucumbers feed on organic matter using elaborate feathery tube feet that surround the mouth. These sticky extensions stroke the bottom, picking up bits of edible debris that are then removed with a wiping motion against the inner margins of the mouth.

There are nocturnal and diurnal species, and the nocturnal forms can be found hiding under the rubble with the brittle stars by day. They are seldom disturbed by predators, as the flesh and organs of several species may be quite toxic. In Samoa the natives use sea cucumbers to catch fish trapped in tidal pools or pockets at low tide. Women of the villages wander over the reef flat carrying small sea cucumbers, and when a likely tidal pool is found the animal is squeezed like a tube of toothpaste. This causes it to eject its internal organs into the pool, poisoning the fishes hiding within. As the stunned fish are scooped into a basket, ready for the fire, the expended sea cucumber is discarded, whereupon it presumably begins regenerating a new batch of organs. Only the fishes are the losers in the long run. In other portions of the Pacific, different species are eaten as *bêches-de-mer*—no doubt another acquired taste.

The crinoids are a beautiful and intriguing group, probably similar in form to the ancestral echinoderms. Many of them begin life as a stalked, sessile creature but later detach from the stalk and become mobile. The delicate featherstars can be seen over the reef at night, with their long feathery limbs extended and trapping small animals in the plankton. During the day you may chance upon them as you turn over loose debris in search of adventure. Figure 6–3 shows some of the unifying characteristics of the echinoderms in a diagrammatic form.

The worm phylum *Annelida* (*annelus*, "ring") consists of about 8,800 species. None of the worms has a skeleton, and all are segmented into a chain of segments that are very similar to one another. The earthworm is a terrestrial annelid that is probably familiar to you, and the marine forms are simply more varied and colorful. Some have bristly "feet" on each segment that can be used for moving across the bottom, or even swimming in some species. The larger worms are usually found under rubble on the reef floor, in the crevices between corals, or deep within the body of a branching coral colony. Few of the free-living worms are out and about during the day, probably because they are considered delicacies by most fishes. Some of these worms are carnivorous, feeding on smaller invertebrates that they seize and puncture with an extensible set of mouthparts. More sedentary worms live in tubes that they either assemble or secrete. The featherduster worms secrete a hard shell, and they are usually seen attached to massive coral colonies. The colonies gradually grow around them, hiding the worms from potential predators. The featherduster worms get their name from an impressive, often colorful set of filaments that they extend from the ends of their hideouts. These bristles are covered with

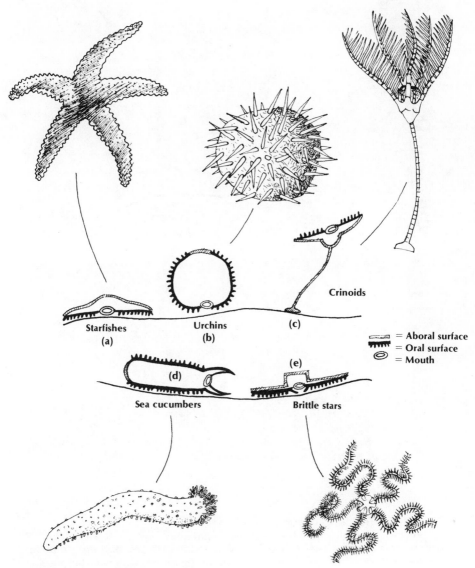

Crinoids

Starfishes
(a)

Urchins
(b)

(c)

(d)

Sea cucumbers

(e)

Brittle stars

= Aboral surface
= Oral surface
= Mouth

Figure 6–3. The echinoderms
All echinoderms share a number of features, although their external
appearances may differ widely.

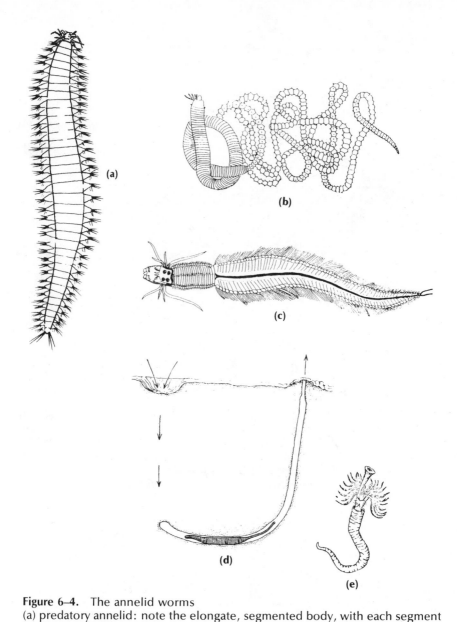

Figure 6–4. The annelid worms
(a) predatory annelid: note the elongate, segmented body, with each segment bearing small "feet." These animals may be found over soft bottom and under debris on the reef or reef flat. They should be handled with care because of the irritating character of the bristles, which can penetrate the skin and produce an unpleasant rash. (b) and (c): two reproductive buds in formation; in (b), the Samoan palolo worm, the reproductive robot is long and slender, whereas in (c), a different species of palolo worm, the sexual cargo carrier is more robust and bears special swimming paddles. (d) a burrowing lugworm that filters incoming water through the sand and then swallows the sand to extract the nutrients; note the raised area surrounding the exit, where the processed sand is excreted. (e) a tube-dwelling worm with specialized bristles around the mouth, which represent specialized gills.

cilia and mucus, and any plankton or organic matter that is carried through them by local currents will be trapped in the mucus and passed to the mouth by the beating cilia. Featherduster worms are very wary of strangers, and a movement nearby will cause them to whip their dusters back inside the security of their shells. They are not always quick enough, but any missing portions are rapidly regenerated. A particularly cooperative featherduster worm is shown in Plate 8.

Other worms live in burrows in sandy areas. The walls of their tunnels are composed of sand grains held together by a cementlike secretion of the worm. Some use sand grains to filter organic particles and plankton from the water, later swallowing the sand. A more ingenious method involves the secretion of a mucus bag that extends in front of the animal, blocking the tunnel. Water enters the burrow and passes through the mucus on its way to the exit, and any particles are trapped in the mucus net. Periodically the worm rolls up the mucus bag, swallows it whole, and makes another net. Some of these burrowing worms produce prominent burrows, and mounds of sand several inches high mark the entrances or exits.

These are the annelids most commonly observed on or near the reef, but there are many more tropical species. However, most prefer muddy, silty environments, and unless you are especially fond of worms, insects, muck, and a rather startling aroma, I doubt that you will have occasion to seek them out. Several of the larger reef-dwelling annelids are considered delicacies by inhabitants of the tropical Pacific and Caribbean. Some of the predatory worms reproduce by budding off smaller, wormlike miniatures that have specialized swimming feet. These are sexual robots, which have only the most rudimentary nervous systems and no digestive systems at all. What they do have are plenty of reproductive organs. At a certain phase of the moon each year they are released from the body of the adult worms, whereupon they swarm to the surface, form enormous concentrations, and break apart releasing the eggs and sperm into the plankton where fertilization occurs. Different islands experience this remarkable show at different times, but November to February is the most likely season. Whenever it occurs the swimming stages are highly prized by the natives, who draw them to boats with bright lights and net them by the pound. The slender objects of their affection taste a bit like old clams, and rumor has it that their aphrodesiacal effects are strongest when they are eaten raw. Needless to say they are only cooked when it is absolutely necessary.

The shellfish are members of a large phylum that contains over 100,000 species. The phylum *Mollusca* (*molluscus*, "soft-bodied") includes many species that long ago reduced or eliminated their shells, but the term *shellfish* is still popular for the group. Primitive molluscs were equipped with simple, flattened shells, rather like that of a limpet. Later forms elaborated on this theme to produce larger, roomier shells with a spiral twist, and still others evolved paired, hinged shells or eliminated the shell entirely. These evolutionary pathways and diversions can be reduced to three categories; examples of each will be found around the reef.

The *gastropods*, or snails, include all those molluscs that have a distinct head, a muscular foot used for locomotion, and a specialized tooth-bearing structure called a *radula*. If a shell is present, it is single and not paired. Gastropod shells are extraordinarily beautiful and varied. They are formed by specialized cells of the mantle, using calcium carbonate extracted from sea water and various proteins manufactured by the snail. Shells may twist to the right or to the left, depending on the species or even the individual snail.

A radula is rather like a tongue that bears numerous small teeth whose shapes vary with the habits of the animal. Limpets feed on algae growing on hard surfaces exposed to heavy wave action, and they have flattened scraping teeth on the radulae. The flattened, conical shape of the shell allows the limpet to inhabit areas subjected to strong surf and surge, and each individual has its own particular territory. In many areas limpets are eaten raw, but collecting them can be a tricky operation. Because of the exposed coastlines favored by the limpets, sets of large waves may come in and carry away the unwary epicure, and limpet-collecting accidents have made them the most dangerous marine animal in Hawaii.

Cone shells are predatory, feeding on other shellfish or fishes, and their radulae bear sharp cutting teeth and sometimes carry a potent venom. These gastropods are highly valued by collectors, and cone shells can be found by day under the bottom rubble or hidden inside of branching coral colonies. Some of the toxins produced by the cone shells can have disastrous effects on humans, so you should approach them with caution. (Refer to the Appendix for more details.)

The spectacular Triton's trumpet is particularly voracious, feeding on other invertebrates including the rather unappetizing crown-of-thorns starfish. Like most other gastropods, the trumpets are hidden in cavities in the reef during daylight hours. Because the shells are rather valuable, Triton's trumpets are disappearing in many portions of the Pacific, and it has been suggested that this may have played a role in the increased populations of crown-of-thorns starfish. A closely related species inhabits Caribbean reefs; the Caribbean also hosts the beautiful, edible queen conch, a large herbivorous gastropod found over

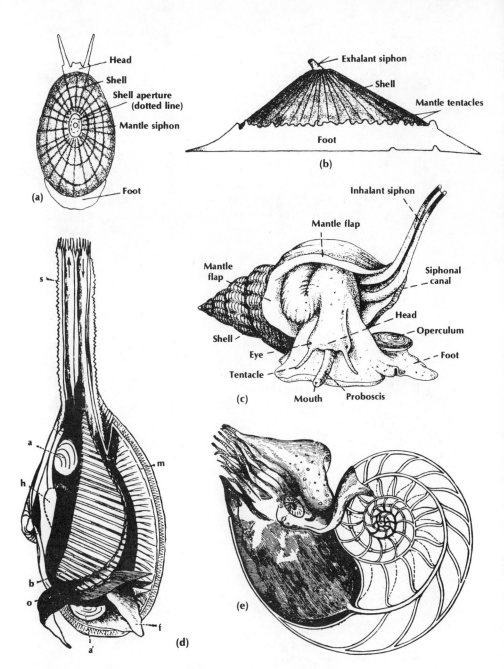

Figure 6–5. The diverse molluscs of tropical waters

(a) and (b): top and side views of a limpet, a simple gastropod with an uncoiled shell that probably illustrates a form characteristic of ancestral molluscs.

(c) a gastropod with a coiled shell. (d) a bivalve mollusc viewed with the shell of the left side removed (a: closing muscle; b: gills; h: heart; o: mouth; f: foot; m: edge of mantle lining the remaining shell; s: incurrent and excurrent siphons). (e) chambered nautilus viewed with half the shell cut away to reveal the inner, gas-filled chambers.

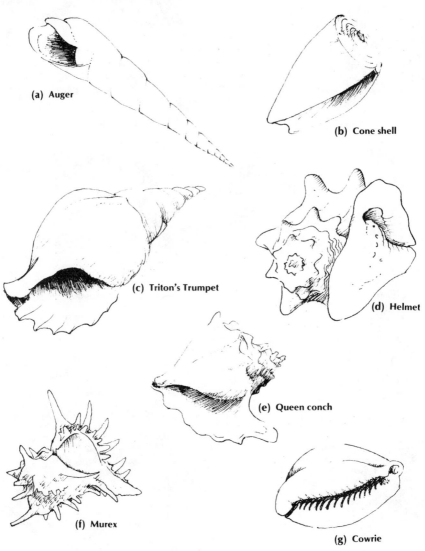

(a) Auger

(b) Cone shell

(c) Triton's Trumpet

(d) Helmet

(e) Queen conch

(f) Murex

(g) Cowrie

Figure 6–6. Tropical gastropods

sandy bottoms. In both oceans augers, predatory moonsnails, and mitres spend their days beneath the sand in shallow waters; the helmets and larger murexes are most often found in deeper waters of 100 feet or more. You will have to spend time poking around in sand and rubble if you want to accumulate a reasonable collection of gastropods.

The bivalve molluscs have paired and hinged shells. Bivalves lack heads and radulae and feed by drawing water through the mantle chamber and over a complex system of cilia-covered gills. These cilia are once again involved with moving a stream of mucus toward a mouth. Some sorting is done along the way and undesirable items are ejected. In most cases there are intake and outflow siphons that lessen the chances for repeated processing of the same water. Although they lack heads, the edges of the mantle are often provided with an elaborate network of eyes, and the shells are quick to close when the resident feels threatened.

Large numbers of young giant clams can be found on some islands by looking on the inner margins of the reef flat. The shallower portions of calm atoll lagoons, such as those of Ahe or Raraka in the Tuamotus, may be carpeted with them. More mature specimens may be scattered over the reef if local hunting pressure is light, but in most places the older animals are only found in deeper, less accessible portions of the reef.

Some bivalves excavate chambers in solid objects, where they can filter in complete privacy. Several species choose to burrow into the skeletons of coral colonies, and the notorious shipworm uses its modified shells to rasp a tunnel into unprotected wood. Most of the rest of the bivalve population remains on sandy ground, where the burrowing is much easier.

Both gastropods and bivalves rely on hydraulic pressure transmitted through their body fluids to move themselves around. As a result they are rather slow moving. The *cephalopods*, on the other hand, are large active animals, the most sophisticated of all invertebrates. All cephalopods have horny beaks that are used in conjunction with prominent radulae. Some species have poisonous salivary glands as well, and even the smallest should be handled carefully. Cephalopods have eight to ten tentacles arranged around the beak, and each tentacle is equipped with rows of sucker discs. These can be used to seize, hold, and otherwise manipulate objects, a faculty lacking in many of the "advanced" vertebrates. Their brains, speed, and eyesight are also unsurpassed among invertebrates.

Cephalopods rely on jet propulsion for rapid movement, with a powerful stream of water ejected from the mantle cavity. Combining less powerful streams of water with a variety of fin movements gives them the ability to make slow progress, either forward or backward, or to hover. Unlike other members of this phylum they have no planktonic larval stages, and the young are usually retained by the female or tended in a nest until the miniature adults have hatched into the world.

The chambered nautilus is the only member of the group that still retains the shell of the ancestral cephalopods. The beautiful coiled structure contains a regulated volume of gas that is secreted by the nautilus and makes the animal neutrally buoyant. Locomotion is accomplished as in other cephalopods, with a jet of water ejected through a movable siphon. These interesting creatures are found in the western Pacific and Indian Oceans. A simpler, less elegant relative, whose shells are more delicate and who lack buoyancy chambers, is found in the tropical Atlantic.

The small cuttlefish that are sometimes seen over coral reefs during the day have lost vestiges of the shell, but they secrete gas into a rugged, membranous cuttlebone, which thus serves a similar purpose to the gas chambers of the nautilus or the swim bladders of bony fishes. The related squids use a different approach, relying, much as the sharks do, on the lightweight oils contained in their oversized livers to reduce their underwater weight.

Squids come in all sizes and colors. Smaller squid are common visitors to the reef, but you will have to look around constantly, for their camouflage is very effective. Squids have pigment cells in the epidermis that are under direct nervous control, and they can change colors in the blink of an eye. Offshore they may be found in immense schools, and because they are quite tasty these species are the basis for a substantial commercial fishery. Plate 9 gives you a look at one of the more impressive species. Larger squids are more secretive, and much of the information we have about them has come from the bellies of slaughtered sperm whales and the post-mortem examination of an occasional beached carcass. Several have been reported in recent years by fishermen working over the deeper reefs of the Hawaiian islands. One was brought to the surface that was estimated to weigh almost 400 pounds, and the head of a second, estimated to have been 20 feet in total length, weighed 75 pounds. Unfortunately for biologists, but probably fortunately for the fishermen, these were dead animals, and between the sharks and the killer whales the remains reached shore in less-than-mint condition. How large a really big squid might grow is an open question. Specimens of 60 feet have been taken, but pieces of animals that could have been over 150 feet long have been examined. The latter would make giant squids the largest animals on the planet, although the blue whales would still retain title as the heaviest. Squids are fierce carnivores, and one can only speculate about the appetite of a 150-foot specimen. Let's just say that I hope never to have an opportunity to see one while I'm diving!

Octopus get quite large, up to 30 feet anyway, but animals of that size are very rare. The average individual on the reef will be about a yard across the tentacles, and you will probably see it hiding within small caves or pockets in the reef face. Smaller specimens may be found inside the reef flat among loose blocks of coral, or within discarded cinder blocks or other debris. Their favorite prey are crabs, which they bite with their beaks and stun with a toxin. One species at least is potentially dangerous to humans (see note in the Appendix) but the reverse is more often the case, for like squid, octopus are delicious.

There now remains but a single phylum. The one phylum, however, contains almost 80 percent of all living species of animals, and its history spans at least 450 million years. The phylum *Arthropoda* (*arthros*, "joint"; *pod*, "foot") is bewildering in its diversity, but by ignoring the insects, spiders, and many other of its members I can narrow the field to a "mere" 28,000 species. These are included in the class *Crustacea* (*crusta*, "shell"). All crustaceans have characteristic larval stages that usually develop in the plankton, and all possess a jointed skeleton that is worn on the outside and controlled by muscles working on the inside. This is essentially the reverse of the system we humans depend on, and it poses several interesting limitations on the animals. Because the skeleton is carried outside the rest of the body, growth must be preceded by a complicated process wherein the animal sheds its old skeleton, or *carapace*, and grows a newer, larger one. During these periods of molting the animal lacks its accustomed protective covering, and usually takes special steps to avoid predators, often including others of its own kind.

The bodies of crustaceans are segmented, or clearly formed from segments fused while the larva is developing. The segments bear a series of paired appendages, starting at the head with two pairs of antennae, followed closely by a series of mouth parts, and finally limbs used for walking and/or swimming. The basic body plan of most crustaceans resembles that of the common shrimp, shown in Figure 6–7. Note the divisions into segments and the collection of segments near the head that support various sense organs.

Spiny lobster are probably the most popular tropical crustaceans because they are excellent eating. These animals are opportunistic predators and scavengers, prowling over the reef at night. Most successful hunting for them is done on very dark nights, when the moon is new or the skies heavily overcast, and the chase requires good reflexes

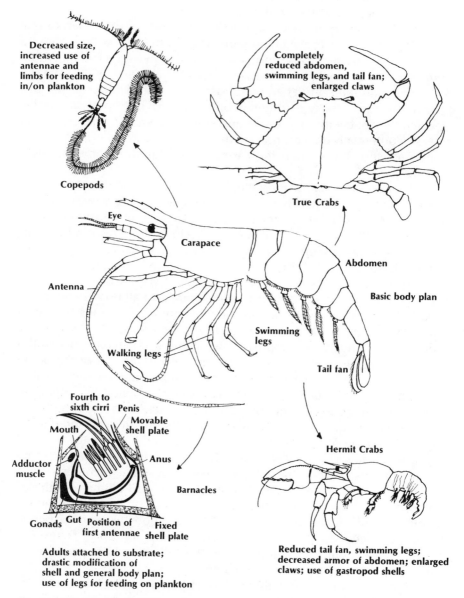

Decreased size, increased use of antennae and limbs for feeding in/on plankton

Copepods

Completely reduced abdomen, swimming legs, and tail fan; enlarged claws

True Crabs

Eye

Carapace

Abdomen

Antenna

Basic body plan

Swimming legs

Walking legs

Tail fan

Fourth to sixth cirri   Penis

Mouth

Movable shell plate

Adductor muscle

Anus

Barnacles

Gonads   Gut   Position of first antennae   Fixed shell plate

Adults attached to substrate; drastic modification of shell and general body plan; use of legs for feeding on plankton

Hermit Crabs

Reduced tail fan, swimming legs; decreased armor of abdomen; enlarged claws; use of gastropod shells

Figure 6–7. Crustacean diversity

and a powerful flashlight. Spiny lobster are seldom seen during the day, and in areas close to civilization they are rarely seen at all, although patrolling the reefs in search of them is often a major social event.

Small snapping shrimp are more common on tropical reefs because they are both smaller and less appetizing. They inhabit small pockets and burrows in the reef and get their name from the loud popping sound they produce. The noise is made by closing at least one enormous claw that has an unusual hinge joint, and the sound is accompanied by a high-pressure stream of water. When these shrimp are present in large numbers the sound is loud enough to be heard above water, and in addition to startling predators the shrimp use the water jet to stun and capture other crustaceans and probably small fishes as well. Cruising sailors who anchor over large congregations of snapping shrimp often wind up peering nervously over the side and checking the bilges hourly. This is because the snapping and popping of the multitudes below is mistaken for the sound of barnacles or shipworms attacking the hull of their boat.

The basic crustacean body plan is modified in some species. In hermit crabs the abdomen is reduced in size and armor, and it is completely useless for swimming. Hermit crabs use the uninhabited shells of gastropods for protection, and when the crab outgrows one shell it simply shops around for a larger one. Hermits are versatile predators and scavengers, and when really hungry they will mouth bits of debris or eat sponges. The edible, terrestrial coconut crab is a larger relative of the hermit that is valued for food throughout the tropical Pacific.

In the true crabs the abdominal segments are permanently folded under the body, and movement is accomplished by walking or swimming motions of the forward limbs. Small crabs live throughout the reef, usually close to the bottom or under the scattered rubble. Other species, which inhabit burrows, are found wherever there are sandy patches. Most crabs will seize and dismember anything they can get their claws on, from sponges to small fishes, and some can supplement their diet by filtering organic debris from the water or off sandy surfaces using fine bristles on their mouth parts.

The smallest, but most important, crustaceans are members of the *zooplankton* (zoo, "animal"). These animals share prominent features with their larger cousins, including a jointed external carapace, paired antennae, mouth parts, and limbs, and various internal structures. There are many different species and a wide range of sizes. Zooplankton, like phytoplankton, show adaptations that retard sinking

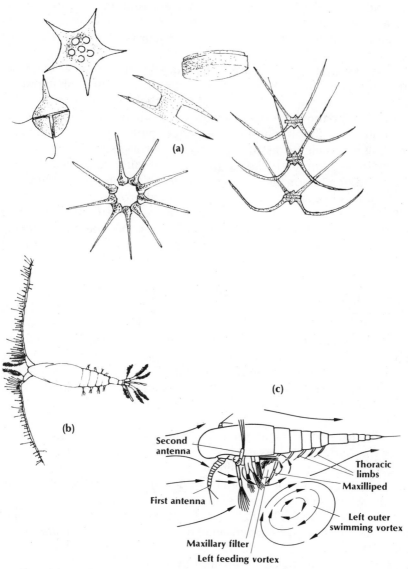

Figure 6–8. Phytoplankton and copepods
(a) different forms of phytoplankton; (b) a typical copepod; (c) feeding currents produced by the movements of a copepod.

rates. They also tend to be transparent, which both protects them from potential predators and prevents them from being damaged by the high-intensity portion of the visible spectrum.

Zooplankton can be divided into two groups on the basis of origin and ultimate fate. The *meroplankton* are members of the zooplankton that spend only a portion of their lives feeding and growing in the surface waters. Most of the marine phyla considered in this chapter use the plankton as a distribution and food source for juvenile or larval stages. Thus their young grow and travel within the plankton before developing further and adopting the appearance and habits of the adult organism. *Holoplankton* spend their entire lives in the plankton, and the most important of the holoplankton are the crustaceans known as *copepods*. Copepods feed primarily on phytoplankton that they capture with marvelously complex filtration systems. Brushlike extensions of their antennae and/or limbs create eddies in the water around them, and when particles swirling about are caught by the fine filters at the mouth parts they are promptly swallowed. Because there are so many different species, it is impossible to state that copepods eat *only* phytoplankton, for like many of us, these animals are opportunists. If a large copepod happens to catch a smaller one, so much the better. Some of the larger phytoplankton are actually bigger than the smallest copepods, so incidents are bound to occur. It is safe to say, however, that copepods as a group are the heaviest consumers of phytoplankton in the ocean.

The barnacles are crustaceans that have profoundly altered the basic body plan of the phylum. Barnacle larvae go through the larval stages common to all crustaceans, but after they settle to the bottom, or contact some solid foundation like the hull of a ship, they attach themselves with special glands on their heads. They then proceed to produce a stout and rather unorthodox skeleton. Wherever the larva chooses to attach will determine the success or failure of the adult. Barnacles feed best in areas with a good water flow, and their sturdy casings allow them to survive despite heavy wave action. They are often encountered right near the high tide line, for they can even withstand lengthy periods of exposure to the air. Other species settle on bare patches around the bases of coral colonies, where they later excavate burrows within the coral skeleton. Mature barnacles feed by extending their long limbs, which bear numerous bristles. Curved into a basket, this network is pulled through the water toward the mouth, and any particles trapped in the process are immediately consumed.

We have briefly summarized the representative characteristics of the six most notable reef invertebrate groups—the sponges, coelenterates, echinoderms, annelids, molluscs, and crustacean arthropods. Each of these groups is, in effect, competing with one another and with the vertebrates of the community for a portion of the energy that is trapped and retained by plants. A great deal can be learned by comparing the ways in which widely separated groups of animals have converged in adapting to obtain a portion of the same energy base—egged on by natural selection and about 500,000,000 years.

In several instances the members of different phyla do not actually compete at all, but instead work together. In addition to the cleaner fishes mentioned earlier, at least one species of shrimp feeds on the parasites found on the body surfaces of fishes that approach their cleaning stations. Many readers will also be familiar with the symbiotic relationship existing between certain fish and larger sea anemones. The resident fish live within the stinging tentacles of the anemone, continually touching them and somehow receiving immunity from the nematocysts. This continual contact appears to be essential, for if the fish is removed and later replaced it may be stunned and eaten. Obviously, anemones have short memories. Most of the fish involved in these partnerships are brilliantly colored, which probably serves to attract the attention of other fishes, and when predators appear the resident fish flit back and forth from the safety of the tentacles. When the anemone feeds, the resident fish get table scraps, so this may be an invitation to attack. Plate 10 shows an anemone fish at home.

Other fish have evolved partnerships with different predatory coelenterates such as the Portuguese man-o-war. Once again, how identification of the resident fish is accomplished is not known. Hermit crabs may show a different form of arrangement with the anemones, because some hermits carry small specimens around on their backs or even in their claws. This helps the crab by discouraging predatory fishes, and it helps the anemone by moving it around to new locations and sources of food. When either eats, the meal may be shared, and when the hermit changes shells it carefully moves its anemone(s) to their new home.

Although these cooperative ventures are interesting, they are hardly the general rule, and there is much to be gained by examining direct competition. First let us consider the transfer of energy trapped in the phytoplankton. Phytoplankton are small, averaging around 1/2500 inch, and they may be seized individually (by the very small zooplankton), trapped or swept into the mouth of ciliary currents (most larval invertebrates), or filtered from the water (copepods). Perhaps because of the great variety of kinds and sizes of plants and animals in the plankton, few of the animal residents appear to care about the identity of the item consumed. Big copepods eat littler ones, and larval invertebrates begin by competing with the small copepods and often end up feeding on them during later stages of development. The same is true of larval fishes, which may also feed on (or be fed on by) other planktonic animals. For our purposes we will reduce such confusion to the statement that zooplankton are the primary consumers of phytoplankton, and add as a footnote that the copepod crustaceans sit at the head of the table.

Next we should look at the primary consumers of energy collected and stored by the algae growing near the bottom. There are only so many ways that an animal can harvest these plants: They may be clipped off near the bases, or gnawed, chewed, or scraped off the bottom. Surgeonfish, triggerfish, and puffers clip or prune filamentous algae from the bottom or off the surface of dead corals. (There is even some indication that groups of surgeonfish may farm these algae by killing isolated portions of healthy coral colonies.) Surgeonfish, some species of damselfish, triggerfish, and parrotfish also gnaw on projecting portions of the reef to remove the algal cover. Limpets and sea urchins graze over wide areas, the limpets using their rasping radulae and the urchins their oral scraping structures. Finally, the angelfish use their flexible teeth to brush or scrape algae from the reef surface. Competition between these groups is reduced by location: limpets in exposed areas, urchins over the reef flat and down the seaward slopes, and grazing fishes spread over the reef either inside or outside the reef flat, and over it when the tide is right. Time sharing is also important, because the herbivorous fishes feed during the day and the urchins roam most freely at night.

The third important energy source is the recycling of the earthly remains of the dead and the waste products of the living. Many reef animals supplement their diets with portions of carcasses when these are available, but this is more an example of opportunism than a particular specialty. For the most part, the bulk of the organic material trapped in bodies and wastes is recycled through bacterial activity. In the process of decomposition a variety of nutrients are released into the surrounding waters, and nutrients and organic fragments are mixed with the bottom sediments. The bacteria themselves may be trapped and consumed in mucus nets by corals, or by mucus feeding worms living in the bottom sediments. The dissolved nutrients are essential for phytoplankton reproduction, as well as for algal growth along the bottom, and recent research has indicated that many reef invertebrates are able to absorb some of these nutrients directly from the water when they are required. It is important to note that the reef structure is so complex that it traps most of what dies in the community. This permits rapid recycling, which would otherwise take 1,000 years or so in the open ocean.

The organic materials released by decomposing bacteria or mixed into the bottom sediments is termed *detritus*, and the major problem facing animals utilizing this energy source is that the organic matter is likely to be widely dispersed. Often it is mixed with or stuck to grains of sand or on the surface of bottom litter. Some more effective techniques used on the reef consist of searching and plucking bits of material with modified tube feet (brittle stars and sea cucumbers) or actually eating and processing large quantities of sand (some burrowing worms).

Those animals that eat either phytoplankton or larger marine plants can be considered to be primary consumers, alias herbivores. Larger animals that feed on the primary consumers are called secondary consumers or carnivores. *Microcarnivores* will be our term for those secondary consumers who specialize in capturing zooplankton. Zooplankton can get as large as one fifth of an inch, so a microcarnivore can use a number of different techniques. Briefly, zooplankton may be harpooned, plucked from the water individually, trapped in mucus nets, or filtered in other ways. In addition, the animal may move to the plankton or the plankton may go to the animal. Corals and jellyfish harpoon with nematocysts; fishes like the cardinalfish, some damselfish, and several wrasses spot the plankton drifting by and snap them up. Bivalves use the ciliated, mucus-coated tracts that line their gills, actively pumping water across them. Sponges rely on their ciliated inner chambers to move the necessary water. Worms buried in the sand may use a catch bag of sand or secreted mucus to filter the currents they produce. Other worms, such as the featherduster, use feathery extensions to passively trap plankton that the local currents bring to their mucus-covered surfaces. Barnacles, meanwhile, sweep their filters *through* the water, and rely on neither mucus nor cilia. There is a segregation, both spatially and temporally. Many worms and bivalves feed in sandy areas; tubeworms, sponges, and corals live within the reef proper. Hard corals, soft corals, and sponges all compete for attachment sites with varying success depending on the local conditions. Whereas damselfish, anemones, featherduster worms, and some jellyfish feed by day, cardinalfish, many corals, and different jellyfishes are most active at night.

We have now discussed the primary consumers of the algae on the reef, and the primary and secondary consumers of the plankton. It was once fashionable to consider all carnivores as living rather two-dimensional lives, with events happening in conveniently logical chains. The food-chain approach assumed a consistent sequence of events, sort of a snapper-eats-damselfish-eats-copepod-eats-phytoplankton-collects-sunlight system. Although this is indeed a useful concept when sorting out energy transfer through a community, which we will get to presently, it is not an accurate summary of life on the reef. A more acceptable statement would be that large animals eat smaller ones, with a couple of exceptions as noted below. Trying to identify animal X as a secondary, tertiary, or quaternary consumer (in the above chain, you would be quaternary if you ate the snapper) is very difficult. A large fish that eats either of two small fishes might become a secondary or tertiary consumer, depending on whether the victim had dined on algae or zooplankton. For this reason I will simply discuss small versus large predators. We are at a convenient point, for in terms of size the secondary consumers of the plankton are roughly the same size as the primary consumers of the algae growing at or near the bottom.

Small carnivores can catch their prey by harpooning (anemones and jellyfish), seizing and gulping (squirrelfish), seizing and piercing (some worms and crabs), seizing and digesting (starfishes), plucking (puffers or butterflyfish), crushing (parrotfish), or stunning (snapping shrimp). Parrotfishes also benefit, as do some predatory starfish, from the algal partners of the coral polyps, but because they presumably have evolved to cope with the animal component (which might in this sense be considered a primary consumer) I am including them in this category.

Large carnivores usually rely on either catching and gulping (grouper) or seizing and rasping (Triton's trumpet and cephalopods). Seizing and tearing, a method utilized by sharks and killer whales, is a special technique that permits feeding on very large primary consumers, microcarnivores, or other large carnivores.

Carnivores large and small specialize in terms of time on the reef, location, or size of prey. Squirrelfish are nocturnal, snappers are diurnal, and groupers feed most often at dusk and dawn. Yet none of the larger reef predators, which in terms of their position in a food chain might be considered tertiary or quaternary consumers, shows much in the way of specialization for *particular* prey. Why is this?

Animals are just not that efficient in passing energy to one another, and a reef can only support a limited number of large predators. As an example, let's consider the food chain described earlier. We have already noted that only about 17 percent of the solar energy trapped by a marine plant ends up producing new biological materials, the rest being lost as heat or used to keep the plant alive at night when there is no sunlight for photosynthesis. Animals lead much more demanding lives, and they are even less miserly when it comes to conserving energy. During the life of an animal only around 10 percent of the energy consumed ends up as surplus that supports growth. The rest is either lost or devoted to essential activities and reproduction. Roughly speaking, this means that a one-pound fish that is a primary consumer must have eaten ten pounds of marine plants to have reached that size. Unfortunately for the secondary consumer that eats him (or her) there is still only one pound's worth of energy retained in the body of the primary consumer. Now suppose that the secondary consumer weighs ten pounds. All fish are bound by the same rules, so this fish must have eaten *100* pounds of primary consumers. The pattern now emerges.

When this kind of hierarchy is illustrated it is often set up as a pyramid with the marine plants at the bottom. The different steps of the pyramid correspond to the various primary/secondary/tertiary consumer positions in the food chain. These are called *trophic levels* and all rely on the activity of the plant "produced" at T–I. By looking at a pyramid you should begin to understand the limitations facing an animal living at T–III, T–IV or higher. Look at a 500-pound grouper sitting on the reef. It is probably a T–V consumer some of the time, but if it were always locked into that role, just consider the problems it would face. A 500-pound T–V consumer would represent the consumption of (for instance) 5,000 pounds of snappers, which ate 50,000 pounds of damselfish, which fed on 500,000 pounds of copepods, which filtered 5 *million* pounds of phytoplankton from the local waters. The message here is that a given area will support far more animals at the lower trophic levels than at higher levels simply because each step up the pyramid wastes another 90 percent of the energy originally reaching the herbivores. Because of this, most upper-level predators are opportunists, feeding at the lower trophic levels whenever possible. This requirement for versatility has discouraged intense specialization. Even with an opportunistic approach, predators higher than T–V are rare, generally solitary, and often highly territorial. The largest animals, such as the baleen whales, whale sharks, or manta rays, rely on feeding entirely on the T–III level because they require an enormous amount of energy and benefit from as short a chain as possible from sunlight to stomach. Human beings are only now beginning to learn this lesson, as we have traditionally devoted most of our attention to pursuing creatures that are themselves upper-level carnivores, such as mackerel, tuna, snapper, or grouper. In the years to come there will be an increasing interest in processing the lower levels of the pyramid as these energy relationships are more widely appreciated—and as there are more mouths to feed. Right now the Poles and the Soviets are harvest-

Trophic level	Percentage of energy received	Percentage of energy retained	Number of individuals supported	Average weight per individual	Total body mass at this trophic level	Identity
T–V	0.017	0.0017	1	500 lbs.	500 lbs.	Grouper
T–IV	0.17	0.017	100	50 lbs.	5,000 lbs.	Snappers
T–III	1.7	0.17	100,000	0.5 lbs.	50,000 lbs.	Damselfish
T–II (primary consumers)	17.0	1.7	enormous	minute	500,000 lbs.	Copepods
T–I (primary producers)	100.00	17.0	even larger	even smaller	5,000,000 lbs.	Phytoplankton

The same example as an energy pyramid:

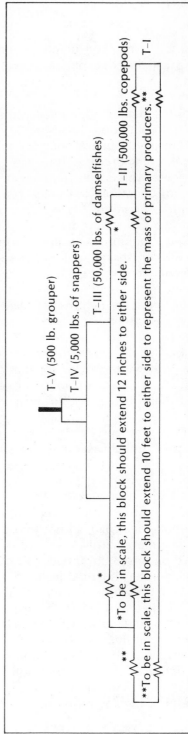

T–V (500 lb. grouper)

T–IV (5,000 lbs. of snappers)

T–III (50,000 lbs. of damselfishes)

T–II (500,000 lbs. copepods)

T–I

* *To be in scale, this block should extend 12 inches to either side.*

** *To be in scale, this block should extend 10 feet to either side to represent the mass of primary producers.*

Figure 6–9. Energy relationships on the reef
This man, feeding at T–VI, gets only 50 pounds of useful energy out of 5 million pounds of plant productivity. Feeding lower on the pyramid is clearly more efficient, and must occur if we are to obtain enough protein in the years to come.

ing krill for human consumption, and there are other nations experimenting with the concept. The effect that this shift in focus will have on other organisms is not known, but it is apparent that it will place us in direct competition with the great whales.

Future commercial exploitation of the coral reefs will probably be limited to local efforts. This is partly due to the difficulties involved in harvesting amid such a complex environment and partly because large-scale commercial ventures tend to specialize in large numbers of large species. This is quite feasible in temperate waters, but it is hardly suitable for operations in tropical coastal waters for reasons discussed earlier in this section. Mariculture, or sea farming, is being studied with an eye toward producing quantities of valuable species under controlled conditions, usually in shoreside tanks or pens. Operations rearing lobster, shrimp, eels, and algae are reasonably successful, and experiments are in progess with other marine species as well. However, none of these projects will influence the reefs in general, for the conditions must be tightly controlled, which is best accomplished in some separate facility or location, such as a penned portion of the reef flat.

Unfortunately, even though we are not intent on plundering the reefs we are still destroying them at an alarming rate. The most common causes of death are landfill projects, which extend over the reef flat, and road cutting, both of which produce high levels of erosion. Initially this may simply lower the light intensity near the deeper portions of the reef, and corals at these depths will then be replaced by other forms, probably sponges and soft corals. As the amount of sand or silt increases on the reef flat, surge and backwash will carry it down the reef slopes, burying the corals. The remaining colonies soon suffocate, and soft corals take their place as filamentous algae coat the exposed portions of the weakening skeletons. The fish and invertebrate populations change in response to these alterations in the environment, as more herbivores move in, and the coral grazers and plunkers move on in search of better living conditions. More bivalves and gastropods enter the area, to the delight of shell collectors, and the barnacles, boring forms, or filtering creatures that are unable to move away are buried and killed. In extreme cases only the sands and the sand-dwelling organisms will remain at deeper levels, and the churning of sand and silt near the surface will prevent the attachment of new plants or animals in the area until the influx of sand and debris has slowed or ceased altogether. Landfill or if you prefer, reef-fill and other sources of increased runoff such as strip mining or road building have been responsible for producing such changes in the reefs of New

Caledonia, Samoa, Hawaii, Tahiti, and other islands on the large scale, and localized effects will almost surely be found around any heavily populated island in the tropics.

A trickle of sewage, as from a small village or a few anchored yachts may actually increase the reef population locally. Bacteria multiply, algae flourish, and many organisms find more to eat. But larger amounts of sewage, particularly in enclosed areas like lagoons, will kill reefs in two ways. The light levels are reduced, and particulate matter in the water increased, and this combination alone might distress some corals. In addition, however, bacterial decomposition of the sewage requires oxygen, and with enough sewage the oxygen levels in the water may decrease enough to asphyxiate the corals. The effects of such pollution are particularly evident in highly urbanized areas.

Blasting usually has more restricted effects on the reefs. In many tropical areas the use of dynamite as a fishing method is popular because it is simple and effective. Sticks are tossed over the reef face, and after the blast many fish float to the surface where they can easily be picked up. Most of the fish and other animals killed by the explosion remain trapped in whatever remains of the reef below, and of course the same area is seldom used for fishing the next day. Blasting a new passage through the reef will change regional patterns of circulation both through the lagoon and along the coast, but other than noting that corals are killed for fifty yards or so to either side of the entrance, studies have not been conducted to determine what the long-term effects might be. Even more drastic changes result from nuclear weapons testing, which still occurs in the southern Tuomotus. How the radiation affects reefs and reef animals regionally and further downstream has yet to be determined. There are some disquieting rumors about fishes becoming contaminated on distant reefs.

Ironically the effects of mere garbage dumping are the least severe, but probably the most discouraging because the practice indicates the general level of disregard for the reef community held by many island inhabitants and visitors. The rather unsightly practice of removing garbage ranging from beer cans to old buses by throwing or driving them onto the reef flat is remarkably widespread and difficult to restrict. There can be a great deal of physical destruction when the larger items crash about in the surf, and although they may attract interesting animals it may be a bit hazardous to snorkel around them in the surge. A potentially more dangerous practice has appeared in the Caribbean, where mangrove swamps are being utilized for dump sites. As inhabitants of the eastern United States have found when using salt marshes for landfill or development, these nursery areas are essential to the health and well-being of the adjacent coastal communities. For the small Caribbean islands, many of which have already decimated local fish populations through unmonitored fish trapping, the destruction of the mangrove forests could ruin chances for an eventual recovery of local fisheries.

A reef is a complex community, with diverse inhabitants that have evolved and specialized under normal conditions for hundreds of millions of years. As we noted earlier in the section such specialization and diversity implies a certain fragility, for the system can function smoothly only as long as normalcy is the order of the day. Maintaining the submarine status quo is especially important around tropical islands, for in many cases the only significant asset held by the inhabitants is the beauty and accessibility of the local reefs. The potential value of that asset should not be overlooked or underestimated when planning coastal projects—filling in a reef to build a hotel for visiting divers does show a certain lack of foresight. Constructing a sea level canal from the Atlantic to the Pacific before comprehensive studies have been done could be disastrous on a larger scale. How would sea snakes and crown-of-thorns starfish like a Caribbean holiday? No one can say at present. In any case, as we increase our presence around the islands and reefs of the tropics we must always take care to insure that seemingly minor alterations in the local environment do not lead to the destruction of the delicate balance of the community. On this cautionary note I will conclude the discussion of the marine biology of the tropics. In Part II of this book we will consider the formation and evolution of the islands whose ultimate fates are so tightly interwoven with those of the surrounding reefs.

Part Two

Islands in Paradise

(a)

Plate 1. Climatic differences due to location relative to the prevailing winds on the island of Maui. (a) Near the southeast corner of the island, facing directly into the tradewinds. (b) Five miles southwest of the photo above, within the rain shadow of Haleakala volcano (alt. 10,400 feet approx.).

(b)

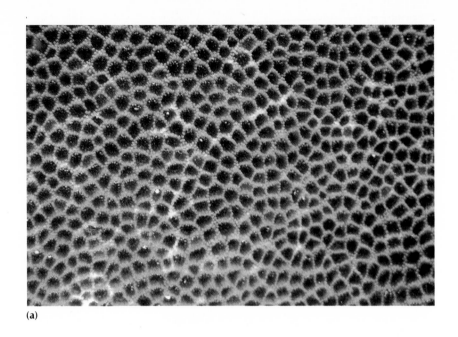

(a)

Plate 2. The varied forms of coral skeletons. Seen with the aid of a close-up lens, coral thecae are beautiful, intricate structures that retain features characteristic of the species of polyp that created it, regardless of the ultimate shape of the colony as a whole.

(b)

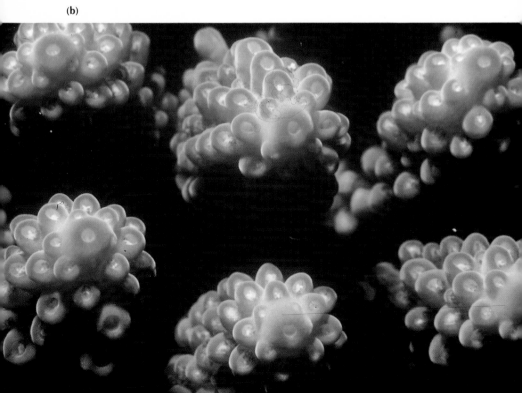

(a)

Plate 3. A closer look at atolls. (a) Inside the lagoon at Ahe atoll in the Tuamotu Archipelago; notice the clear shallow water just this side of the islet. (b) Exploring an islet on Raraka atoll, another of the Tuamotu group.

(b)

Plate 4. The Galapagos marine iguana. Like characters in a creature-feature, these unique animals form lines along ridges as they bask in the sun.

Plate 5. The sperm whale. Largest of the odontocetes, sperm whales have more than once been hunted to the edge of extinction. Note the distinctive location and angle to the blowhole and the slanted blow that is produced upon exhalation.

(a)

Plate 6. The humpback whale. (a) A humpback swimming directly toward the camera; notice the prominent bumps on the edges of the upper jaw and the "splashguard" that keeps water from entering the nasal passageways. The blow is clearly double, in contrast to that of the odontocetes (as in Plate 5). (b) A feeding humpback surfacing with a mouthful of prey; note the distended pleats of the throat.

(b)

Plate 7. The crown-of-thorns starfish. A small group of individuals dine on a coral colony; almost all of the living polyps have been removed and the white colonial skeleton is exposed.

Plate 8. A featherduster worm spreads its mucus-coated bristles above the protective confines of an encrusting coral colony.

Plate 9. The giant squid. The photograph shows the head and portions of the tentacles of a giant squid. Note the 8-inch eye (pale blue) just above the formidable beak and the 1-inch sucking discs that line the inner aspects of the tentacles. The entire animal was estimated to be 20 to 25 feet in length.

Plate 10. An example of interphylum cooperation. A clownfish watches cautiously from its sanctuary within the stinging tentacles of a large anemone.

Plate 11. A caldera on the island of Maui. After the initial eruptive pressures have eased and the lava within the central shaft has cooled, the crater at the summit may collapse inward to form a broad depression known as a caldera. The central caldera at Haleakala, on the island of Maui in the Hawaiian islands, is almost five miles across at its widest point. Later volcanic activity has produced striking formations within the caldera, and this volcano is still classified as dormant rather than extinct.

Chapter Seven

The Life of an Island

The next three chapters will discuss the formation and history of islands and island groups, and once again we will begin with a simple model and develop it until some useful principles become apparent. Let's consider what happens when a break in the oceanic crust allows molten lava to reach the surface of the ocean floor. Such eruptions may occur from a single hole or vent, from several related vents, or along cracks or rifts. The type of lava that is released from mid-ocean vents or rifts is of a distinct type, and one of its most important features is that it flows quickly and easily, spreading over a wide area before solidifying. Thus in contrast to continental-type volcanoes, which often have steep sides, it takes a lot of lava to raise a submarine volcano very far off the bottom. Roughly 10,000 submerged seamounts have been identified to date, representing islands in the making or volcanoes that ceased to erupt before reaching the ocean surface. Those that persist in their erupting will eventually emerge above the waves as a new island.

Islands can appear rapidly, from a geological standpoint anyway, and the rate of lava release can be staggering. The island of Hawaii has reached its present dimensions in about 750,000 years, rising from depths of around 16,000 feet to peaks of almost 14,000 feet above sea level. In general, the slope of a new island is very gentle, only about 6°, and this broad lava formation is called a volcanic shield. For our model we will follow the fate of a volcanic shield that formed from a single vent and ceased to erupt when its summit projected a few thousand feet above the ocean surface. The summit may remain peaked and gradually become more angular with age. In other instances, as the magma beneath the summit cools and contracts, the entire peak may collapse inward to form a large, bowl-like depression called a *caldera*. A spectacular caldera is shown in Plate 11.

One of the key concepts of modern geology is that the light, solid materials of the earth's crust are floating on a more dense, yet plastic molten layer much like ice cubes float in a drink, or a raft on a lake. Floating is a dynamic balance, even on this grand scale. If you place extra weight on a raft it settles into the water, and as an island is forming the floating crust beneath is being loaded with an enormous amount of weight. In the case of the island of Hawaii the loading is something like 77,750,000,000 tons! So it should not be a great surprise to find that when the eruptive pressures have eased, sooner or later the ocean floor supporting the island begins to settle deeper into the molten mantle beneath. The island then begins to submerge or *subside*. This subsidence strongly affects the appearance and fate of the island both directly and indirectly, through interactions with two other forces, erosion by waves (submarine erosion) and erosion by rain and wind (subaerial erosion). From the moment that our model island approached sea level, waves driven by the prevailing winds began pounding away at its shoreline, but the periodic discharge of new lava minimized the visible effects. Once volcanic activity stops, however, the waves begin to alter the contours of the young island on a more permanent basis. The waves pound into the shoreline, cutting into the slopes to create a shallow submarine platform. As the waves advance they cut deeper into the mountainside, removing support for higher portions of the slopes, which then tumble into the sea. With time, substantial cliffs are formed, and the continual wave action churns the fallen debris, turning blocks to boulders, boulders to pebbles, and pebbles to sand that may be swept back over the platform and down the submerged slopes or carried by currents to other portions of the island.

Your first look around a volcanic island will show you that cliff height varies, both from island to island and along the coast of an individual island. One reason is that although we like to speak of the prevailing winds and seas, or the northeast and southeast tradewinds, the winds that you actually encounter vary from day to day. Even during the tradewind season the winds arrive not from a specific direction, but from a statistically predictable range of directions centered around either northeast or southeast. Most often during the rainy season, but whenever storms arrive, there are strong westerly winds and seas that strike otherwise sheltered portions of the coast. The cliffs thus represent a visual record of these events, their frequency, and relative intensity. Cliffs are most prominent over the range of the tradewinds, and of lesser height in regions affected by storm seas. There is little or no cliff development in completely sheltered areas. The effects of trade-driven seas can be seen along the northeast coasts of Molokai or Hawaii (Hawaiian Islands, northern hemisphere), Aruba or Barbados (Caribbean, northern hemisphere), or the southeast coast of Aunu'u or Tutuila (Samoan Islands, southern hemisphere). The southwest coast of Lanai (Hawaiian Islands) or Martinique (Caribbean) or the northwest coast of Tutuila have recorded the seasonal impact of storm seas.

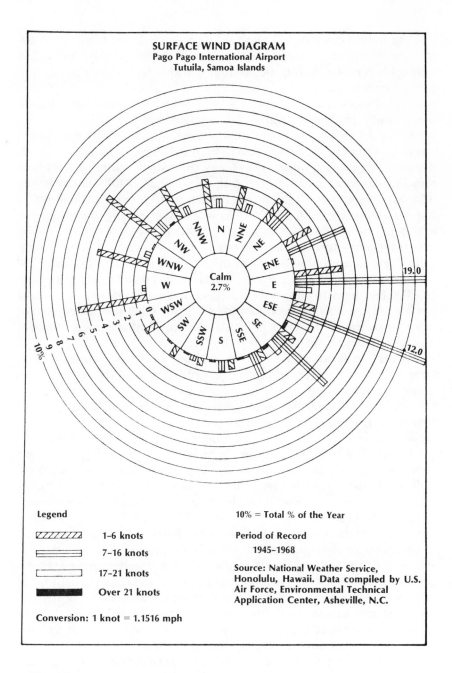

Figure 7–1. Sector diagram indicating average wind directions and frequencies for an island located within the zone of the southeast tradewinds (courtesy National Weather Service, Honolulu, HI).

The height of cliffs will also vary, less predictably, because of differences in the character of the lava rock. If the lava is weak the waves advance easily, landslides are frequent, and high cliffs are produced. But if the rock is more dense and resistant huge caves may develop at sea level before the rock above finally yields, so the waves advance more slowly and the cliffs are relatively lower.

It should be pretty obvious that waves can only advance and cliffs can only retreat for a finite length of time before running out of island. If wave erosion continues, eventually only small spires of rock will remain, like Kicker Rock in the Galapagos or St. Paul's Rocks in the Atlantic. When even these visible remnants have been conquered by the seas the waves still continue to work, leveling off the top of the island in a process known as *planation*. If later subsidence places the now truncated island beyond the reach of wave action, its flattened top will remain as evidence that it was once a bona fide island. Around 200 of these submerged *guyots* have been discovered so far, some as deep as 6,000 feet below the surface. This is quite a ways down, and might lead you to ask how one goes about estimating what the normal rate of subsidence might be for a particular island. I will give you one approach now and a second later in the chapter.

As the waves advance, creating cliffs and cutting a submarine platform, they are also recording the rate of subsidence. If the island is subsiding rapidly, the wave-cut platform will have a steep grade, but if the island is stationary or only slowly settling there will be a broad, almost flat plateau. Things should be kept in perspective, however, as rapid geological movement may be only a few yards per millennium.

Although it is presenting an obstacle to the prevailing seas, our new island is also blocking the prevailing winds, with predictable results. As discussed in Chapter 1, this is grounds for precipitation, but in addition the young island is bleak, barren, and black. It is therefore subject to intense heating, which further encourages the formation of updrafts, clouds, and rain. On our model island of low to medium height the rainfall produced will drench the upper slopes fairly evenly, and as the water flows down to the sea it will collect into rivulets, perhaps following the trails of erupted cinders and larger boulders. At first there will be innumerable small rivulets meandering down the gentle slopes, but as the lighter surface layers of cinders and ash are carried away these channels will deepen and the rivulets merge to form streams. On the leeward side of the island these will ultimately flow into the sea, pouring their accumulated loads of debris down the submerged slopes. On the weather side of the island things are different, and the streams cascade over the growing cliffs in spectacular waterfalls.

Figure 7–2. Cliff formation
top: Recent landslides can be seen along the bottom of these cliffs along the windward coast of Eiao Island in the Marquesas group. Heavy rainfall and general subsidence has produced small bays between cliffed spur ends such as the one shown.
middle: The cliffs along the southern coast of Lanai (Hawaiian Islands) are the result of intermittent storms that strike an area normally quite dry. Because subaerial erosion is slow, the coast here shows a line of cliffs, not a series of embayments.
bottom: The cliffs around this island in the Galapagos have gone about as far as they can go—soon this island will be only a shoal on the charts.

Gradually the general appearance of the island changes. The stream channels deepen to become valleys separated by ridges with steep sides. The island is being dissected by rainfall, and the gently rounded ridge peaks that separated the rivulets become increasingly angular as the valleys deepen. Meanwhile the island is gradually subsiding. As the seaward ends of the valleys are submerged, bays are created. Once bays have formed, even though the streams continue to discharge debris into the ocean, most of the transported materials will settle to the bottom within the quiet confines of the bays before reaching the outer slopes. The valley floors then become collection sites for these eroded materials, and the heads of the valleys may fill in to form deltas. Despite the accumulation of debris, the shape of the valley/bay walls above the water can give information about the amount of subsidence that has occurred, as shown in Figure 7–4.

The formation of bays has an additional effect on the coastline by limiting wave action and erosion to the seaward tops of the ridges or spurs that separate adjacent bays. Embayment is most characteristic of the leeward side of a small island such as our model, where most of the valleys reach the sea. On the windward side there is a continual interplay between the rainfall, the waves, and subsidence. High rainfall produces deep valleys, and rapid subsidence helps to bring them to sea level, but a high rate of cliff formation tends to cut off the valleys to produce waterfalls.

On larger, loftier islands such as those of Hawaii or Caribbean islands like Jamaica, Cuba, or Hispaniola, the local climatic variations described in Chapter 1 have pronounced effects. Nevertheless there is a continual interplay between subaerial and submarine erosion that determines the location and relative prominence of cliffs, valleys, and waterfalls.

Thus far we have created a reasonably straightforward picture of a typical island with its coastal cliffs, valleys, bays, and other scenic attractions. Although we could almost stop here, particularly if we were dealing with islands in high latitudes, few tropical islands are so simply described. We need to look at a few sources of variation from our model that have widespread application. Foremost among these is the activity of coral animals.

During the early life of a tropical island the runoff is so extreme, and the waters so dirty, that the submerged coast is an inhospitable site for the settlement of coral planulae. While the light, easily eroded and transported materials such as ash or cinders continue to be carried into the sea the surrounding waters remain murky, but the coastal waters clear as the initial washdown phase ends. Gradually the streams reach

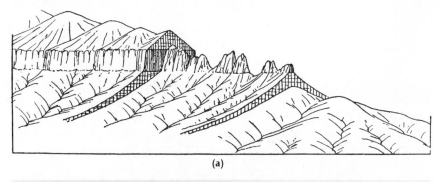

(a)

(b)

(c)

Figure 7–3. The changing shapes of ridge peaks
(a) diagram, showing evoution of spur forms on Moorea; (b) appearance of
ridge line in Cook's Bay, Moorea; (c) ridge line along the northern coast
of Nuku Hiva, Marquesas Islands.

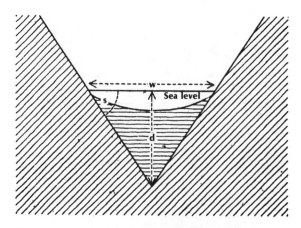

Figure 7–4. Hypothetical section across a partly submerged and partly silted up V-shaped river valley (w, width of bay; s, angle of slope of sides; d, rock bottom depth). Even after considerable sedimentation has occurred the shape of a valley may still give information about the amount of subsidence that has taken place. Sometimes the valleys can be tracked offshore with the aid of modern depth-sounding equipment; this was done off the island of Oahu, where stream-cut valleys are now 1,200 feet below sea level.

deeper and more dense lava, and as plants arrive and begin to cover the slopes erosion is further reduced. As the waters clear and the valleys become bays that trap much of the remaining debris, reefs may begin to appear in discrete locations.

The larvae may settle first on the edges of the wave-cut platforms, if the churned sand and rock is limited, and near the spur ends that separate bays. Corals may remain indefinitely in isolated patches, as along the shores of the Marquesas Islands, but if the coral reef can grow successfully and rise toward the surface it will begin to lessen the force of the waves on the shoreline, and the rate of cliff formation will slow. With less wave erosion the waters will clear further and the corals will be able to colonize new portions of the coast. Eventually the reefs may spread completely around the island, following the shoreline and extending into each bay, broken only in regions where the fresh water run off is high, such as seaward of streams, or siltation is heavy, such as the delta-headed bays. At this stage the reef complex is known as a *fringing reef.*

Figure 7–5. Additional effects of heavy rainfall
(a) Tutuila Island, American Samoa: You are looking into a large caldera whose
seaward wall was breached by waves, forming the natural harbor of Pago Pago.
Note the broad valley at the head of the harbor and the accumulated sediments
washed down from the surrounding walls. (b) Nuku Hiva, Marquesas: Part of
the north side of this island is sheltered from trade-driven waves and storm
seas, and erosion by rainfall is the major force at work. Notice the huge piles of
material washed from the steep sides (left portion of photograph) and the
strange contours of the ridge-line to the right, seen in greater detail in Figure
7–3. (c) St. Lucia, Lesser Antilles: A delta plain fills a drowned-valley
embayment along the western coast.

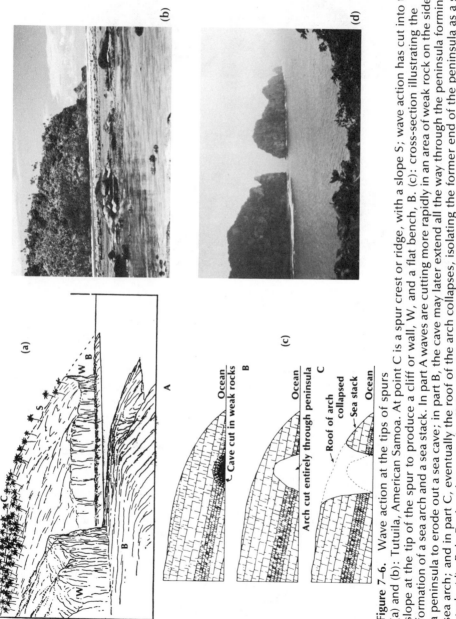

Figure 7-6. Wave action at the tips of spurs

(a) and (b): Tutuila, American Samoa. At point C is a spur crest or ridge, with a slope S; wave action has cut into the slope at the tip of the spur to produce a cliff or wall, W, and a flat bench, B. (c): cross-section illustrating the formation of a sea arch and a sea stack. In part A waves are cutting more rapidly in an area of weak rock on the side of a peninsula to erode out a sea cave; in part B, the cave may later extend all the way through the peninsula forming a sea arch; and in part C, eventually the roof of the arch collapses, isolating the former end of the peninsula as a sea stack. (d): Pola Rock, a large stack off the northern coast of Tutuila Island.

As the island continues to subside the coral reefs will grow toward the surface, and the island will appear to be receding from its reefs. The space between the reef and the shoreline deepens and becomes a lagoon. This enclosed body of water traps coralline sand, which is carried across the top of the reef by the waves that now expend their energies against the structure of the reef. Cliff formation is at an end, and the reef is now termed a *barrier reef*.

Although we try to classify islands as representing either fringing or barrier reef systems, things are not always so clear-cut. Certainly the islands of the Society group or Fiji include many classical examples of barrier reefs, whereas the reefs of Hawaii and much of the Caribbean are clearly fringing reefs. But because fringing and barrier reefs are part of a continuum, intergrades are common. The submerged slopes of an island are seldom precisely the same all along the coastline, and even minor variations will be exaggerated by associated differences in exposure to the waves, freshwater run off, shading, and/or siltation that combine to influence the rate of coral growth. Even when a typical island with a barrier reef is examined, you will find that the windward and leeward lagoons are seldom the same width, nor do they have the same number and types of passes leading to the open sea. Geological events may also result in variations because not all islands subside in a precise and even fashion. If the island tilts to one side as it settles, reef and lagoon formation will be relatively accelerated along one coast and retarded on the other.

If reef growth and subsidence continue, when the island slips beneath the surface an encircling reef will remain to mark its former location. As this massive reef traps sand and coral rubble on its upper plateau it will create another kind of island, a coral island or *atoll*. Because we have already examined the structure of atolls in Chapter 2, I will not belabor the topic here. Charles Darwin was the first to suggest the correct relationship between various reef forms in his book *Coral Reefs*, but it was almost 120 years before it received analytical attention although it did generate some terrific armchair arguments among the intellectuals of the nineteenth century. Darwin's theory indicated that the age of an atoll and the depth of its subsidence should be roughly estimated by the distance one could drill into the coral rock before reaching the dense lava on which the original planulae settled. To date, drillings have shown that the conglomerated coral rock can extend almost a mile beneath the surface, to a rough age of 43 million years, and there is little doubt that emergence, erosion, and subsidence are the primary forces that shape islands and lead to the formation of fringing reefs, barrier reefs, and atolls. Because of a variety of physical factors, some of which will be considered in Chapter 8, the

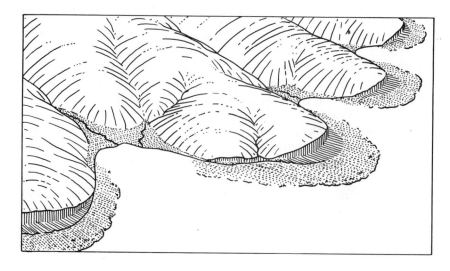

(a)

(b)

Figure 7–7. Fringing reefs
(a): The appearance of an island with young fringing reefs;
note the stream deltas within the bays, the wave-cut
spur ends, and the coral reefs that fail to penetrate to the
heads of the embayments due to heavy siltation and
fresh-water flow. The hatched area short of the cliffs
indicates the extent of the wave-cut shore bench. (b): The
fringing reef at Tutuila, American Samoa, is generally
awash at low tide, when the natives harvest shellfish and
other reef edibles almost without wetting their feet.
Notice the cliffed spur ends and the coastal highway to the
right of the picture.

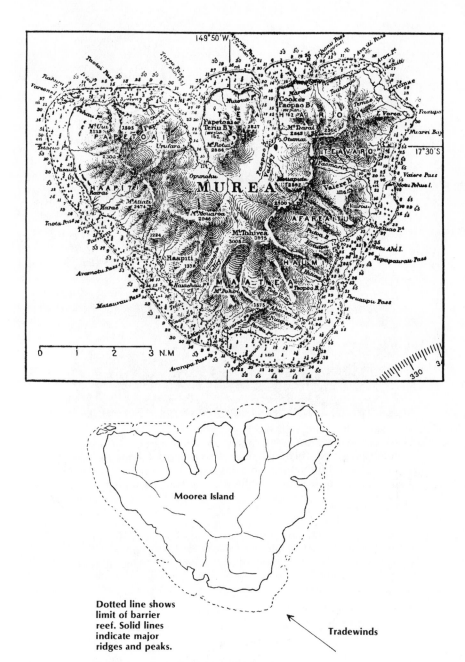

Figure 7–8. The barrier reef at Moorea Island
The island of Moorea in the Society Islands is a close neighbor of Tahiti.
Moorea (spelled Murea in the top illustration) is an excellent example of an
island surrounded by a barrier reef that closely follows the general contours of
the coast.

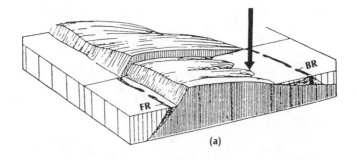

(a)

(b)

Figure 7–9. Fringing/barrier reef intergrades
Islands may be difficult to assign to either fringing or barrier reef categories. This is largely due to the fact that the two are part of a continuum, and many variations are possible. Part (a) shows an island where the lee side has subsided more rapidly than the windward side. As a result the island has a barrier reef on one side and dringing reefs on the other. Part (b) shows one portion of the fringing reef of Tutuila, American Samoa, which is approaching barrier reef status; the reef to the right is almost 400 yards in width, and encloses a small lagoon with depths of over 6 feet. (FR: fringing reef; BR: barrier reef).

ratio of fringing reefs to barrier reefs to atolls is rather different in the tropical Atlantic and Pacific, and most Caribbean islands would be classified as fringing reefs or fringing/barrier reef intergrades.

If you look around carefully while visiting any tropical island you will probably see some island features that our expanded model still fails to predict. Although we cannot hope to cover all the possibilities without treating each island as a separate entity, we can look at a few additional factors that may have been involved in shaping your particu-

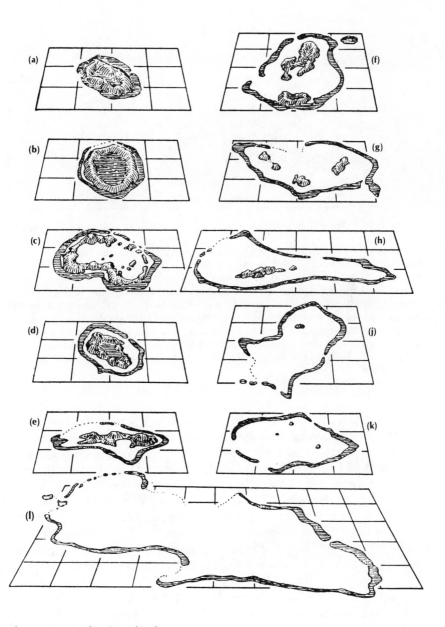

Figure 7–10. The Fiji Islands
The Fiji Island group has somehwere around 900 islands. Scattered among
them are excellent examples of the stages of development along the fringing
reef–barrier reef–atoll trail. (A, Naiau, B, Kambara; C, Fulanga; D, Tuvutha; E,
Namuka; F, Ongea; G, Yangasa; H, Oneata; J, North Argo; K, Reid; L. Great
Argo; the small squares are two miles on a side.)

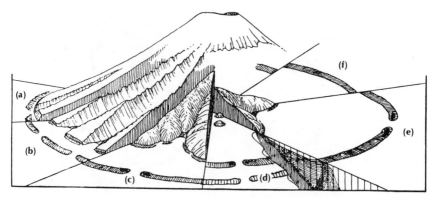

Figure 7–11. Sector diagram summarizing the evolution of a typical tropical island.
A: volcanic shield with spur end cliffs and fringing reefs. B: later subsidence produces barrier reef with passes opposite stream-cut valleys. C: mature barrier reef system, with no spur end cliffs visible and narrow fringing reefs found along highly eroded shoreline. D: "almost atoll" stage, with only the tops of the island structure showing above the surface; in this case a double barrier has formed, with the original fringing reef of C producing a second barrier reef through subsidence. E: more typical later stage than C, with a single barrier reef and broad lagoon; shaded area indicates submarine contours. F: atoll that remains after subsidence has taken the island beneath the surface.

lar island. Over the past one to two million years there have been four cycles of world-wide changes in climate and temperature as the glaciers advanced and retreated. During glacial periods sea level fell hundreds of feet (around 240 feet during the last glacial period 10,000 to 20,000 years ago). Naturally such changes destroyed many a coral reef as they were gradually exposed to the air. With the protective reefs out of their way, the waves once more carved platforms from the exposed slopes of the mountain or reef base until new living reefs became established along the lower sea level. When accurate depth profiles are examined, submarine slopes have a staircase appearance, with most islands showing at least two to five narrow terraces, with the deepest at around 440 feet below the current sea level. These represent wave-cut platforms, and as such they record the long-term pauses during the glacial oscillations of advance and retreat. On the islands of Curacao, Aruba, and Bonaire a series of terraces have been elevated to a maximum height of about 250 feet, and the evidence can be examined—and the once flourishing corals—without getting your feet wet.

When sea level fell, drying reefs were eroded by storms and rain, and when sea level rose the reefs that had managed to form at the lower level were drowned as soon as they were removed from the warm, sunlit surface waters. Each time the sea level cycled, any of the old reef structure that remained intact could be recolonized, but it was sometimes in less-than-original condition. Tutuila island, for example, formed from a series of rifts and subsequent dissection has given it a rather tortuous profile. As the island subsided around 400 feet, bays were formed and waves breached the southern wall of a large central caldera, forming the natural harbor at Pago Pago. This subsidence also produced an extensive barrier reef, but during the glacial periods these reefs were repeatedly exposed and eroded. Now only scattered remnants of the barrier reef complex remain, but a healthy fringing reef survives along the modern coastline.

Other evidence of glacial changes in sea level are found exposed in regions not subjected to uplift. Roughly 125,000 years ago, and again more recently, sea level was higher than it is today, and waves cut small cliffs and platforms along the exposed shores of most of the tropical Pacific islands. This elevated shore bench has proved to be ideal for paving, and with minimal effort many islands have a ready-made coastal highway. On Oahu, in the Hawaiian islands, a large embayment enclosed a coral reef and lagoon when sea level was around 25 feet higher than it is today. When sea level fell to its present level this region was exposed, and then filled with additional debris washed down from the surrounding mountains. The resulting plain, which encloses a small vestige of the original embayment, is the site of Pearl Harbor and the surrounding communities.

Islands such as those of Hawaii or Bermuda, near the northern limits of coral growth, the Marquesas, which receive the waters of the cool Peru Current, or the Caribbean islands, which are strongly affected by conditions on the adjacent continents, faced additional problems during glacial periods due to a world-wide drop in sea-surface temperatures. The change was considerable, dropping 2 to 4°C in the north Pacific and Caribbean and 4 to 6°C around the Marquesas. These areas today have noticeably fewer species of corals than the tropical western Pacific, as we noted in Chapter 2. Sometime over the same period conditions altered around the Bahamas sufficiently to produce a shift from a coral-dominated reef system to an algal/calcareous precipitate system.

A number of more extensive crustal activities may make an island look rather more complicated than our model. Although a young island may not subside at all, later subsidence may be uneven or inter-

Aunu'u Island

Approx. scale
1" = 3 miles

N

mittent. If the volcano becomes active after a long pause, whether or not subsidence has occurred the avalanche of fresh lava will bury portions of the island and its reefs. This was the case on Tutuila, where a late eruption buried a portion of the southern reef complex. The crust may move as a unit, raising or lowering an island abruptly. Dead reefs are found on seamounts now thousands of feet beneath the surface, whereas the island of Eua (Tonga group) is an atoll with its reef flat now located 1,000 feet in the air. There are many other elevated islands in the tropics, and reefs over 900 feet high have been found in the Solomons, Fiji, and Tonga. There are many less strikingly elevated atolls in the tropics, as in the Phoenix Islands of the Pacific or the islands of Marie Galante, Sombrero, Antigua, Navassa, and a few of the Bahamas islands in the tropical Atlantic. A single island may pop up and down at a dizzying pace; for example, Fonuafoo (Falcon) Island in Tonga is said to have "changed size and form many times, and has at times disappeared" (SD Pub 80). Although it is still indicated on some of the charts of that area, it was completely submerged when I passed through the region in 1977.

The island of Nuku Hiva, one of the northern Marquesas islands, has had an interesting history that involved some extensive crustal movements. It formed as a large, single-vent volcanic shield. A broad caldera developed, and some time before the island subsided completely, additional volcanic activity produced a second volcanic cone within the original caldera. Eventually the island disappeared beneath the surface, and wave action scoured its upper surface into a submarine platform. Then crustal activity elevated the northern half of the island nearly 3,000 feet, and the once wave-swept platform became a lofty plateau. The southern portion of the island, including sections of both the caldera and its enclosed crater, separated along a long fracture or fault, and apparently failed to emerge above the surface. As a result, the southern coast of Nuku Hiva now consists of a line of near-

Figure 7–12 (opposite page). Tutuila Island
This sketch presents the general appearance of the island and its off-lying submarine platform and reef structures. Figure 7–1 presents wind frequency and directional information for this island. (Black areas: altitudes over 1,000 feet; coarse stippled areas: altitudes between 200 and 1,000 feet; white areas: sea level to 200 feet in elevation; fine stippled areas: remnants of barrier reef; broken lines: edge of submarine platform.) 1: Pago Pago harbor (see also Figure 7–5). 2: typical fringing reef (see also Figure 7–7). 3: fringing/barrier reef (see also Figure 7–9). 4: large isolated stack (see also Figure 7–6). 5: lava field over older reef (see text).

vertical cliffs. Around 300 feet of subsidence has occurred since the elevation, and when entering the principal harbor at Taio Hae you are sailing into the younger crater. The less popular anchorages at Comptroller's Bay and Taie Oa represent the eastern and western entrances into the older, larger caldera.

Similar reemergence and faulting is found elsewhere in the Marquesas group, and also in the Hawaiian islands. The islands of Lanai and Kahoolawe have plateaus 1,200 feet above sea level, which may have been cut by waves; the appearance of Oahu and the windward cliffs of Molokai are graphic examples of faulting. Other instructive cases can be seen in Figure 7–14.

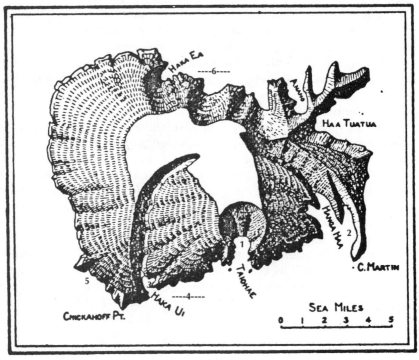

(a)

(b)

(c)

(d)

(e)

Figure 7–13. Nuku Hiva Island
(a) On Nuku Hiva, one of the Marquesas Islands, the effects of elevation and faulting are very apparent. 1: Taio Hae Bay, inside of younger crater. 2: Comptroller's Bay (east) and 3: Tai Oa Bay (west), which represent the remains of the older crater. 4: exposed and cliffed coast (see (c)). 5: sheltered coast with low rainfall (see (d)). 7: sheltered coast with high rainfall (see (e)). (b) sketch of Nuku Hiva Island from the south, showing the flattened summit. (c), (d), (e) are photographs taken from the locations indicated in part (a).

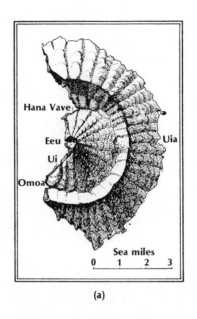

(a)

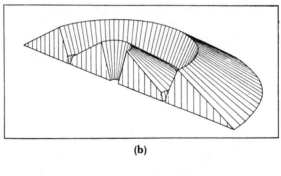

(b)

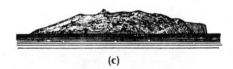

(c)

Figure 7–14. Other islands in the tropics that show evidence of reemergence and/or downfaulting
(a) Topographic sketch of Fatuhiva Island (Marquesas). (b) Diagrammatic sketch of an island of the type of Fatuhiva. The moat between inner and outer craters is represented as having been deepened by streams, and its end embayed by subsidence. Otherwise the effects of marine and subaerial erosion are ignored. (c) Sketch of Fatuhiva Island from the north, showing the volcano slopes on the eastern and northern sides, and the steep or precipitous western coast. (d) Sketch of Hivaoa Island (Marquesas Islands). The extent of the plateau is not known accurately. (e) Sketch of Tahuata Island (Marquesas Islands). (f) Bird's-eye diagram of Oahu, Hawaii.

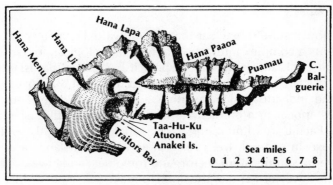

(d)

(e)

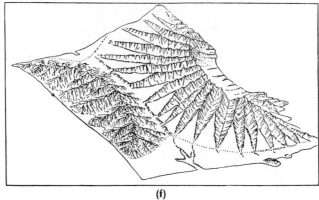

(f)

193

By now it should be clear that the individual character of an island represents a complex interaction between geological, meteorological, and biological factors. In this respect it is curious that island *groups* exist that share a remarkable number of features. Moreover, in many cases the individual islands within a group will differ, but the differences appear in a predictable fashion. For example, islands in the tropical Pacific are often found in lines that trend roughly southeast to northwest. In general, the youngest and highest islands are found in the extreme southeastern sector, and the oldest and lowest are located at the northwestern end of the line. To make sense out of this we must look more closely at just what causes volcanic eruptions and crustal movements. These topics form the basis for Chapter 8, "Island Arcs and Chains."

Chapter Eight
Island Arcs and Chains

The idea that the world's land masses could be fitted together like an enormous jigsaw puzzle is not a new one. In the seventeenth century the rough contours of western Africa and South America were known, and the suggestion made that the two had been separated by the Great Flood. This "catastrophic theory" persisted through the nineteenth century, with embellishments to include the birth of the moon from the floor of the Pacific Ocean. By the early 1900s several calculations had shown that continental and oceanic rocks differed in density, with the continental elements being relatively light. Other investigations had shown that the continental rocks extended farther beneath the surface, and it was generally accepted that the solid crust was floating on some deeper layers of molten rock. This idea of dynamic floating was called *isostasy*, which received additional attention when researchers in northern Europe demonstrated that the retreat of heavy glaciers was being followed by a rapid rise or rebound of that portion of the continent.

Over the next twenty years several investigators, championed by Alfred Wegener, proposed that all the modern continents had once been joined together in a single super-continent named *Pangaea*. Biological and geological evidence was mustered to support this theory, not just a simple recounting of the coastal similarities. This theory of continental drift generated some violent arguments, as most of the proponents were in Europe and most critics lived in the United States. (You could say they had drifted apart!) Until the mid-1950s the critics held the upper hand, for no one could manage to explain how a continent of solid materials could move through or over an even more dense ocean floor. The geographic evidence was seen merely as coincidence, and the biological data was held to be the result of land bridges that had conveniently subsided without a trace.

The first chink in the conservative armor appeared when a solid ridge of undersea mountains was traced right down the center of the Atlantic Ocean. Something strange was obviously going on down there. Since that time geology has gone through a revolution compar-

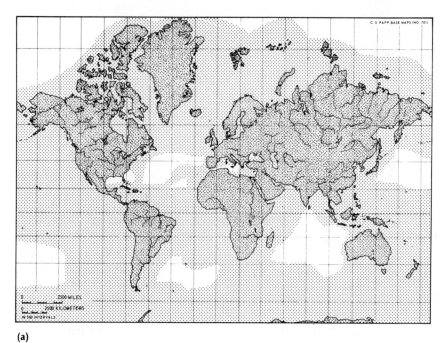

(a)

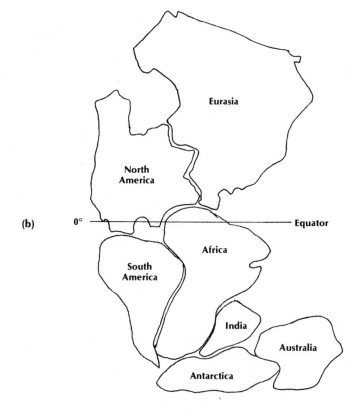

(b)

able to the reorganization of astronomy after Copernicus or biology after Darwin. By 1965 the modern theory of continental drift had won over a majority of geologists, and the years that followed have witnessed the (almost) unconditional surrender of the rest. No one really had any choice, faced with the results of coastal surveys, satellite mapping, laser technology, computer profiles, radioactive datings, and other new techniques all pointing in the same direction. This does *not* mean that today's interpretation of the theory is etched in stone. We have only begun to grasp the mechanics and forces involved, and although we have no idea *why* such things happen, at least we can prove that they do happen. With this in mind I will not waste space providing you with details demonstrating that the earth's crust really does float and move. Any reader who still harbors doubts when this chapter closes should consult the Additional Readings list at the back of this book. What's important here is that the concepts of modern geology can help explain some interesting aspects of island structure and history that you might otherwise miss. In Chapter 7 you looked at the life history of a typical mid-ocean volcano, and then considered several variations on the basic theme. In this chapter we will broaden our perspective to explain regional patterns of variation and discuss the formation of other kinds of volcanoes and volcanic islands.

The information gathered by modern geologists has resulted in significant deviations from Wegener's ideas about continental drift. The most interesting bit of information is that the mass of a continent is not separated from the adjacent ocean floor. Instead, the two are firmly attached, and the entire complex is called a *plate*. The earth's crust is currently fragmented into about six large plates and many smaller ones (which we will ignore for the most part). All these plates are in complex motion with respect to one another. What controls their movement? Well, we know that oceanic rock is continually being formed along ridges in the ocean floor, like the mid-Atlantic ridge, where molten materials are forced to the surface. The plates on either side move away from these ridges. You might then wonder why molten lava is appearing along such restricted formations and not popping up at random all over the surface of the planet.

Figure 8–1 (opposite page). Two opposing views of earth's history (a) map of the world, showing the combined area of land bridges that several authors postulated for the Cretaceous and Tertiary, up to 1913. As can be seen, hardly any ocean bottom remained after all the postulated land bridges had been superimposed on the map. (b) the supercontinent of Pangaea as envisioned by modern geologists.

Compressed by gravity and heated by pressure and radiation, the earth's core is extremely dense and hot. Although the very center is probably solid, it is surrounded by superheated molten metals. This layer is in turn surrounded by a mantle of molten rock, called *magma*, which underlies the relatively thin but solid crust of the planet. The mantle is heated from below, and even though molten rock is rather dense and viscous it still must behave like other fluids. Hot magma rises, and cold magma sinks, and with a little imagination you should be able to envision great molten currents moving slowly beneath the crust in giant advection cells. This should sound familiar, because we talked about the movements of another material heated from below when we looked at the formation of wind systems in Chapter 1. Volcanic ridges thus form where hot magma wells up and breaches the relatively thin and cool crust. "Thin" is almost too massive a term for the crust, as the oceanic crust has an average thickness of about four miles, and continental crust an average of 28 miles, whereas the earth's diameter is about *8,000* miles. In any event, since molten magma, as lava, is continually reaching the surface, piling up, and solidifying, the entire area could theoretically rise to the surface, but in fact this does not ordinarily occur. This is because the two sides of the ridge continually move away from the centerline. The two sides of a volcanic ridge thus represent the growing edges of two separate crustal plates, and the height of the ridge reflects how fast the magma is finding its way to the surface and also how fast the new ocean floor is moving away to either side. Europe and North America, attached to plates on either side of the mid-Atlantic ridge, have been moving apart for roughly 180 million years. Another long ridge is located in the eastern Pacific, known as the East Pacific Rise, and there are several others scattered around the planet. All are sites where new ocean floor is being created and plates are growing and moving. We know that the earth isn't expanding like an inflating balloon, so something else must either be destroying or altering oceanic materials elsewhere on the globe. This hypothesis is supported by the fact that there are continental rocks that are billions of years old, but the oldest ocean floor formed less than 200 million years ago. Let's develop another manageable model, so we can examine the situation more carefully.

I will suggest that we visit an earth shaped like a beer can, which is covered with nothing but ocean and oceanic crust. There are only two plates in the crust, and they intersect at opposite sides of the can. One seam becomes an active volcanic ridge, where new ocean floor is produced. The ridge grows, and as the local crust is loaded the pressures of gravity, subsidence, and movement of the underlying magma away from the ridge all work to drive the two plates apart. At the opposite side of the can, the pressures build as the two edges are pressed more firmly together. Eventually some critical limit is reached, and one of the plates is forced to ride up over the other. The defeated plate is said to be *subducted*. This subduction lessens the resistance to movement, because compression along the plate edges is greatly reduced and the plates can move away from the volcanic ridge and toward the area of subduction. As this occurs the subducting plate is gradually driven into the mantle below. Where it bends to begin its descent, a deep oceanic trench is created. As it descends, the subducting plate is heated and the plate edge begins to melt. The lower portions of the plate become areas of intense magma activity. In addition to recycling the lava of the ocean floor, the remelting process incorporates sea water and marine sediments as well, and because of this odd mixture of ingredients the magma formed in this region is quite distinct from that which wells up along the volcanic ridge.

Subduction is not a gentle process. The subducting plate resists such bending, and there is always considerable friction between the opposing plates. The result is that the subducting plate moves in fits and starts, and each time the pressures are released by plate movement there are earthquakes that shake the crust around the trench. The plate that is *not* subducting does not have an easy time of it either. Its edge is still subjected to some compression and jolted by earthquakes at the same time. Fractures appear along the edge facing the trench and volcanoes form parallel to the trench. These are created because the magma that forms as the subducting plate is remelted is less dense—hence lighter—than the surrounding materials.

Volcanic activity continues, building up a long line of islands, then joining them together to form a super-island of volcanic materials. As more lava reaches the surface, the local crust is loaded with more and more weight. The principles of isostasy result in subsidence, which effectively means that as the growing volcanoes extend higher into the air they are also extending deeper into the mantle below. The rocks and minerals nearest the magma are heated, compressed, partially melted, and reformed. The ever loftier peaks are eroded by rain, scoured by winds, and the sediments produced are washed over the lower slopes. There they accumulate, are baked, compressed, and form new and even lighter combinations. In essence our super-island is becoming more continental in structure.

Now let's refer to Figure 8–2, where things are becoming more interesting. A second advection cell becomes established right under the center of the super-island. A line of volcanoes appears, then a ridge

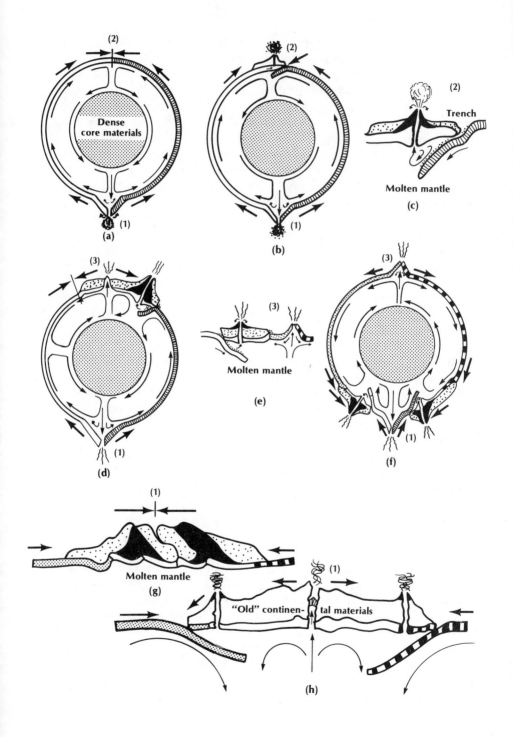

(2)

Dense
core materials

(1)

(a)

(2)

(1)

(b)

(2)

Trench

Molten mantle

(c)

(3)

(1)

(d)

(3)

Molten mantle

(e)

(3)

(1)

(f)

(1)

Molten mantle

(g)

(1)

"Old" continen-
tal materials

(h)

that emits magma characteristic of mid-ocean ridges. Ultimately the entire island is torn in two, and one fragment is driven out over the subducting oceanic plate. The other fragment faces a dilemma because both edges of this plate are bordered by volcanic ridges. Because the lighter, more continental rocks are too light to subduct, the impasse is resolved when the oceanic portion of the plate fractures and turns beneath the continental fragment.

At this point we have four separate plates, two oceanic and two bearing continental-type materials. Let's go a bit further and depict a form of oscillating system. The growing plates bordered by continental fragments are increasing in size as they move over the subducting oceanic plates. Material is added along the lines of volcanoes facing the trenches, and redistributed by subsequent erosion. Eventually the two new plates collide over the volcanic ridge that has been producing the subducting oceanic plates. The collision further alters the character of the continental materials. Neither can subduct, so what used to be seaward volcanoes and continental margins are compressed and folded to create mountain ranges. Pressures continue to build until

Figure 8–2 (opposite page). Crustal events on a beer-can world
(a) *starting point:* a midocean ridge at (1) is enlarging the plates, which are being compressed at (2). (white plate: A; hatched plate: B; fine arrows indicate currents in the molten mantle; coarse arrows indicate tendency for plate movement). (b) *Step 1:* Pressure is released somewhat through the subduction of plate B. A trench is created in the process. (c) *Step 1:* Enlarged view of region (2). Compression of plate A has produced a low range of hills, over which fresh lava is erupting from the turbulent mantle below. Subaerial erosion is reshaping and redistributing these materials, and under the increased load this portion of plate A is settling deeper into the mantle. (black areas: erupted lava; stippled area: "continental" rocks). (d) *Step 2:* A second advection cells forms and fractures the young continent, driving one fragment over plate B and increasing compression at point (3). (e) *Step 3:* This is an enlarged view of region (3). Plate A has fractured along the continental margin, forming a new trench and a new line of volcanoes parallel to it. This midocean ridge is producing two new plates, plate C (grey) and plate D (striped). (f) *Step 4:* The plates bearing continental fragments are about to collide, riding over the ocean ridge at (1) in the process. (g) *Step 5:* The region at (1) has been enlarged and turned rightside-up for your convenience. The two continental fragments are being combined and compressed. (h) *Step 6* (oriented as in g): Pressures are eased as plates C and D fracture and subduct. The old volcanic ridge has split the continent, and the fragments are being driven toward the opposite pole as plates E and F grow and spread. You can now return to Step 3 and repeat as often as you like. (black areas: newly erupted lava; stippled areas: new continental materials)

something gives, and the dense oceanic portions of the plates on either side buckle and subduct beneath the continental mass. This eases compression, and now the upwelling magma beneath the center of the continent creates a line of volcanoes, then a volcanic ridge that is producing more oceanic crust. This splits the continent yet again, driving the enlarged fragments out over the subducting plates on their way to an eventual collision at the opposite pole.

These movements, disruptions, subductions, and recombinations could be continued indefinitely. In many respects this is precisely what has been going on for the past two billion years! But before we look at the real world in this light, we should pause to summarize the primary features illustrated by our model, as follows:

1. Ocean floor is created at a volcanic ridge that emits a characteristic type of dense magma (lava).

2. When two sections of ocean floor collide head on, they are both compressed and one or the other will subduct to form a deep ocean trench.

3. The border of the nonsubducting plate will be marked by earthquakes and volcanoes that eject a lava different in composition from that in (1).

4. Continental rocks are the result of repeated erosion, compression, remelting, and reforming of the lava produced in (3). They are lighter than oceanic materials.

5. A continent will grow along its seaward edge where an oceanic plate subducts and magma is released by volcanoes parallel to the trench.

6. When two continents collide, neither subducts and the resulting compression produces mountain ranges.

7. Continents may grow, shrink, or change shape through combination or fragmentation.

8. Continental rocks continue to age because they are too light to subduct, whereas those of the ocean floor have a finite life span. Oceanic rocks are continually being created at volcanic ridges and destroyed at ocean trenches.

All that must be done to approach reality is to recognize that (a) new ocean floor can be forming at different rates along many ridges all at the same time, and (b) these processes are underway on the surface of a sphere, not a simple cylinder. The effects of these variations are more easily seen than explained, so I will proceed with an examination of the structure of the Pacific and Atlantic oceans.

The long East Pacific Rise (EPR, for short) is the site of active ocean floor formation in that ocean. It extends from the high southern latitudes in a long, crescentic track until ending abruptly just off the North American coast. As in our model, the plates on either side of this rise are growing and new portions of each plate are moving away from the central ridge.

The large plate that extends to the west is the Pacific plate, the only one of the six principal plates that does not include a sizable portion of a continent. The general movement of the plate is shown in Figure 8–3. To the north it dives beneath the Alaskan portion of the North American plate, descending into the broad arc of the Aleutian trench. As you might expect, samples collected from the ocean floor in this area are the oldest in the Pacific, for they have traveled quite a distance since their formation roughly 150 million years ago. The same may be said for the northwestern limits of the plate where it dives to destruction at the Kurile, Japan, and Marianas trenches.

The fate of the northern portion of the EPR can be reconstructed fairly easily. Driven by the pressures that split Pangaea and opened the Atlantic some 180 million years ago, the North American plate has overridden the Pacific plate and portions of the East Pacific Rise in the process. This was not a peaceful undertaking. The resistance and compression buckled the western portion of the continent, creating the Sierra Nevada/Cascade range and perhaps the Rocky Mountains. This event must have drastically affected living conditions on the continent—North America moves west, compression crunching its coastline, and mountains rising. The entire continent elevates slightly as a result, causing an arm of the sea to retreat, exposing the lowlands of the interior. With these waters removed, daily temperature fluctuations become more severe, and at the same time the western ranges are blocking the prevailing winds. Weather patterns are changed for the entire hemisphere. Winters become more severe and the eastern portions of the continent become less humid as the moisture condenses over the windward slopes of the new mountain range. All these factors were probably involved in the elimination of the large marine and terrestrial reptiles, which of course paved the way for the evolution of writers and readers.

When North America finally reached the EPR, the seaward trench was obliterated. The activity along what was once a volcanic rise then interacted with the pressures driving America west, creating a sliding, shearing motion that began forcing portions of California, now fused to the Pacific plate, toward the Aleutian trench. At this time the volcanic islands that were strung along the continental side of the trench were compressed into the body of the continent to form the California Coastal Ranges. One portion of the northern EPR remains fragmented off the coasts of Oregon and Washington, and reminders of the tre-

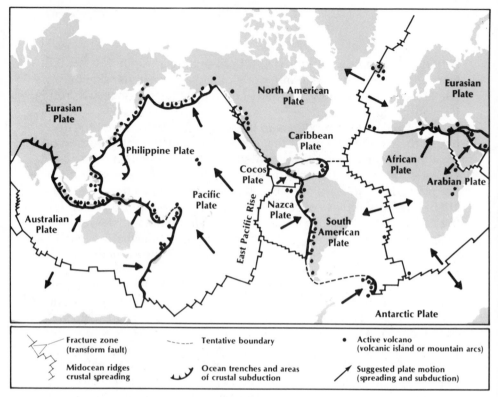

Figure 8–3. Crustal plates and the structure of the ocean floor.

mendous forces involved in the collision between volcanic rise and continental mass appeared in the recent eruptions of Mount Saint Helens.

The situation in the southern Pacific is a bit more complicated. To the east of the EPR a fragment of the Antarctic plate is subducting before the advance of South America, and the attendant compression and vulcanism has produced the lofty Andes range. To the west of the EPR, the Pacific plate is engaged in a complex battle with the Australian plate. At the deep trench east of the Tongan Islands the Pacific plate dives beneath the Australian plate, whereas south of the Solomon Islands the Pacific plate emerges unscathed, and it is the Australian plate that slides into oblivion. Near the bight, where these two processes converge, there are several poorly described plate fragments that jostle one another about.

The Atlantic was born when the supercontinent of Pangaea began to break apart along the line of the Mid-Atlantic Ridge roughly 180 million years ago. It continues to enlarge because Europe and North

America are moving apart at around three inches a year. There are four major plates in the Atlantic floor (see Figure 8–3) and one small plate fragment. The latter is called the Caribbean plate, and it underlies most of the tropical Atlantic islands of special interest to us. To the east, the North and South American plates subduct beneath the Caribbean plate. To the north the Caribbean plate is sliding along the edge of the North American plate. To the south, the Caribbean plate is all but fused with the South American continent, but there is some shear/sliding movement between the two. On the western front, a small plate fragment east of the EPR is subducting beneath the Caribbean plate along the western coast of Central America. The situation is further complicated by the fact that there are two plate pieces in the area, one beneath the Panamanian isthmus and a second supporting a small portion of the South American coast and the adjacent sea floor. The geological history of this entire region has been very complex, and we still lack a complete and satisfactory reconstruction of the fine points.

If you were able to see the floors of the Pacific or Atlantic oceans you would see a few additional details. As indicated in Figure 8–3, a volcanic rise appears to consist of a series of fragments, each separated by long fractures or faults that run at right angles to the axis of the ridge. The rate of magma release differs slightly, both in terms of the time of activity and the amount of lava released, so there are relative differences in the rates of movement along either side of these faults. The fractures, called transform faults, are one of the results of operating the system on the surface of a sphere rather than on a beer can. Similar factors are involved in determining that the major subduction zones at trenches always seem to curve along their length.

Before going any further, take a moment to consider what all these movements, rearrangements, and collisions have meant for living organisms. We have already mentioned the climatic changes that may accompany mountain building ashore, but the movements also directly affect marine organisms. The tropical fauna of the Atlantic is an excellent example of the interplay underway between the physical environment, geological processes, and natural selection. Following the break-up of Pangaea, tropical marine organisms were free to travel from the Indo-Pacific region through the Mediterranean and into the tropical Atlantic, because Africa did not collide with Europe to close the Mediterranean until around 65 million years ago. In Chapters 2 and 3 we noted the difficulties facing planktonic larvae drifting east across the tropical Pacific as far as Hawaii or the Marquesas. Crossing the expanse of open water between these islands and the coast of North or South America is even more difficult because there are no island way-stations. Biologists refer to the intervening waters as the East Pacific Barrier, and only a few of the shallow water organisms found along the tropical west coast of the Americas arrived there from the Central Pacific. The rest either moved into the region from cooler coastal waters to the north or south or reached the western coast from the Caribbean in some fashion. The latter conclusion was reached before plate tectonics was considered fashionable and is based on the fact that the tropical western coast of the Americas has twice the number of genera in common with the Caribbean as it has with the western Pacific. Geological evidence now has shown that the small plate fragment that bears the isthmus of Panama only sealed off the Caribbean 1 to 2 million years ago, and that before that time tropical organisms were free to pass between the Atlantic and Pacific. Natural selection underway since that closure has resulted in the evolution of twin species on either side of Central America from common ancestral populations. As a semi-enclosed body of water, the Caribbean was subsequently affected by the temperature changes that accompanied the glacial periods, perhaps decreasing the total number of species on the reefs.

Our descriptions, definitions, and qualifications are at an end, and we can proceed with our investigation of island formation and structure. In broad terms we can sort the tropical island groups into five discrete categories according to their mode of formation. Each merits separate treatment.

Category I An *island arc* is created when subduction is underway beneath an oceanic plate or the submerged margin of a continent. The curve of this arc follows the curve of the trench nearby. In general island arcs are sites of frequent earthquake activity, cycles of subsidence and emergence, and active volcanism, with volcanoes scattered throughout the arc. The erupted lava differs from that produced at volcanic ridges, and the volcanoes themselves are steeper and more sharply defined than the volcanic shields described in Chapter 7. All the volcanic activity is not confined to exposed volcanoes, and the ocean floor near an island arc is usually littered with seamounts, shoals, and other hazards to navigation. With these guidelines in hand we should be able to identify the principal island arcs within our areas of interest.

In the southwestern Pacific, the Pacific plate moves beneath the Australian plate along the Tonga trench. On the Australian side of the trench lies the island arc of Tonga, produced by the volcanic activity that accompanies the melting and recombination of plate materials and their overlying sediments deep in the mantle below. As you may recall from Chapter 7, this is an extremely active area, and the crust may move enough to elevate or submerge entire islands. Small earthquakes are common, and larger ones are not unusual. Near the northern limits of the Tonga trench, extremely complex forces are at work. Seven hundred and fifty miles to the west the Australian plate is subducting beneath the Pacific plate, the reverse of what is happening along the Tonga trench. The Fiji islands lie in between, within this zone of transition. They are perched atop a portion of the crust that is being subjected to enormous pressures, twisting, flexing, and bending. Volcanic activity within the region has produced the approximately 900 islands in the group. Many of the islands show signs of having been uplifted at one time or another during their histories, and the crust is rising and falling not just within the Fijian and Tongan islands, but also at some distance away. The eastern Fijian, or Lau, group of islands consists mainly of low islands and atolls, whereas the larger western land masses have substantial barrier reefs. Relatively recent volcanic activity has occurred in the western sector, but there are no volcanoes erupting in Fiji at the present time.

Farther west, the island arcs of the New Hebrides, Banks, Santa Cruz, and Solomon islands are found along the Pacific side of the trenches. In the New Hebrides the volcanoes of Tana and Aneityum islands are active, and there are several other peaks that are candidates for future eruptions. The New Hebrides are relatively young islands, or at least there has been sufficient overflow of new lava to prevent the development of extensive reefs along the shores of most islands in the group. The Banks Islands are even younger in appearance, scarcely dissected and surrounded by narrow fringing reefs. The Santa Cruz arc is more varied, with one active volcano (Vanikole I.) and other islands that have subsided to produce fringing and barrier reefs. There are many poorly charted reefs and shoals in the region. The Solomon Islands include seven large islands and twenty to thirty smaller ones. Several of these islands support active volcanoes, and there are fumaroles (sites where hot gases are released) and hot springs scattered throughout the islands. Most islands are encircled by massive reefs, there are numerous shoals, banks, and pinnacles, and the region has only been superficially surveyed. Some reefs in the area have been elevated repeatedly, and the region is in a state of seismic unrest.

We have now entered the northern Pacific. Along the continental margin of the Marianas trench lies the Marianas island arc. These islands are all high and volcanic, and there are no atolls in the arc. Active volcanoes are found on several of the islands. Continuing north along the line of trenches we encounter the Volcano and Bonin islands, the islands of Japan, the Kurile Islands, and finally the Aleutian island arc. As all of these lie outside our primary area of concern, I will only note that they follow the pattern of shoals, earthquakes, volcanoes, and general instability that has typified the island arcs considered above.

Much of the northeastern portion of the EPR has been altered following the collision with North America, and along with the obliteration of the coastal trench the attendant volcanic arc was incorporated into the body of California. South of the equator no volcanic arcs have been produced because the trench is located directly off the coast of South America, and the volcanic activity is appearing within the coastal Andes range. So even without island arcs, the eastern boundary of the Pacific is marked by earthquakes and volcanoes. In circling the Pacific we have defined the Pacific "Ring of Fire," an area bordered primarily by trenches, and invariably marked by intense volcanic and/or seismic activity.

The Caribbean has a ring of fire of its own, and this area is one of the most seismically active portions of the planet. Most of the islands in the region formed as island arcs, although due to the complex movements of the plate and its neighbors all of the arcs are not matched with trenches at the present time. The Windward and Leeward Islands, stretching from Grenada in the south to Anguilla in the north, form a fine example of an island arc, however. The islands are young, somewhere under 50 million years of age, and lie along the edge of the Caribbean plate in a curve that follows the trend of the trench just to the east.

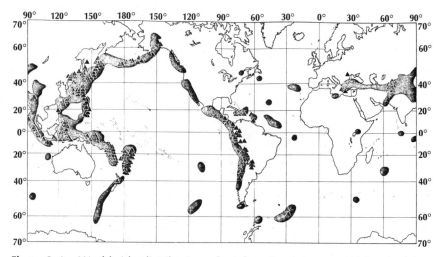

Figure 8–4. Worldwide distribution of earthquakes between 1904 and 1952. Deep earthquakes are indicated by triangles, shallow ones by shading. Compare with Figure 8–3 and note the correlation with plate boundaries, as discussed in the text.

Many of the islands harbor active volcanoes, earthquakes are common occurrences, and many of the islands show signs of having been uplifted and/or submerged at times during their histories. Continuing along the curve leads you into the Greater Antilles, where the Virgin Islands, Puerto Rico, Jamaica, Hispaniola, southern Cuba, and the Cayman Islands are found along either trenches or troughs; northern Cuba may have formed in association with a trench/subduction system that was obliterated as Cuba collided with the Bahamas bank. Completing our circuit brings us off the coast of Venezuela to the Netherlands Antilles, which are thought to have formed as a small plate (which includes a portion of the South American coast) moved to the north over the subducting Caribbean plate.

So far so good, but a quick look at the maps included in Chapter 9 will be enough to remind you that we have only managed to account for about half of the islands in the tropical Pacific and Atlantic. Obviously there must be other processes at work, processes that function far from the edges of an individual plate. In Chapter 7 we focused attention on the history of typical mid-ocean volcanoes and volcanic shields, and now we must address their mode of formation. Let's make one key assumption that is not unreasonable, that is, that the deep mantle is not always heated exactly evenly. This would mean that there would be localized regions of more intense heating that we will call *hotspots*.

Now suppose a hotspot were located somewhere beneath the axis of a volcanic ridge. Because more heat is provided to the deep mantle at this point, the upwelling of magma is increased beneath a localized portion of the ridge. The movement of the ridge materials away from the center is relatively slow, so magma piles up over the hotspot. Soon a volcano reaches the surface, or perhaps two, one on each plate. As the entire rise continues to produce new oceanic materials, the plates move away from the midline and the volcano(es) are carried farther away from the center of the hotspot. Eventually the volcano will have moved so far from the ridge axis that it is cut off from the source of magma and volcanic activity ends. Shortly thereafter, the upwelling magma over the hotspot produces a second volcano (or pair) over the ridge. With time we find a third, a fourth, and so on, as depicted in Figure 8–5. As long as the hotspot remains in place, and the plates move away at a steady pace, these islands will string out in a nice even line or chain oriented at right angles to the axis of the volcanic rise.

Category II This group consists of those island formed by the "hotspot-on-a-ridge" method. Many islands in the Atlantic formed in this fashion, the most famous being Iceland, which is situated right

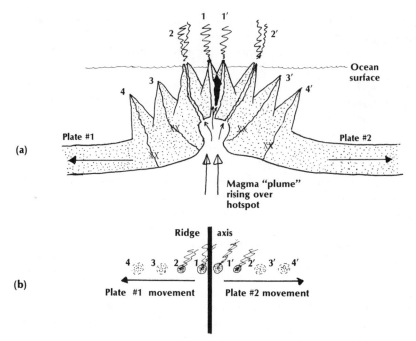

Figure 8–5. The effects of a hotspot under a volcanic rise
(a) This sketch presents a diagrammatic illustration of the formation of an island chain over a rise due to the activity of a hotspot beneath the ridge axis. Volcanoes are forming in pairs as the plates continue to move apart. (black: ridge axis; XX: vent closed.) (b) The events in (a) as seen from above the ocean surface. (dashed outline: submerged seamount).

over the Mid-Atlantic Ridge (MAR) and growing larger and larger as time passes. Farther to the south, closer to our area of investigation, the islands of Bermuda, Ascension, and St. Helena arose over the MAR. In addition to the exposed islands, there are many submerged seamounts that extend to either side of the ridge in a symmetrical array, and that have been useful in reconstructing the "fit" of the continents in Pangaea. In the Pacific, such islands are few and far between, and only the islands of Sala-Y-Gomez and Easter Island in the southeastern Pacific have been suggested as likely candidates for membership. The hotspot approach would be more useful in analyzing the Pacific islands if we could make another adjustment in our model. If a hotspot can appear under a ridge, it could just as easily appear someplace else, so let's see what happens when we place it under the center of a plate.

The localized upwelling of magma weakens and then erodes the overlying crust. Eventually it reaches the surface and voilá, we have a mid-ocean volcano. The volcanic ridge that created the plate is still active, so the plate keeps moving, but the hotspot is located deep in the molten layers below, and it stays put. Soon the magma pocket that feeds our volcano has moved, and its supply of fresh lava is cut off. It might continue to erupt for a time, because any trapped magma is still under considerable pressure, but in the long run the volcano is done for. The hotspot plume is still active, so when the next weak spot appears or is created in the crust a second volcano will arise, and then a third, and so forth until an entire chain has been formed.

Category III This sizable collection of island groups includes all those that clearly have formed from isolated hotspots. What are their distinguishing characteristics? First of all, the youngest islands are closest to the hotspot, and the oldest farthest away. Second, each island represents a load on the underlying crust, so it begins to subside as it moves away from the hotspot. If all processes continue at a steady pace, the highest island will be closest to the hotspot, and in waters that support coral reefs we should find a steady gradation through fringing reefs, barrier reefs, almost-atolls, atolls, and finally guyots as we move farther along the chain.

This is a rather simplified setup, because we have made two oft-violated assumptions: that the hotspot always produces lava at a constant rate and that the plate always moves at a steady pace. Before going any further we need to consider the effects of such variations on our model. Let us increase and decrease the activity of the hotspot so that the amount of magma erupted varies. When the flow rate is high, a large and lofty island is created, and when it is low a smaller island forms. If the plate is moving at a steady pace the islands will each be a different size, but the distance between the peaks will remain constant. This should be the case even if lava flow is sufficient to join several peaks into an elongate super-island. Suppose the hotspot quits altogether? The chain will continue to move away, and through subsidence the islands will settle gradually, potentially even forming a chain consisting entirely of atolls or guyots. Regardless of their location and general appearance, the relative ages of the islands within the chain will reveal their common and sequential origins.

What if there are two or more vents leading from a common magma chamber? Then you'll find several islands that formed roughly simultaneously, parallel to the axis of the chain. How about a situation where the hotspot remains constant, but the rate of plate movement changes? The islands will once again vary in size, because when the plate movement is slower the islands will be over the plume for a longer period. If the plate moves very slowly, even small volcanoes

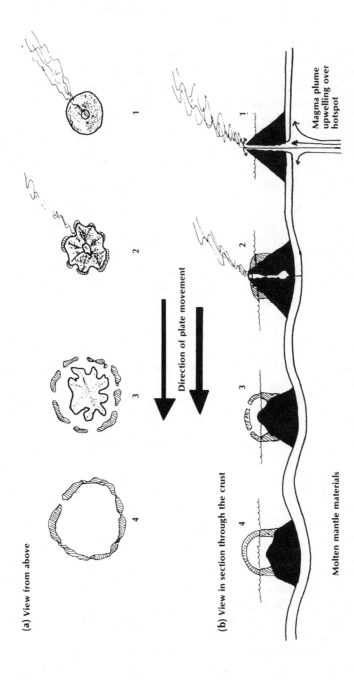

(a) View from above

1   2   3   4

Direction of plate movement

(b) View in section through the crust

1   2   3   4

Molten mantle materials

Magma plume upwelling over hotspot

Figure 8–6. Formation of an island chain over a midplate hotspot. Note reef development, subsidence, and embayment. (1: island building; 2: fringing reef; 3: barrier reef; 4: atoll; hatching: coral reef)

may overlap to form a compound island. In any case, the volcanic peaks will then be relatively close together, and if the plate picks up the pace the islands will become both smaller and farther apart.

Finally, what happens if the plate changes direction? In our model we could accomplish this by shutting down the original ridge and starting another at right angles to it. Because the hotspot is unaffected by such goings-on, islands will continue to form, but now they will string out in a new direction, once again perpendicular to the ridge axis. This is a particularly interesting point: Island chains must therefore represent a permanent record of the direction of movement of the plate that bears them! Even if we did not know where or when a volcanic rise was operating, the island chains could provide us with the information needed to back-calculate the direction of plate movement as it passed over a stationary hotspot. No doubt you are wondering about what might happen if the hotspot itself started moving around. For the moment we can safely ignore this possibility because it appears that the hotspots analyzed to date have held their present positions for at least 120 million years. You might also wonder if hotspots are phenomena limited to the mantle beneath ocean floors, and here the answer is a definite no. Out of 122 hotspots identified around the world, 57 percent are found beneath continents. How hotspots interact, perhaps to form volcanic ridges, is the subject of discussion in some of the Additional Readings listed at the back of the book.

We can now begin to examine Category III island chains in detail, starting with those of the tropical Pacific. We have already noted the direction of motion of the Pacific plate, which is roughly heading from SE at the EPR to NW at the Asian/Alaskan trench system. This is the trend or course line that should typify recent island chains formed by hotspot activity beneath the plate. The Hawaiian archipelago has been the most thoroughly examined island chain in the entire Pacific basin, so we had best begin there.

The Hawaiian Islands extend from the island of Hawaii to the submerged guyots at the farthest limits of the Leeward Islands almost 2,200 miles away. The island chain trends roughly SE to NW, active volcanoes are restricted to the southeastern portion of the group, and the islands get progressively older and lower as you travel west from the active volcano on the island of Hawaii. There are only two significant variations from our model that should concern us.

When the ages and positions of the islands are plotted, it becomes apparent that eruptions have occurred in pairs, with the two volcanoes separated by at least thirty miles. This can only be explained by assuming that the hotspot plume is quite broad, and that at least two vents

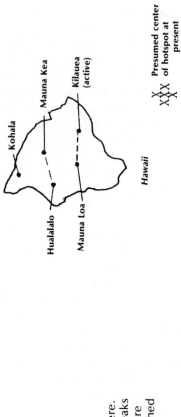
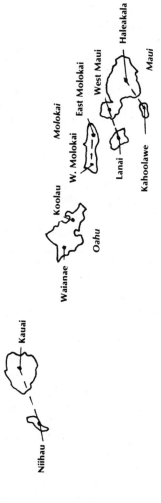

Figure 8–7. The Hawaiian archipelago
The inhabited islands of the chain are shown here.
Composite islands are listed in smaller type, individual peaks
are underlined, and peaks that were/are
active contemporaneously are connected by dashed
lines.

can be provided with magma at a given time. Research has indicated that the hotspot is roughly 180 miles in diameter, while the individual vents are each a mere twenty miles across. The second variation is the fact that both hotspot activity and the rate of plate movement have changed over time. How do we know this? The ages of the islands range from around 750,000 years for the island of Hawaii to roughly 46 million years for the submerged Koko Seamount near the tail end of the Leeward Islands. The consistent trend of the chain over this distance would indicate that the direction of plate movement has been fairly constant. But when you examine the ages of the volcanoes with the distance between the peaks you find that the rate of plate movement (distance covered per unit time) has been accelerating. The average rate of movement over the entire 40+ million year history of the chain has been under 5 inches per year, but the current rate may be considerably greater. At the same time you will find that the younger volcanoes are larger, and because plate motion has increased, the rate of lava flow must have increased even more over the same period. In fact, it has increased tenfold since the formation of Kauai 4.5 million years ago.

The Hawaiian chain is an exquisite example of a mid-ocean hotspot in action. By going between the inhabited islands of the chain you are, in a sense, traveling in time as well as space. Millions of years ago Kauai was not only located where the island of Hawaii is today, but it had the same stark, undissected landscape, and the same smooth shield form typical of recent, active volcanoes. By the same token Kauai now shows us the dissection, erosion, reefs, and embayments that will typify the island of Hawaii millions of years from now. Each island is like a frame from a movie about island history; the larger islands are separate frames spliced together. On composite islands like Maui you can stand in one spot and compare the effects of natural forces on two volcanic shields differing in age by 500,000 years.

Earlier we noted that the Koko Seamount, located near the end of the Hawaiian chain, dated at roughly 46 million years. Actually the Koko Seamount is not just the end of this story, but the beginning of another, for stretching NNW from Koko is a chain of submerged seamounts and guyots that extend all the way to the Aleutian trench. Although this line of submerged islands is called the Emperor chain, it quite clearly must represent a northern extension of the Hawaiian chain. This conclusion is borne out by the fact that radioactive dating shows a gradual increase in age along the chain, to an age of at least 70 million years for the Meiji Seamount near the northern end of the Emperor chain. We can only explain this by assuming that these volcanoes must have formed when the Pacific plate was moving on a more

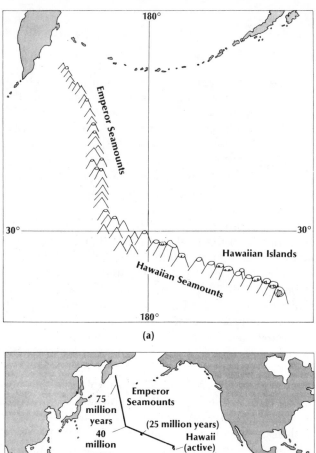

(a)

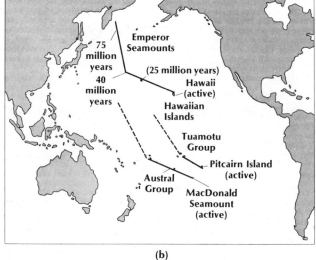

(b)

Figure 8–8. Alterations in the direction of plate movement as recorded by volcanic island chains in the Pacific
(a) Emperor seamount chain, a sequence substantiated by radioactive dating techniques. (b) Two other island chains that may have formed in similar fashions and at similar times; accurate dating has yet to be performed throughout these island groups.

northerly heading. Although more detailed research will provide additional bits of information, we can now comfortably state that from around 40 to at least 70 million years ago the Pacific plate was heading NNW. The reason for the change in direction 40 million years ago is still unknown, but the presence and character of the Emperor chain tells us that such a change did occur.

Grouping other island chains according to their rough orientation will therefore tell us something about the approximate ages of the member islands. This information is useful, because very few of the other Pacific isles have been examined in as great detail as have those of the Hawaiian chain. Pacific island chains younger than 40 million years should follow the approximate trend line of the Hawaiian islands, while those older should closely approximate that of the Emperor chain. I will designate the former as III(a) and the latter as III(b). Four tropical Pacific island chains are contemporaries of the Hawaiian chain, and included in Category III(a).

The axis of the Society islands extends from Tahiti'iti (elevation 4,300 feet; age 480,000 years) to the attached island of Tahiti (elevation 7,300 feet; age 650,000 years) through the nearby island of Moorea (elevation 4,000 feet; age 1.65 million years) and so forth along the chain until the atoll of Bellinghausen is reached, over 1,000 miles to the WNW. Subsidence has been more pronounced here than in Hawaii, and reef growth more prolific, so even the island of Tahiti supports a narrow barrier reef.

The Tuomotu Archipelago (sometimes spelled Tuamotu) lies several hundred miles to the east of the Societies. There are seventy-eight islands in the group, and they are oriented roughly parallel to the Hawaiian and Society islands. High islands are found in the southeastern portion of the chain, but they are few. The island of Pitcairn lies far to the southeast, near the current location of the hotspot, and it is volcanically active. Like the almost-atoll of Mangareva,* which is closer to the body of the chain, it is not a lofty island, and neither has peaks over 1,500 feet in height. Only Pitcairn is without organized reefs; Mangareva is an almost-atoll, and all the other islands to the north of Mangareva are atolls. The entire region is famous for its uncharted reefs and shoals, and bears the nickname "The Dangerous Archipelago" for good reason.

To the west of the Society islands lie the Austral and Cook island chains, which are separated politically but not geologically. The hotspot is now presumed to be located near the active MacDonald Seamount, and the chain extends roughly NW through Rapa, Taievavae,

*Mangareva is sometimes considered part of a subgroup, the Gambier Islands.

Tubae, Rurutu, and so on, until reaching the atoll of Palmerston. In general the islands become lower as one proceeds along the chain from Rapa (2,100 feet) to Palmerston (almost awash). Yet there are indications that some late elevation of the surrounding sea floor has occurred. Mauke Island has elevated reefs, and close by there are other islands with similar features. Mangaia Island, for example, now wears its barrier reef 200 feet above sea level. As with the Tuomotus we have very sketchy information to work with, and a more detailed chronological picture is impossible at the moment. In both chains there are more islands than one would expect were there but a single vent erupting at one time, and often it seems that there are shorter chains of islands that parallel the main body of the group. In any event, accurate soundings, surveys, and radioactive datings must be done before things can be sorted out as neatly as was possible for the Hawaiian chain.

The fourth island chain to be included in Category III(a) is the Galapagos islands. Because these islands are located east of the EPR, they are strung out in a different direction, with the youngest islands to the west. There are six large islands, nine smaller ones, and many pinnacles, spires, and seamounts. The large western islands of Isabella and Fernandina are high and actively volcanic. There are no atolls in the group, and because of the cool Peru Current there are few coral reefs anywhere in the chain.

Category III(b) will be used to group island chains that formed around the same time as the Emperor seamounts. In general these are older and lower, consisting solely of atolls and seamounts or guyots. The islands have few inhabitants, and there is little detailed information available concerning island age or structure. Despite these reservations, two chains have been suggested as representing northern extensions of III(a) chains, so I will discuss them briefly. The Ellice-Gilbert-Marshall island chain begins near Funafuti Atoll and extends roughly NNW for 1,600 miles before apparently ending near Bikini Atoll. This long series of atolls has been linked to the Austral-Cook island chain. Meanwhile, the islands scattered between Flint Island, 750 miles south of the equator, to Kingman Reef at latitude 6°N have been suggested as the northern predecessors of the Tuomotu chain. They are called the Line Islands.

Now I would dearly love to tell you that we have accounted for all of the tropical island groups at this point, but of course that isn't the case. We can lump the remaining islands into two additional categories. In general, we know less about these islands than about some of the groups we have already covered, and it is likely that there will be some shuffling into Categories I to III as more data become available.

Category IV The histories of these island groups are poorly understood, but they are the result of either hotspot activity or trench-associated vulcanism. Our crystal balls are a mite hazy about the details. In the Pacific most of the areas of confusion are found near especially active portions of the plate. The clustered islands of the Carolines are a good example. The group extends into the pocket formed between the Pacific plate and a fragment of the Eurasian plate. Altogether there are 570 islands scattered over roughly 20° of longitude. Research to date has shown that the Eastern Carolines, now part of the Federated States of Micronesia, can be attributed to the activity of a hotspot that we could include in Category III(a). The trend line runs from Kusaie Island (elevation 2,100 feet; age around 1 million years) through Truk Island, an almost-atoll roughly 12 million years old. It appears likely that further surveys will show that most of the rest of the eastern and central Caroline group formed in some similarly logical sequence, but there are too many islands in too small an area for me to try and guess what the pattern might be. (It has been proposed by some geologists that the region may represent a now extinct mid-ocean ridge, and that many of the islands formed over the ridge.)

A portion of the *western* Carolines, now part of the Federated States, and the Palau Islands seem to have formed in a different fashion. Ngulu and Yap Islands lie on the Asian side of the Yap trench, which appears to be a southern extension of the Marianas trench system. A separate mini-trench lies to the east of the Palau group. Thus it is possible that both Ngulu and Yap, as well as Palau, will ultimately be assigned to Category I.

The Samoan Islands of the tropical Pacific are generally accepted as having formed over a hotspot. Yet it does not fit the patterns established above for either Category III(a) or (b). In Samoa the islands to the east are lower, smaller, and more highly dissected, whereas it is the *western* islands that are larger, higher, more shield-like, and actively volcanic. Lava from Tutuila Island, one of the eastern members of the chain, has been dated at 3 to 12 million years, so certainly the plate was moving east to west at the time that island was forming. That leaves two possibilities, one being that the hotspot was widely active early in its career, and a large trapped pocket of magma was carried off by the westernmost island, Savai'i. Present eruptions would then represent releasing pressures from the trapped lava mass, but the western island would still be the oldest. The eastern islands would have formed later, and as hotspot activity faded it would have produced smaller and smaller islands. This is logical, but one is left wondering about the relationship between this proposed hotspot and that of the Austral-Marshall series, which would presumably have involved this portion of the plate at some point. Another possibility would be that the hotspot itself had moved beneath the plate. Of course no hotspot motion has been detected as yet, but then no one is any more certain of the rules governing their movement than they are about how they form in the first place. Postulating a moving hotspot could actually enable us to sort out another problematic Pacific island chain, the Marquesas Islands.

Dating of rocks from the various islands of this group has produced a nice sequential picture, with dates from 1.3 to 6 million years, occurring along the chain from Fatu Hiva to Nuku Hiva. Unfortunately the trend line of the Marquesas cannot be reconciled with that of any other young island chain. These islands are not located near an area of subduction, as the Samoan Islands or Carolines are, but there is a large fault extending through the area. It is clear that the crust has been very active beneath the chain, as noted in Chapter 7, but the effects of such crustal action on hotspots (or vice versa) are unknown.

Category V These island groups have varied histories that differ markedly from the arcs and chains described above. In this category you will find islands formed of continental materials, produced by biological activity in shallow waters, or created through the uplifting of sedimentary materials from the ocean floor.

The beautiful island of New Caledonia is located on the Australian plate just shy of the trench that borders the New Hebrides island arc. New Caledonia is continental in structure and much older than other islands in the region. The continental rocks that form the elongate island must be a relic of some earlier collision and subduction cycle, and it has been suggested that it may represent a fragment of the Australian continent that has broken away. At the moment the coast of the island is subsiding, and for the most part it is enclosed within a barrier reef. In the Caribbean the islands of Trinidad and Tobago are built of continental rocks that represent an eastern extension of the compression and folding that produced the Andes range. The islands became isolated from the South American mainland only around 10,000 years ago as sea level rose following the last glacial cycle. New Caledonia, Trinidad, and Tobago are strikingly different from other islands in their areas because of their continental histories. New Caledonia is old, low, weathered, and rich in mineral deposits, whereas islands on the other side of the nearby trench are lofty, little dissected, and actively volcanic. Trinidad and Tobago are also more rounded than their volcanic neighbors, and because of their long-term communication with the mainland their flora and fauna show less of a distinctive character than do those of more isolated islands.

The Bahamas Banks began forming with Florida as corals first established themselves along the shallow edge of the continental shelf following the opening of the Atlantic. The entire region has subsided slowly since that time, and as the reef platform grew in width the enclosed lagoon behaved as lagoons usually do. Coralline sands were deposited as coral skeletons were demolished by wave action or processed by living organisms. These sands were mixed with other calcium carbonate debris produced by biological activities, and the mixture was compacted and cemented together by coralline algae, other small organisms, and chemical reactions with the warm lagoon waters. Sometime around 60 million years ago, plus or minus, the Florida Bank and the Bahamas Bank became separated. Conditions changed further as the glacial cycles exposed, eroded, and resubmerged the banks. Erosion carved channels that further subdivided the Bahamas Bank into discrete segments separated by deep channels. The islands we see at the moment represent resistant, emergent windward reef and/or lagoon deposits, and calcium carbonate is still being deposited in the surrounding shallows. Yet although corals are growing around these islands, particularly along their windward coasts, biological activities are no longer the major source for the accumulating carbonates. Because of an unusual combination of factors, chemical processes now predominate. The extensive shallow banks are areas of high evaporation, and the waters that flow over them become very warm and very salty. Under these conditions calcium carbonate will precipitate out of the water and form small granules, called *oolites*, which may grow progressively larger. The shifting and scouring action of the oolite sands over the shallow interior and leeward portions of the banks discourages the settlement of coral planulae and other attached organisms.

The island of Barbados is unusual in that it is composed of layers of deep-ocean sediments that were compressed into rock and then elevated to an altitude of over 1,000 feet above sea level. Barbados lies close to the axis of the trench that borders the Lesser Antilles, and it may have formed as sediments that accumulated in the southern portion of the trench were squeezed between the colliding plates. Overlying the sedimentary rocks are a series of exposed and eroded coral reefs. These are layered in tiers or terraces rather like a wedding cake, with the oldest at the very top.

Now I must admit that there are still a number of relatively small islands and even island groups that we have failed to consider in this overview. Most of them are sparsely populated, poorly known, and extremely difficult to reach, or in some cases, even *find*. Because I doubt that any of us will have an opportunity to visit them, describing them in detail would serve little purpose, but it is safe to say that a careful analysis would enable you to assign them to one of our five categories. With this accomplished I will close the strictly theoretical portion of this book and we will move on to see how the details of earlier chapters may be combined to produce three-dimensional profiles of specific islands and island groups.

Chapter Nine
A Review of Tropical Island Groups

In the first eight chapters of this book you have examined many aspects of life in the tropics. Although we have only had the chance to consider the most superficial details you should by now have sufficient background to ask your own questions and find the answers while you are traveling. Whatever islands you care to visit will greet you with comfortable temperatures and hospitable inhabitants. Yet what today seems idyllic is actually a calm that was preceded by centuries of conflict and crisis.

Almost 30,000 years ago the world was locked into the last of the great ice ages. At the time, sea level was 200 to 300 feet lower than it is today, because of the vast amount of water tied up in glaciers. Old Stone Age tribes from Asia took advantage of the situation and, using exposed land bridges, spread through Indonesia and on to Australia. Following the recession of the glaciers and the corresponding rise in sea level these primitive settlers were isolated. Thousands of years passed before boats and rafts were invented by the New Stone Age peoples, who promptly invaded Malaysia and Indonesia. As this wave of immigrants traveled from island to island, they usually surprised and eliminated their less sophisticated predecessors. The Solomon Islands, the New Hebrides, New Caledonia, and eventually the islands of Fiji were colonized by these New Stone Age peoples, now known as Melanesians. Not all the older inhabitants were eliminated, and a few Old Stone Age cultural holdouts managed to survive, even into the twentieth century. Invariably they persisted in isolated, relatively undesirable, and inaccessible regions such as the mountains of New Guinea. They also survived in Australia in the societies of the Australian aborigines, because Australia was protected by an intervening expanse of treacherous water.

About 5,000 years ago the first Polynesians entered the Pacific, equipped with better boats and a flair for celestial navigation. Over the next 3,000 to 4,000 years they ventured as far east as Easter Island, a lonely outpost facing the 3,000 miles of empty ocean that separated Polynesia from South America. Polynesian settlers also spread north across the equator to the islands of Hawaii and south as far as the temperate islands of New Zealand. This long period of exploration was not a smooth continuum. Instead the migrations began when local population pressures, family feuds, or minor wars drove new groups into unexplored areas in search of a little peace and quiet. Predictably, encouraged by their initial success, later voyages were undertaken for rematches or conquests, and eventually regular trading routes became established.

The final wave of pre-European colonization began sometime around 1000 B.C. when a Malaysian/Polynesian hybrid stock entered from the northwest and spread across the scattered islands and atolls of the northern Pacific. These Micronesians voyaged as far east as the Gilbert Islands, populating the Marianas and Marshalls along the way.

Meanwhile, back in the Atlantic, North America itself was probably uninhabited until Asian peoples migrated across the Bering straits around 10,000 years ago. Some North American Indians did reach the Caribbean islands, but other than some arrowheads and the like they did not leave extensive cultural remains, and their fate is unknown. Around 1,700 years ago, the Arawak Indians entered the Caribbean islands from the Venezuelan coast, island hopping to the north. They were followed by the Carib Indians, who also originated in South America. The Caribs were notable for having a particularly belligerent attitude and a fondness for baked-outsider. The arrival of the Caribs usually meant the departure or consumption of the Arawak inhabitants, and by the sixteenth century, when the Spaniards began paying a lot of attention to the area, most of the Lesser Antilles were under Carib control, and they were making inroads into the Greater Antilles as well.

The Europeans entered the tropics impelled by a particularly devastating combination of greed and religious fanaticism. The Spaniards led the charge into the Caribbean, and found the primitive Caribs to be formidable opponents. Side-stepping the Carib islands, the Spaniards focused on the Arawaks, who were more tractable. As the islands were seized, the Arawak inhabitants were shipped throughout Spanish holdings as slaves. The demand was great and the mortality so high that islands like Barbados and Jamaica were almost depopulated. This had long-range effects, for when colonial ventures tried to develop the islands they had to import African slaves to take the place of the vanished native work force. The resultant blend of cultures, ethnic backgrounds, and attitudes created unique island societies. The British and French, who arrived after the Spanish, were left with the task of ousting the Caribs from the remaining unclaimed islands. It was not an easy task and the Caribs were able to discourage settling of some islands for decades. Even after the native inhabitants had been brought under control, the fighting continued, as the Spanish, French, and British squabbled over various islands and island groups.

Although the Spaniards were the first to reach the Pacific by sea, they failed to play a major role in the development of the Pacific islands. This is understandable, because their society was already involved with the Inquisition as well as the demolition of Central and South American civilizations. In 1520 Magellan found the western gateway to the Pacific and sailed into uncharted waters. Because the Pacific is truly the home of islands, with over 4,000 of them, it is nothing short of remarkable that Fernando managed to sail almost all the way across without seeing a single one. By the time he reached Guam, 110 days out, roasted rats were selling for a ducat apiece and most of the leather goods aboard had been boiled and eaten. Despite the hardships, his crew ultimately completed the voyage—but without their fearless leader. Like many of his contemporaries Magellan proved to be a little too fearless, meeting his end while leading a band of sixty Spanish zealots in a punitive action against about 1,500 armed Philippine natives. The return of what remained of Magellan's party provided little in the way of useful information about the Pacific. They had demonstrated that the world was round, but that conclusion had already been reached by others, mainly mathematicians who relied on less arduous methods. Actually the most significant result of the entire venture was that the Spice Islands, alias Philippines, were shown to lie within the Spanish sphere of influence, a fact with direct economic and political consequences.

In the years that followed, European politics became increasingly complex. Exploration of the vast expanse of the Pacific was disorganized, because when military, religious, and commercial interests are jockeying for power, information is kept under wraps. It wasn't until the close of the eighteenth century that the published reports of expeditions such as those of Bligh, Cook, and Bougainville permitted a general understanding of Pacific geography. Unfortunately this was accompanied by the use, abuse, and gradual destruction of the native civilizations and inhabitants. The Pacific Islands were carved up among the powers of the day and changed hands as dictated by alliances, wars, and treaties signed thousands of miles away. New diseases ravaged the island populations. In the Marquesas the population declined from an estimated 200,000 to around 10,000. Yet throughout the Pacific the native cultures still survive to a degree. Even in Hawaii, where the native population and culture have become absorbed into twentieth-century American life, there is still a distinct Polynesian flavor. In most other island groups, whether Polynesian, Melanesian, or Micronesian, the surviving populations displayed a remarkable flexibility, selectively absorbing parts of European culture and technology while completely ignoring others. Samoans in thatched houses watch color television at the same time as Fijian policemen dress in colorful skirts and pith helmets. The combinations are fascinating, and occasionally highly amusing.

The remainder of this chapter will summarize useful information concerning the principal islands and island groups in the tropical Atlantic and Pacific. Although there will be some historical tidbits mixed in, the main emphasis will be on providing information to assist you in your personal explorations. Planning where, when, and how to go are just as important as knowing what to see after you have arrived. The islands will be examined proceeding from east to west across the tropical Pacific, beginning with the Galapagos islands and ending in Palau, and then around the curve of the Caribbean, beginning with the Bahamas and ending in the Netherlands Antilles. In each instance a brief introduction summing up pertinent data about the island group—its size, population, mode of formation, local politics, languages, currency, and other details applicable to the group as a whole—is followed by a diagrammatic chart of the region, showing its layout. However, don't try to navigate by it!

For ease of reference, additional information is condensed into tabular form. One table contains data on the individual islands of the group, including reef structure, island height, and accessibility by commercial transportation. A second table presents weather survey data, which should assist you in determining the most equitable time for your visit. It is impossible to answer all the potentially useful questions about all the islands because of space and data limitations, but this should not keep you from deducing answers to questions not directly addressed in the tables. For example, an island without commercial air or steamship service usually lacks a commercial bank or a reliable post office, and for yachts the chances are that provisioning or mechanical services will be unavailable.

The tables will make use of the following abbreviations and symbols:

Table I: Island Characteristics

RC = reef classification
    P = patch reefs or coastal patches only
    F = fringing reef

```
    B = barrier reef
   AA = almost-atoll
    A = atoll
    R prefix = raised or elevated, as in:
   RA = raised atoll
```

This information should be considered in light of the mode of formation of the island group, which is indicated in the introduction for each group. Should your memory fail you, Category I is an island arc formed parallel to a trench; Category II is an island chain formed by a hotspot located beneath a volcanic ridge; Category III is an island chain formed by a hotspot located away from the edges of a plate, with (a) Pacific chains contemporary with Hawaii and (b) Pacific chains of ages similar to the Emperor seamounts; Category IV are Pacific and Atlantic islands formed by hotspot activity, but not fitting the neat pattern of Category III; and Category V includes islands that are continental in structure, islands formed by biological activity, and those comprised of uplifted sediments.

IH = island height

```
    A = awash (less than 50 feet)
    L = low (50–1,500 feet, approx.)
    M = medium (1,500–5,000 feet, approx.)
    H = high (5,000–9,000 feet, approx.)
   VH = very high (9,000+ feet)
```

Pop = population of island (total persons)

```
    0 = uninhabited
    S = settlement (1–1,000)
    V = village (1,000–10,000)
    T = town (10,000–50,000)
    C = city (50,000+)
```

Med = medical facilities available

```
    − = no organized services
    C = local clinic
    H = hospital
```

Air? = commercial air service available?

```
    Y = yes
    N = no
```

Note: The lack of commercial service does not always mean that there is no airfield or charter flights available.

Ship? = commercial passenger ship service available?

> Y = yes
> N = no

Note: The lack of commercial service does not imply the absence of interisland freighters, but these should be examined before use, and their schedules are frequently unreliable.

Harbor? = Is there available passage and shelter for yachts?

> 0 = no lagoon, pass, or harbor of refuge
> S = passage for vessels of 5–10 feet draft
> D = passage for vessels of 10+ feet draft

Note: An open roadstead or anchorage may exist, but unless it is reliable and safe it is scored as a 0.

Volc? = is there volcanic activity on the island?

> + = active volcano(es)
> − = none

Table II: Weather Survey Information

Air Temp = average monthly temperature, °F; (ADH) = average daily high

Sea Temp = average surface temperature, °F

Surf Winds = prevailing winds from the direction indicated

Swell Dirn = prevailing swell arrives from the direction indicated

Overcast Percentage = percentage of sky covered with clouds, usually at 9 A.M. and 3 P.M., averaged for the month

Rainfall, days = average number of rainy days

Rainfall, inches = average amount of rainfall

Cyclones/Gales = average number of days with 40 knot or higher winds

Note: A value covered by a bar, as in $\bar{x}$ indicates an average value for a three-month period centered around that month. You should also be aware that data collected from ocean stations do not take into account the effects of island height, winds, and so on, on local weather patterns and should be considered minimal cloud and rain estimations.

Notes on Island Charts

1. All drawings should be taken as diagrammatic only because no attempt has been made to make them precise.

2. Dry land areas are shown as stippled regions, reefs are either hatched (fringing or barrier reefs) or dotted (atolls).

3. With the chart facing you so that you can read the various island names, the top of the page will be North, the bottom will be South, and East and West will be right and left respectively.

A final word of advice: Once you have planned your trip, decided on the season, and made your reservations, take a moment to refer to the Appendix dealing with tropical hazards. You will find that even in paradise there are potential problems. Although these are generally minor it would be a shame to ruin a perfectly good vacation because you left home without planning for all eventualities. The more you learn, the lower your chances of being unpleasantly surprised!

The Tropical Pacific Islands

The Galapagos Islands

Category: III(a)
Islands: 15, plus numerous spires and pinnacles
Area: 3,000 sq. mi.
Total population: 4,000 (1973)
Political status: Territory of Ecuador, SA
Currency: Ecuadorian sucre
Language: Spanish

These interesting volcanic islands are rigidly controlled by the Ecuadorian military establishment, and all visitors to the islands must be cleared through the proper channels. For the most part this means that your arrival will be by an Ecuadorian carrier (airline or vessel) and your tour will be conducted by agents licensed to conduct business in Ecuador. All the wildlife, with the exception of introduced pests like feral goats, are protected by law. Reef formation is very limited around these islands, but there are several patch reefs and interesting shoal areas, and underwater visibility is excellent. Terrestrial wildlife is abundant, well-mannered, and very unusual. Most of the islands are parched and dry along their leeward (northern) slopes, although vegetation may survive along the southerly exposures and internal valleys. In the lowlands the rainy season extends from January to April, but precipitation is unreliable at best. Along the higher windward slopes rainfall is scarce but possible year round. Fogs are common around the islands because of the large temperature difference between the air masses and the cool waters of the Peru Current that bathe the islands throughout most of the year.

Visiting yachts are not welcome, although they may be tolerated for brief visits (seventy-two hours or less) if all protocol, papers, and fees are in perfect order. Those familiar with the methods of fee determination prevalent elsewhere in South America will not be surprised. The principal ports of entry are at San Cristobal (Wreck Bay) and Santa Cruz (Academy Bay). Yachts must enter at Wreck Bay before visiting any other destination in the group. Academy Bay is the more hospitable port of the two, and the Charles Darwin Research Station is located along its shores. Provisioning, communications, and services are extremely limited, and you would be wise to boil your water.

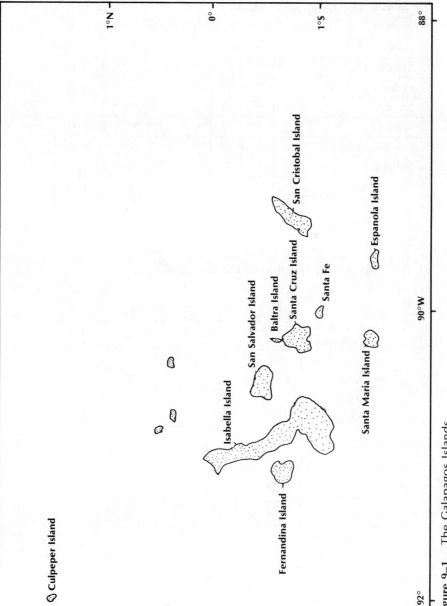

Figure 9–1. The Galapagos Islands

Table 9-1: The Galapagos Islands

Island	RC	IH	Pop.	Med.	Air?	Ship?	Harbor?	Volc?
San Cristobal	P	M	V	C	N	Y	D	–
Espanola	P	L	O	–	N	Y	D	–
Santa Maria	P	M	S	–	N	Y	D	–
Santa Cruz	P	M	V	C	Y	Y	D	–
San Salvador	P	M	O	–	N	N	D	–
Isabella	P	H	V	–	N	Y	D	+
Fernandina	P	M	O	–	N	Y	D	+

Table 9-2: Weather in the Galapagos

	Air Temp. °F	Sea Temp. °F	Surf. Winds	Swell Dir'n.	Over-cast %	Rainfall days	Rainfall inches	Cyclones/ Gales
January	86		S			8	0.8	0
February	86	78	SE	SSE	62	9	1.4	
March	88		SE			6	1.1	
April	87		SSE			6	0.7	
May	86	68	S	SSE		4	0	0
June	83	72	S			4	0	0
July	81	69	S			9	0	0
August	81	70	S	SSE		8	0	
September	80		S			7	0	
October	81	70	S			2	0	
November	81	73	S	SSE		4	0	0
December	83		S			6	0	

Data Source: various, primarily ocean station reports

The Marquesas Islands*

Category: IV
Islands: 10, plus numerous shoals
Area: 1,274 sq. mi.
Total population: 5,593 (1971)
Political status: French territory
Currency: Central Pacific franc
Language: French, Marquesan, and various combinations of the two

In the Marquesas you are struck by the enormity of the catastrophe that befell the Polynesian civilizations as European influence grew. These islands once supported a population of 100,000 to 200,000 natives; today only a handful remain. The islands are covered with ruins, deserted villages, and empty valleys that once supported thriving communities. Melville's books *Typee* and *Omoo* describe his experiences on the island of Nuku Hiva, now the administrative center for the group, and to read these accounts and then explore the area is certainly an educational, if sobering, experience.

In this group, the isolated islands and villages are *really* isolated, and even on Nuku Hiva you should not expect standard postal, radio, or telephone services to be available 100 percent of the time. There are several inter-island freighters that wander between these islands and the Tuomotus on an irregular basis, but in general you should not expect to utilize these for transportation because of the extremely primitive conditions onboard. There are regularly scheduled flights to several of the islands and limited tourist services are available.

The reefs are not spectacular and the waters are often turbid due to erosion and siltation, but marine life is abundant. Cetaceans seem to congregate around these islands.

The islands are physically striking and cruising among the islands is a memorable experience. As with other French possessions, all visitors should obtain the necessary visas *before* arrival. Some knowledge of French is recommended, although *fluent* French is not essential because the islanders speak Marquesan. French is as much a second language to them as it is to you.

*Note: Because of its isolated location in the eastern Pacific, the Easter Island group will be appended to this section (see page 236).

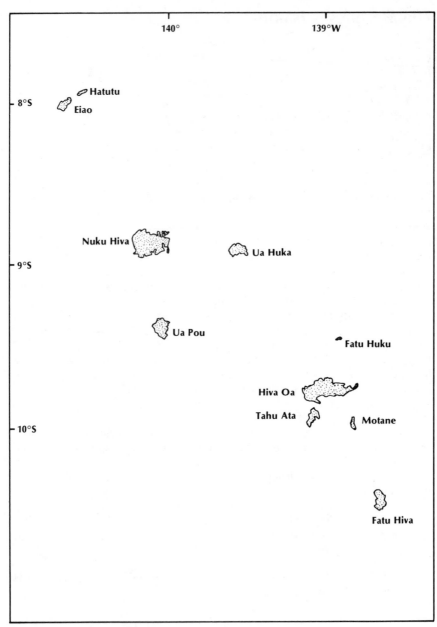

Figure 9–2. The Marquesas Islands

Table 9-3: The Marquesas Islands

Island	RC	IH	Pop.	Med.	Air?	Ship?	Harbor?	Volc?
Fatu Hiva	P	M	V	–	N	N	D	–
Motane	P	L	O	–	N	N	O	–
Tahu Ata	P	M	V	–	N	N	D	–
Hiva Oa	P	M	V	–	Y	Y	D	–
Fatu Huku	P	L	O	–	N	N	O	–
Ua Pou	P	M	V	–	Y	Y	D	–
Ua Huka	P	M	V	–	Y	Y	D	–
Nuku Hiva	P	M	V	C	Y	Y	D	–
Eiao	P	M	O	–	N	N	D	–
Hatutu	P	L	O	–	N	N	O	–

Table 9-4: Weather in the Marquesas

	Air Temp. °F	Sea Temp. °F	Surf. Winds	Swell Dir'n.	Over-cast %	Rainfall days	Rainfall inches	Cyclones/ Gales
January		80	E		49	10		0
February			NE		41	4		0
March			ENE		48	2		0
April			E		42	3		0
May			E		35	8		2
June			E		45	3		0
July			E		42	4		0
August		80	E		34	1		0
September			E		40	4		0
October			E		51	5		0
November			E		40	4		0
December		80	E		54	7		0

Data Source: ocean station reports

Easter Island

Category: II
Islands: 3 (1 inhabited)
Population: 1,500
Political status: Possession of Chile
Language: Spanish

Easter Island is overseen by a military officer who doubles as the Captain of the Port. Although the anchorages are very poor and few yachts visit the islands, there are weekly flights to the mainland and/or Tahiti. Easter Island is famous for its gargantuan carvings that face the open sea along the coastline.

Table 9-5: Weather at Easter Island

	Air Temp. °F	Sea Temp. °F	Surf, Winds	Swell Dir'n.	Over-cast %	Rainfall days	Rainfall inches	Cyclones/ Gales
January	73		E		53	20	5.2	0
February	74		ESE		49	13	1.6	0
March	73		E		57	19	9.0	1
April	70		SE		55	21	5.1	0
May	68		SE		61	18	3.9	0
June	65		SSE		67	20	9.5	1
July	63		S		62	20	3.2	1
August	64		SE		63	17	2.6	0.7
September	64		SSE		63	20	3.5	0.7
October	65		SE		58	12	2.2	0.3
November	67		SE		63	13	5.0	0
December	70		ESE		49	15	2.9	0.7

Data Source: Easter Island

The Tuomotu Archipelago

Category: III(a)
Islands: 82, plus numerous shoals
Area: 780 sq. mi.
Population: 8,537 (1977)
Political status: 78 of the islands are French possessions; four are British
Currency: Central Pacific franc (French islands)
Language: French, Tahitian, or some combination (French islands); English
    (Pitcairn Island)

French area. The Tuomotus are a collection of atolls and a few low islands. These islands are also known as the Dangerous Archipelago because navigation among the isles is extremely difficult. Available charts are accurate as far as depicting the location and rough contours of each island, but updating is infrequent, and soundings offshore are likely to be either incorrect or inadequate in many regions.

The weather is mild, and cyclones are rare this far to the east (but they do occur). The islands are monotonous in appearance, but the entire area is famous for its marine life, and the diving is superb. Fresh water, provisioning, medical services, and reliable communications are not to be found on most of the islands in the group.

These islands are part of French Oceania and are administered by the authorities headquartered in Papeete, Tahiti. Islands in the southern portion of the chain are now off limits to visitors without special clearance because of the nuclear testing conducted by the French military.

British area. Of the four islands, only one is inhabited. They are geologically tied to the other islands of the Archipelago but are administered separately. Pitcairn is inhabited by the descendants of the HMS *Bounty* mutineers. Its total population was 86 in 1964.

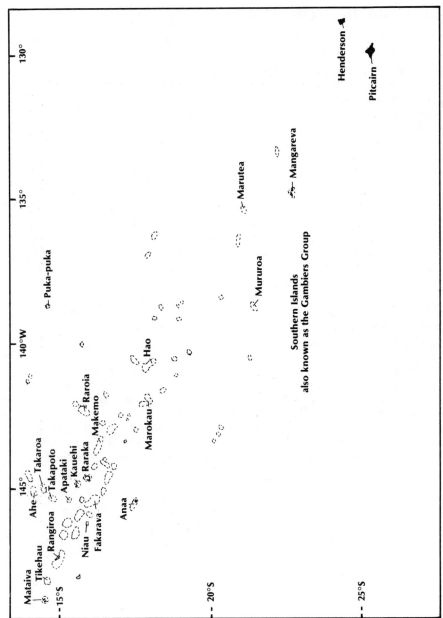

Figure 9–3. The Tuamotu Archipelago

Table 9-6: The Tuamotu Islands

Island	RC	IH	Pop.	Med.	Air?	Ship?	Harbor?	Volc?
Pitcairn	P	L	S	–	N	N	O	+
Mangareva	AA	L	S	–	Y	N	D	–
Hao	A	A	V	C	Y	Y	D	–
Makemo	A	A	S	–	Y	N	D	–
Tahanea	A	A	S	–	N	N	D	–
Anaa	A	A	S	–	Y	N	O	–
Arutua	A	A	S	–	Y	N	O	–
Fakarava	A	A	V	–	Y	N	D	–
Raraka	A	A	S	–	N	N	S	–
Kauehi	A	A	V	–	N	N	D	–
Apataki	A	A	S	–	Y	N	D	–
Tikehau	A	A	S	–	Y	N	S	–
Takapoto	A	A	S	–	Y	N	O	–
Niau	*EF/EA	A	S	–	N	N	O	–
Mataiva	A	A	S	–	Y	N	O	–
Rangiroa	A	A	V	–	Y	Y	D	–

*This island has been described as a raised atoll by one author, and as an elevated, reef-rimmed crater by another. Based on the experience of diving on the site, the latter appears most likely.

Table 9-7: Weather in the Tuamotus

	Air Temp. °F	Sea Temp. °F	Surf. Winds	Swell Dir'n.	Over- cast %	Rainfall days	Rainfall inches	Cyclones/ Gales	
January	80		E		49	20	7.4	0	
February	80		ENE		41	20	6.8	0	
March	79		ENE		48	17	4.3	0	
April	78		E		42	13	4.3	0	
May	76		E		35	25	14.2	0	
June	73		E		45	22	7.6	2	
July	72		ESE		42	24	5.8	0	
August	75		E		34	13	2.5	2	
September	74		E		40	14	10.9	0	
October	75		E		51	26	19.9	0	
November	76		E		40	24	10.5	0	
December	79		E		54	23	13.3	0	

Data Source: Mangareva Atoll and ocean station reports

The Society Islands

Category: III(a)
Islands: 14
Population: 117,703 (1977)
Political status: French possession
Currency: Central Pacific franc
Language: French and Tahitian

These lovely islands are the cultural and administrative center for French Oceania. Papeete, on the island of Tahiti, is the principal city and port of entry for the entire territory. There are no better facilities available to the visitor anywhere in the tropical Pacific outside of Hawaii.

Visiting yachts are welcome, but a substantial security deposit is required from each member of the crew to cover possible deportation expenses. In 1980 this was approximately $850 in U.S. currency. All visitors, whatever their method of arrival, will find that entry procedures are much more relaxed and congenial if you arrive with a visa *already* in hand and bearing a *round-trip* ticket.

Airlines service most of the islands in the group, and the swimming and diving are marvelous everywhere; the sheltered lagoons are particularly nice for novices.

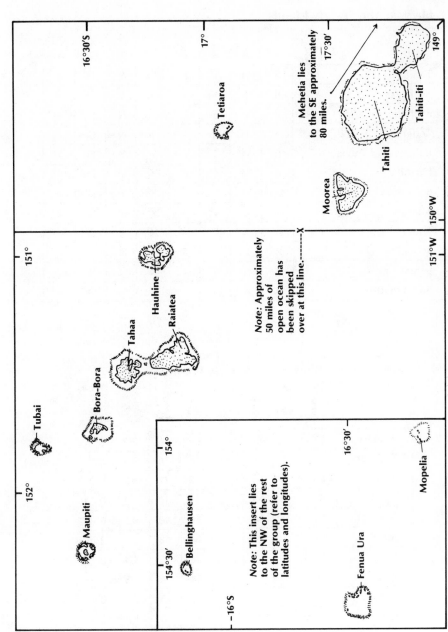

The following text labels appear within the figure:

16°30'S

17°

Tetiaroa

Mehetia lies
to the SE approximately
80 miles.

17°30'

Tahiti-iti

Tahiti

Moorea

149°

150°W

151°

Hauhine

Raiatea

Tahaa

Bora-Bora

Tubai

Maupiti

152°

Note: Approximately
50 miles of
open ocean has
been skipped
over at this line.------X

151°W

150°W

154°

154°30'

Bellinghausen

Note: This insert lies
to the NW of the rest
of the group (refer to
latitudes and longitudes).

16°30'

Mopelia

16°S

Fenua Ura

Figure 9–4. The Society Islands.

Table 9-8: The Society Islands

Island	RC	IH	Pop.	Med.	Air?	Ship?	Harbor?	Volc?
Tahiti	B	H	V	H	Y	Y	D	–
Moorea	B	M	V	–	Y	Y	D	–
Mehetia	B	L	S	–	N	N	O	–
Tetiaroa	A	L	S	–	Y	N	O	–
Raiatea and Tahaa	B	M	T	C	Y	Y	D	–
Huahine	B	M	V	C	Y	Y	D	–
Bora Bora	AA	M	V	C	Y	Y	D	–
Maupiti	B	L	V	–	Y	N	D	–
Tubai	A	A	S	–	N	N	O	–
Mopelia	A	L	S	–	N	N	S	–
Fenua Ura	A	A	S	–	N	N	O	–
Bellinghausen	A	A	S	–	N	N	O	–

Table 9-9: Weather in the Society Islands

	Air Temp. °F	Sea Temp. °F	Surf. Winds	Swell Dir'n.	Over-cast %	Rainfall days	Rainfall inches	Cyclones/ Gales
January	81		NNE		69	16	7.2	0
February	81		NNE		66	16	9.4	0
March	81		NE		69	17	10.1	0
April	81		NE		58	10	2.7	0
May	79		NE		58	10	4.5	0
June	77		ENE		60	8	2.8	2
July	76		NE		46	5	1.4	0
August	76		NE		54	6	1.5	2
September	78		NNE		55	6	3.0	0
October	79		NNE		57	9	5.6	0
November	79		NNE		60	13	8.4	0
December	80		NNE		65	14	15.7	0

Data Source: Papeete, Tahiti

The Line Islands

Category: III(b)
Area: 193 sq. mi.*
Population: 1,472 (1973)
Currency: Australian dollar
Language: English or Gilbertese

*Excluding Johnston Island

This collection of islands is divided administratively into several groups. Most have been included in the newly formed Kiribati Republic, formerly known as the Gilbert and Ellice Islands. The few British possessions and three of the four U.S. islands are uninhabited. Johnston Island is the site of a major U.S. military establishment, and is off limits.

None of these islands is heavily populated, and the only export at the present time is copra (dried coconut meat), although guano was once a major industry in this region. General services and reliable communications are not to be found outside of Christmas and Johnston Islands. Although cruise ships occasionally pause at Christmas Island momentarily, the other islands in this portion of the Kiribati Republic are only occasionally visited by inter-island freighters.

Caution is the rule when navigating among these islands, because the local charts are generally of poor quality and the currents in this region are quite variable.

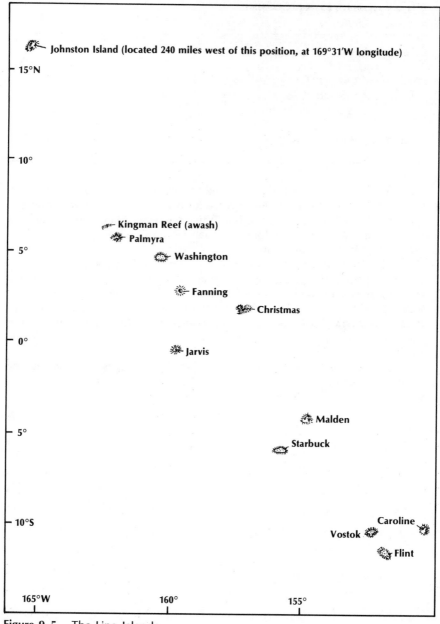

Figure 9–5. The Line Islands

Table 9-10: The Line Islands

Island	RC	IH	Pop.	Med.	Air?	Ship?	Harbor?	Volc?
Caroline (Br.)	A	A	O	–	N	N	O	–
Starbuck (Br.)	A	A	O	–	N	N	O	–
Malden (U.S.)	RA	A	O	–	N	N	O	–
Jarvis (U.S.)	RA	A	O	–	N	N	O	–
Christmas	A	A	V	–	Y	Y	S	–
Fanning	A	A	V	–	N	N	D	–
Washington	RA	A	V	–	N	N	O	–
Palmyra (U.S.)	A	A	S	–	N	N	D	–
Johnston (U.S.)	A	A	V	H	Y	Y	D	–

Table 9-11: Weather in the Line Islands

	Air Temp. °F	Sea Temp. °F	Surf. Winds	Swell Dir'n.	Over- cast %	Rainfall days	Rainfall inches	Cyclones/ Gales
January	81		ESE		59	13	10.8	0
February	81		ESE		59	15	10.5	0
March	82		E		59	18	10.7	0
April	82		E		63	20	14.1	0
May	82		ESE		59	19	12.6	0
June	82		SE		58	16	10.0	0
July	82		SE		54	14	8.2	0
August	83		SE		50	10	4.4	0
September	83		SE		49	8	3.2	0
October	83		SE		50	8	3.6	0
November	83		ESE		49	8	2.9	0
December	82		ESE		55	11	8.0	0

Data Source: Fanning Island

The Hawaiian Islands

Category: III(a)
Area: 6,450 sq. mi..
Islands: 7 inhabited, numerous islets, atolls, and shoals
Population: approx. 1,000,000 (1980)
Political status: U.S. state

We have discussed these islands all through the text, and I will devote little additional attention to them here. All the inhabited islands are located in the southeastern portion of the chain, and the long string of atolls and seamounts known as the "Leeward Islands" are a conservation zone administered by federal and state authorities.

Actually there are eight large islands in the southeast; one of them, Kahoolawe, has been controlled by the U.S. Navy since World War II, and it is used for bombing practice and military maneuvers of one kind or another. For obvious reasons, this island is strictly off limits, as are its surrounding waters.

Niihau, a small island off Kauai, and Lanai are both privately owned. Niihau has a population of about 240, 95 percent of whom are of Hawaiian descent, and the island is closed to uninvited guests. Lanai is essentially an enormous pineapple plantation, but there is also a small town and commercial flights are available to the island.

Scheduled flights and cruise ships make all the other islands easily accessible, and if you are going to Hawaii you should be sure to travel beyond the confines of Honolulu, where you will find a variety of diversions, distractions, and general hubbub that you probably thought you were leaving behind on the mainland. Tourism is a major industry in these islands, and so the facilities are excellent.

For the yachtsman, Hawaii offers services unavailable elsewhere in the tropical Pacific. The only precautionary note is that good harbors are in short supply, and open roadsteads are the general rule. Although gales are rare, gale-force winds are created locally, as winds funnel through valleys and/or between islands, particularly from January to April.

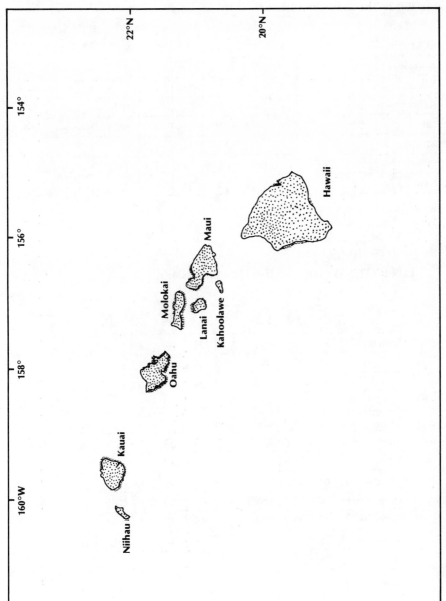

Figure 9–6. The Hawaiian Islands

Table 9-12: The Hawaiian Islands

Island	RC	IH	Pop.	Med.	Air?	Ship?	Harbor?	Volc?
Hawaii	P	VH	T	H	Y	Y	D	+
Maui	F	VH	C	H	Y	Y	D	−
Kahoolawe	F	M	O	−	N	N	O	−
Lanai	F	M	V	C	Y	N	D	−
Molokai	F	M	V	H	Y	N	D	−
Oahu	F/B	M	C	H	Y	Y	D	−
Kauai	F	H	T	H	Y	Y	D	−

Table 9-13: Weather in the Hawaiian Islands

	Air Temp. °F	Sea Temp. °F	Surf. Winds	Swell Dir'n.	Over- cast %	Rainfall days	Rainfall inches	Cyclones/ Gales
January	71	73	NE		53	14	3.5	0
February	71	73	NE		48	10	3.7	0
March	72	73.9	ENE		54	13	3.2	0
April	73	75.2	ENE		55	12	2.1	0
May	75	77.4	ENE		51	11	1.4	0
June	77	79.5	ENE		50	11	1.0	0
July	78	79.5	E		49	13	1.0	0
August	78	80.2	E		47	13	1.2	0
September	78	80.1	ENE		47	13	1.4	0
October	77	79.3	ENE		46	13	2.0	0
November	75	76.8	ENE		52	14	3.3	0
December	73	73.8	ENE		51	15	4.1	0

Data Source: Honolulu, Oahu

The Austral and Cook Islands

Category: *III(a)*
Islands: *19, plus numerous reefs and shoals*
Area: *Austral islands—174 sq. mi./(So.) Cook Islands—230 sq. mi.*
Population: *Austral Islands–5,208 (1977)/(So.) Cook Islands—21,227
    (1977)/North Cook Islands—2,290 (1977)*
Political status: *Austral Islands—possession of France, part of French
    Oceania/(So.) Cook Islands—self-governing territory of New
    Zealand/North Cook Islands—dependency of New Zealand*
Language: *English (Cook Is.)/French (Austral Is.)*
Currency: *Central Pacific franc (Austral Islands)/New Zealand dollar (Cook
    Islands, both groups)*

Few visitors go so far afield, but these are extremely interesting and hospitable islands. Tourism has yet to become a major industry, so facilities and services are rather limited in the outer islands and absent altogether in the North Cooks.

The Cook Islands as presented here are more a political assemblage than a geological one. The eight islands of the "South" Cook Islands, simply called the Cook islands, are clearly part of the Austral/Cook volcanic chain. The five islands of the North Cooks are of uncertain origin and are located some distance away near the equator.

Rarotonga is the principal island of the New Zealand-affiliated island groups; Avarua is the major city on the island. Flights to other islands in the Cooks originate here; there are no commercial flights to the North Cook Islands. Principal exports of the Cook Islands include copra, fruit juices, and canned fish.

The administrative heart of the French islands is located on Tubai (also spelled Tubuai) Island. Flights to the Austral Islands originate in Papeete, Tahiti.

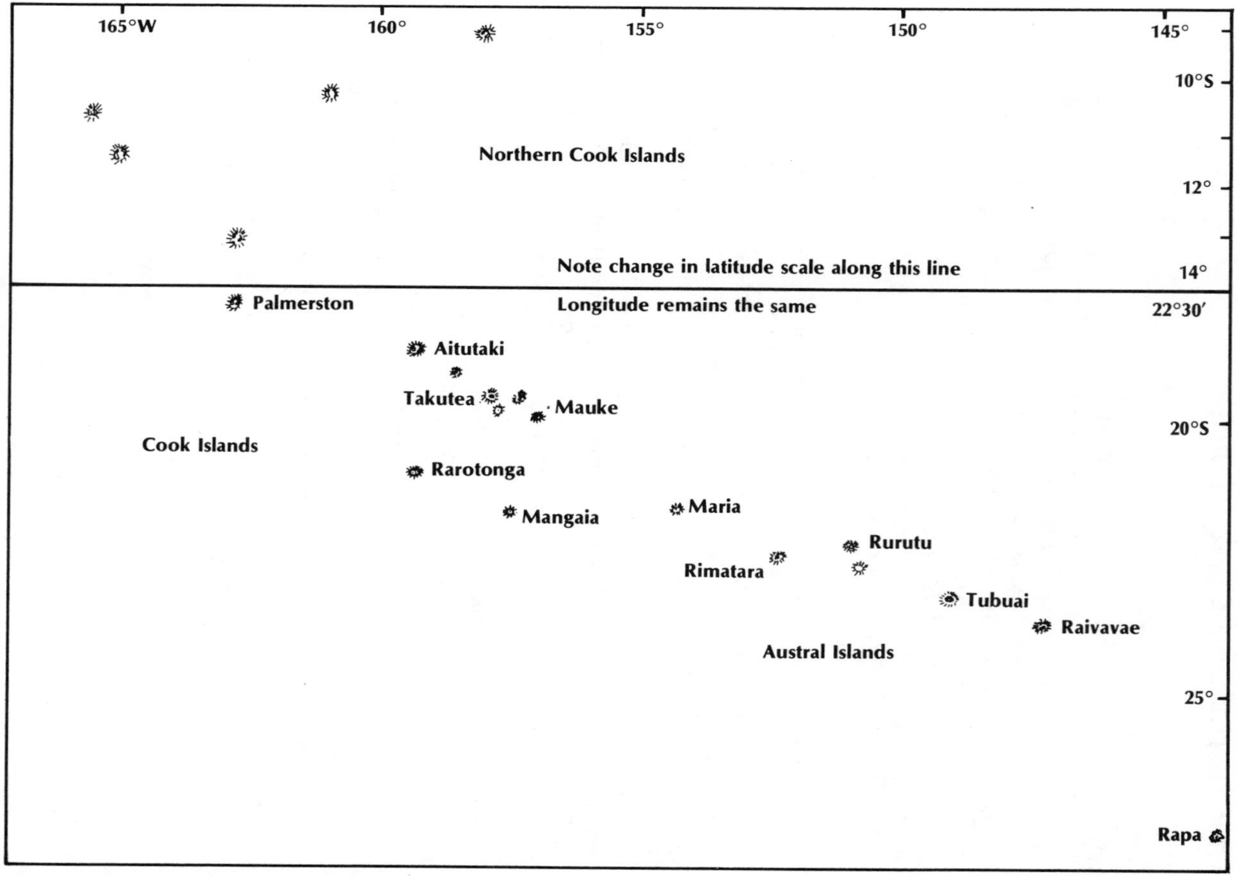

Figure 9–7. The Austral and Cook Islands

Table 9-14: The Austral and Cook Islands

Island	RC	IH	Pop.	Med.	Air?	Ship?	Harbor?	Volc?
Rapa (Fr.)	F	M	S	–	N	N	D	–
Raivavae (Fr.)	B	L	S	–	N	N	S	–
Tubai (Fr.)	B	L	V	C	Y	N	D	–
Rurutu (Fr.)	RF/B	L	V	–	Y	N	D	–
Rimatara (Fr.)	RB	L	S	C	N	N	O	–
Maria (Fr.)	A	A	S	–	N	N	O	–
Mangaia	RA	L	V	–	N	N	O	–
Rarotonga	RB	M	V	H	Y	Y	D	–
Mauke	RA	A	S	–	N	N	O	–
Atiu	RA	L	V	–	N	N	O	–
Aitutaki	F/B	L	V	C	Y	N	D	–
Danger	A	A	S	–	N	N	O	–
Nassau	A	A	S	–	N	N	O	–
Suvarov	A	A	O	–	N	N	D	–
Manihiki	A	A	S	–	N	N	O	–
Penrhyn	A	A	S	–	N	N	D	–

Table 9-15: Weather in the Austral and Cook Islands

	Air Temp. °F	Sea Temp. °F	Surf. Winds	Swell Dir'n.	Over-cast %	Rainfall days	Rainfall inches	Cyclones/ Gales
January	78		E		60	19	9.2	
February	78		ESE		65	19	10.1	
March	78		ESE		70	20	11.2	
April	76		ESE		57	17	7.7	
May	73		SE		58	17	5.9	
June	71		SE		58	15	4.8	
July	70		SE		52	13	4.4	
August	70		SE		54	15	4.7	
September	71		ESE		59	14	5.0	
October	73		ESE		55	13	5.3	
November	74		ESE		65	14	6.4	
December	76		E		66	16	8.1	

Data Source: Rarotonga, Cook Is.

The Samoa Islands

Category: IV
Islands: 8, plus several satellite islets
Population: W. Samoa: 146,635 (1971); Area = 1,101 sq. mi./Am. Samoa: 27,233
   (1970); Area = 76 sq. mi.
Currency: Western Samoan dollar (talla)/U.S. currency
Language: Samoan and (some) English

The Samoan Islands are administratively separate, despite the fact that the native inhabitants travel back and forth continually, visiting relatives and friends. The larger islands of Western Samoa contain most of the population. Formerly a territory of New Zealand, these islands are now independent. Most of the economic interest is agricultural. Tourist services are available and visitors are very well received. These islands have massive fringing reefs, so good harbors are scarce. The capital city is Apia, on Upolu Island.

The population of American Samoa is concentrated on the island of Tutuila, site of the beautiful natural harbor of Pago Pago. American Samoa (also called Amerika Samoa) is a U.S. territory, with the same status as Puerto Rico or the Virgin Islands. The two major industries are government and tunafish, each employing about half the working population. There are two large canneries on the island that receive the catch of most commercial vessels operating in the region. The government shipyard is large and busy servicing this fleet, but yachts may haul out at reasonable rates. Tourism is not a priority and tourist services are extremely limited. Jet airline services, and a U.S. Post Office connect the island with Hawaii on a reliable basis. The outer islands are very rural in character, with no tourist services whatever. Rose, the easternmost island of the group, is an uninhabited atoll maintained as a nature preserve that is off limits without special clearance. Diving and snorkeling are excellent, both off the outer reef slopes and on isolated banks and shoals close to the islands.

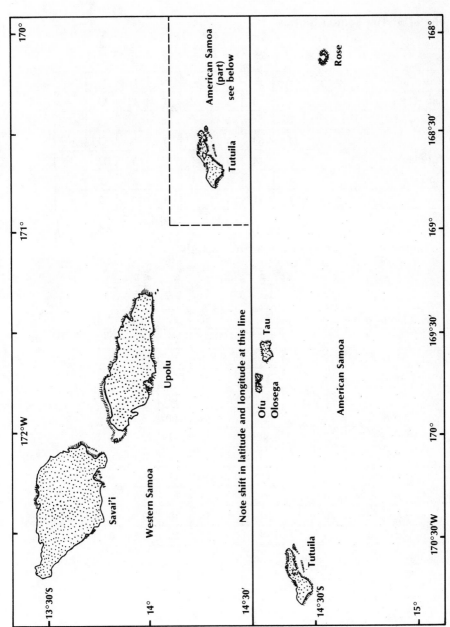

Figure 9–8. The Samoan Islands

Table 9-16: The Samoa Islands

Island	RC	IH	Pop.	Med.	Air?	Ship?	Harbor?	Volc?
Rose (U.S.)	A	A	O	–	N	N	D	–
Tau (U.S.)	F	M	V	–	Y	N	O	–
Olosega (U.S.)	RF	M	V	–	Y	N	O	–
Ofu (U.S.)	F	M	V	–	Y	N	O	–
Tutuila (U.S.)	F	M	T	H	Y	Y	D	–
Upolu	F	M	T	H	Y	Y	D	–
Savai'i	F	H	V	C	Y	N	D	+

Table 9-17: Weather in the Samoa Islands

	Air Temp. °F	Sea Temp. °F	Surf. Winds	Swell Dir'n.	Over-cast %	Rainfall days	Rainfall inches	Cyclones/ Gales
January	79		E		66	21	16.8	2
February	79		NE		67	19	15.7	1
March	79		NE		60	19	13.5	2
April	79		E		57	18	10.2	0
May	78		E		48	13	5.5	0
June	78		E		44	11	5.2	0
July	77		ENE		42	11	2.6	0
August	78		E		41	11	3.2	0
September	78		E		48	12	5.1	0
October	78		E		51	15	6.1	0
November	79		ENE		55	18	9.3	0
December	79		ENE		59	20	13.6	0

Data Source: Apia, W. Samoa

The Tonga Islands

Category: I
Islands: 169, plus reefs
Area: 385 sq. mi.
Population: 90,000 (1975)
Political status: Independent kingdom embraces all islands except Niue, which
  is a self-governing N.Z. dependency
Currency: Tonga Pa'anga (N.Z. dollar on Niue)
Language: English and/or Tongan

The King of Tonga resides in a modest "palace" in Nuku'alofa, the principal city, on the island of Tongatapu. All administrative activities focus on this island, and it is provided with excellent air and water connections with other portions of the Pacific.

Tonga is divided into three groups: the southern section, including Tongatapu; the middle region, centered around the Ha'apai islands; and the northern section, headquartered at Vava'u. The inhabited islands are primarily raised islands and banks. Volcanic activity over the past 100 years has been restricted to the regions west of Ha'apai and southwest of Tongatapu. Earthquakes are common, and occasionally severe.

Several outlying islands are included in the kingdom: Tafahi, Niuatobutabu, Niuafoo, and Ata. None has connections with the outside world on any regular basis.

Tonga is not thriving economically and agriculture remains the primary source of support for the native population. Limited tourist facilities are available, especially in Tongatapu and Vava'u. Visitors are warmly received and the snorkeling is exquisite.

The isolated island of Niue has an anchorage suitable for large vessels and maintains regular airline connections with the outside world. Flights originate in either Tonga or Samoa.

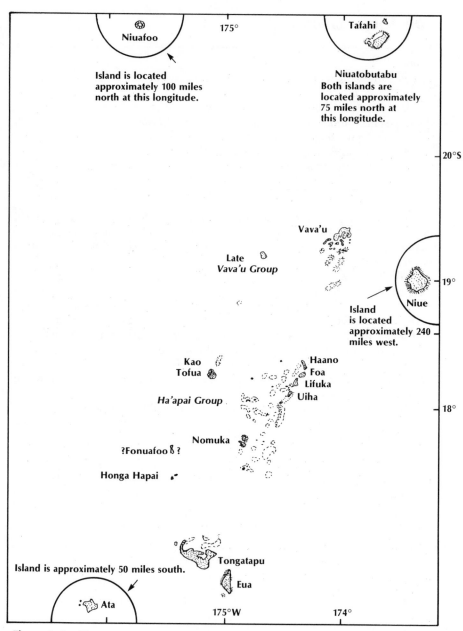

Figure 9–9. Tonga

Table 9-18: The Tonga Islands

Island	RC	IH	Pop.	Med.	Air?	Ship?	Harbor?	Volc?
Ata	P	L	O	–	N	N	O	–
Eua	RA	L	S	–	Y	N	O	–
Tongatapu	RA	L	T	C	Y	Y	D	–
Lifuka	RA	L	V	–	Y	N	D	–
Haano	RA	L	S	–	N	N	O	–
Vava'u	RA	L	V	C	Y	N	D	–
Tafahi	F	M	S	–	N	N	O	–
Niuatobutabu	RA	L	V	–	N	N	O	–
Niue	RA	K	V	C	Y	N	D	–
Niuafoo	F	L	S	–	N	N	O	+

Table 9-19: Weather in the Tonga Islands

	Air Temp. °F	Sea Temp. °F	Surf. Winds	Swell Dir'n.	Over-cast %	Rainfall days	Rainfall inches	Cyclones/ Gales
January	78		ESE		66	16	8.0	0.3
February	79		ESE		62	12	5.0	0.3
March	78		ESE		70	17	8.6	1.0
April	77		SE		64	13	10.2	0
May	73		SE		63	10	1.0	0
June	73		S		65	11	3.7	0
July	71		SSE		64	9	0.8	0
August	71		SE		65	6	3.0	0
September	72		ESE		68	11	4.2	0
October	74		ESE		65	9	4.0	0.5
November	75		SE		63	9	4.8	0
December	77		ESE		63	11	4.4	0.5

Data Source: Nuku'alofa, Tongatapu

The Fiji Islands

Category: I
Islands: 844 islands and islets (106 inhabited)
Area: 7,055 sq. mi.
Population: 600,000 (approx.)
Political status: Independent member of the British Commonwealth
Currency: Fijian dollar
Language: English, Fijian, and Hindi (Indian)

Fiji was once a British colony where large numbers of Indians (from India) were brought in as a cheap source of labor. Today Fiji is independent, with roughly equivalent numbers of Indian and Fijian residents. The capital is located at Suva, on the island of Viti Levu. This is the largest and most heavily populated island in the group.

Viti Levu is located in the western portion of the country, which is characterized by high islands. The eastern or Lau group of islands consists primarily of low atolls and reefs. Flights to other islands originate on either Viti Levu or Vanua Levu. International air and sea passengers arrive at either Suva or Lautoka (Nadi airport), both located on the island of Viti Levu.

Fiji is active in a number of industries, including copra, sugar, and gold mining. Suva is a bustling duty-free port and a center for shoppers interested in products originating in the Orient. Tourism is considered very important, and visitors are treated like royalty in most areas. Fishing, snorkeling, and shelling are all excellent.

Harbors are plentiful, and visitors on yachts could wander among the islands for years without seeing everything. Caution must be exercised, however, because charts are inadequate, the weather is unpredictable, and currents are irregular both in strength and direction.

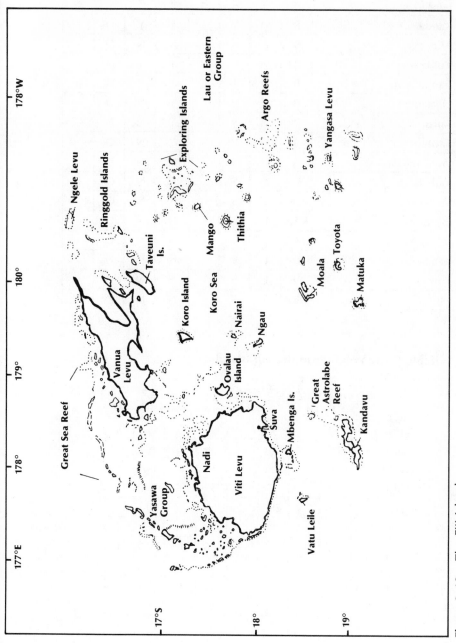

Figure 9–10. The Fiji Islands

Table 9-20: The Fiji Islands

Island	RC	IH	Pop.	Med.	Air?	Ship?	Harbor?	Volc?
Kandavu	B	M	V	–	Y	Y	D	–
M'Benga	B	L	S	–	N	N	D	–
Viti Levu	B	M	C	H	Y	Y	D	–
Vanua Levu	B	M	T	C	Y	Y	D	–
Ovalau	B	M	V	–	Y	N	D	–
Koro	B	M	S	–	Y	N	D	–
Taveuni	B	M	V	–	Y	N	D	–
Wailangilala	A	L	S	–	N	N	D	–
Yathata	RA	L	S	–	N	N	O	–
Vatu Vara	RA	L	S	–	N	N	O	–
Exploring Isles	RAA	L	V	–	N	N	D	–
Lakemba	RAA	L	V	–	N	N	D	–
Kambara	RA	L	V	–	N	N	D	–
Toyota	RB	L	S	–	N	N	D	–
Moala	B	L	S	–	N	N	D	–

Table 9-21: Weather in the Fiji Islands

	Air Temp. °F	Sea Temp. °F	Surf. Winds	Swell Dir'n.	Over-cast %	Rainfall days	Rainfall inches	Cyclones/ Gales
January	79		E		57	23	11.4	0.1
February	80		ENE		56	22	10.7	0.1
March	80		ENE		56	24	14.5	0.2
April	78		E		55	23	12.2	0
May	76		ESE		59	21	10.1	0
June	74		ESE		56	18	6.7	0
July	73		ESE		56	17	4.9	0
August	73		ESE		63	19	8.5	0
September	74		ESE		62	19	7.7	0
October	75		ESE		61	18	8.3	0
November	77		ESE		63	19	9.8	0
December	79		ESE		59	21	12.5	0.1

Data Source: Suva, Viti Levu

The Gilbert and Ellice Islands
(The Kiribati Republic and Tuvalu)

Category: III(b) (main chains)
Islands: 17*
Area: 124 sq. mi.*
Population: 63,633 (1973)*
Political status: Independent members of the British Commonwealth
Currency: Australian dollar
Language: English and Gilbertese predominate

*This does not include those islands considered with the Line Islands.

The Kiribati Republic gained independence on July 12, 1979. Administrative activities in the main portion of the group are centered around Ocean Island, also known as Banaba Island, and at the town of Betio on Tarawa Atoll. Commercial air transportation is available at each of these islands, connecting them to other Pacific nations, and small inter-island planes reach several outlying atolls in the group. Visitors are few and far between, but the islanders are hospitable and the snorkeling is fascinating.

At the moment, 99 percent of the revenue to this republic results from phosphate (guano) mining on Ocean Island, a raised atoll. Strip mining of these resources has almost eliminated this source of income, however, and it seems likely that in the future there will be an increasing interest in the development of commercial fisheries. Although this nation is small in area, the territorial waters that they may claim include a large portion of the western north Pacific.

Tourist facilities are limited, but exist on the more populous islands of the main chains. The Phoenix Islands, of separate geological origin, are raised atolls with few inhabitants; they are included on the chart because the island of Canton was formerly considered a U.S. possession and housed military personnel.

The nearby island of Nauru is another raised atoll rich in phosphate. Although geologically tied up with the other islands of the region, it is a separate nation of its own. It is fabulously wealthy, with its own international shipping company and airline. Most of the citizens live elsewhere and receive substantial subsidies from the government; applications for naturalization will no doubt be discouraged!

The Tuvalu Islands, formerly called the Ellice Islands, were administratively separated from the Gilberts in 1976. These islands were originally colonized by Polynesian peoples and their local languages and cultural histories are distinct from the Micronesian groups that inhabit the islands to the north. The administrative center is located on Funafuti. The entire group of islands totals only 9¼ square miles and has a population of about 5,000 people. Tourist facilities are extremely limited.

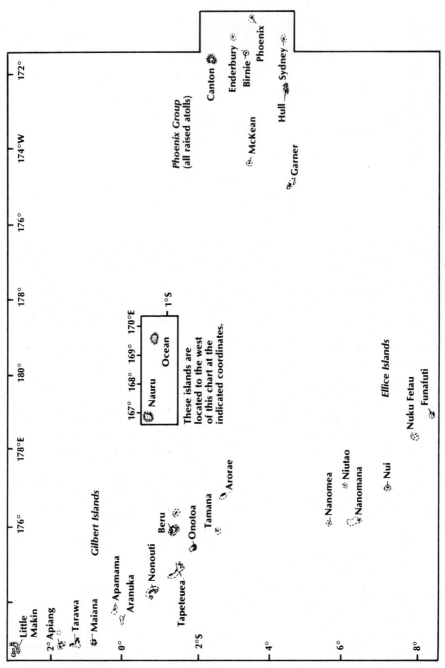

Figure 9–11. The Gilbert and Ellice Islands (Kiribati Republic and Tuvalu)

Table 9-22: The Gilbert and Ellice Islands

Island	RC	IH	Pop.	Med.	Air?	Ship?	Harbor?	Volc?
Funafuti	A	A	S	–	Y	N	D	–
Nuku Fetau	A	A	S	–	N	N	D	–
Vaitupu	A	A	V	–	N	N	O	–
Nui	A	L	S	–	N	N	O	–
Niutau	RA	A	V	–	N	N	O	–
Nanomana	RA	A	S	–	N	N	O	–
Nanomea	A	A	V	–	N	N	D	–
Tamana	A	A	V	–	N	N	O	–
Beru	A	A	V	C	Y	N	O	–
Tapeteua	A	A	V	–	N	N	D	–
Nonouti	A	A	V	–	Y	N	D	–
Apamama	A	A	V	–	Y	N	D/S	–
Tarawa	A	A	T	C	Y	N	D	–
Apaiang	A	A	V	–	N	N	D	–
Makin	A	A	V	C	N	N	D	–
Ocean	RA	L	V	H	Y	N	D	–

Table 9-23: Weather in the Gilbert and Ellice Islands

	Air Temp. °F	Sea Temp. °F	Surf. Winds	Swell Dir'n.	Over-cast %	Rainfall days	Rainfall inches	Cyclones, Gales
January	81		NNE		44	17	12	0.3
February	81		NE		45	13	8.2	0.3
March	81		ENE		31	13	7.9	0.1
April	81		ENE		48	11	6.6	0
May	81		ENE		46	11	4.9	0
June	81		E		43	12	4.8	0
July	81		ESE		31	15	6.1	0.1
August	81		ENE		44	13	4.2	0
September	81		ESE		36	12	3.9	0
October	81		ESE		42	10	4.4	0
November	81		ESE		45	11	4.9	0.1
December	81		E		45	14	8.5	0.1

Data Source: Ocean Island, plus ocean station reports

The Islands of New Caledonia

Category: V
Population: 150,000 (approx.)
Political status: French overseas territory
Currency: Western Pacific franc (Noumea)
Language: French, some Pidgin English spoken in villages

The territory is dominated, politically and physically, by the island of New Caledonia. This elongate island is the fourth largest land mass in the Pacific, exceeded only by the two islands of New Zealand and the island of New Guinea.

The capital city is Noumea, located near the southeast coast of New Caledonia. Noumea has a large population and is linked with other portions of the Pacific by commercial air and water service. Port facilities and services are excellent.

The island is old and extremely well dissected by rainfall. It is rich in minerals, including nickel, chrome, silver, and gold. Industrial growth so far has been based on the mining of nickel, but increasing attention is being paid to other valuable minerals.

Tourism is primarily restricted to the area centered around Noumea. The nearby Isle of Pines is an exquisite islet devoted to tourism, and Isle Ouen (Wen) also has good facilities. Diving, snorkeling, fishing, and shell-collecting opportunities are superb.

The climate is surprisingly temperate. Near Noumea there may be morning frosts in July despite the warm waters and luxuriant coral growth along the coast. This produces occasional fogs, which may concern those arriving by yacht. In other respects this is one of the finest sailing grounds in the tropical Pacific.

Cyclonal storms are relatively common in this portion of the Pacific, and caution is advised when sailing during the tradewind season as well as at other times of the year (see Table 9–25 for weather data).

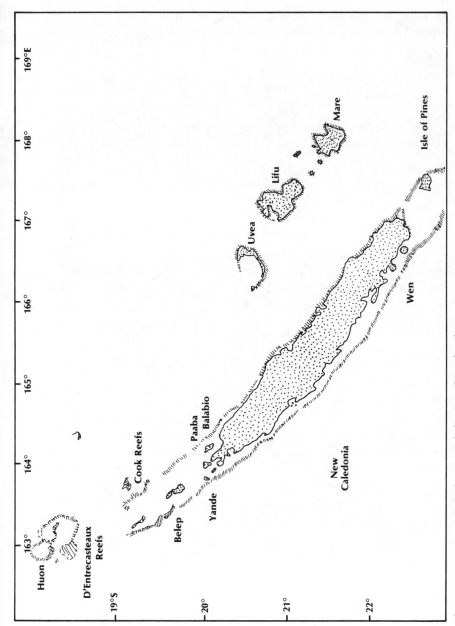

Figure 9–12. New Caledonia and the Loyalty Islands

Table 9-24: The Islands of New Caledonia

Island	RC	IH	Pop.	Med.	Air?	Ship?	Harbor?	Volc?
Pines	B	L	S	–	Y	N	D	–
New Caledonia	B	H	C	H	Y	Y	D	–
Ouen	B	L	S	–	Y	N	D	–
Belep	B	L	S	–	N	N	D	–
Mare	RA	L	V	–	Y	N	D	–
Lifu	RA	L	V	–	Y	N	D	–
Uvea	A	A	S	–	Y	N	D	–

Table 9-25: Weather in New Caledonia

	Air Temp. °F	Sea Temp. °F	Surf. Winds	Swell Dir'n.	Over-cast %	Rainfall days	Rainfall inches	Cyclones/Gales
January	80		ESE		43	10	3.7	1.8
February	80		E		43	12	4.3	1.5
March	78		E		40	15	5.4	2.1
April	76		E		42	13	5.4	0.3
May	72		E		44	15	4.5	0
June	70		ESE		47	13	3.9	0.1
July	68		ESE		44	13	3.7	0
August	68		ESE		41	12	2.7	0
September	70		ESE		42	8	2.4	0
October	72		ESE		40	7	2.2	0.1
November	75		ESE		44	7	2.3	0.2
December	78		ESE		37	6	2.7	0.4

*Cyclone data is gathered from reports covering the entire region, not Noumea specifically. Gales are *not* reported.

Data Source: Noumea, New Caledonia

The New Hebrides Islands (The Republic of Vanuatu)

Category: I
Islands: 14 large islands and numerous smaller islands, islets, and shoals,
    including the Torres and Banks island groups
Area: 5,700 sq. mi.
Population: 112,496 (1979)
Political status: Independent (July 29, 1979)
Currency: pound
Language: Pidgin English and innumerable tribal dialects

Tourism in these islands is just beginning and centers around the island of Efate, where the capital city of Vila is located. Luganville Santo, on Espiritu Santo Island, is a secondary port of entry to the country. Only these two islands maintain airline and cruise ship connections with the outside world and could be considered westernized.

With the possible exception of certain portions of the Solomons, these islands have been *least* influenced by European civilization of any of the Melanesian groups we will be discussing. This should be remembered by the visitor. Tourists are welcome, but when visiting the outer islands you should keep your eyes and ears open. Inter-tribal wars continue to occur, and as late as 1977 headhunting was still being reported (albeit infrequently) from some areas.

Farming provides the major source of support to the native inhabitants, most of whom live in small, separate villages. Each community may have its own language, and Pidgin English is the only universal means of communication. With some practice, it is fairly easy to pick up.

Industrial development is underway, with mining and fish processing most important. This was momentarily disrupted in May 1980, with the attempted secession of Espiritu Santo, but the situation has stabilized and both industry and tourism are expected to increase over the next few years.

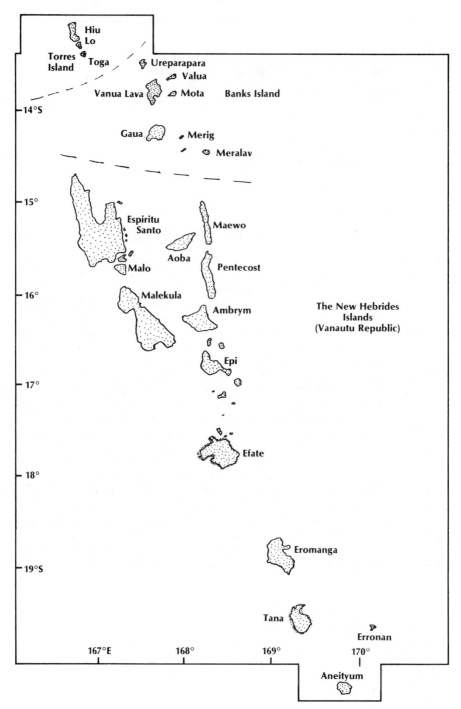

Figure 9–13. The New Hebrides Islands (Vanuatu)

Table 9-26: The New Hebrides Islands

Island	RC	IH	Pop.	Med.	Air?	Ship?	Harbor?	Volc?
Aneityum	F	M	V	–	Y	N	D	+
Tana	RF	M	T	–	Y	N	D	+
Erronan	RP	M		–	N	N	O	–
Efate	RB	M	T	H	Y	Y	D	–
Epi	B	M	V	–	Y	N	D	–
Malekula	F	M	V	–	Y	N	D	–
Ambrym	B	H	V	–	Y	N	D	–
Pentecost	F	M	V	–	Y	N	D	–
Espiritu Santo	RF	H	V	–	Y	Y	D	–
Aoba	F	M	V	–	N	N	D	+
Maewo	F	M	V	–	N	N	D	–
Gaua	F	M	S	–	N	N	D	–
Vanua Lava	F	M	S	–	N	N	D	+
Ureparapara	F	M	S	–	N	N	D	+
Lo	F	L	S	–	N	N	D	–
Hiu	F	M	S	–	N	N	O	–

Table 9-27: Weather in the New Hebrides

	Air Temp. °F	Sea Temp. °F	Surf. Winds	Swell Dir'n.	Over- cast %	Rainfall days	Rainfall inches	Cyclones/ Gales
January	81		ESE		60	20	10.4	0.4
February	81		SE		60	18	11.4	0.3
March	81		SE		50	20	6.6	0
April	79		SE		60	17	7.7	1.2
May	77		SE		60	16	5.8	0.3
June	74		SE		60	17	5.0	0
July	74		SE		60	14	3.2	0
August	73		SE		60	13	5.7	0.9
September	75		SE		60	12	3.7	0.2
October	76		SE		60	11	3.7	0.1
November	77		SE		50	12	4.3	0
December	79		SE		50	16	5.5	0

Data Source: Erronan

The Solomon Islands

Category: I
Area: 11,500 sq. mi.
Islands: 7 major islands, 20 to 30 smaller islands, and the islands of the Santa
    Cruz group
Population: 196,823 (1976)
Political status: Independent Republic
Currency: Solomon dollar
Language: English, Pidgin English, and various tribal dialects

The Solomon Islands, like the islands of Vanuatu, are very isolated and contain numerous, semi-autonomous villages. In the entire nation there are fewer than 1,000 automobiles, and less than sixty miles of paved roads. The only real city is the capital city of Honiara, on Guadalcanal Island. It has a population of around 15,000.

Like the Marquesas Islands, these islands were decimated following the arrival of the Europeans. From an estimated population of 250,000+, the total population was around 70,000 at the turn of this century. Since that time the situation has changed for the better, and at the moment over 50 percent of the population is under 20 years of age.

The islands of Guadalcanal, San Cristobal, and Gizo have substantial port facilities. Principle exports are copra, fish, and timber. International air service arrives at Honiara, where connections can be made with a local airline servicing many of the outer islands. Tourist accommodations are limited but available around Honiara and KiraKira (San Cristobal Island).

The huge island of Bougainville, usually considered to be part of the Solomons, is at this writing still a territory of Papua (New Guinea). There have been a series of uprisings on that island to demand seccession or union with the Solomons. It, and the satellite island of Buka, are included in Tables 9–28 and 9–29.

This is a fascinating area to sail through, but the charts are woefully inadequate, even concerning the general contours of the islands. Weather and currents are unpredictable, and scattered unexploded World War II ordinance makes anchoring especially titillating, if not actually disastrous.

Figure 9–14 (opposite page). The Solomon Islands

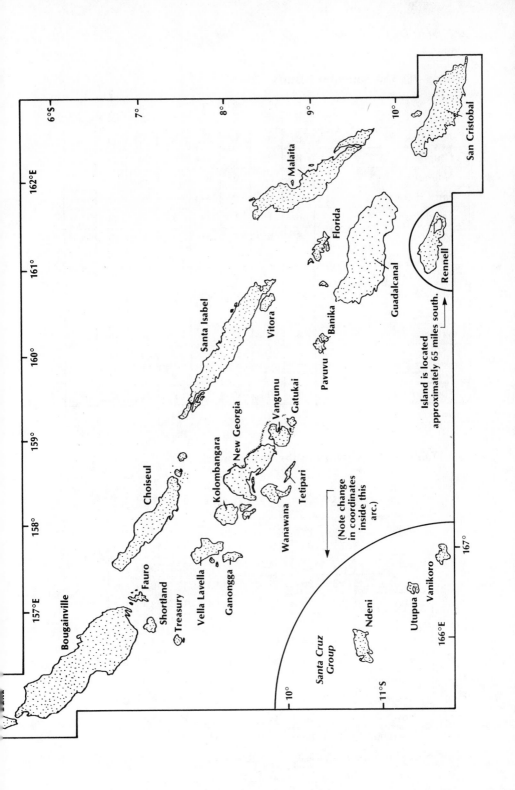

6°S
7°
8°
9°
10°

162°E
161°
160°
159°
158°
157°E

Bougainville

Fauro
Shortland
Treasury

Vella Lavella
Ganongga

Kolombangara
New Georgia
Vangunu
Gatukai

Choiseul

Wanawana
Tetipari

Santa Isabel

Vitora

Malaita

Florida

Pavuvu
Banika

Guadalcanal

San Cristobal

Rennell

Island is located
approximately 65 miles south.

(Note change
in coordinates
inside this
arc.)

Santa Cruz
Group

Ndeni

Utupua
Vanikoro

10°
11°S

166°E
167°

Table 9-28: The Solomon Islands

Island	RC	IH	Pop.	Med.	Air?	Ship?	Harbor?	Volc?
Vanikole	B	M	V	–	N	N	D	+
Utupua	B	L	V	–	N	N	D	–
Ndende	F	M	V	C	Y	N	D	–
San Cristobal	B	M	V	H	Y	N	D	–
Guadalcanal	B	H	T	H	Y	Y	D	–
Malaita	B	M	T	H	Y	Y	D	–
Florida	B	L	V	–	N	N	D	–
Santa Isabel	B	M	V	–	Y	N	D	–
New Georgia	RB	M	V	C	Y	N	D	–
Choiseul	B	M	V	–	Y	N	D	–
Balalei	B	L	V	–	Y	N	D	–
Gizo	B	L	V	C	Y	N	D	–
Vella Lavella	B	M	V	–	N	N	D	–
Bougainville	B	VH	V	C	Y	N	D	+
Buka	RB	M	T	C	N	N	D	–

Table 9-29: Weather in the Solomon Islands

	Air Temp. °F	Sea Temp. °F	Surf. Winds	Swell Dir'n.	Over-cast %	Rainfall days	Rainfall inches	Cyclones/Gales
January	82	85	NW		59	21	14.3	0.5
February	82	85	NW		58	21	15.8	0.3
March	82	85	NW		57	22	15.0	0.3
April	82	86	E		53	19	10.0	0
May	82	86	E		54	18	8.1	0.2
June	81	85	E		56	16	6.8	0.8
July	81	84	E		56	17	7.6	0.8
August	81	84	E		59	16	8.7	0.6
September	81	84	E		55	18	8.0	0.5
October	82	84	E		57	18	8.7	0.1
November	82	86	NW		55	16	10.0	0
December	83	86	E		53	19	10.4	0.1

Data Source: Guadalcanal Island

The Marshall Islands

Category: III(b)
Islands: 36 low atolls
Area: 70 sq. mi.
Population: 25,044 (1974)
Political status: Independent with U.S. commonwealth status
Currency: U.S. dollar
Language: English and Marshalese

These are all low atolls, strung out in two roughly parallel chains. The presence of the U.S. military has left a lasting impression on the entire group. Bikini, Enewitok, and Kwajalein Atolls are off limits except with special clearances. The former pair of islands were used for testing nuclear weapons, and resettlement attempts have not been resoundingly successful due to residual contamination. There is a small marine research facility operating on Enewitok under the aegis of the U.S. government. Kwajalein Atoll is an active Air Force base.

Rongerik Atoll is said to have been seriously contaminated by fallout from the nuclear tests, and prior to 1959 this was also reported for Ailinginae, Rongelap, and Utirik. The latter islands have since been given a clean bill of health, but you might find the information interesting anyway.

On the remaining islands, copra is the main export crop, and most islanders subsist on local farming and fishing. Marine life is plentiful and the waters are clear and warm. Outside of the main islands, tourist facilities are nonexistent, but the natives are hospitable in the extreme.

As with other islands in this region, charts are unreliable and the weather frequently unpredictable. Visiting vessels should be on the alert for typhoon (cyclone) warnings because these low islands do not offer sufficient shelter. Waves 20 feet high have completely devastated islands in the group just within the past twenty years.

Wake Island, located well to the north of the region shown on the chart, is geologically separate from the Marshalls. It is a U.S. airbase that is closed to the public.

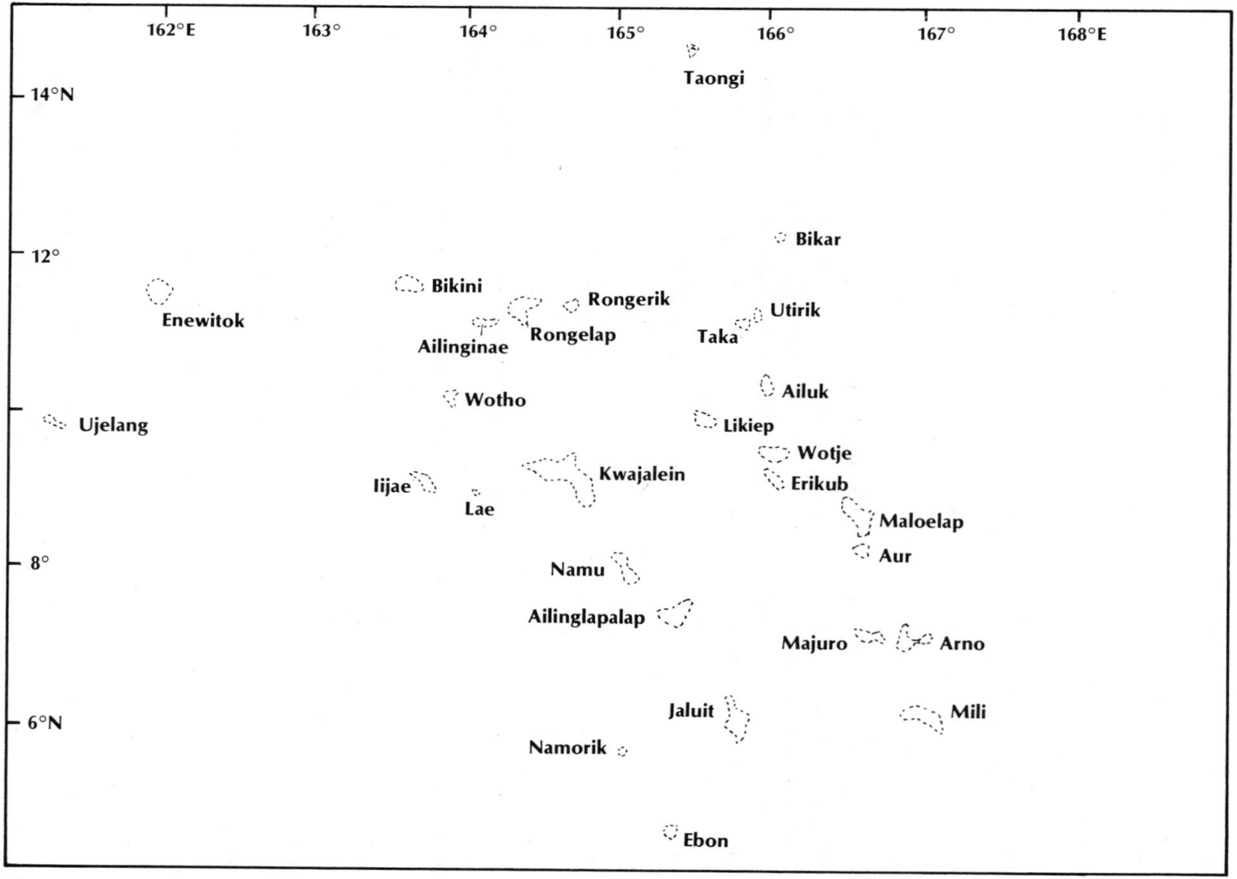

Figure 9–15. The Marshall Islands

Table 9-30: The Marshall Islands

Island	RC	IH	Pop.	Med.	Air?	Ship?	Harbor?	Volc?
Ebon	A	A	S	–	N	N	D	–
Jaluit	A	A	V	–	Y	N	D	–
Majuro	A	A	V	H	Y	Y	D	–
Arno	A	A	V	–	N	N	D	–
Likiep	A	A	S	–	N	N	D	–
Maloelap	A	A	S	–	N	N	D	–
Kwajalein	A	A	V	H	Y	N	D	–
Ailinglapalap	A	A	V	–	N	N	D	–
Ujae	A	A	S	–	N	N	O	–
Ujelang	A	A	S	–	N	N	S	–
Enewitok	A	A	S	–	Y	N	D	–
Bikini	A	A	O	–	N	N	D	–
Rongelap	A	A	S	–	N	N	D	–
Wake	A	A	S	C	Y	N	D	–

Table 9-31: Weather in the Marshall Islands

	Air Temp. °F	Sea Temp. °F	Surf. Winds	Swell Dir'n.	Over-cast %	Rainfall days	Rainfall inches	Cyclones/ Gales
January	80	81	ENE		74	16	3.6	0.3
February	80	81	ENE		58	14	2.2	0.1
March	81	82	ENE		73	16	6.5	0.3
April	81	82	NE		79	19	5.0	0.6
May	81	82	ENE		85	21	8.2	0.8
June	81	83	ENE		75	23	8.7	0.8
July	82	83	NE		84	23	8.9	2.6
August	82	84	NE		80	24	9.5	4.4
September	82	84	NE		88	22	10.2	3.2
October	81	84	NE		79	23	10.9	2.9
November	81	83	ENE		86	24	12.1	1.9
December	81	82	ENE		78	19	9.0	0.8

*Data for the entire western north Pacific; cyclones only, gales *not* recorded.

Data Source: Kwajalein Atoll

The Federated States of Micronesia
(formerly the Eastern and Central Carolines)

Category: IV
Islands: roughly 950, not all inhabited
Area: 510 sq. mi.
Population: 62,720 (1974)
Political status: Independent, with U.S. commonwealth status
Currency: U.S. dollar
Language: English, Yapese, Trukese, Ponapean, Kusaiean, etc.

Ports of entry to these interesting islands are located on Ponape, Truk, and Yap. At the moment, copra and cacao are the two leading exports; interest in commercial fisheries is growing. The western section consists of islands certain to be assigned to Category III(a), as discussed in Chapter 8; the small trench extending along the eastern coast of Yap and neighboring islands suggests that these may belong in Category I. Linguistically these islands are just as diverse; almost every island has its own dialect, often mutually unintelligible.

Tourist facilities are restricted to the more heavily populated ports of entry. Sailing in the region is fascinating, as long as you pay proper attention to the navigational and weather precautions mentioned for other western Pacific island groups. Swimming, snorkeling, and so on are excellent to superb.

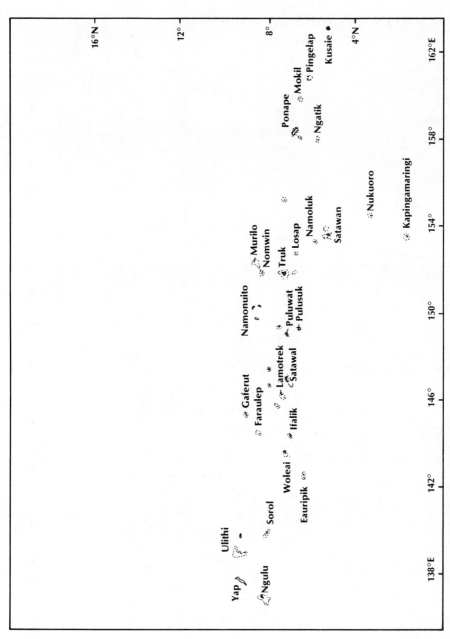

Figure 9–16. The Federated States of Micronesia

Table 9-32: The Federated States of Micronesia

Island	RC	IH	Pop.	Med.	Air?	Ship?	Harbor?	Volc?
Kusaie	B	M	V	–	Y	N	D	–
Pingelap	A	A	S	–	N	N	O	–
Ponape	B	M	T	H	Y	Y	D	–
Kapingamaringi	A	A	S	–	N	N	D	–
Satawan	A	A	V	–	N	N	D	–
Lukunor	A	A	V	–	N	N	D	–
Namoluk	RA	L	S	–	N	N	D	–
Losap	RA	L	S	–	N	N	D	–
Truk	AA	L	T	H	Y	N	D	–
Puluwat	A	A	S	–	N	N	O	–
Woleai	A	A	S	–	N	N	D	–
Ulithi	A	A	S	–	N	N	D	–
Yap	B	L	V	H	Y	N	D	–

Table 9-33: Weather in the Federated States

	Air Temp. °F	Sea Temp. °F	Surf. Winds	Swell Dir'n.	Over-cast %	Rainfall days	Rainfall inches	Cyclones/Gales
January	81	82	NNE		90	19	8.4	*
February	81	82	NNE		92	17	6.3	*
March	81	82	NNE		91	19	7.8	*
April	81	83	NNE		92	23	12.3	*
May	81	83	NNE		90	26	14.1	*
June	81	83	NE		90	26	11.9	*
July	81	84	SE		87	25	12.3	*
August	80	84	S		90	26	12.8	*
September	80	85	SW		89	25	12.6	*
October	81	85	S		89	24	13.5	*
November	81	84	NNE		91	25	12.4	*
December	81	83	NNE		92	23	13.2	*

*Consult data presented in Table 9-31 for the Marshall Islands.

Data Source: Truk Atoll

Guam and The Commonwealth of the Northern Marianas

Category: I
Islands: 13, plus 3 islets (CNM)
Area: 225 sq. mi. (Guam); 479 sq mi. (CNM)
Population: 86,926 (1970, Guam); 14,355 (1974, CNM)
Political status: Guam is an unincorporated territory of the United States; the
    commonwealth of the North Marianas is an independent U.S. affiliate
Currency: U.S. dollar
Language: English; Chomorro

Guam. Guam is a relatively high island, formed along the edge of the trench system involved with the Marianas as well. Guam is dominated by U.S. military presence and is of great strategic importance. Almost one third of the land is assigned to the U.S. Navy and Air Force. The major port is Apra at the capital city of Agana.

The native language, Chomorro, is of Indonesian origin, as are the natives themselves. Subsistence farming and fishing were the original sources of support for the population; commercial fishing is now under development and economic salvation may have arrived in the form of tourists. There were roughly 250,000 tourists to the island in 1976, three quarters of them from Japan. Guam is the logistical center for the entire region. International flights arrive there, and passengers can connect to smaller flights to various outer islands, including the Marianas, Palau, and the Federated States of Micronesia. Goods exported from the region are transshipped through Guam. Good tourist facilities and excellent snorkeling are to be found on the island.

Commonwealth. Many of the tourists arriving at Guam are spreading to outer islands and the regional economy is benefiting. Saipan is the center.

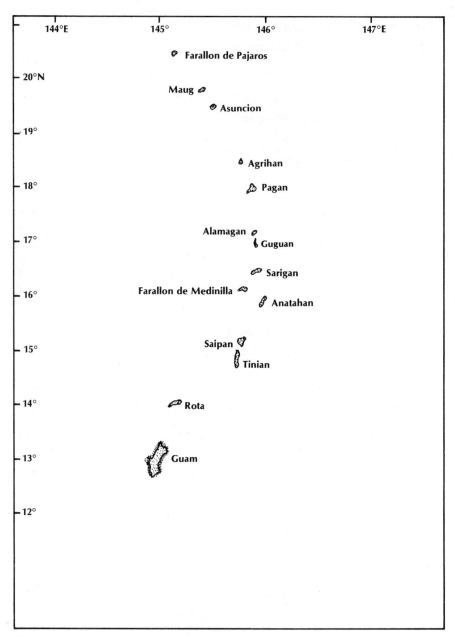

Figure 9–17. Guam and the Commonwealth of the Northern Marianas

Table 9-34: Guam and the Commonwealth of the Northern Marianas

Island	RC	IH	Pop.	Med.	Air?	Ship?	Harbor?	Volc?
Guam	RB/F	L	C	H	Y	Y	D	–
Aguijian	P	L	O	–	N	N	O	–
Rota	RF	L	V	C	Y	N	D	–
Tinian	RF	L	S	–	Y	N	D	–
Saipan	RF	M	T	H	Y	Y	D	–
Sarigan	F	M	S	–	N	N	O	–
Guguan	F	L	O	–	N	N	O	+
Alamagan	F	M	S	–	N	N	O	–
Pagan	F	M	S	–	N	N	D	+
Agrihan	F	M	S	–	N	N	O	–
Asuncion	P	M	O	–	N	N	O	+
Maug	F	L	O	–	N	N	O	–
Farallon de Pajaros	P	L	O	–	N	N	O	+

Table 9-35: Weather in Guam and the Marianas

	Air Temp. °F	Sea Temp. °F	Surf. Winds	Swell Dir'n.	Over-cast %	Rainfall days	Rainfall inches	Cyclones/Gales
January	78	81	NE		71	24	4.6	0
February	78	81	ENE		71	16	3.5	0
March	79	81	ENE		70	19	2.6	0
April	80	82	ENE		66	19	3.0	0
May	80	83	E		65	19	4.2	0
June	80	84	E		68	23	5.9	0
July	80	85	ESE		78	24	9.0	0.2
August	79	85	ESE		81	26	12.8	0.1
September	79	85	ESE		80	26	13.4	0.2
October	79	85	E		77	27	13.1	0.2
November	79	84	ENE		70	24	10.3	0.1
December	79	82	ENE		70	23	6.1	0.1

Data Source: Guam

The Palau Islands

Category: IV
Islands: 8 large islands, approximately 235 smaller ones
Area: 185 sq. mi.
Population: 12,674 (1974)
Political status: Independent member of U.S. commonwealth
Currency: U.S. dollar
Language: English, Palauan, Sonsorolese

This island group is dominated by Babelthuap Island, which among U.S. affiliates in Micronesia is second in size only to Guam. Only the northern islands in the group have exposed volcanic rocks, and most of the Palau islands have elevated reefs along their coasts. Recent subsidence has resulted in the formation of extensive barrier reefs, especially along the western coasts of the islands, whereas fringing reefs may occur off the eastern shores. This suggests that the region around the islands may be settling with a slight tilt with subsidence more pronounced to the west.

Most of the islands are heavily forested. Cacao is the main export crop, but commercial fishing is being developed as well. All imports and exports arrive via Guam, and all visitors must do likewise. Snorkeling is spectacular, and the islands vary in structure and appearance. There are good harbors and sailing in this region is said to be very good (accepting the usual precautions concerning charts and weather conditions in the western Pacific).

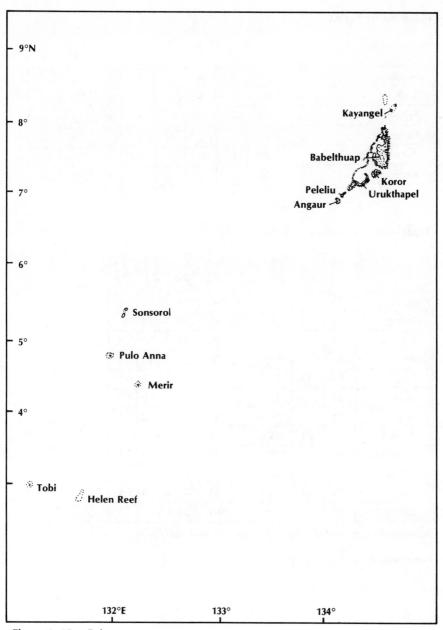

Figure 9–18.　Palau

Table 9-36: Palau

Island	RC	IH	Pop.	Med.	Air?	Ship?	Harbor?	Volc?
Sonsorol	RA	A	S	–	N	N	O	–
Angaur	RA	L	O	–	N	N	O	–
Peleliu	RA	L	V	–	N	N	D	–
Koror	RB	L	V	H	Y	N	D	–
Babelthuap	RB	L	V	–	N	N	D	–
Kayangel	A	A	S	–	N	N	S	–

Table 9-37: Weather in Palau

	Air Temp. °F	Sea Temp. °F	Surf. Winds	Swell Dir'n.	Over-cast %	Rainfall days	Rainfall inches	Cyclones/Gales
January	80		NE		90	23	11.7	*
February	80	81	NE		86	19	7.1	*
March	81		NE		86	18	7.6	*
April	81		ENE		86	21	10.4	*
May	81	83	E		88	26	14.6	*
June	81		E		91	26	13.0	*
July	81		SW		91	26	15.2	*
August	81	84	SW		94	25	15.8	*
September	81		SW		91	25	14.3	*
October	81		SW		87	22	13.1	*
November	81	84	ENE		89	23	12.9	*
December	81		ENE		93	26	11.7	*

*Consult data presented in Table 9-31 for the Marshall Islands.

Data Source: Koror Island

The Tropical Atlantic Islands

I. THE BAHAMAS GROUP
The Bahamas and the Turks and Caicos Islands

The Bahamas Islands

Category: V
Islands: 700, with numerous islets and bays; roughly 30 inhabited
Area: 4,404 sq. mi.
Total population: 203,946 (1976)
Political status: Independent member of the British Commonwealth
Currency: Bahamanian dollar, but U.S. currency gratefully accepted
Language: English

The islands of the Bahamas represent exposed and eroded portions of an extensive reef that began forming more than 100 million years ago. Two large submerged banks support the islands—Little Bahamas Bank to the north and Great Bahamas Bank in the south. Because the waters are shallow and the sands shift frequently, navigation among the islands requires considerable attention, but the underwater scenery makes it all worthwhile.

The islands were discovered by America's most famous tourist, Christopher Columbus, on his first voyage. Subsequently the Spanish shipped the Indian inhabitants to Cuba and Hispaniola as mine workers, but they did not establish any settlements on the islands. A British colony was founded in the seventeenth century, but there were so many islands and islets that settlers without official sanction gradually took control of many of the islands. These immigrants ranged from disgruntled Revolutionary War veterans to assorted brigands and thieves who used the islands as a pirate headquarters. The latter proved very difficult to dislodge, primarily because of the difficulties in navigating through the maze of islands. Modern-day drug entrepreneurs seem to have followed this pattern. Both the Americans and the Spanish have tried to take over the islands at one time or another, but they remained under British control until independence was attained in 1973.

These are probably *the* most accessible islands from a tourism standpoint, because the group extends to within fifty miles of the U.S. mainland. Although these are not tropical islands in the strict sense—because they lie north of 23½°N—the clear and sunny skies, brilliant sandy beaches, and relaxed atmosphere would be enough to fool anyone. Commercial transportation is available to most of the inhabited islands, and there you will usually find some form of tourist facility waiting with open arms, for more than 70 percent of the country's income and employment depends on contented visitors. Whatever you consider appropriate for a vacation is available. There are gambling casinos and swinging nightlife, charter fishing expeditions, scuba tours, and plush hotels on the populous islands such as New Providence. If you'd sooner disappear there are charter flights to more tranquil islands where swimming and beach-combing are the major forms of entertainment. A large fleet of sail-it-yourself charter sailboats, called "bareboat charters," and many more luxurious crewed charter boats are available for hire if you would prefer to see the islands at a more leisurely pace.

The Turks and Caicos Islands

Category: V
Islands: 30; 7 inhabited
Area: 92 sq. mi.
Total population: 5,675 (1970)
Political status: British Crown colony
Currency: Jamaican dollar
Language: English

Physically these islands are virtually identical with those of the Bahamas, and the same navigational cautions and meteorological delights are found in both groups. Although the two are separated politically, the Turks and Caicos represent the southeastern limits of the Bahamas Bank formation discussed in Chapter 8.

The histories of these small islands are tied up with their main commercial export, salt. Admittedly that doesn't sound like much now, but in the days when refrigeration was just a dream, a supply of salt was essential to any country attempting to maintain trading routes and empires abroad. Without salt beef, or more typically salt cod, your ships' crews would starve or wind up like Magellan's party, eating the soles of their shoes or the leather chafing gear from the rigging. With visions of expansion driving them, various nations took control of the islands, and they passed from Bermudan to Spanish to French to Bahamanian to Jamaican hands before attaining independent colony status in 1962. A declining demand for salt has virtually eliminated the business, and the local economy is now based on fishing and the exportation of fisheries products, such as shells and lobsters. Any island with good beaches, clear waters, and enough shells or lobster to export would seem destined for stardom, but so far these islands haven't been developed appreciably. There is a notable lack of luxuries, and the islands need better runways and roads, but if you are after an out-of-the-way spot and have a fondness for clear waters and steamed lobster these may be the islands for you.

Winds and weather. The entire region is influenced by the northeast tradewinds throughout the year, but the northern islands are influenced by the proximity of the North American continent. The northwestern portion of the group experiences E/SE winds during the summer and NE/E winds in winter; the remainder of the islands have easterly winds in summer and northeasterly winds in winter. Hurricanes are very common over the months of July through September.

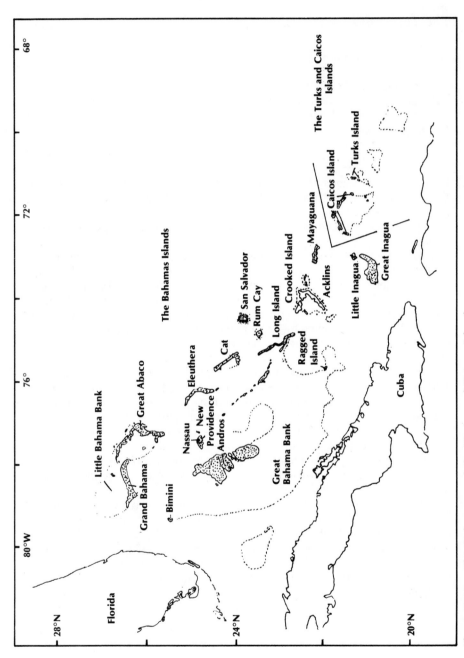

Figure 9–19. The Bahamas and the Turks and Caicos Islands

Table 9–38: The Bahamas and the Turks and Caicos Islands

Island	RC	IH	Pop.	Med.	Air?	Ship?	Harbor?	Volc?
Grand Bahama	F*	L	T	H	Y	Y¹	D	–
Great Abaco Island	F*	L	V	C	Y	Y	D	–
Bimini	F*	L	V	H	Y	Y	D	–
Eleuthera	F*	L	V	–	Y	Y	D	–
New Providence	F*	L	C	H	Y	Y	D	–
Andros	B*	L	V	C	Y	Y	D	–
Long Island	F*	L	V	C	Y	Y	D	–
Great Exuma	F*	L	V	H	Y	Y	D	–
Cat	F*	L	V	–	Y	Y	D	–
Crooked Island	F*	L	S	C	Y	Y	D	–
Acklins Island	F*	L	S	H**	Y	Y	D	–
Mayaguana	F*	L	S	C	Y	Y	D	–
Great Inagua	F*	L	V	H	Y	Y	D	–
Grand Turk	F*	L	V	H	Y	Y	D	–
Salt Cay	F*	L	S				D	–
Caicos Group (4)	F*	L	V	C	Y	Y	D	–

*fringing reefs surrounding banks produced through biological and chemical processes

**staffed part-time

Table 9–39: Weather in the Bahamas

	Rainfall days	Rainfall inches	Air Temp. °F (ADH)
January	6	1	77
February	5	2	77
March	5	1	79
April	6	3	81
May	9	5	84
June	12	6	87
July	14	6	88
August	14	5	89
September	15	7	88
October	13	7	85
November	9	3	81
December	6	1	79

Data Source: Nassau, New Providence Island

II. THE CARIBBEAN ISLANDS

THE GREATER ANTILLES GROUP The islands of Cuba, Jamaica, Hispaniola, Puerto Rico, and the Virgin Islands make up the Greater Antilles arc. The member islands have similar geological histories, forming over oceanic crust adjacent to a trench system. Portions of the trench array that existed during their formation have since been obliterated, and further compression occurred when Cuba and the North American continent collided. Trenches or troughs are still found near most of the islands within this assemblage, with the Puerto Rico trench to the northeast and the Bartlett trough between Cuba and Jamaica/Caymans. With the exception of the Virgin Islands these are high, volcanic islands, and in all cases they are as old or older than the Category I islands of the Lesser Antilles arc.

Because these are predominantly large islands, generalizations about local climate are difficult. Complex mountain ranges, strong land and sea breeze systems, and the channeling of winds between the islands may all affect the observed weather at the local level. This should be kept in mind when reviewing the meteorological data for the individual islands or island groups.

Jamaica and the Cayman Islands

Jamaica

Category: I
Islands: 1, plus small coastal islets
Area: 4,411 sq. mi.
Total population: 1,911,400 (1971)
Political status: Independent member of the British Commonwealth
Currency: Jamaican dollar
Language: English

Jamaica is a beautiful tropical island, complete with lush forests, sandy beaches, coral reefs, and sheltered anchorages. To the east a lofty peak in the Blue Mountain Range reaches 7,402 feet, and along the ridge there are other summits reaching heights of over 6,000 feet. Subsidence was followed by a period of elevation, and a limestone plateau is now exposed on the western coast at an altitude of 3,000 feet.

Columbus reported this island in 1494, and the Spanish moved in fifteen years later, much to the dismay of the Arawak inhabitants. Once the latter had been either killed by disease or eliminated by more direct methods the resourceful Spaniards imported African slaves to do the manual labor. Spain used the island as a central supply base for operations in the New World until late in the seventeenth century, when the British took over the island. With an eye toward discomfiting the Spanish further, the capital city of Port Royal was unofficially turned over to bucaneers who raided Spain's shipping lanes. This period of sanctioned high-times is still fondly recalled by the inhabitants, but it was already fading when a massive earthquake in 1692 flattened the city. A more sedate government subsequently shifted to the present capital of Kingston, and the British remained in control until Jamaica became an independent nation in 1962.

Tourism is important to Jamaican economy, but the island has many other sources of income. Jamaica is the world's largest exporter of bauxite, an aluminum ore, and there are mines producing asbestos as well. Agricultural products including citrus fruits, sugar, cocoa, and tobacco are also exported with some success.

The Cayman Islands

Category: 1
Islands: 3
Area: 100 sq. mi.
Total population: 10,249 (1970)
Political status: Member of the British Commonwealth
Currency: Cayman Islands dollar
Language: English

The Cayman Islands are so small and so far off the regular sailing routes that they remained unnoticed until Columbus' fourth trip, when he sighted one of the northern islands. Other than noting a plentiful supply of sea turtles there was not any great interest shown in the region. Because everyone else was ignoring these islands, and especially the northern island of Little Cayman, which is low and rather mosquito-plagued at times, pirates moved in and set up a camp so large that it took a major British amphibious assault to dislodge them.

The islands are elevated coral reefs that grew over volcanic foundations, in this case a portion of a mountain range that extends through eastern Cuba. Tourism is the major industry, but in recent years the favorable policies toward banking operations have made Grand Cayman a little-Switzerland for the region. There are no rivers to carry debris into local waters, so diving is excellent, especially in the outer islands of Little Cayman and Cayman Brac where development is rather leisurely. The inhabitants of all the islands are extremely warm and hospitable toward visitors.

Winds and weather. These islands are directly in the path of the northeast tradewinds; the winds are NE in winter and NE/E in summer. Because of its large size and high mountains, Jamaican climate is strongly influenced by land and sea breezes that develop and affect portions of the lee (SW) side of the island in opposition to the prevailing tradewinds. Hurricanes strike the islands every few years, and during the winter cold air masses called *northers* may bring high winds and rain. Throughout the year there is a marked difference in rainfall between windward and leeward coasts of Jamaica; the northeast coast averages 100 to 200 inches per year, whereas Kingston averages a mere 27½ inches.

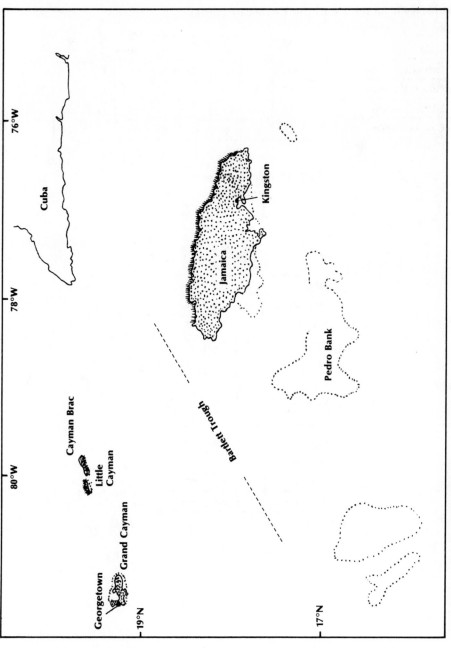

Figure 9–20. Jamaica and the Cayman Islands

Table 9-40: Jamaica and the Cayman Islands

Island	RC	IH	Pop.	Med.	Air?	Ship?	Harbor?	Volc?
Jamaica	F/B	H	C	H	Y	Y	D	–
Grand Cayman	RA	A	C	H	Y	Y	D	–
Little Cayman	RA	A	S	–	Y	N	D	–
Cayman Brac	RA	L	V	C	Y	N	O	–

Table 9-41: Weather in Jamaica

	Rainfall days	Rainfall inches	Air Temp. °F (ADH)
January	3	0.9	86
February	3	0.6	86
March	2	0.9	86
April	3	1.2	87
May	4	4.0	87
June	5	3.5	89
July	4	1.5	90
August	7	3.6	90
September	6	3.9	89
October	9	7.1	88
November	5	2.9	87
December	4	1.4	87

Data Source: Kingston

C. Hispaniola*

The Dominican Republic _____

Category: I
Area: 18,700 sq. mi.
Total population: 4,000,000 (1972)
Political status: Independent nation
Currency: Gold peso
Language: Spanish

Haiti _____

Category: I
Area: 10,700 sq. mi.
Total population: 4,750,000 (1972)
Political status: Independent nation
Currency: Gourde
Language: French, Creole

Hispaniola is a fertile, mountainous island, second only to Cuba in total area in the Caribbean. The mountain ranges of this island run roughly east to west. The northern coastline is often rugged and cliffed; the southern coast has adjacent lowlands and numerous bays. The internal valleys and windward slopes are among the most verdant of the Caribbean, and scenically the island as a whole is very alluring. Unfortunately this poor island has had an almost unbelievably troubled history.

Columbus discovered the island for the Europeans in 1492, and the eastern town of Santo Domingo is the oldest settlement in the New World. In 1697 the French settled the western end of the island, and eighty years later the two powers divided the island between them. In 1795 the Spanish turned over their holdings to the French, but the inhabitants of eastern Hispaniola didn't care for this very much. A rebellion followed that returned Santo Domingo to Spain. A dozen years later the Spanish colony declared its independence, whereupon the French invaded and conquered it. The Spanish inhabitants responded by establishing the Dominican Republic and bringing it once more under the protection of the Spanish Crown. However, not everyone liked that arrangement either, and there was an almost immediate rebellion against Spain. The pattern was now firmly established: The next fifty years witnessed twenty-eight revolutions and thirty-five governments.

Meanwhile, Haitian politics were almost as confusing. Haiti declared independence from France in 1804, and the years that followed saw one Emperor

*Additional data on this island can be found in Table 9–63, p. 341.

(assassinated), one King (suicide), and a President simultaneously, followed by a second President and another Emperor before a Republic was formally established. Changing the governmental title did little to stabilize the region, and in 1915 the U.S. government decided to add to the island's rich political history by sending in the Marines to take over. One year later the Dominican Republic was brought under the same administration.

The United States remained in control of Haiti until 1934. A working constitution was accepted in 1950, but did not prevent the subsequent election of a President-for-Life, whose son has succeeded him. The Dominican Republic was on its own for a time after the United States departed in 1924. A coup was followed by an iron-clad rule for thirty-one years, but in 1962 things reverted back to business as usual. An election was followed by a coup, followed by an Army revolt and then a civil war, and the U.S. Marines returned from 1965–1966. Since that time general elections seem to have worked well (ignoring the coup attempt of 1973).

With all this going on, it is not surprising that despite its scenic splendor Hispaniola has not grown into a popular tourist resort. The economies of both nations are in poor repair, and severe famines have struck the island in the past decade. The problems have been aggravated by the fact that Haiti has the highest population density of anywhere in the Caribbean, coupled with the least economic base to support it. This is a shame, because there are few islands in the Caribbean with as great a potential for generating tourist revenue if the assets were properly managed and the political situation were a bit less volatile.

Winds and weather. Hispaniola is the highest of the Caribbean islands, and localized interactions between the tradewinds and land/sea breezes produce a varied climate. The basic tradewind pattern is shared with the rest of the Greater Antilles—NE winds in winter and NE/E winds in summer. As you might predict, the western side of the island has the least rainfall, and along the northern coast the amount of rain increases as you travel east. The southern shore, markedly influenced by land and sea breezes, varies on a day-to-day basis, but is generally warmer than the northern coast.

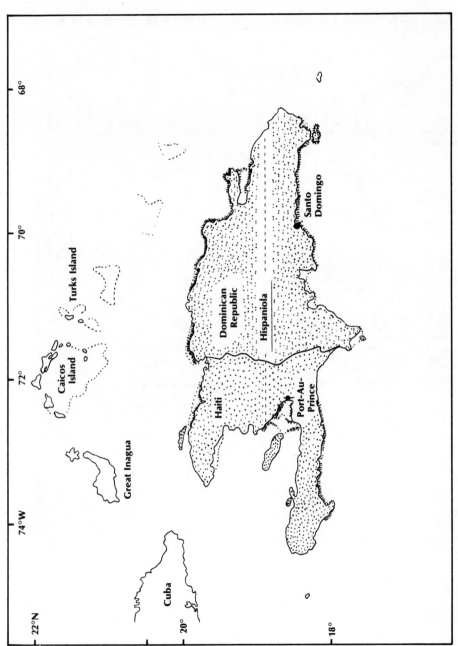

Figure 9–21. Hispaniola

Table 9–42: Weather in Haiti

	Rainfall days	Rainfall inches	Air Temp.°F (ADH)
January	3	1.3	87
February	5	2.3	88
March	7	3.4	89
April	11	6.3	89
May	13	9.1	90
June	8	4.0	92
July	7	2.9	94
August	11	5.7	93
September	12	6.9	91
October	12	6.7	90
November	7	3.4	88
December	3	1.3	87

Data Source: Port-au-Prince (Haiti)

Table 9–43: Weather in the Dominican Republic

	Rainfall days	Rainfall inches	Air Temp.°F (ADH)
January	7	2.4	84
February	6	1.4	85
March	5	1.9	84
April	7	3.9	85
May	11	6.8	86
June	12	6.2	87
July	11	6.4	88
August	11	6.3	88
September	11	7.3	88
October	11	6.0	87
November	10	4.8	86
December	8	2.4	85

Data Source: Dominican Republic (Santo Domingo)

Puerto Rico*

Category: I
Islands: 1, plus coastal satellites
Area: 3,423 sq. mi.
Total population: 2,688,269 (1970)
Political status: unincorporated territory of the United States
Currency: U.S. dollar
Language: English and Spanish

The volcanic activity that formed the island of Puerto Rico was followed by a period of elevation and subsequent erosion before a general subsidence became the rule. The island spine is a mountain range that runs roughly west to southeast with peaks of 3,000 to 4,000 feet. To the northeast the coast is often rugged and cliffed, whereas the remainder of the northern coast and the entire southern shore have broad coastal plains. As you might expect, the wettest region lies short of the mountains in the northeast section, whereas the southwest corner of the island is extremely dry. Elsewhere along the southern coast there is a strong daily sea breeze that brings frequent showers to the coastal plains.

The ever-vigilant Columbus discovered this island in 1493, giving it an unpopular name that failed to stick. Although the British and Dutch both attempted to seize it at one time or another, the Spaniards held on until 1898, when they lost title to the United States. Modern Puerto Rico is rather different from the other Caribbean islands, thanks to the Americanization that has brought it closer and closer to trading its territorial status for statehood. The main city of San Juan is heavily tourist-oriented, and legalized gambling hasn't hurt the local economy. Outside the city you can begin to relax and feel as if you are on vacation and not hustling and bustling along at a pace set by hotels, discos, and casinos, although every year you must travel a little farther to make good your escape.

Winds and weather. These conditions are as noted for other islands of the Greater Antilles, with local variations due to land and sea breeze systems.

*Additional data on this island can be found in Table 9–63, p. 341.

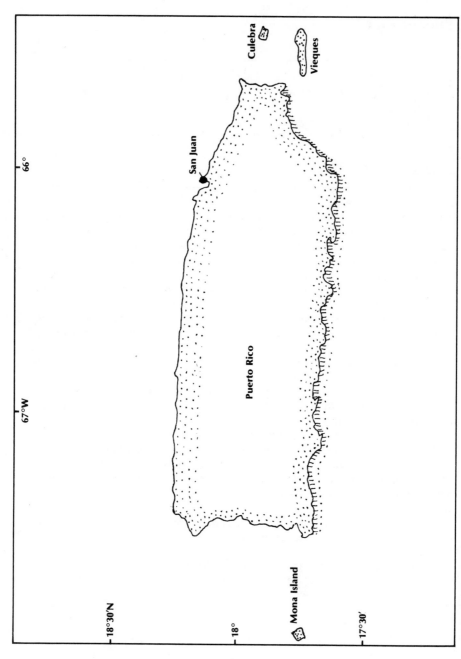

Figure 9–22. Puerto Rico

Table 9-44: Weather in Puerto Rico

	Wind Dir'n.	Rainfall days	Rainfall inches	Air Temp. °F (ADH)
January	ENE	20	4.3	80
February	ENE	15	2.7	80
March	ENE	15	2.9	81
April	ENE	14	4.1	82
May	ENE	16	5.9	84
June	ENE	17	5.4	85
July	ENE	19	5.7	85
August	ENE	20	6.3	85
September	ENE	18	6.2	86
October	ENE	18	5.6	85
November	ENE	19	6.3	84
December	ENE	21	5.4	81

Data Source: San Juan

The Virgin Islands

The U.S. Virgin Islands _____

Category: I
Islands: 50; 3 with significant populations
Area: 132 sq. mi.
Total population: 63,200 (1970)
Political status: unincorporated territory of the United States, under the
    Department of the Interior
Currency: U.S. dollar
Language: English

The three main islands of the U.S. Virgin Islands are rather different in appearance and atmosphere. St. Croix is the largest and most agriculturally oriented of the islands; St. Thomas is the most extensively developed for tourism; St. Johns is close to pristine. St. Croix has a varied structure. Subsidence was accompanied by the development of a barrier reef that was later elevated and eroded. The low mountains that run the length of the island increase in height to the west, and this feature has a pronounced effect on local climate. The eastern end of the island is characterized by rocky, desert-like conditions whereas to the west, where the tradewinds ascend the rising slopes, veritable rainforests can be found. For cruising enthusiasts, this is the island with the least to offer in terms of safe harbors and anchorages. St. Thomas is mountainous, with 1,500 foot peaks and excellent harbors for both yachts and cruise ships. The capital of Charlotte Amalie is located on one of these harbors, and up to half a dozen passenger ships may be found within its boundaries at one time. St. John is similar to St. Thomas in general appearance, but almost two thirds of the island has been declared a National Park. This has limited development, and associated environmental problems, and the population is very low. There are many good anchorages, but sailors should be aware that the Park Service takes a dim view of collecting shells or smashing coralheads with a dragging anchor.

These are relatively rich islands from a regional standpoint, yet they are not without problems. The influx of American tourists and American products has led to problems with the disposal of waste products, and some of the beaches are suffering as a result. The waters around the islands are clear, but some of the reefs have been virtually stripped of corals and shellfish by visitors with an unconquerable desire to take a piece of the tropics home with them. My only comment would be that the honeymooning gentleman who stuffed a fire-coral into his swimming trunks as a souvenir probably had an experience that should be more widely appreciated by those who refuse to heed pleas for conservation and restraint. If you are interested in getting away from the tourism hub of St. Thomas and seeing the "real" Virgin Islands, then you should plan a visit to St. John. There are many yachts available for charter in St.

Thomas, and cruising through this group and the British Virgin Islands is a worthwhile project.

Columbus discovered the islands, but it took the Spanish until 1555 to beat the Caribs into submission and establish a firm claim. In the seventeenth century the French, British, and Dutch argued over ownership, but it was the Danes who began actually developing them. Almost 250 years later Denmark sold these islands to the United States for 25 million dollars. The original mainstay of the economy was sugarcane, but tourism has taken over the lead in recent years. The islands are a natural tourist mecca—the waters are warm and clear, the climate is superb, and the Danish history gives some of the scenery ashore a unique character. The inhabitants enjoy a good bash now and again, and as a result twenty-seven major holidays are celebrated in the course of a year.

The British Virgin Islands

Category: I
Islands: 60; 16 inhabited
Area: 59 sq. mi.
Total population: 10,500 (est.)
Political status: Member of the British Commonwealth
Currency: U.S. dollar
Language: English

As usual, Christopher Columbus found and named these islands. Pirates were the only settlers until 1773, when the British established a colony. Three islands are significantly populated, Tortola, Virgin Gorda, and Anegada. The latter is an elevated atoll, now fringed with living reefs; Virgin Gorda and Tortola are mountainous with peaks to 1,780 feet. As with the U.S. Virgin Islands, the reefs are primarily fringing reefs, but in a few locations they are approaching barrier reef status. The waters are extremely clear, and in general the islands are closer to St. John than St. Thomas in ambience. Toward the eastern portion of the group there are more extensive reefs and numerous shoals that make cruising rather interesting. Traveling in a group by land or water is almost a necessity because many of the most entertaining local businesses and restaurants are only open when there are enough visitors to make it all worthwhile.

Winds and weather. There is little you can say about the weather in the Virgin Islands other than that it is idyllic. The tradewinds arrive from the East almost all year, temperatures are comfortable, and rainfall gentle but reliable.

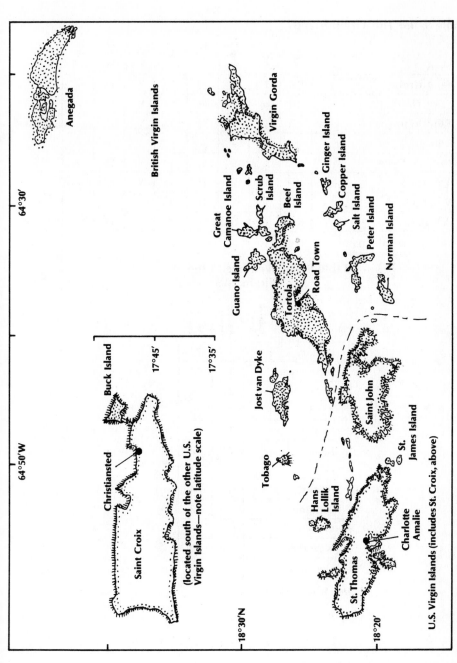

Figure 9–23. The Virgin Islands

Table 9-45: The Virgin Islands

Island	RC	IH	Pop.	Med.	Air?	Ship?	Harbor?	Volc?
Saint Croix	RB	L	T	H	Y	Y	D	–
Saint Thomas	RB	M	T	H	Y	Y	D	–
Saint John	RB	L	V	C	Y	Y	D	–
Tobago	F	L	–	–	–	–	–	–
Jost van Dyke	F	L	S	C	Y	Y	D	–
Tortola	F	L	V	H	Y	Y	D	–
Virgin Gorda	F	L	S	H	Y	Y	D	–
Anegada	RA	L	S	–	Y	Y	D	–

Table 9-46: Weather in the Virgin Islands

	Rainfall days	Rainfall inches	Air Temp. °F
January		4.3	77
February		1.9	77
March		2.0	78
April		7.5	79
May		1.3	80
June		2.9	82
July		5.6	84
August		4.1	84
September		6.6	83
October		5.6	83
November		5.4	80
December		3.8	78

Data Source: U.S. Virgin Islands

II. THE CARIBBEAN ISLANDS (continued)

THE LESSER ANTILLES GROUP This is an artificial collection of islands with varied histories. Aves Island, a Venezuelan possession to the west of the body of the group, is probably a contemporary of the Greater Antilles. It is an elevated reef that is awash during storms, and the area around it is a marine preserve. The Lesser Antilles are further subdivided into the Windward and Leeward Islands. The Leewards lie to the north, and like most of the Windward Islands they have formed in the past 85 million years along the edge of a trench. One of the Windwards, Barbados, formed separately, probably as trench sediments were compressed and uplifted. The remainder of the Lesser Antilles are strung along the Venezuelan coast. Trinidad and Tobago are portions of the mainland that have become isolated relatively recently. The series of islands between Aruba and Islas Testigos have complex histories, beginning with the establishment of a volcanic base along a now obliterated trench. Here the most recent volcanic activity, within the past 85 million years, has been along a trench formed where the Caribbean plate is subducting beneath a fragment of the South American continent.

THE LEEWARD ISLANDS
The Netherlands Antilles (northern sector)

Category: I
Islands: 2½
Area: 33 sq. mi.
Total population: 12,600 (1973)
Political status: Integral portion of the Netherlands
Currency: Netherlands Antilles guilder
Language: Dutch (and French on St. Maarten)

Two of these islands, Saba and St. Eustatius, are volcanic peaks that rise abruptly from the sea. Their coasts are steep and often cliffed, ascending to summits of 2,820 feet (Saba) and 1,969 feet (St. Eustatius). Neither island is noted for reliable anchorages or harbors of refuge, but St. Eustatius was once the principal trading port of the entire region. The historical sites on St. Eustatius island can make a fascinating focal point for a tour, but the success story of the island came to a sudden halt when a miffed British admiral plundered the island in a fit of pique over a presumed insult to the Crown.

As is often the case in the Lesser Antilles, the northern coast of St. Maarten is battered by swells and all but inaccessible from the sea. The southern coast is more hospitable, with numerous embayments and good diving and fishing. This island has been divided between the Dutch and the French, who call it St. Martin. Tourism on all three islands has been increasing steadily, and St. Maarten supports a commercial fishery and a rum factory as well.

Winds and weather. These islands have in common with the other Leeward Islands easterly tradewinds that are present throughout the year, and rainfall that is not excessive.

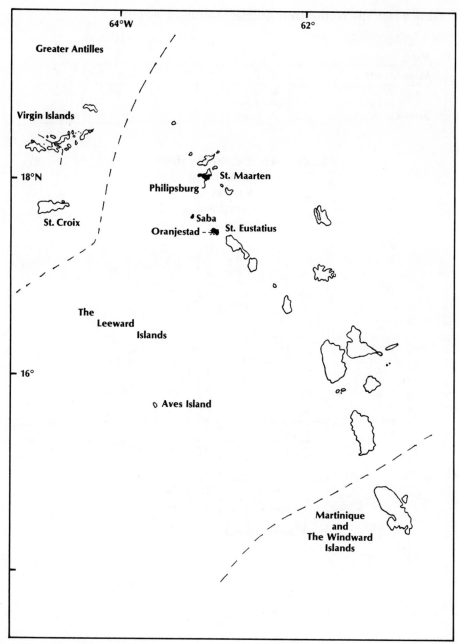

Figure 9–24. Netherlands Antilles (northern sector)

Table 9-47: The Netherland Antilles (Northern sector)

Island	RC	IH	Pop.	Med.	Air?	Ship?	Harbor?	Volc?
Saint Maarten	P	L	V	H	Y	Y	D	–
Saba	P	M	V	–	Y	Y	D	–
Saint Eustatius	P	M	V	–	Y	Y	D	–

Table 9-48: Weather in the Netherland Antilles (Northern sector)

	Rainfall days	Rainfall inches	Air Temp. °F
January		0.5	76
February		1.5	75
March		3.9	75
April		1.1	77
May		4.7	77
June		2.3	79
July		6.5	79
August		5.2	79
September		2.8	79
October		2.1	79
November		1.2	78
December		3.5	75

Data Source: Oranjestad

Guadeloupe and its dependencies

Category: I
Islands: 10½, plus islets
Area: 657 sq. mi.
Total population: 334,900 (1974)
Political status: French Overseas Department
Currency: New francs
Language: French (and Dutch on St. Martin)

This island assemblage is headquartered in Guadeloupe, an interesting pair of islands separated by a narrow channel. The western island of Basse-Terre is actively volcanic and rises to 4,900 feet, whereas the eastern island of Grand-Terre is composed of a series of low hills that are the eroded limestone of an elevated reef. Both islands are embayed and the effects of subsidence are evident along the tortuous coasts. To the south, the islands of Desirade and Marie Galante are elevated atolls. The small Iles des Santes are satellites of Guadeloupe. To the north the island of St. Barthelemy (St. Barts) has a rugged, rocky coastline fringed by coral reefs. The southern islands lack extensive reefs, and although the waters are clear there is very little diving done locally.

The first inhabitants were the Arawaks, who were chased out or eaten by the Caribs around 1000 A.D. The Spanish tried to occupy the islands following their discovery by Columbus, but they were unable to overcome the determined Carib defenders. When the French arrived in the early seventeenth century the Caribs fled to Dominica, which was the major Carib stronghold in the region. France and Britain passed the islands back and forth once or twice, but France's claim was not seriously threatened except on St. Barts, which Sweden controlled for over 100 years, and on St. Martin, which was eventually divided between the French and the Dutch.

Modern Guadeloupe has yet to be developed extensively for tourism, despite its scenic beauty. St. Barthelemy is becoming increasingly popular with visitors, probably because of the fringing reefs and a large local population of lobsters.

Winds and weather. The NE/E tradewinds blow all year round and the temperatures are comfortable. July through October marks the wettest season.

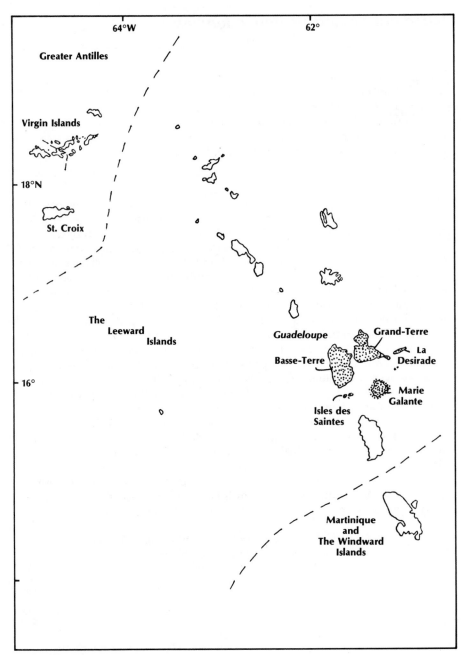

Figure 9–25. Guadeloupe

Table 9–49: Guadeloupe and Dependencies

Island	RC	IH	Pop.	Med.	Air?	Ship?	Harbor?	Volc?
Basse Terre	P	M	T	H	Y	Y	D	+
Grande Terre	P	L	T	H	Y	Y	D	–
Marie Galante	RA	L	T	H	Y	Y	D	–
Les Saintes	P	L	V	C	N	Y	D	–
Desirade	RA	L	V	C	N	Y	D	–
St. Barthelemy	F	L	V	C	Y	Y	D	–
St. Martin	P	L	V	H	Y	Y	D	–

Table 9–50: Weather in Guadeloupe

	Rainfall days	Rainfall inches	Air Temp. °F (ADH)
January	23	9.2	77
February	18	6.1	76
March	20	8.1	77
April	20	7.3	79
May	23	11.5	80
June	25	14.1	80
July	27	17.6	81
August	26	15.3	82
September	23	16.4	82
October	24	12.4	81
November	22	12.3	80
December	23	10.1	78

Data Source: Guadeloupe

Antigua, Anguilla, and their dependencies

Category: I
Islands: 7, plus islets and rocks
Area: 170 sq. mi. (Antigua and dependencies)/153 sq. mi. (Anguilla and
   dependencies)
Total population: 63,000 (Antigua and dependencies)/53,500 (Anguilla and
   dependencies)
Political status: Antigua and dependencies: independent members of the
   British Commonwealth; Anguilla and dependencies: members of the West
   Indies Associated States, associated with Great Britain
Currency: East Caribbean dollar
Language: English

Administratively these islands are separated into Antigua-Barbuda-Redonda
and Anguilla-St. Kitts-Nevis-Sombrero. Several of the islands have undergone
cycles of subsidence, reef growth, emergence, and erosion. Antigua is an
elevated almost-atoll, with a low volcanic peak in the southwest. The rest of the
island is rather flat, composed of uplifted and eroded reef deposits. Barbuda,
Sombrero, Anguilla, and Redonda are elevated atolls, some of which have
been mined for phosphate deposits. St. Kitts (i.e., St. Christopher) and Nevis
are paired volcanic islands, the latter rising to a peak of almost 3,600 feet.
Barbuda and Antigua are perched atop the Barbuda Bank, an extensive shoal
area that has tilted slightly upward along the eastern edge. Anguilla is based on
a bank that extends to the south, supporting St. Martin/Maarten and St. Barthelemy as well. Uninhabited Redonda is parked on a small bank of its very
own.

The islands were discovered by Columbus, but the Spanish abandoned
their attempts at colonization because the islands were too dry. The French
gave the islands a try, but departed with similar complaints. The British arrived
and settled down to grow tobacco, despite raids by the Caribs, and later diversified to growing sugar cane. At the moment Antigua is the tourism capital, but
commercial production of sugar, cotton, fruits, salt, and fisheries are scattered
throughout the islands. Life on Anguilla is a bit unsettled because after an
attempt to become independent of their dependencies their political status has
been up in the air. Right now the island is on the fence, administratively tied to
its "dependencies" but demanding separate consideration by Great Britain.

Winds and weather. The weather is consistently fine, with very little rain
and a lot of sunshine. The trades persist throughout most of the year.

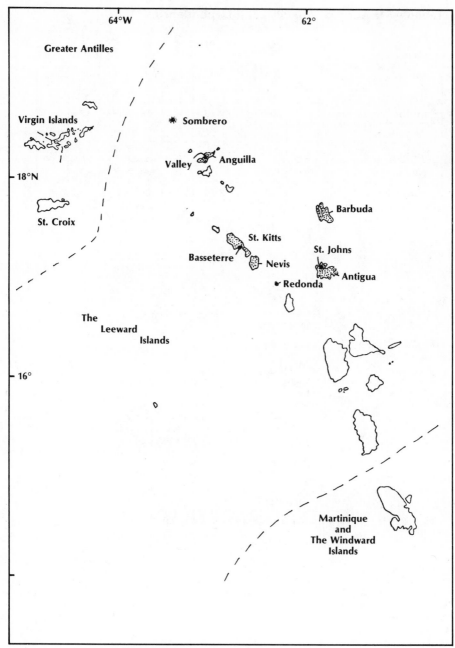

Figure 9-26. Antigua, Anguilla, and their dependencies

Table 9-51: Antigua, Anguilla, and Dependencies

Island	RC	IH	Pop.	Med.	Air?	Ship?	Harbor?	Volc?
Antigua	RA	L	C	H	Y	Y	D	–
Barbuda	RA	L	S	–	Y	N	O	–
Redonda	RA	L	O	–	N	N	O	–
Anguilla	RA	L	V		Y	Y	D	–
St. Kitts	P/F	M	T	H	Y	Y	O	–
Nevis	P/F	L	T		Y	Y	O	–
Sombrero	RA	A	O	–	N	N	O	–

Table 9-52: Weather in Antigua

	Rainfall days	Rainfall inches	Air Temp. °F
January		0.2	74
February		0.8	
March		1.4	
April		1.4	
May		3.0	
June		0.6	79
July		4.2	79
August		3.7	79
September		4.4	81
October		6.2	
November		2.8	80
December		3.3	78

Data Source: Antigua

Table 9–53: Weather in St. Kitts

	Rainfall days	Rainfall inches	Air Temp. °F (ADH)
January	17	4.1	80
February	11	2.0	81
March	11	2.3	82
April	10	2.3	83
May	12	3.8	84
June	12	3.6	85
July	16	4.4	86
August	16	5.2	86
September	16	6.0	86
October	15	5.4	85
November	17	7.3	84
December	15	4.5	82

Data Source: St. Kitts

Montserrat*

Category: I
Islands: 1
Area: 39.5 sq. mi.
Total population: 13,292 (1973)
Political status: Crown Colony of Great Britain
Currency: East Caribbean dollar
Language: English

Montserrat is a rugged, heavily forested island with peaks of up to 3,000 feet. The coast from east to northwest is cliffed and fringed with rocks and reefs, whereas the southwest coast has more gradual slopes. There are a few small indentations along the latter shoreline that provide anchorage to yachts. This island has had a relatively tranquil history, remaining uninhabited until a group of Irish folk settled there in the seventeenth century. There were a couple of incidents in which the French took over the island briefly, but nothing out of the ordinary (for this region anyway). Agricultural products, including fruits and cattle, are more of an income source than tourism at the moment, but the government is encouraging the development of the visitor industry.

Winds and weather. The climate of Montserrat is quite comfortable, with temperatures averaging in the low 80s and rainfall around average for the Leewards at 62 inches per year.

*Additional data on this island can be found in Table 9–63, p. 341.

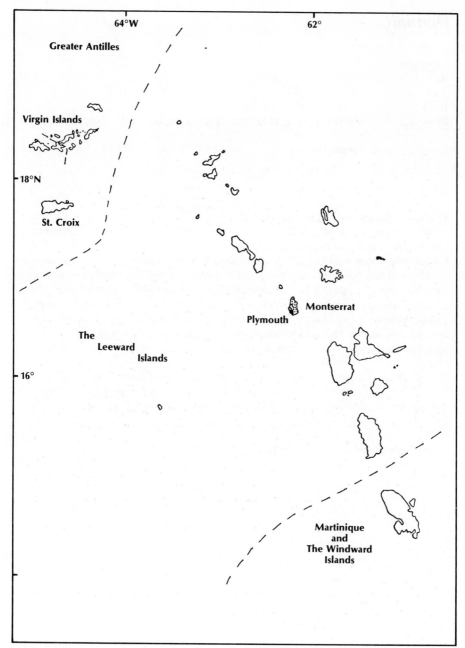

Figure 9–27. Montserrat

Dominica*

Category: I
Islands: 1
Area: 289.5 sq. mi.
Total population: 70,302 (1970)
Political status: Member of the West Indies Associated States, associated with
    Great Britain
Currency: East Caribbean dollar
Language: English

This is a high, mountainous island similar to Montserrat in appearance. Rainfall is plentiful on the slopes and there are hundreds of waterfalls and even rivers. The island was a Carib stronghold, and on a reservation here roughly 1,000 Caribs still retain vestiges of their culture. European domination came very slowly, and much of the early history of the island represents a three-way war, with the French fighting the British and the Caribs fighting everybody. The northern and western coasts are cliffed, and although the eastern and western coasts do have some small embayments there are few trustworthy anchorages around this island. The scenic beauty of the island is further tempered by the fact that in recent years tourists have not been made to feel especially welcome.

Winds and weather. This is a very lush island, and rainfall in the interior forests may be close to 200 inches per year. There are warm and cool seasons, but neither is unpleasant. The winds are predominantly easterly, as is the case with the other islands of this region.

*Additional data on this island can be found in Table 9–63, p. 341.

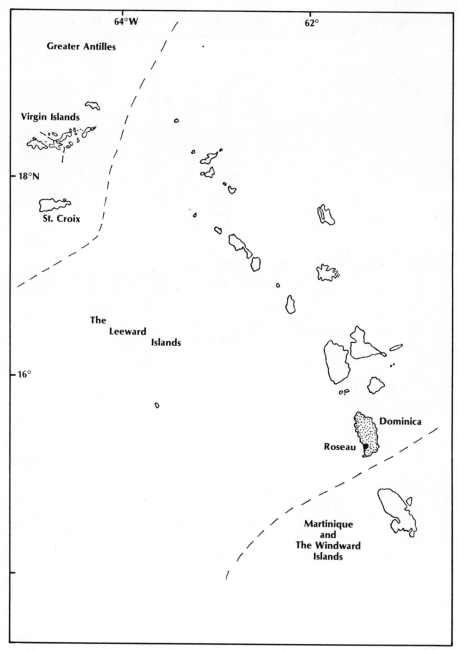

Figure 9–28. Dominica

Table 9-54: Weather in Dominica

	Rainfall days	Rainfall inches	Air Temp. °F (ADH)
January	16	5.2	84
February	10	2.9	85
March	13	2.9	87
April	10	2.4	88
May	11	3.8	90
June	15	7.7	90
July	22	10.8	89
August	22	10.3	89
September	16	8.9	90
October	16	7.8	89
November	18	8.8	87
December	16	6.4	86

Data Source: Roseau

THE WINDWARD ISLANDS

Martinique*

Category: I
Islands: 1
Area: 420 sq. mi.
Total population: 320,000
Political status: Overseas Department of France
Currency: New francs
Language: French

Like the last two islands considered, Martinique is mountainous and volcanic, with a ridge line reaching 4,800 feet in altitude trending northwest to southeast across the island. The highest mountain, Mt. Pelee, stands in the northwest portion of the range. Martinique is reminiscent of the evenly subsiding islands of the tropical Pacific, with numerous embayments and cliffed spur ends. Also, a submerged barrier reef surrounds much of the island.

Like Dominica, Martinique's history was fairly quiet, only changing hands (French to British) four times since 1635. Geologically the history of the island has been more cataclysmic. Pelee is actively volcanic, and a devastating eruption in 1902 destroyed the capital city of Saint Pierre and killed all but one of its 30,000 inhabitants. It erupted less disastrously in 1932, and has been resting since then. I doubt that property values have recovered. Tourism today is not a booming industry, and most of the revenue of the island community is derived from agricultural pursuits. Things are bound to change, however, because the inhabitants are friendly, the weather is fine, and the island is one of the loveliest in the Caribbean.

Winds and weather. Patterns are similar to those of other islands of the Windward and Leeward groups, with east winds in spring and summer and northeast winds in autumn and winter. The trades blow throughout the year. The rainy season and the hurricane season are one and the same; the climate is rather dry the rest of the year.

*Additional data on this island can be found in Table 9–63, p. 341.

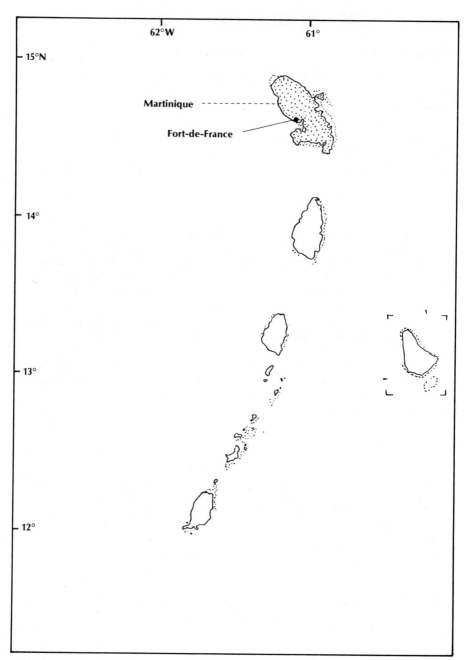

Figure 9–29. Martinique

Table 9–55: Weather in Martinique

	Rainfall days	Rainfall inches	Air Temp. °F (ADH)
January	19	4.7	83
February	15	4.3	84
March	15	2.9	85
April	13	3.9	86
May	18	4.7	87
June	21	7.4	86
July	22	9.4	86
August	22	10.3	87
September	29	9.3	88
October	19	9.7	87
November	20	7.9	86
December	19	5.9	84

Data Source: Fort-de-France

St. Lucia and St. Vincent*

Category: I
Islands: 2
Area: 238 sq. mi. (SL)/150 sq. mi. (SV)
Total population: 114,000 (SL)/22,000 (SV)
Political status: Members of the West Indies Associated States in association
    with Great Britain
Currency: East Caribbean dollar
Language: English

St. Lucia and St. Vincent are very similar in general appearance; both are
mountainous and heavily forested. The highest peak on St. Lucia reaches 3,145
feet and the highest on St. Vincent barely exceeds 4,000 feet. Both islands are
actively volcanic. There are hot springs on St. Lucia and a volcano on St.
Vincent that erupted as recently as 1972. The eastern coasts are steep and
cliffed because they are exposed to the full force of the tradewind-driven seas.
Portions of the interior mountain ranges have been strongly dissected, and
subsidence has produced a number of beautiful bays along the western shores.
The beaches are superb and offer excellent sailing, fishing, and diving. A
few of the embayments on St. Lucia have filled in with washed-down sediments
to form picturesque deltas crossed by meandering streams.

Saint Lucia was inhabited by the Caribs when the Europeans took notice of
it, and the scrappy indians were able to hold the intruders offshore until 1650.
The French and British played ping-pong with the island for well over a century, passing it back and forth fourteen times before England won the volley.
The Caribs were even tougher on St. Vincent, and while the British and French
sparred over ownership of the island it was usually done at some distance away
until the British finally succeeded in deporting both the French and the Caribs
at the close of the eighteenth century.

These are very scenic and interesting islands that have yet to be extensively
developed. The tourism industry is just beginning in St. Lucia, but none of any
consequence has yet begun on St. Vincent. The economies of both islands are
agriculturally based.

Winds and weather. Patterns are similar to those described for the islands
of Dominica and Martinique.

*Additional data on these islands can be found in Table 9–63, p. 341.

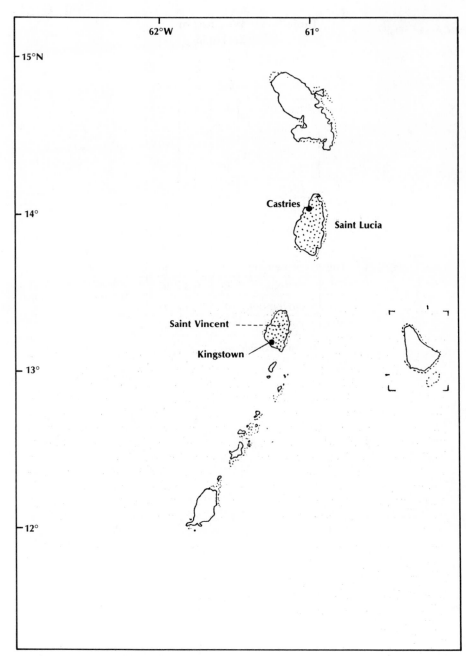

Figure 9–30.　Saint Lucia and St. Vincent

Table 9-56: Weather in St. Lucia

	Rainfall days	Rainfall inches	Air Temp. °F
January	18	5.3	82
February	13	3.6	83
March	13	3.8	84
April	10	3.4	87
May	16	5.9	88
June	21	8.6	88
July	23	9.3	87
August	22	10.6	88
September	21	9.9	88
October	19	9.3	87
November	20	9.1	85
December	19	7.8	83

Data Source: Soufriere

Grenada and the Grenadines

Category: I
Islands: 1 (Grenada)/600 islands and islets (Grenadines)
Area: 133 sq. mi.
Total population: 93,000 (Grenada)/14,000 (Grenadines)
Political status: Independent member of the British Commonwealth
    (Grenada)/Grenadines are divided between Grenada and St. Vincent
Currency: East Caribbean dollar
Language: English

Grenada is a lush, mountainous island seated atop an extensive shallow bank. Grenada's peaks are relatively low, reaching only 2,700 feet, and there has been no recent volcanic activity on the island itself. The same is not true of the surrounding ocean floor, for only five miles north of the island volcanic activity was observed during a series of earthquakes forty years ago. The eastern shores of Grenada are exposed and cliffed, with wave-cut platforms extending up to three quarters of a mile offshore. There are several bays along the eastern and southern coasts, but the shoreline is most hospitable along the western shores, where the capital city and harbor are located. Because of the orientation of the mountain range to the prevailing winds, the rainfall is plentiful, and because the range is low the rain is largely restricted to the areas on either side of the ridge line. The beaches are extensive and the inhabitants congenial. While tourism is currently an also-ran as compared with agriculture, I doubt that this situation will continue now that political events have put this tiny country "on the map."

The Grenadines are low volcanic islands that lie between Grenada and St. Vincent. Carriacou and all the islands to the south are dependencies of Grenada, whereas the northern islands are administratively tied to St. Vincent. With the exception of Carriacou these islands are sparsely inhabited, and the waters around the Grenadines support extensive coral reefs. In short, it is an exquisite area for visitors to enjoy cruising. There are also commercial vessels that travel in and amongst the scattered islands on a more or less regular basis.

Winds and weather. Patterns are similar to those described for Dominica and Martinique, although unlike the latter islands, Grenada and the Grenadines lie outside the normal hurricane pathways.

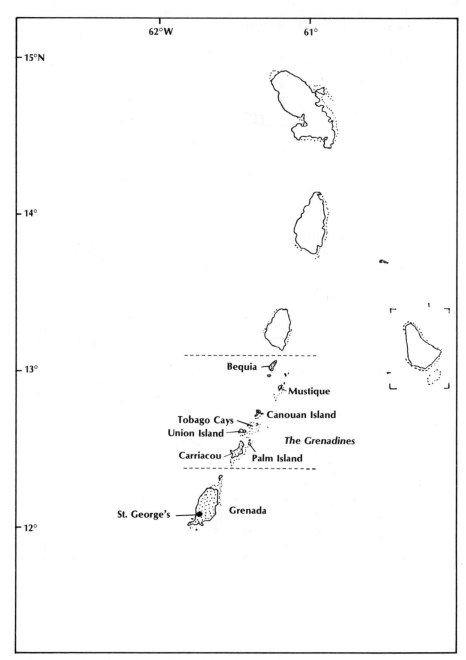

Figure 9–31. Grenada and the Grenadines

Table 9-57: Grenada and the Grenadines

Island	RC	IH	Pop.	Med.	Air?	Ship?	Harbor?	Volc?
Grenada	F	M	C	H	Y	Y	D	–
Bequia	F	L	V	H	N	Y	D	–
Mustique	F/B	L	S	–	N	N	D	–
Canouan	F	L	S	–	N	N	D	–
Union	F/B	L	S	–	N	N	D	–
Carriacou	B	L	V	H	N	Y	D	–

Table 9-58: Weather in Grenada

	Rainfall days	Rainfall inches	Air Temp. °F
January		4.2	78
February		4.4	79
March		2.0	79
April		2.1	81
May		3.3	81
June		5.9	81
July		7.1	81
August		6.0	81
September		7.0	81
October		7.1	81
November		10.6	80
December		6.5	80

Data Source: Grenada

OTHER ISLANDS OF THE LESSER ANTILLES
Barbados*

Category: V
Islands: 1
Area: 166 sq. mi.
Total population: 245,000 (1975)
Political status: Independent member of the British Commonwealth
Currency: Barbados dollar
Language: English

Barbados is composed of sedimentary rocks capped by a series of uplifted reefs now found to heights of over 1,100 feet. The exposed reef materials have been extensively eroded, and as a result the island contour is very uneven. The uplifting of the island has been intermittent, producing a series of reef terraces or platforms that are now exposed with the oldest on top. Reef growth is extensive around the current shoreline, with a barrier reef extending along the windward coast.

Barbados history is quite unusual for the region. The original settlers were Arawaks, but the Spanish either killed them with introduced diseases or shipped them to Hispaniola as slaves. No settlements existed until the British arrived, and for its entire history up to the present, the island's status has not changed even a single time! Tourism has been increasing in recent years, and at the moment is running third behind rum and molasses as the island's main industry. The waters surrounding the island are rich in fisheries resources and commercial development seems inevitable. If *that* doesn't prove to be enough, oil may be trapped in the sediments beneath the island. For the visitor to Barbados, the night life is not much, but the reefs and beaches are all you could ask for.

*Additional data on this island can be found in Table 9–63, p. 341.

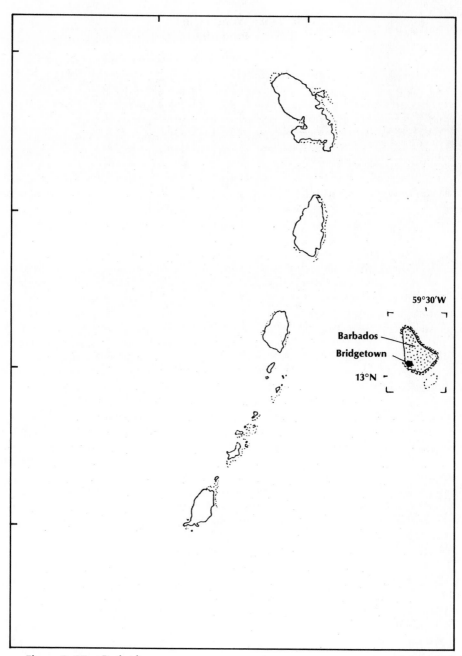

Figure 9–32. Barbados

Table 9-59: Weather in Barbados

	Rainfall days	Rainfall inches	Air Temp. °F (ADH)
January	13	2.6	83
February	8	1.1	83
March	8	1.3	85
April	7	1.4	86
May	9	2.3	87
June	14	4.4	87
July	18	5.8	86
August	16	5.8	87
September	15	6.7	87
October	15	7.0	86
November	16	8.1	85
December	14	3.8	83

Data Source: Barbados—Bridgetown

Trinidad and Tobago*

Category: V
Islands: 2, plus minor islets
Area: 1,980 sq. mi.
Total population: 931,000 (1970)
Political status: Independent member of the British Commonwealth
Currency: Trinidad and Tobago dollar
Language: English

Trinidad and Tobago represent portions of mainland South America isolated by the sea. The separation occurred a mere 10,000 years ago. There are three mountain ranges in Trinidad running East to West, which represent a northern extension of the Andean fold system. The highest mountain is just over 3,000 feet high. Tobago is by far the smaller of the two islands, but like Trinidad it is rather mountainous over much of its length. The northern two thirds of the island has peaks reaching 1,900 feet, whereas the southern region is low and rather flat. Both Trinidad and Tobago are surrounded by reefs, some of them extensive, and fringed with excellent beaches.

Trinidad is undergoing extensive industrial development, primarily related to oil exploration but aided by a busy agricultural complex. The cost of living is quite high, and it is a very bustling island. Tobago is evolving as the vacation retreat for Trinidad, and has so far escaped heavy industrialization.

Winds and weather. These islands lie near the southern extent of the northeast tradewinds. Easterly and northeasterly winds are present throughout the year; Trinidad is large enough that land and sea breeze systems may modify this pattern along the leeward coast. Hurricanes generally pass to the north of these islands, but thunderstorms may appear from the nearby mainland during any season. In general the climate is more humid and mainland-tropical than you will find on the islands to the north.

*Additional data on these islands can be found in Table 9–63, p. 341.

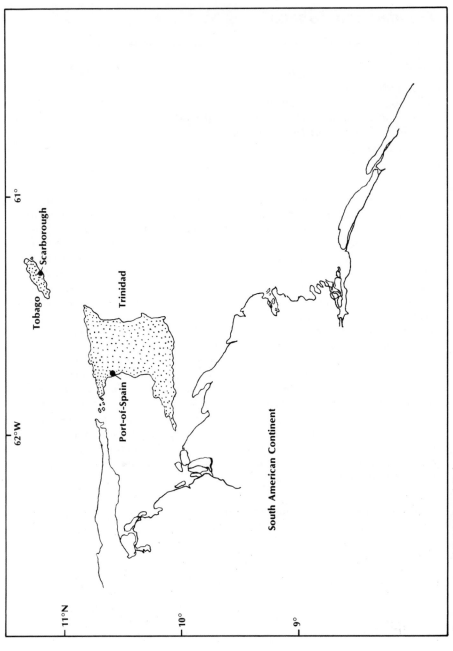

Figure 9–33. Trinidad and Tobago

Table 9-60: Weather in Trinidad

	Rainfall days	Rainfall inches	Air Temp. °F (ADH)
January	18	3.4	86
February	15	2.5	86
March	13	1.2	88
April	11	2.4	89
May	21	5.9	89
June	26	11.8	87
July	26	10.2	87
August	24	9.8	88
September	18	6.1	89
October	20	5.7	89
November	22	7.5	88
December	21	6.7	86

Data Source: Trinidad

The Netherlands Antilles (southern sector)

Category: I
Islands: 3
Area: 925 sq. mi.
Total population: 225,000 (est.)
Political status: Integral portion of the Netherlands
Currency: Netherlands Antilles florin
Language: Dutch and English

The southern Netherlands Antilles are older than their northern comrades. Current reconstructions indicate that along with one of the islands to the east, Balanquilla, the islands of Aruba, Curacao, and Bonaire formed about 120 million years ago along a trench that has since been obliterated. When a new trench formed sometime around 80 million years ago, volcanic activity was rekindled not only at these sites but also along a line of small islands to the east. None of the Dutch "A-B-C" islands is volcanically active today, and over the intervening years they subsided completely and then were uplifted. All three islands are elevated atolls that have been eroded and dissected to some degree while younger reefs became established along their submerged slopes.

The islands were first claimed by Spain, but the Dutch invaded and used the islands as bases for trading operations. They have held onto them ever since. With a tranquil history, a fine climate, crystalline waters, and extensive reefs you might expect this group to have a rather peaceful, laid-back tropical atmosphere. You would be quite wrong, because shortly after oil was discovered on the nearby mainland these islands began gearing up to handle oil refining and processing. Curacao is an international shipping center, moving large ships in and out of five major harbors. There are petroleum refineries and phosphate mines on Curacao, refineries and deep-water harbors on Aruba, and although Bonaire lacks refineries, it does have a salt plant. Tourism is on the increase, and although visitors arriving by air or sea are warmly received, I would imagine many of them are surprised at the hustle and bustle that greets them as they debark.

Winds and weather. The weather patterns here resemble those reported for the islands of Trinidad and Tobago.

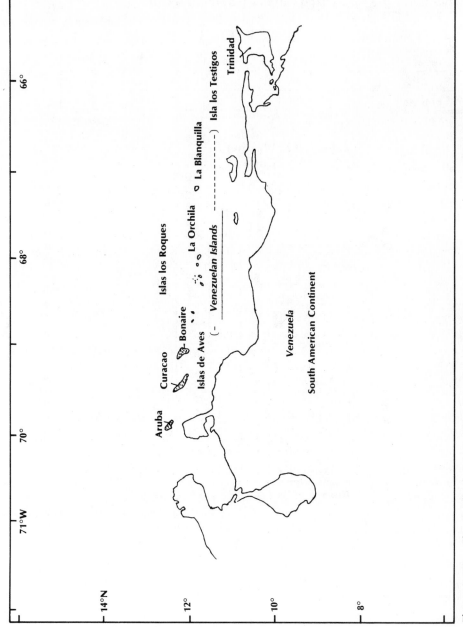

Figure 9-34. The Netherlands Antilles (southern sector)

Table 9-61: The Netherland Antilles (Southern sector)

Island	RC	IH	Pop.	Med.	Air?	Ship?	Harbor?	Volc?
Aruba	RAA	L	C	H	Y	Y	D	–
Bonaire	RA	L	V	C	Y	Y	D	–
Curacao	RA	M	C	H	Y	Y	D	–

Table 9-62: Weather in Curacao

	Rainfall days	Rainfall inches	Air Temp. °F (ADH)
January	14	2.1	83
February	8	1.0	84
March	7	0.8	84
April	4	1.1	86
May	4	0.8	87
June	7	1.0	87
July	9	1.5	87
August	8	1.2	88
September	6	1.1	89
October	9	4.2	88
November	15	4.4	86
December	16	3.9	84

Data Source: Curacao

Table 9–63: Summary Data for Caribbean Islands

Island	RC	IH	Pop.	Med.	Air?	Ship?	Harbor?	Volc?
Hispaniola	F/B	VH	C	H	Y	Y	D	–
Puerto Rico	F	M	C	H	Y	Y	D	–
Montserrat	P/F	M	T	H	Y	Y	O	+
Dominica	P	M	C	H	Y	Y	D	+
Martinique	P/F	M	C	H	Y	Y	D	+
St. Lucia/St. Vincent	P/F	M	C	H	Y	Y	D	+
Barbados	RA	L	C	H	Y	Y	D	–
Trinidad	F	M	C	H	Y	Y	D	–
Tobago	F	M	T	H	Y	Y	D	–

Appendix:
Advice Concerning Tropical Hazards

DANGEROUS MARINE ORGANISMS

Sharks have a bad reputation, which they deserve despite the fact that attacks are few and far between. *Any* event that results in a fatality one third of the time is worthy of special attention. Unpleasant interactions with other marine animals are far less serious, but because they are also much more common they merit consideration as well. In this brief addendum you will learn which marine animals are potentially dangerous, how best to avoid them, and what you should do if your precautions prove to be inadequate.

Which marine animals are dangerous? You are already familiar with the basic characteristics of the most common reef inhabitants, members of six phyla of invertebrates and one that includes the vertebrates. We will now look at the dangerous representatives of each group.

Coelenterates (corals, anemones, jellyfish, etc.) As a group the coelenterates have a particularly nasty reputation. Nematocysts are used for attack or defense as needed, and the sensations induced in a human victim range from intense pain, muscle spasms, and respiratory difficulties to a slight tenderness, anxiety, and itching, depending on the species involved and the sensitivity of the individual victim. The site of contact is recorded as a raised reddish or purple/red welt, which follows the path of the offending tentacle(s). Despite the intense pain that may be experienced, fatalities are very rare. Symptoms such as pain, cramps, and nausea may persist for hours but will gradually subside thereafter.

In order of increasing frequency of occurrence and decreasing order of severity of effects, coelenterate-related problems may be listed as:

cubomedusa stings (sea wasps)
Portuguese man-o-war stings
poisonous anemone stings
fire coral stings
miscellaneous jellyfish stings
miscellaneous coral stings
coral cuts and scrapes

Cubomedusae, alias sea wasps, are small jellyfishes with one complex tentacle trailing off each corner of the angular swimming bell. A severe stinging may prove fatal for sensitive individuals. There are several species in the tropics, but to date fatalities have been reported only from the southwest Pacific, near the Australian coast.

A Portuguese man-o-war is a colonial hydrozoan equipped with a large, gas-filled float that allows the colony to drift from place to place. There are several species, ranging from small colonies with silvery-blue floats and delicate tentacles to massive ones whose floats may be over a foot in length, with robust tentacles nearly 100 feet long. Although the toxin is weaker than that of the sea wasp, the intended prey are fishes, and a swimmer who becomes entangled in one of the tentacles is sure to receive a large dose of the poison.

Although Portuguese men-o-war are usually seen well out to sea, a strong onshore wind or westerly storm may bring them close to the coast. At such times swimmers should be extra careful in looking around before diving in. When beachcombing after squalls, watch for the floats washed up on the sand, and give them a wide berth. The nematocysts will continue to fire on contact even after most of the rest of the colony has been sunbaked to mush.

The anemones, hydrozoans, jellyfishes, and corals each have species noted for the unpleasant sensations that follow a contact with their tentacles. In general, large anemones should always be treated with respect. In Hawaiian waters this courtesy should be extended to small ones as well, because there is an endemic species that is fond of rocky tidepools and whose sting is quite dangerous. Fire corals look like true corals, but they are actually colonial hydrozoans. They produce a calcareous skeleton, but the skeleton is on the outside rather than the inside of the colony. Rather than getting up close with a hand lens to make an identification, you would be better off avoiding all "corals" that are white, golden brown, bright yellow, or fluorescent in color. If you have questions, the native inhabitants will probably be happy to point out the local varieties to you. They are found throughout the Caribbean and the central and western Pacific, but fire corals have not been reported from Hawaii. When dealing with *any* coelenterates you should always remember that all nematocysts contain some kind of toxin, and some people will show a reaction to species considered innocuous by the rest of the world.

Coral cuts often accompany and complicate the effects of coelenterate strings. Coral colonies have innumerable sharp edges, the effects of which may initially go unnoticed because your sensitivity to pain is dulled while you are in the water. For obvious reasons, the tips of branches or the broken edges of fractured plates are the worst offenders, but even massive forms can act as oversized cheese graters if you are slammed against them by a breaking wave.

Echinoderms (starfish, urchins, etc.) We need to consider the sea urchins in two groups, those that possess a formidable array of long spines and those that bear short, apparently harmless spines. Many species defend themselves with very long, very sharp, and very brittle spines. These spines are usually adorned with barbs and ridges that prevent their easy removal, and even the slightest contact with such spines will result in their penetration of the skin. Some species make their defenses even more impressive by including venom sacs at the tips of the spines or along the grooved edges of each shaft.

When you have had the misfortune to bump into one, the immediate sensation is burning pain. The area around the injury reddens and swells, and the fragments of the spine will be visible as a bluish central spot. The acute pain fades within hours, but a dull aching may persist for several days.

The short spined urchins are, for the most part, less of a threat. Many species have spines so stubby and blunt that you would be hard-pressed to injure yourself seriously when contacting one. However there are species that are quite well defended, despite their lack of spines. These urchins have tiny pincers, each equipped with a poison gland, scattered across their upper surfaces. Some of these short-spined forms do not look like typical sea urchins, so the unwary snorkeler may be tempted to examine one much too closely. One of the most dangerous has large, wavy tube feet almost a quarter of an inch in diameter. These may completely obscure the upper surface of the urchin, and with their bright yellow rims and purple centers they are fascinating to observe. A second dangerous form uses its tube feet to accumulate coral fragments and other debris that mask its outline. A nip from one of the pincers of these urchins produces effects far out of proportion to its size. Intense, burning pain, numbness, paralysis, respiratory troubles, and even death may follow. Although the pain itself may vanish within the hour, the other symptoms may continue to mount for several hours after contact. If the area is not cleaned properly the pincers will remain attached to the wound, and they are quite capable of continuing to inject toxin into the victim even after their separation from the urchin. It is fortunate that these urchins are far less common than their more benign relations, and that the pincers are too small and weak to be effective unless exposed to bare skin.

The crown-of-thorns starfish bristles with spines that cover its aboral surface. The spines look blunt, but they are not. Each spine is sheathed by an epidermis containing glands that produce toxic secretions. The slightest touch at the tip of a spine slides the sheath away from the end and coats the shaft with venom. The spines are brittle at intervals along their length, and pieces usually remain in the wounds. The severely spined victim experiences intense, burning pain, and perhaps nausea. The puncture site turns blue with a pale margin and the surrounding area reddens and swells. Weakness, disorientation, and fever may follow. Recovery from a severe incident may take longer. The Fijian name for the crown-of-thorns starfish can be literally translated as "eight months of pain." For those who work with these adorable beasts, as I did, or who are attracted to them for some reason, subsequent spinings produce increasingly severe reactions. Crown-of-thorns starfish are restricted to the tropical Pacific at the moment, and barring the construction of a sea level canal, they will probably remain there.

Molluscs (shellfish and associates) Shell collectors love cone shells because their color variations are delightful. To show off a specimen it must ordinarily be cleaned because the shell usually has a heavy encrustation on it that makes identification difficult in the field. This is most unfortunate because several species have radulae that function as injectors of a severe toxin, and handling the wrong species the wrong way invites disaster. An injection of toxin is followed by a stinging or burning sensation because the poison acts to block the passage of signals from nerves to muscles. A serious dose of the poison will produce a spreading numbness, paralysis of voluntary and involuntary muscles, coma, and even death. Recovery from a nonfatal dosage may take from hours to weeks, depending on the amount of toxin received and the sensitivity of the individual.

All cephalopods use their beaks with great effectiveness, and their bites can be quite unpleasant, rather like a bee or wasp sting. In addition there are species whose bites may prove fatal. One of the most dangerous species is an octopus marked by beautiful blue blotches that measures less than a foot across the tentacles. It is an inhabitant of Australian waters, but the lesson here is that you should handle even small cephalopods with proper respect. The immediate sensation following a toxic bite is one of severe, throbbing pain that may spread throughout the affected limb or portion of the body. Swelling and redness develop rapidly, and bleeding may be profuse. Blurring of vision, numbness around the mouth, and muscular paralysis may follow in the worst cases.

Vertebrates (Class Chondrichthyes–sharks, rays, etc.) We have already considered the cartilaginous fishes involved in the production of biting injuries (Chapter 4). Skates and rays are related to sharks but differ in having enormously expanded pectoral fins. With these wings they are able to flap their way through the water. The pectorals extend along the sides above the gill slits, which are therefore located on the underside of the flattened body. Most skates and rays are carnivores who rely on commando tactics. They lie flat on the bottom and may cover themselves with a thin dusting of sand, concealing their outlines but leaving their eyes exposed. As we saw when considering other commando-style fishes, such animals are often equipped with some form of protection against predators.

The skates may have a series of enlarged denticles along the midline of the back, or scattered over the upper surface of the body. These are very sharp and most disagreeable to step on. The sting-rays have large, serrated spines with venom glands attached. These formidable structures are located partway along the slender tail. The spine can be thrust with startling speed and accuracy by flexing the body and moving the tail up and over the back. These are not brittle, delicate elements, so there may be considerable tissue damage to complicate the injury. An altercation with a specimen 6 feet across the wings, with a 6 to 8-inch spine, may be very serious indeed. Spining is followed by severe pain in the area immediately around the wound. The pain usually peaks within the first two hours, but it may taper gradually for days afterwards. The area swells considerably, and of course there may be severe bleeding as well because of the accompanying lacerations. Deaths are rare, but they have occurred, and panic, drowning, or poor first aid may make matters worse than they otherwise would be.

Vertebrates (Class Osteichthyes–bony fishes) Most of the common reef fishes are equipped with spiny rays in their dorsal, anal, and perhaps pectoral fins, and many have ornamented gill covers and edges as well. These make them tricky to handle, and small puncture wounds are common but not unduly alarming.

We have already noted the stern armament of the surgeonfishes, and some species are also equipped with fin spines that bear a weak venom. Surgeonfish injuries usually consist of slashing cuts on the hands, forearms, or legs of spearfishermen who lose control of their prey (these are not aggressive animals). The pain may be throbbing, intense, and accompanied by swelling, and some discomfort may persist for a week after the injury.

The scorpionfish are worth noting because of their elaboration of normal spines and ridges with not-so-normal poison glands. Venom glands are associated with their dorsal pelvic, and anal fins as well as over their gill covers and heads. The typical scorpionfish remains concealed by its camouflage in crevices, among the corals, or in areas of rubble or coral litter. If actually threatened they become quite agitated, and may rush their attacker to deliberately make contact with their spines. They are found throughout the tropics. Two variations on this pattern deserve attention.

The stonefish is an extremely poisonous relation of the scorpionfish. It is very well camouflaged, and its reaction to a potentially hostile intruder is to remain perfectly still. Stonefish live in the southern and western Pacific, but have not been reported from the Marquesas, Galapagos, Hawaii, or any of the Atlantic islands. The poisonous lionfish, which was discussed in Chapter 3, has a more widespread distribution, being found throughout the tropical Atlantic and Pacific. Because it is an "advertiser" a lionfish is more easily seen and avoided than other more cryptic members of the scorpionfish/stonefish/lionfish assemblage. A contact with the spines of any of these animals is decidedly memorable, creating intense throbbing pain that spreads and lasts for hours. Swelling and discoloration of the wound ensues, and delirium, convulsions, cardiac arrest, and death may occur in especially severe spinings or when the victim is particularly sensitive to the toxin.

Barracuda have been involved in attacks on humans, and they have an unsavory reputation in many areas. These predators often dart from rest to seize their prey, and their success lies in their quick reaction times and rapid acceleration. Tissue losses can be considerable, but there is no toxin associated with the injuries.

Moray eels are seldom seen out and around the reef by day, but on occasion they may leave the security of a cave to take a particularly tempting morsel, such as a speared fish or octopus. They may also take offense at your intrusion into their private portion of the reef, and divers have often been bitten while reaching for a lobster or interesting shell deep within a pocket or cavern. The bite of a moray is not poisonous, but their oral hygiene habits are deplorable, and their mouths and teeth are usually covered with slime and bacteria that can infect an uncleaned wound.

Vertebrates (Reptiles) If there are crocodiles in the water, stay out of it. Where they are common they are more feared than sharks, and you should watch your step on land as well. As the hunting pressure for skins continues, the ranges of the marine crocodile and the Atlantic crocodile are gradually shrinking. Although they are not judged to be a severe problem within any of our areas of interest, you should be alert to any local gossip concerning sightings in the Solomon Islands or the southern Caribbean.

Sea snakes are a concern in the tropical Pacific, but not (as yet) in the tropical Atlantic. Their mouths are small, but the venomous fangs within are very sharp. The toxin is actively injected through a groove or canal in each fang. Sea snakes seem to have variable moods. In some reports they are regarded as mild-mannered; and in others, as aggressive. Most often, incidents result from the snakes being handled in a fish net, stepped on, or bumped into while swimming. At first the bite may seem to produce no ill effects, and this latent period may last for hours. A pronounced reaction at the site of the bite never does appear, but what does appear is a gradually increasing number of unpleasant symptoms that affect the victim's entire body. Aching and muscular stiffness may be followed by difficulties in speech or swallowing. Weakness becomes paralysis. Nausea and vomiting make the situation even more discomfiting. The general nervous and circulatory systems are affected, and in an estimated 3 percent of the cases death follows within a week. In the remaining cases, recovery may take several weeks or even months.

Vertebrates (Mammals) We have already discussed killer whales and boats. There has been a single report of a sea lion attacking a diver, but the details are sketchy. The truth of the matter is that your worst mammalian enemy will be other human beings, with their outboards, spear guns, fishing lines, nets, broken bottles, and general inattention.

How do I avoid such incidents? The animals we discussed above can be sorted into just three groups. These animals are dangerous because they either bite, spine, or sting. The appropriate precautions differ in each instance. Biting animals are predators that rely on powerful jaws and sharp teeth to obtain their food. Such animals tend to use the same strategy to repel invaders from their territory or to defend themselves against attack by other predators. In this group we would include the cephalopods, sharks, barracuda, marine crocodiles, and sea snakes. To avoid potentially distressing problems, you should pay heed to the following:

1. *Never pursue, spear, or otherwise harass a biting animal.* You are an awkward visitor to their world, and there is nothing to be gained by bravado. Larger barracuda seem to be as territorially minded as sharks, and they are equally unlikely to be intimidated by threatening gestures. Even if you are a crack shot, most of these biting animals are difficult to kill with a spear, and some (the moray, for example) have a reputation for writhing right back up the spear at you. As for the cephalopods, although you might want to try and catch one for dinner, teasing or playing with one is very risky entertainment.

2. *Avoid wearing bright, intense colors or highly reflective objects.* In Chapter 4 we considered the effects of color on shark behavior. The lightning-fast reactions of a barracuda to potential prey have the unfortunate corollary that the animal does not take much time to carefully analyze the nature of the intended victim. Any bright, silvery, fluttering object may remind it of a delicacy and invite an attack. Divers or snorkelers have been struck on the silvery surfaces of new weight belts, at the wrist where a watch glitters, or even had a sparkling pendant or necklace torn from around their necks. At such times more personal portions of your anatomy are endangered as well.

3. *Look before you leap into the water or reach into a confined space.* You don't want to startle anything lurking in the area. Barracuda or shark attacks will be even more likely, even in clear water, when a startled predator is face to face with a large, noisy, unfamiliar creature that lands right on top of it. Jumping on a sea snake also indicates rather poor planning. When seeking shells or lobster, blind groping around in a dark pocket is foolish, for a resident moray will object by fastening its teeth onto your hand or arm. Despite folklore to the contrary, leaving your appendage in its mouth until it shifts its grip requires more control than my kind of human being can muster, and the injury gets more severe as you pull yourself away.

4. *When in doubt, get out.* This should be done as quickly and quietly as possible. Don't stick around to prove anything to anyone once you begin to feel uneasy.

Spining or stinging animals are using their equipment for defensive purposes. Usually, problems arise when the victim makes an error in judgment due to inattention or simple ignorance of the possible danger. The animal is merely trying to mind its own business when suddenly some enormous creature stomps on it, careens into it, grabs it for a handhold, or otherwise molests it. Spining animals include the long-spined sea urchins, the crown-of-thorns starfish, sting rays, and various fishes including the surgeon fishes and scorpionfishes. To avoid problems with spining animals, you should first amend rules 1 and 3 above to include them as well as biting animals. In addition you should consider the following items.

5. *Avoid handling animals with potentially dangerous spines.* Even heavy leather gloves may prove to be inadequate because the spines are so long and sharp.

6. *Always wear sneakers with heavy socks, or thick-soled diving booties when snorkeling or strolling over the reef flat.* This will drastically reduce the chances for severe cuts and stings as well.

7. *Always look carefully before planting your feet on the bottom.*

8. *Shuffle your feet while walking over sand.* A flat-footed shuffle gives plenty of advance notice concerning your imminent arrival, and most mobile animals will take the hint and leave. If you come upon a stonefish you will probably avoid the most dangerous, dorsal spines; if you encounter a sting ray the odds are good that you will merely pinch the edge of the body-disc. Rays are defensively inclined, and they will scoot off rather than stand and fight if you are not planted on the middle of their backs.

9. *Swim whenever possible.* In four feet of water you will be much safer floating over the reef than trusting your ability to see what you are about to tromp on.

Stinging animals use injection systems to introduce toxins of varying potency. The injection mechanisms are very small, and most are effective only against bare skin or very light clothing. Coelenterates, short-spined urchins, and cone shells belong in this category. Two important precautions—looking around before jumping into the water, and wearing diving booties or sneakers—have already been mentioned.

10. *Wear heavy gloves whenever you snorkel or stroll over the reef flat.* This will protect you from most stings and cuts that would otherwise occur should you grab the "wrong" item or slip and fall.

11. *Always use a catch bag when collecting shells.* Stuffing cone shells in your pants, after collecting them with gloves, is not advisable. Once securely placed in a catch bag, you should also pay attention to where the catch bag ends up. Letting it bounce against your unprotected body is just as dangerous and will potentially affect some very tender portions of your anatomy.

Finally I should make two general remarks about safety precautions and principles:

12. *Clothing is your best defense against many marine hazards.* Small biters, stingers, and coral cuts are rendered harmless by a heavy long-sleeved shirt and a good pair of jeans (in addition to the items

mentioned in 6 and 10 above). When snorkeling around shallow corals, in areas where there is heavy surge, or when entering and leaving the water over a reef edge, good clothing is a must. You might feel a bit out of fashion while others are sporting their designer bikinis, but you will have the satisfaction of returning from your exploration minus the stabs and scratches that plague those less conservative individuals.

13. *Always swim with a buddy, and make certain that your partner knows the rules as well as you do.* Your cautious avoidance of a moray will do very little good if your buddy decides to spear it, and your knowledge of first aid will not help you a bit if you are the one who ends up being bitten as a result.

"What do I do if . . .?" First and foremost, *remain calm* and help the victim out of the water. You may have to do this quickly, which is one good reason why buddies are supposed to stay within sight of one another at all times. In the case of a severe bite or some other injury with extensive tissue damage you may need to restrict bleeding through direct pressure on the wound or through the use of pressure points; in the case of severe spine injuries or stings the victim may become disoriented or unable to swim without assistance.

Once you are both safely out of the water, you need to determine the general nature of the injury, with or without the assistance of the victim. Classify the injury as:

I. An injury not involving a toxin:

A. bites of sharks, moray eels, barracuda, and so forth. These will be large slashes or tears, and there may be extensive tissue damage or loss.

B. spine injuries from any of a number of fishes, including the surgeons. These are usually small cuts or puncture wounds, and the victim will probably tell you all about it.

II. An injury accompanied by the injection of a toxin:

A. bites with associated poisons, such as those of octopus or sea snakes. These will resemble puncture wounds or small bites.

B. spine injuries with venom involvement, such as those from long-spined urchins, crown-of-thorns starfish, scorpionfish, and so forth. The injuries resemble I(B) but produce more severe reactions in the victim.

C. stings, which always involve some toxin, due to jellyfish, corals, short-spined urchins, cone shells, and so forth. These may be raised welts or small puncture wounds.

These two classes of injuries require different treatment, so we will consider them separately. As we do so you should be aware that I am describing the procedure recommended for patients who are beyond the reach of immediate professional care. Traditional first aid protocol would require you simply to stabilize the patient and seek medical assistance. However, such activities would do little good if the nearest clinic is hundreds of miles away. You are on your own, so you will need to respond immediately if you intend to minimize the damage, eliminate the possibility of further, subsequent injury, and prevent complications. It is thus important for you to know the entire range of response to these injuries. If a physician appears and can take over at step 2, good. If *not* then you should be prepared to reach step 3 on your own and at the proper time.

If you find medical details disquieting, you may elect to gloss over these matters. After all, if you follow the rules and keep alert you will probably never need any medical knowledge, no matter how often you splash around. But you will be ignoring your responsibility to those around you, perhaps your diving partner or some child or stranger who might be a trifle less attentive to detail.

After you get the victim out of the water, try to keep him or her—and yourself—as relaxed as possible. If there is no pressing, immediate problem such as blood loss or the possibility of the injury becoming more severe with time, have the victim dry off and lie down. If he or she is cold, cover the individual with a blanket or towel. *Be reassuring and sympathetic*, and don't force food or drink. If needed, give the victim something to ease the pain (even aspirin is effective and should not be overlooked).

In an injury without toxin injection the major problems are possible loss of blood, tissue damage, and secondary infections that may develop at a later date. A really massive bite, such as that produced by a large shark or barracuda, will require professional medical attention to repair the damage. Your primary involvement should be to control bleeding, treat for shock, and get help as soon as possible. Standard Red Cross First Aid is applicable. Smaller bitings and spinings should be treated in the same way as more familiar cuts received ashore. Follow this sequence:

1. Clean the wound thoroughly with soap and water, and remove any foreign matter.
2. Apply stitches or butterfly bandages as needed.
3. Apply an antibiotic ointment, and cover with a clean dressing.
4. Alleviate pain; treat for shock as needed.

It is crucial that you take number 1 literally. A rinsing with fresh water and a dab of soap will not suffice, even on a minor spining from the fins of a fish you cleaned for dinner. Plain soap or the antiseptic variety will do, and a small soft brush is a useful tool. A good scrubbing is neither simple nor painless, but any pain or discomfort you might cause or experience will be negligible compared to the possible results of a tropical infection. If absolutely necessary, you can use a local anesthetic prior to this scrubdown. After the whole procedure is over you should, of course, try to make the victim as comfortable as possible.

Wounds involving the introduction of a venom are more complicated. Unfortunately, there has been very little work done with marine toxins, and the chemical nature and action of many of the toxins described earlier are still unknown. This makes accurate treatment rather difficult, and for the most part you are left treating the symptoms as they appear. Your primary goal here is to let the body's defenses take care of the details while you try to make the patient feel at ease during the recovery period.

For a toxic bite you should do the following:

1. Encourage some bleeding to help flush the wound. This does not mean that you should enlarge the wound or cut large criss-crosses as they do in the movies, which would just make matters worse.

2. Clean the site thoroughly, with soap and water.

3. Apply an ice pack to the region for at least fifteen minutes, if possible. This reduces pain and may help to keep swelling to a minimum.

4. If a sea snake was involved, try to obtain an antitoxin injection.

5. Treat the symptoms and wait it out. For the most part you will be relieving pain, but in severe cases artificial respiration may be required.

For a toxic spining follow these procedures:

1. Remove any remaining spines, even if you have to use a local anesthetic and do some digging, unless the spines have entered a joint. If this has occurred, or in the event that the spines have penetrated so deeply that removal is out of the question, clean and dress the wound and await medical assistance or advice.

2. Reduce the effectiveness of the toxin. Most of these poisons are proteins, and you can destroy or change them by using mild chemicals. Apply meat tenderizer or green papaya skin, both of which break down proteins, or flush the site with ammonia (urine is the traditional remedy, and may be easier to obtain), vinegar, lemon juice, or alcohol.

3: Clean the wound thoroughly.

4. Apply ice, treat for shock, administer pain medication as needed.

5. Reduce swelling if necessary with systemic (i.e., oral or injectible) steroids; reduce allergic reactions with antihistamines such as benedryl.

6. If a stonefish was involved, seek antivenom therapy.

For poisonous stings do the following:

1. Remove any undischarged nematocysts or clinging pincers with sand or a towel, being careful not to trigger them against your own skin in the process. Be gentle, so you do not encourage additional injections of toxin.

2. Follow procedures two to five for poisonous spines.

3. If a sea wasp was involved, seek antivenom therapy.

You will no doubt hear about other possible treatments for poisonous stingings or spinings. These may take the form of local remedies, stories told fifth-hand, and perhaps down-right quackery. For example, many Pacific islanders insist that sticking the offended portion of your anatomy into the oral chamber of a crown-of-thorns starfish will remove the spines, pain, and swelling that accompany the injury. I can say from personal experience that this treatment is ineffective and rather messy to boot. The same is true of other medical rumors common in the region. If you are inclined to experiment, that is your right, but please consider doing so only *after* you have followed the steps outlined above.

So ends our discussion of the identification, prevention, and treatment of dangerous marine animals and the injuries they may inflict. The next portion of the appendix tackles problems that are much more common in tropical waters—those that result from *people* attacking and devouring *marine animals*.

SEAFOOD POISONING IN THE TROPICS

Mild cases of seafood poisoning are actually fairly common, and most residents of the tropics have either experienced it firsthand or have acquaintances who have done so. Surprisingly enough this has not led to any great interest in the problem, although it has produced a remarkable variety of half truths, sure-fire test methods, and folk remedies for real or imaginary incidents. Heated discussions may occur over whether you should soak your future meal in brine (or fresh water), cook it into oblivion (or eat it raw), look for "green highlights" (or other unusual signs), or see if flies/cats/birds will eat it before you do. Such arguments are amusing, but not very productive, because none of these approaches to the problem will help you reduce your chances of exposure.

The matter is more complicated than the local sages suppose, for several unrelated factors can be involved in the creation of a poisonous entrée. In general terms, human poisonings can be assigned to one of three categories:

1. Literally selecting the wrong meal, which we can define as any animal that produces and stores a toxin within its body.

2. Eating seafood that has "gone bad" due to improper preparation or stowage. This can result in the growth of toxic bacteria or the liberation of chemicals that trigger a severe allergic reaction in the consumer.

3. Eating seafood that is normally edible but that has become contaminated with a chemical or biological toxin that has appeared in the local environment.

These categories are different enough to justify the consideration of each form individually. In doing so we will examine aspects of fish poisoning, which is by far the most common cause of human poisonings, and then branch out to include other potentially poisonous organisms as well.

1. Selecting the Wrong Meal

Fishes As you will recall from the discussion of bony fishes in Chapter 3, several fishes produce and store poisons within their bodies. The puffer fish are an excellent example, because they produce a poison that has been intensively studied. It is called *tetrodotoxin*, or TTX, and it affects the activity of nerve and muscle cells. Symptoms usually appear within an hour after the meal, in the form of a numbness around the mouth and a tingling of the fingers and toes that leads eventually to total body numbness. Nausea and vomiting may or may not occur. In severe cases there is gradually increasing paralysis and difficulty in breathing, with eventual coma and death within twenty-four hours. The respiratory paralysis is probably the major cause of death, and the fatality rate is fairly high because the toxin is quite powerful. In some of the puffers only certain organs are toxic, and with careful preparation the flesh may still be eaten. In Japan *fugu* is prepared by licensed chefs, and puffers are considered a delicacy. Accidents still happen, even with experts in charge, so your best course of action is to avoid potentially toxic species entirely. Puffers are "advertisers," and there are several other potentially dangerous advertisers, such as boxfishes, filefishes, and triggerfishes.

Invertebrates Sea anemones and sponges should be mistrusted, and unless you have a reliable local guide you should not take chances with any echinoderm, even an urchin.

A related form of poisoning results from eating the toxic organs of certain animals. Some, such as many sharks, several mackerel, sea turtles, and cetaceans, may store toxic levels of Vitamin A in their livers.

2. Eating Seafood That Has "Gone Bad"

Fishes The proper preparation of fish for consumption is fairly simple, but such details are often ignored for one reason or another. Bacteria thrive in tropical climes, and unless your catch is protected from invasion it will become host to a burgeoning population of organisms in short order. Your inattention will become apparent to all concerned from eight hours to three days after the meal is served. Symptoms include abdominal pain, diarrhea, chills, and fever. In essence, your body is trying to get the offending materials out of the works as fast as possible, so your innards are in an uproar! A severe case will resemble a mild form of cholera, and even a light dosing will be memorable.

A special type of spoilage poisoning results from improper preparation of fishes such as the mackerel and tuna, which have very dark and bloody flesh. This kind of poisoning is called *scomberotoxin* (*scomber*, "mackerel") poisoning. As their tissues decompose over a period of hours, bacterial action and enzymes in the flesh combine to release large quantities of histamine, a chemical that produces an extremely unpleasant allergic reaction in a human consumer. Symptoms develop quickly, with headache, dizziness, abdominal pain, vomiting, and diarrhea. The face of the victim may swell, and there may be some problems with breathing. The worst effects usually pass within twelve hours.

To avoid such unpleasantness, fishes should always be cleaned as soon as possible after they are caught. Cleaning a fish should at least involve the removal of all viscera and a good flushing of the body cavity. In the case of extremely bloody fishes, take special precautions. Pay attention to the dark red tissue lying just beneath the vertebral column. These are the kidneys, and their rich supply of blood makes this a region that quickly breaks down after the death of the animal. Sliding a thumb along the undersurface of the spinal column, with the thumbnail breaking the slender sheath covering the kidneys, is the easiest way to insure that the region is thoroughly cleaned and flushed out. You should also remove the head of the animal as well as the viscera because this removes potential trouble sites at the gills and heart. The cleaned fish should be stowed out of the sun in as cool a location as possible. If you have no refrigeration, a damp cloth laid over the surface of the fish will help. If the fish dries out severely, if the flesh smells strangely, if the skin bulges or lifts away from the muscles beneath, then you have probably failed to take adequate precautions and the fish should be discarded.

Invertebrates The basic precautions indicated above would also hold true for handling invertebrates such as crabs, octopus, lobster, and shellfish. The notable exception is that because you seldom clean these before cooking, they should be stored out of the sun, covered with a damp cloth or seaweed, and cooked alive. If the animal looks strange, or has been dead for quite a while, you should discard it or risk taking a chance you may later have reason to regret. In general the symptoms resemble those of standard bacterial food poisoning. Some incidents involve an allergic response to histamine and are therefore similar to scomberotoxin poisoning, but the chemical and clinical details have yet to be worked out.

3. Eating Contaminated Seafood

Fishes In our consideration of the energy relationship of the coral reef we examined the structure of food webs, food chains, and trophic levels. Think for a moment about how these relationships influence the distribution of a toxic substance that arrives at a reef. Let us assume that this poisonous substance is absorbed, or at least surrounds, the primary producers. This would be the case if it appeared in the plankton or along the bottom. A one-pound primary consumer grazes on ten pounds of algae (seaweed or phytoplankton) and in the process absorbs and stores the accompanying toxin. A ten-pound carivore then eats one hundred of these small herbivores, and receives the accumulated toxin from half a ton of algae. A carnivore at T-III or T-IV ends up carrying around a massive dose of the poison.

Many environmental poisons, such as pesticides, and biological poisons such as TTX are stored in fatty tissues. The liver and reproductive organs are prime areas of the body that contain abundant fats, and these are the regions that may contain toxic chemicals even when the rest of the beast is quite innocuous. With the stakes so high, there is no use taking chances, and you would be advised to avoid eating the internal organs of any marine animal.

Not all the poisons introduced into the food web are confined to the internal organs, however. Ciguatera poisoning results from the consumption of contaminated fish flesh. The active chemical ingredient is called *ciguatoxin*, or CTX. CTX is produced by small, single-celled algae related to the zooxanthellae found within the reef-building coral polyps. Colonies of CTX-producing algae grow near the bottom, apparently concentrating on the surfaces of certain kinds of seaweeds. The herbivorous fishes that browse on these plants consume the toxic colonies as well, and the CTX is stored within their tissues. Later it may be passed along, in an increasingly concentrated form, to other reef predators and possibly to the human diner who selects any of the herbivorous or carnivorous links in the local energy chain. For some reason it appears that fishes are unaffected by the concentrations of CTX they consume; however, you and I are not so fortunate.

Large fields of host algae are not found in any quantity on the average reef. But when a reef is disturbed, whether by seasonal storms, heavy rains, or human activities such as blasting or dredging, large denuded areas are produced that may then be colonized by the seaweeds and their toxic companions. At the moment our knowledge of additional details is incomplete. Why do the algae appear at one site and not another? Is there only one host species, or several? Is there some natural cycle involved, and can it be controlled? We have no answers as yet. We *do* know that the toxin accumulates in the bodies of fishes in "hot" areas, and that they retain the poison within their bodies for years afterward. It also seems that the problem can spread from one reef to adjacent reefs over time. In the Marshalls, Hawaii, and the Line Islands there are indications that the appearance, spread, and decrease in the number of toxic fishes on a reef may follow a pattern lasting up to eight years.

The toxin itself is a lipid (fatty) molecule absorbed into the walls of the cells and in fatty areas of the body such as the liver. Current opinion is that an animal that is contaminated gradually accumulates and stores the toxin throughout its life. This does not affect the fishes, but for mammalian consumers such as human beings or marine mammals, sooner or later the symptoms of ciguatera poisoning may appear. Over a period of years, the amounts of toxin consumed and stored will vary among different individuals. This means that each person may have a different "dose" of CTX required to produce a reaction. This is probably why some diners may become quite ill after a particular meal, whereas others in the party remain unaffected. It is important to note, therefore, that continued exposure to even mildly contaminated fish may eventually cause problems. Although there seem to be slightly different chemical forms of this poison that yield slightly different clinical pictures, the overall pattern is the same. Problems appear within six hours after the CTX has been consumed. In cases involving an extremely toxic fish, the onset may be much more rapid. Typically the symptoms include a general uneasiness, a tingling around the mouth and lips, weakness, nausea, diarrhea and vomiting, chills, and abdominal pain. These usually fade in a day, and the mortality rate is very low, probably because the toxin is so strong, and its effects so severe, that the contaminated meal is rejected or rushed through the digestive tract before the poison has been completely absorbed.

Because ciguatoxin can be passed through a food web by so many different routes, almost any species of reef fish might be toxic at some locality at one time or another. But we can use our knowledge of the source and transmission of CTX to make a few general rules concerning fishes you should avoid eating.

1. Avoid large snappers, all surgeonfish, barracuda, and moray eels. Surgeonfish seem to feed on the algal source of the toxin, and the other fishes are predators who are likely to have stored large amounts of CTX in their systems. Remember that the toxin is accumulated over long periods of time, and larger fish will presumably contain larger amounts of ciguatoxin. This means that if you have a particular fancy for snapper or barracuda, indulge yourself with small specimens. Under no circumstances should you eat even a small moray, however. They are likely to be dangerous regardless of size and age, perhaps because of the large amounts of fat within their bodies.

2. If local villagers assure you that the above fishes are perfectly good to eat, pay no attention. In Micronesia moray eels are considered a delicacy, despite the fact that severe poisonings result. You *should* listen carefully if they indicate that there are other *toxic* species in local waters.

Invertebrates Paralytic shellfish poisoning (PSP) shares a number of features with ciguatera poisoning. The source of the poison in this case is a related single-celled alga that is planktonic in habits. When present in large numbers the surface waters take on a characteristically reddish tinge, which explains the term *red tide*. Shellfish and other filter-feeding invertebrates absorb the toxin as they strain their food from the overlying waters. Although this kind of poisoning most often appears following the consumption of shellfish, other animals such as shore crabs may also be poisonous following a red tide. Symptoms usually appear within thirty minutes after the meal. A tingling of the mouth, lips, and fingertips is followed by a spreading numbness and weakness. Dizziness, headache, rapid pulse, and other symptoms may follow; nausea, vomiting, and diarrhea may or may not occur. In extreme cases, progressive weakness leads to paralysis that involves both the voluntary and involuntary muscles. The mortality rate is low, and in most cases the symptoms have abated within twenty-four hours.

Before considering treatment for cases of suspected seafood poisoning, I would like to list the most common misconceptions concerning the prevention of incidents.

Eating raw seafood is dangerous. This is no more true than saying that eating cooked seafood is safe. Any fish must be properly selected, cleaned, stored, and prepared to be considered safe. For example, CTX is extremely tenacious. It cannot be extracted by soaking or washing, and it is unaffected by freezing or heating. Even if the entire fish is reduced to ashes, the cinders will be toxic, and there is just no way to cook, clean, or chill your way to safety. The same is true for TTX and scomberotoxin. So if it is safe cooked, it was probably safe raw. There are potentially serious parasite problems from the consumption of raw fresh water fishes, and from raw salt water fishes from temperate waters, but none reported from tropical marine species. If uncooked shellfish are your favorite snacks you should do your own collecting and avoid polluted harbors.

Only reef fishes are dangerous. In terms of CTX poisoning you are pretty safe when dining on dolphin (mahi-mahi fish), tuna, marlin, and so forth, which are part of the offshore food web. But free-ranging fishes such as these may still produce symptoms of bacterial and/or scomberotoxin poisoning following improper preparation or stowage.

You can always tell by the color. You can't.

Flies/cats/dogs/natives can somehow tell when a fish is poisonous. Of course they can, but only after eating it. Unless you want to carry around an expendable cat or native assistant, this method won't do you much good. Even experienced animals such as Monk seals have been found apparently the victims of CTX poisoning.

Treatment of seafood poisoning is even less standardized than in the case of injected toxins that were considered earlier in this appendix. In most cases the poison is inadequately known, or too little detail is available, to permit determination of an effective medical response. The biggest problem seems to be that many cases of seafood poisoning go undetected and unreported because the symptoms following a mild dosage may be so vague that they are mistaken for something else entirely. Even when the problem is properly diagnosed, most victims will recover without any assistance, so almost any treatment may seem to work miracles. A review of the literature will quickly show that there are widely different and contradictory treatments hailed as effective in combating the same symptoms. Rather than examine the theoretical approach to these problems you should concern yourself with treating the symptoms as they occur and with keeping the patient as comfortable as possible under the circumstances. You will probably be successful if you can:

a. Make certain that the meal is eliminated as quickly and completely as possible. If nausea and vomiting have not started on their own, induce them. Do *not* administer anti-nausea or anti-diarrhea medication, because you will be blocking the only routes available for the elimination of the toxin.

b. Administer pain medication as required, and in general make the victim as comfortable as possible. Be reassuring and sympathetic.

c. Administer an antihistamine for severe allergic reactions, should they occur.

d. Be prepared to administer artificial respiration as needed. The victims are usually alert right up to the time of crisis, and death most often results from a cessation of breathing rather than from some complex chemical reaction. If you can keep the patient supplied with oxygen until the level of toxin declines, you stand an excellent chance of saving a life, even following a very severe poisoning.

e. Replace lost fluids whenever possible. Clear liquids are the rule, that is, any fluids you can see through. Water, soda, and so forth are fine, but avoid milk or fruit juices. If the victim is unable to keep anything down, you may need to replace fluids intravenously, assuming that you have access to the proper equipment.

There are other medical problems peculiar to the tropics that are not primarily marine-related. Because medical attention may be of poor quality or totally unavailable, you should be prepared to act on your own to prevent problems, and even to treat them when necessary. The next portion of the appendix deals with such terrestrial affairs.

MEDICAL PROBLEMS AND PRECAUTIONS

Tropical islands are among the safest places in the entire world, in or out of the water. Central America, India, Africa, Indonesia, or Southeast Asia—these are the places to be approached with at least mild apprehension. In such areas the tropical climate and species diversity have interacted with questionable sanitation practices, overcrowding, and unrestricted travel of human, animal, and insect carriers to produce some truly intimidating health hazards. With the exception of a few diseases that arose in these areas and later entered the tropical Pacific from the west, serious, life-threatening tropical medical problems are almost unknown in Oceania. Similarly, the water barrier around the Caribbean islands has protected them from most of the serious Central and South American endemic diseases. With appropriate immunizations and a few precautions concerning climate, food, and insects, the prudent traveler can remain perfectly healthy, and with fairly simple first aid, health care, and medication the imprudent or unlucky individual will recover without lasting ill effects.

Rather than cover material already treated in detail in other sources, I shall refer readers interested in special topics to the Additional Readings list. The principles and procedures of first aid are concisely summarized in the soft cover edition of *Standard First Aid and Personal Safety*, published by the American Red Cross. It is a handy reference and an excellent traveling companion. Armed with a recent copy, an understanding of this chapter, and the portable medikit described below you will be adequately prepared for any routine emergency.

Cruising yachts have special requirements because a great deal of their time is spent underway, far from outside assistance and advice. For those concerned with the selection and stowage of a seagoing dispensary, I suggest a review of the article "Planning for Emergencies," detailed in the Additional Readings list. Your concern should also encompass the proper treatment of more serious emergencies, and for that information I refer you to Dr. Peter Eastman's excellent work, *Advanced First Aid Afloat*.

My intention here is to focus on the prevention and/or early treatment of those relatively minor problems that might ordinarily arise in the course of a visit to the tropics. In more serious cases, the situation will probably require the services of a physician rather than a first aid specialist, even a skilled one. This should not be a cause for concern, however, because timely preventive measures are particularly effective in avoiding such extreme developments. The textbooks on tropical medicine are filled with discussions of grossly neglected problems that do little to inspire confidence—or to provide useful information to the average traveler. In reality the tropics are no different from any other region, in that the key to good health is prevention backed by prompt recognition and early treatment. Most tropical medical problems are also encountered in the temperate zones, but their frequency and/or severity are increased under tropical conditions of warm temperatures, high humidity, and intense sunshine. On individual islands local factors can adversely affect the sanitation of food and water, exposure to insects that spread disease, and individual susceptibility to disease. We will begin with the most common problems and proceed from there.

The difficulties most often experienced are those that do not require any form of transmitter or carrier. These arise from direct contact with the distinctive tropical environment.

Sunshine

The tropical sun is less filtered by the atmosphere, and independent of how hot it feels on a given day, the sunlight can directly damage the skin and eyes. An all-over, blistered sunburn is no laughing matter, despite what your traveling companions may say. Sun *screens*, not ordinary suntan oils, applied frequently when out in the sun, and reapplied after swimming, are your best defense. Some tanning *will* occur, even through a sun screen, so don't be overly anxious to get that perfect tan, for it will only peel that much sooner if you burn. If you find that you have burned anyway, you will start turning an angry red two to four hours after exposure, and your burn won't peak until fourteen to twenty hours after you leave the sunshine. A bad burn will last around three days. A severe, blistered burn that covers more than 20 percent of your body merits the immediate attention of a doctor; systemic steroids may prove helpful if administered within the first twenty-four hours. If your burn is less severe, you can take steps to minimize the misery. Treat yourself to cool showers or compresses three or four times a day, and apply a soothing cream, steroid if you have it. Taking two aspirin two to three times a day will also help ease your discomfort. Local anesthetic sprays and creams, usually equipped with "-caine" in the brand name, actually do not help much more than cold water, and worse yet, some people can become allergic to them. Blisters, if small, can be left intact, but larger ones (over 2 inches in diameter) should be drained through a small needle hole and covered with a sterile bandage until they dry out. These represent an opening in the skin, and as such, are potential sites for infection. So pay attention to the treatment of cuts and skin infections as recommended below.

Some unfortunate people actually become allergic to the high-energy ultraviolet light that reaches the surface in the tropics. It takes at least one exposure to become sensitized, and then repeated exposure to produce the allergic reaction. If you become sensitized a rash becomes apparent on about the fifth day of your sunny vacation, even though you may already have a tan. This exquisitely inconvenient development may be red, itchy, and bumpy, rather like a forest of mosquito bites, or there may be small (pinhead-sized) blisters. The problem is primarily restricted to areas exposed to the sun, especially the face, chest, arms, and legs. The rash responds to steriods taken internally, steriod creams rubbed onto the rash, and anti-histamines such as Benedryl, which helps to lessen the maddening itch. Unfortunately, once you have become sensitized it will not take much sunshine to bring back the rash, and sun screens are not very effective in preventing this recurrence. Clothing is the only answer, so if you get this frustrating reaction to the tropical sun you should keep covered up, even if it means swimming with long pants and sleeves. Although all the causative factors have not been worked out, you should be aware that certain drugs, such as tetracycline or thiazides, can precipitate such a reaction, so if you are already on such medication when you arrive in the tropics you should be on the alert for early warning signs.

Fair-skinned individuals who have repeatedly burned and peeled their noses, ears, cheeks, foreheads, bald spots, forearms, and/or hands also risk skin cancer in the affected areas. Remember that your face, neck, and arms will be out in the open all day long, so *use sun screens*.

Your skin protects most of your body and bears the brunt of sun damage, but your eyes are vulnerable as well. After years of exposure to the sun, anyone's eyes, even those of dogs and cats, will develop skin growths that progress from the nasal border across the iris (colored portion of the eye). Such problems are easily prevented (in people, at least) by wearing sunglasses. Because of the intense reflection that occurs off the surface of the ocean, a pair of polaroid lenses are a good investment because they are particularly effective at damping the glare.

Humidity

"It's not the heat but the humidity" represents a basic consequence of the strategy used by mammals to control their body temperatures. Excess heat is used to evaporate water, either across the surface of the lungs and mouth (for a fur-covered animal such as a panting dog) or through sweat glands located on naked portions of the skin, which means almost everywhere in the case of a peltless human being. In moist or humid environments the air around us can't absorb our moisture very rapidly, so evaporation and subsequent cooling occurs very slowly. In short, we sweat like crazy but stay too hot. Warm and wet means uncomfortable, and in addition we are letting ourselves in for a variety of unpleasant rashes.

Areas of the body where moist, hot skin rubs against moist, hot skin are especially troublesome; neck creases, underarms, the groin, and under the breasts are good examples. Tight-fitting nylon or polyester clothing, such as underwear, pantyhose, pants, or jeans, and confining shoes neither absorb moisture nor permit evaporation. Wearing these in the tropics is like leaving a baby in wet diapers and plastic pants—in either instance, the wearer will wind up with diaper rash! Just the moisture and normal skin debris can block the openings of sweat glands and cause small red blisters, alias prickly heat. Several hostile biological agents may also become involved, particularly yeasts and fungi. These thrive in warm, moist, dark areas and produce a variety of unamusing rashes.

Yeast-related rashes are red, moist, bumpy, and very itchy. Fungus rashes are more varied. Some are dry and produce white flakes of skin, known as scales, which partially rub off. Other fungal rashes are dark and wrinkled. Some fungus infections spread out in a circular pattern, in which the inner portions heal while the outer margins spread further; one form is called ringworm, despite the fact that worms have nothing to do with the problem. A rather striking form of fungus prefers the surface of the back, over which it ranges widely. Against brown or tan skin, these areas stand out as lighter-colored patches, giving a strange, checkerboard appearance. In Hawaii the local name for this condition is haole rot. (*Haole* is the Hawaiian word used to designate those of light-skinned European ancestry.) Finally, there is the familiar problem of athlete's foot, which survives in temperate regions in the warm, damp confines of locker room floors.

You don't have to analyze these problems too closely to be able to deal with them effectively. Keeping as cool and dry as possible all over is both the prevention and the cure for these problems. Wear loose-fitting clothes, and as few of them as local customs and your own sense of propriety permits. Cotton clothing is best because it absorbs moisture and leaves the skin dry. Open-toed sandals or shoes make sense, unless you are out for a beach or reef walk, in which case a breathable canvas sneaker will be preferable for safety reasons. Talcum powder or corn starch spread in body creases will help reduce chafing, and if all else fails there are medications available that have both anti-fungal and anti-yeast properties. Most rashes of this kind will respond to thrice daily applications of medicated creams, and miconazole or clotrimazole are the chemical ingredients to look for on the label.

Two special variations of these problems deserve mention because they are relatively common, especially disconcerting, and easily prevented and/or cured. First let us consider swimmer's ear, otherwise known as *otitis externa*. The canal leading to the eardrum is a tube of skin about three-quarters of an inch long. It opens just above the earlobe and inside it is warm and dark. When you swim or bathe it gets damp as well—in short, it is a perfect spot for a fungus garden. The trick is to keep your ears dry. If you find that water remains in your ears after a long swim, perhaps affecting your hearing, you may have a chunk of wax blocking the canal and trapping moisture inside. Rinsing the ear canal with a soft squeeze bulb is the easiest way to remove the wax, and you will also be removing a potential rallying point for a fungal invasion. You can also make life more difficult for fungus by rinsing your ear canals once or twice a week with a dilute solution of vinegar, mixed half and half with ordinary water. Ear plugs or Q-tips are definitely not the answer. You may scratch the sensitive ear walls and risk infection, jam a block of wax where it doesn't belong, or even damage the eardrum.

If a maddening itch *does* develop, scratching is obviously out, for the same reasons. Instead, dry out your ear canals using air blown from a fan or a hair dryer. If using a hair dryer, however, be sure that the heat is turned off because the temperature put out by a blow dryer is much too high. Rinsing the canals with the vinegar solution three to four times a day can help cure a mild case, but for more advanced infestations medicated eardrops may be the answer.

The second variation is yeast-related, and is called *moniliasis* or *candidiasis* (sorry about the lack of a more memorable common name). Being warm, moist, and dark, the vagina is prone to yeast infections. Although a small amount of yeast is normal in the vagina, under tropical heat and humidity it may flourish to the point of discomfort. This results in an itching, burning pain and a whitish, lumpy discharge. To help prevent this, all cotton underwear, not just a cotton panel, should be worn, and rinsing the vagina with a very dilute solution of vinegar (two teaspoons per pint of water) may help a mild case. Most cases may require either a specific anti-yeast medicine, such as nystatin, or a broad spectrum cream like miconazole, which also works against fungal infections.

Bacterial Infections

Yeasts and fungi are not the only organisms that flourish on the moist, warm surface of the skin. As was the case with the yeasts and fungi, there is nothing unusual about the presence of bacteria on the body. Even the most infamous "tropical" bacterium, *staph*, can be found on the skin of most people on the planet, in any climate. There seem to be more misconceptions about staph than there are about any other common illness except perhaps the common cold. Staph bacteria are found on the normal individual's skin in small numbers, and they cause no problems because the keratin covering of the skin is an effective barrier. Of course, this protection only works if your skin remains intact. In warm, moist tropical regions, staph can really thrive on your body surface, and it is this increase in sheer numbers that leads to problems, not the fact that tropical staph bacteria are somehow different from staph confronted elsewhere in the world. The population explosion following your arrival in the tropics begins almost immediately—and given enough food, most bacteria double their numbers every twenty minutes! Any cut, broken blister, coral scrape, scratched insect bite, shaving nick, and so forth, releases fluids that provide a nutrient bonanza for the bacteria in the area and also give direct access to the warm, dark inner recesses of the body. Once they have gained entrance they will multiply and spread even more rapidly.

Your system rallies its defenses—special cells flock to the site, attack and destroy the invading bacteria, but die in the process. The pus that oozes from the wound contains their earthly remains. The blood supply to the area is increased, so it swells and reddens. The lymphatic system is mobilized, and as regional portions of the network become involved you may see them through the skin as red streaks that lead from the injury toward the heart. The lymph nodes or glands along this route may become swollen; if the infection is in the arm, the glands of the armpit will swell; if in the leg, those in the groin will be affected. Finally the body thermostat setting is raised in an effort to debilitate the invaders with higher-than-normal temperatures—in other words, you get a fever. Prevention of such goings-on requires a fairly straightforward attention to detail. Avoid breaks in the skin, for one thing, and whenever injuries do occur, it is a safe bet that bacteria have found an entrance somewhere. Thus, the problem becomes one of removing the intruders and barring the entrance of others in the future.

The first step is a familiar one: Wash the injury thoroughly with soap and water. This should be done as soon after the incident as possible in light of the rather short generation time of the bacteria involved. A dab of antibiotic ointment can be placed over the cleaned wound, but slapping a lump of goo on top of a dirty one is futile. Unless they are physically removed, or at least exposed, bacteria deep inside a scratch will never know the ointment is in the area and an infection will probably occur. After washing, the injury should be covered with a clean dressing to keep it free from further invasion until the skin has had a chance to repair the breach in its defenses.

A visit to a tropical island tends to be full of activity, and in the course of a typical day you will probably acquire several unnoticed bumps and scrapes, particularly on your arms and legs. Washing by itself will usually prove to be sufficient to prevent infection of these minor dings, and as a preventative measure you should scrub your entire body every day. If a minor infection has occurred, scrubbing twice a day will probably clear it up; fifteen-minute hot soaks or compresses will help speed up the process by encouraging blood flow to the area and limiting the spread of the infection. More serious infections may require the counsel of a doctor, who will probably prescribe antibiotics. His/her advice may be particularly useful, because certain regions appear to be harboring staph bacteria that have become resistant to penicillin. In the absence of a physician, erythromycin, dicloxacillin, or cephalahexin are usually effective.

To summarize:

1. You can avoid most staph infections by frequent and thorough scrubdowns.

2. You can heal most infections, even without antibiotics.

3. If the infection spreads to the point that you do need antibiotics, it usually means that you have neglected to pay enough attention to either of the two previous points.

A special category of tropical skin infections is the infamous "tropical ulcer." This is a serious, large (2 to 4 inch) chronically oozing crater, which usually develops on the legs or arms. Staph bacteria are not involved; instead, several different, ordinarily harmless bacteria appear to be responsible. Tropical ulcers usually occur in malnourished people with poor circulation to their limbs. You might conclude that this problem would more often affect a relatively underprivileged resident, rather than a healthy visitor, and in general you would be quite correct. There are two important exceptions to be noted that specifically concern readers who are either vegetarians or cruising sailors. If you are both, perhaps you should read these remarks twice.

Vegetarians must be especially careful to balance their protein intake to include all the required amino acids, because you can feel healthy and still be essentially protein-malnourished to some degree. Cruising sailors must also watch their protein and vitamin C intake, particularly on long passages where the tendency exists to select a meal on the basis of which cans are closest to the top of the larder. To make matters worse, peripheral circulation is likely to be restricted because a cruising sailor may spend several weeks without moving farther than the distance between a berth and the cockpit. Tropical ulcers appear at the site of even a minor injury to the skin and grow rapidly in size. Antibiotics alone often fail to save the day. Food, especially protein and vitamin C, elevation of the limb, frequent washing and disinfection of the sore combined with massive doses of penicillin do help. So this is an excellent example of a situation where reliance on modern "miracle cures" such as antibiotics cannot substitute for a continual concern for hygiene, diet, and prompt first aid. The lesson should be remembered.

Temperature

Most of the discussion so far has concentrated on the effects of the tropical climate on the skin or on the organisms normally found living there. Your body is also directly affected by the tropical heat. Temperature and fluid regulation activities are especially subject to disturbance when you first enter the tropics. Your system can adjust to excessive heat through better tolerance of exercise, better temperature control through sweating, and increased fluid and salt intakes, but it takes time for your body to shift gears in so complex a fashion. As a visitor you may not have enough time, or you may simply forget to allow yourself a break-in period.

The term *heat prostration* covers the most commonly experienced overheating problem. The body tries to cope with the unaccustomed heat, but the individual is pushing things a bit. Sweating is profuse, and both fluid and salt loss can be considerable. Then the subject begins to feel weak, nauseated, and faint—and suddenly collapses. What happened? Essentially the temperature regulating system has failed to keep things under tight enough control. You will recall from Chapter 5 that heat is lost at the body surface in naked (i.e., nonfurry) regions. In our case this means almost everywhere, and just beneath our skin there is a vast network of blood vessels whose volume can be closely controlled. If we are too hot, more blood goes to the skin and more heat is lost to the outside world. The sweat glands are provided with additional nutrients so they can work harder, coating the skin with salty fluids that evaporate and remove heat brought to the surface by these blood vessels. Of course as the sweat forms and evaporates, it must be continually replaced. This leads to a series of problems, unless these activities are well coordinated with other systems in the body. The temperature-regulating center is sending messages to the sweat glands to proceed at full steam, and the vessels to the skin are dilated. This means that (a) more and more fluids are being removed from circulations by the sweat glands, and (b) whatever blood volume exists must be distributed not only to those portions of the body that normally require servicing, but also to a large network of vessels in the skin, which are usually shut down.

You might think that the fluid loss through perspiration is insignificant, but you would be very wrong. A person sweating at maximum rates can lose almost a half-gallon of water every hour! As a result, the volume of the circulating blood declines. Blood pressure drops, the pulse rate increases, and the heart works harder to supply all of its dependencies. Despite this increase in activity, sooner or later something, somewhere, is going to get short-changed in its supply of blood. When this happens, a different response is initiated, and the brain shuts down the vessels to the skin, thus lowering to an extent the demand on the circulatory system. Yet those sweat glands are still getting the go ahead, so fluid loss continues. As the blood supply to the brain decreases, nausea, headache, and an eventual crash (faint) will follow. What you see from the outside is someone who appears to be experiencing a fainting spell. The person's skin is moist because the sweat glands are still charging away, but the surface of the skin is cool or clammy because the local circulation has been shut down. The victim's pulse is rapid, sometimes almost too rapid to count, but the body temperature is close to normal when checked with a thermometer.

Proper treatment is simple: Get the person to a cool place in the shade, in front of a fan, or in an air-conditioned bus or room. Encourage the individual to slowly drink a lot of fluids. Recovery will be surprisingly swift and complete. The problem would have been prevented in the first place if the individual had paid attention to the signals being sent by his or her body. When you are sweating heavily, consciously drink more fluids; if you start feeling weak, nauseated, or shaky get to someplace cool and relax with a cold drink (nonalcoholic until you feel a bit better).

Failure to take appropriate precautions can result in more serious problems. Heat stroke is the most extreme, and fortunately least common, problem arising from difficulties in internal temperature regulation. A person who already has health problems affecting circulation and sweating, such as heart disease or diabetes, is particularly susceptible to heat stroke. If you are one of these people you must be especially cautious about exertion in the tropics. As in the case of heat exhaustion, there is some internal conflict of interest, and in this instance the temperature-regulating system of the body just gives up completely. Despite the heat of the sun, sweating stops, the skin becomes dry and hot, and body temperature begins to climb, perhaps reaching levels as high as 106–113°F. Temperatures this high inside the body will kill brain, muscle, liver, and kidney cells. Unless the temperature is quickly reduced, the victim will either die or, at the very least, suffer permanent damage to vital organs. An ice-water bath is the best emergency treatment, as long as you are careful to see that the victim does not drown in the process. Medical assistance should be obtained as soon as possible, but your first priority should be cooling the victim.

Frequently the early symptoms of heat stroke will be the same as those heralding heat exhaustion, so here is one more reason to listen to your body. Cool off when you're uncomfortably hot, drink fluids when you are sweating heavily, and relax when you are so inclined. You are exploring for enjoyment, not participating in an endurance test.

This completes our list of problems produced or exaggerated by the tropical environment. Although they all will at least make you uncomfortable, and heat stroke is potentially fatal, none involves the activity of unusual or especially virulent microorganisms. These will be considered next.

Gastroenteritis

A variety of unpleasant medical problems can be conveniently grouped on the basis of a shared complex of all-too-familiar symptoms: vomiting and diarrhea. Although traveler's trots do not result from a single source, your GI tract (short for gastro-*i*ntestinal) really has only one line of defense against any assault—to try and get rid of the offending materials just as fast as possible. These purging operations are usually brief, but chronic problems can result from worm or other parasitic infestations. The most dangerous forms are the rare diarrheal diseases of typhoid and cholera. If you fall victim to any of these biological troublemakers it means only one thing: You have been exposed to contaminated food or drink.

We have already discussed the bacterial contamination of seafood. Other kinds of food also deserve the same cautious treatment, or you risk food poisoning from a terrestrial source. The more common, not to mention more disquieting, source of trouble involves the transfer of disease-producing bacteria, viruses, or parasites from infested human or animal feces. These problems are not restricted to the tropics by any means; indeed, they occur wherever sanitation procedures are lax. Aspen, Colorado has had outbreaks of diarrhea caused by the parasite *giardia*, and the almost fanatical approach to sanitation in the Panama Canal Zone has virtually eliminated most of the so-called "tropical diseases." Principal routes of transmittance are:

a. the feet or bodies of insects such as flies or cockroaches, which reach your food bearing hitchhikers from an earlier stop;

b. the unwashed hands of an individual who is infected and who also happens to be preparing your meal;

c. swallowing contaminated water; this route is particularly insidious, because it can occur while swimming, brushing your teeth, or (worse yet) via the ice cubes that grace your evening cocktail. Eating raw shellfish from waters contaminated by sewage will have the same end result;

d. any one of a number of devious routes, which can involve several steps: walking barefoot through contaminated sand, then brushing off your feet, or petting a passing dog or cat that has contaminated fur, or any other chain of events that eventually leads bacteria from some such source to your hands, and later, your mouth.

Whether or not a particular region of the tropics is likely to pose a threat to the tranquillity of your GI tract really boils down (no pun intended) to how much money the local government spends on sewage treatment and water purification and how meticulous the food preparers and servers are in refrigeration, insect control, cooking, and personal hygiene. In general, the large and relatively wealthy communities, such as those of Hawaii, and heavily touristed resorts such as those of Tahiti, Puerto Rico, Guam, or Bermuda have sanitation standards comparable to any on the mainland United States. Anywhere outside of these oases you should take a few precautions. To prevent GI surprises, you must either kill the organisms responsible or avoid them entirely. We can summarize the rules as follows:

1. Always select piping hot, cooked meals: Ninety-nine percent of the organisms that thrive at our body temperatures are killed by thorough cooking, making even contaminated food harmless.

2. Always drink bottled or treated water, if you drink the local water at all. It should be boiled for at least one minute, without cheating. You can treat water yourself by adding five drops of tincture of iodine per quart of water, and letting it stand for thirty minutes before drinking. With a collapsible quart container in your luggage, plus a bit of iodine, you can have safe water anywhere. Safe ice cubes are more of a problem.

3. Always use safe water to wash, or at least rinse, anything that will reach your mouth. Many parasites have eggs that resist drying; if contaminated water last rinsed your glass or fork, the carefully prepared drink or meal will wind up bearing perfectly healthy eggs. This applies to your hands, drinking glasses, utensils, toothbrush, and so on.

4. Avoid uncooked salads or you will be headed for trouble. Eat cooked vegetables and peel any fruit yourself, with your own nice clean hands.

5. Avoid local beverages, carbonated or not. Carbonation does

nothing to affect the quality of the drink, and local island beverages, even those with familiar brand names, may be made under wildly unsanitary conditions. The bottled fruity drinks in the Galapagos Islands are affectionately referred to as "amoeba water."

6. Bottled or canned beer is safe, but drink it from the container after rinsing the top. Home brew of one kind or another and local juice drinks should be skipped.

7. Avoid raw fresh-water fish because they can carry parasites that will be delighted to find themselves in your system. Cooking kills them and makes the meal safe.

8. Avoid swimming, walking barefoot, or collecting edible fish or shellfish from that picturesque beach or quiet lagoon in front of the village. In many areas the traditional location for privies was on stilts over the water or at the most convenient beach at low tide. With modernization the raw sewage is often piped to traditional areas, with resultant contamination of local waters. Live cholera bacteria have been found twenty yards from the beach, surviving contentedly in sea water for days.

Keep these precautions in mind and you may avoid an impressive array of potential problems. The following is a partial listing of problems; those with particularly nasty implications are asterisked. I should point out that if we were considering one of the risky areas of the world, the list would ramble on indefinitely.

Food poisoning arising from:

staphylococcus
clostridia
salmonella
shigella

Parasitic infestation by:

giardia
ascaris
strongdyloidias
various tapeworms

Serious infectious diseases:

* polio (Dominican Republic and Haiti)
* typhoid fever
* cholera (tropical Pacific only)
* hepatitis A and B
* ameobic dysentery
* schistosomiasis (certain Caribbean islands only)

No one is likely to be 100 percent effective in following these precautions, I must admit. I once spent several months watching every move I made, and then ran afoul of an ice cube. (I must say, though, that the first cold drink certainly tasted good, and it seemed worth the risk at the time.) If you do find yourself with a mild case of food poisoning, with classic symptoms, you can help yourself by giving your gut a complete vacation. This means eating nothing that requires much digestion. Drink small amounts of clear liquids frequently for a couple of days and the diarrhea will usually cease. Clear liquids includes anything you can see through, such as water, tea, soda, broth, jello, and so on. Gradually advance your diet through bland starches (bread, crackers, rice, noodles) to vegetables and then to meat over a two- to three-day period, which should complete your recovery. If you redevelop the symptoms, backtrack one step and try again. Over the first four to five days following the onset of symptoms you must avoid milk, ice cream, cream (including creamy soups), cheeses, and greasy foods. This might go against the grain because most people link milk with good health, but when diarrhea strikes one of the first casualties is your ability to digest milk products. This loss may persist for up to two weeks, and whenever you consume milk products over this period your system will behave as if you'd just taken a laxative. I am sure you will agree that this is hardly what you need under the circumstances.

Parasitic infestations may make you miserable from time to time, but their presence can usually be tolerated for long periods without any treatment whatever. To remove them, you will need appropriate medication; if you are planning an extended visit to the tropics you might elect to take some with you, just in case. For other travelers, if you have GI problems while in the islands and they persist after you return home, ask your doctor to check you for possible eggs and/or parasitic souvenirs.

You must try to avoid catching any of the more serious infectious diseases listed because medical treatment must be prompt—and may even be ineffective in severe cases. In any event, you will be too sick to worry about treating yourself, so there is little point in describing the routines. Fortunately for everyone, the three most dangerous of the group—typhoid, cholera, and hepatitis—can be thwarted by appropriate immunization procedures. We will describe the approved protocol for these diseases below.

You may have noticed that the "traveler's friend," Lomotil, has not been mentioned. This drug and others, such as donnatal, belladonna, and paregoric, neither cure the infection nor heal the bowel. All they manage to do is paralyze your gut, slowing it down so that you vomit less often, have fewer painful cramps, and have only one or two bouts of diarrhea per day, rather than five or six. These drugs can get you through the airport and over that long flight more comfortably, but you will not be getting any better as you go along. When used by children or infants these drugs can even hide the symptoms and allow severe and dangerous dehydration to occur. So, to be succinct, carry a "plugger" with you, but use the clear-liquids-only diet instead.

Problems with Tropical Insects

In large numbers, insect bites certainly can make you miserable. Some regions have a number of biting insects, such as the tiny "no-no" flies of the Marquesas or the giant green flies of the western Pacific. But by and large, your major concern will be with the familiar mosquito. There is not much you can do to ease the itching of a bite, but ice, calamine lotion, aspirin, and antihistamines may give some relief. In the long run, however, the problem is not the bites themselves, but rather, the number of serious diseases that mosquitos can spread, such as malaria, filariasis, Dengue fever, or encephalitis.

Malaria is restricted to the southwestern portion of the tropical Pacific and Hispaniola in the Caribbean. Table A–1 lists the specifics of this and other mosquito-borne diseases. However, travelers should realize that their itinerary may change unexpectedly, with deviations from the planned route potentially exposing them to unanticipated risks. Advance preparation, including this possibility, can minimize problems and make detours a plus instead of a minus.

You contract malaria from a mosquito that has previously bitten a person already infected with the disease. From five to thirty-seven days afterwards you develop a high fever and chills, and if you recover from the initial episode you can periodically relapse over and over again. With proper treatment malaria can be cured, but you can always be reinfected. By taking low doses of anti-malarial medications, most malaria can be avoided. Chloroquine is the traditional anti-malarial drug, and it is effective in preventing malaria throughout 99 percent of the area we are considering. Dosage instructions are included in the list of portable medikits for the traveler following Table A–1.

Other portions of the world are less fortunate. Some areas of Latin America, Asia, Africa, and the Solomon Islands appear to host strains of malaria that have become chloroquine resistant, so if your trip takes you to these areas you will need to obtain special anti-malaria medications. And even if you have taken anti-malaria drugs religiously, any high fever of long duration, repeated day after day, which develops within one *year* of your travel through a malaria-prone region should prompt you to remind your physician of the trip and your itinerary.

Table A–1
Immunizations and prevalent diseases in various portions of the tropical Pacific and Atlantic

Region	Special Immunizations*						Prevalent Diseases					
	Required[1]		Recommended**									
	YF	CH	TY	GG	CH	YF	MAL	YF	FIL	DEN	RB	SCH
PACIFIC												
Cook Is	–	–	+	+	–	–	–	–	+	+	2	–
Fiji	+	+	+	+	–	–	–	–	+	+	–	–
Fr. Oceania:												
Austral Is.	+	–	+	+	–	–	–	–	+	+	2	–
Marquesas	+	–	+	+	–	–	–	–	+	+	2	–
Societies	+	–	+	+	–	–	–	–	+	+	2	–
Tuamotus[3]	+	–	+	+	–	–	–	–	+	+	2	–
Galapagos Is.	+	–	+	+	–	–	–	–	–	–	2	–
Guam	–	–	+	+	+	–	–	–	–	–	–	–
Hawaiian Is.	–	–	–	–	–	–	–	–	–	–	–	–
Kiribati Rep.	+	–	+	+	+	–	–	–	+	–	2	–
Nauru	+	–	+	+	–	–	–	–	–	–	2	–
New Caledonia	+	–	+	+	–	–	–	–	–	–	2	–
Palau[4]	–	–	+	+	–	–	–	–	–	–	–	–
Pitcairn Is.	+	+	+	+	–	–	–	–	–	–	–	–
Samoa, American	+	–	+	+	–	–	–	–	+	+	–	–
Samoa, Western	+	–	+	+	–	–	–	–	+	+	2	–
Solomon Is.	+	–	+	+	–	–	5	–	+	+	+	–
Tonga	+	–	+	+	–	–	–	–	+	+	2	–
Tuvalu	+	+	+	+	–	–	–	–	+	+	2	–
Vanuatu Rep.	–	–	+	+	–	–	+	–	–	–	2	–

ATLANTIC

	YF	CH	TY	GG	MAL	FIL	DEN	RB	SCH
Antigua[6]	+	+	+	-	-	-	+	-	-
Bahamas[7]	+	+	+	-	-	-	+	-	-
Barbados	+	+	+	-	-	-	+	-	-
Bermuda	-	-	+	-	-	-	-	2	-
Cape Verdes	+	+	+	+	+	-	-	2	-
Dominica	+	-	+	-	-	-	+	2	-
Grenada[8]	-	-	+	-	-	-	+	+	+
Guadeloupe	+	-	+	-	-	-	+	-	+
Hispaniola[9]									
Dominican Rep.	+	+	+	+	+	-	+	+	+
Haiti	+	-	+	-	+	-	+	+	+
Jamaica[10]	+	-	+	-	-	-	+	-	-
Martinique	+	+	+	-	-	-	+	-	-
Montserrat	+	-	+	-	-	-	+	-	-
Neth. Antilles[11]	+	-	+	-	-	-	+	-	-
Puerto Rico	-	-	+	-	-	-	+	-	-
St. Helena[12]	-	-	+	-	-	-	-	2	-
St. Lucia[13]	+	-	+	-	-	-	+	-	+
Trinidad[14]	+	+	+	-	-	+	+	+	+
Virgin Is.[15]	-	-	-	-	-	-	+	-	-

YF = yellow fever; CH = cholera; TY = typhoid; GG = gamma globulin; MAL = malaria; FIL = filariasis; DEN = Dengue fever; RB = rabies; SCH = schistosomiasis.

*Recommended immunizations apply only if traveling outside regions with modern tourist facilities and good sanitation standards. This table is based on World Health Organization certifications; blank portions of the table indicate that no official information is available.

See next page for references.

Table A–1 (continued)

1 = required by the government if you are arriving from an infested area
2 = not officially certified as free of rabies
3 = including the southern Gambier group
4 = including the Northern Marianas, Federated States of Micronesia, and Marshall Islands
5 = chloroquine-resistant strain of malaria present here
6 = including Anguilla, St. Kitts/ Nevis, and other members of the West Indies Federation in the northern Leeward Islands
7 = including the Turks and Caicos Islands
8 = including the Grenadines
9 = travelers should be aware that polio is present on this island
10 = including the Cayman Islands
11 = including the northern and southern groups
12 = including Ascension Island
13 = including St. Vincent
14 = including Tobago
15 = British and U.S. Virgin Islands alike

Filariasis, which occurs in the tropical Pacific but not in the Caribbean or Atlantic, also involves the transfer of infection from individual to individual via mosquitos. The initial illness is a nonspecific fever. Over many years, usually more than ten, with continual exposure the invading organisms may block regional lymph glands in the groin or armpit. This leads to chronic swelling of the nearby limb, which, in severe cases is called *elephantitis*. The basic causative organism can be killed by drugs, but the blockage they have caused is permanent. Fortunately, brief exposure (less than two years) gives no cause for concern, but people residing in filariasis areas should have their blood checked regularly so that medication can be provided before any damage has been done. Even for permanent residents, steps to reduce exposure to mosquitos plus testing and medication as needed should make elephantitis completely avoidable. One interesting aside is that the mosquitos themselves are killed by the disease. Once an infected person has been bitten, the mosquito is only able to fly for 100 yards or so before dying. Severe cases are rare, so even in the most heavily afflicted areas you are likely to remain unexposed as long as you remain reasonably isolated from potential carriers.

Mosquitos also spread viruses for which there are no specific treatments. Although in Africa and South America some of these may prove fatal, the tropical Pacific and Caribbean have only Dengue fever and (rarely) Japanese-B encephalitis, neither of which is so severe or common to merit acute anxiety attacks. Dengue fever, alias break-bone fever, is characterized by severe, immobilizing muscle pains and a fever that lasts for up to a week. Although the victim is miserable and weak through it all, recovery is usually slow but uneventful. All you can do is make the patient as comfortable as possible. Encephalitis is more severe and frequently requires intensive medical care; but again, recovery is the rule. The symptoms include blinding headaches, high fever, stiff neck, convulsions, and coma, so it is not the sort of problem you would be inclined to tackle on your own. Therefore, I will not detail the rather technical possibilities for treatment.

Treatable or not, the best solution to all mosquito-borne diseases is prevention. As a visitor you can hardly be expected to drain local swamps, but sleeping in a screened enclosure, perhaps using your own mosquito netting, and prudent use of mosquito repellents will go a long way toward eliminating the problem.

Other Infectious Diseases

There are three other infectious diseases that rank high on the list of tropical terrors: tuberculosis, leprosy, and trachoma. Before you begin to think about them, you should know that these diseases are only caught through prolonged, close contact with an infected person. *Short-term visitors do not risk catching these diseases.* You would only stand a very small chance of contracting one of these illnesses if you lived in the same house with an infected individual for months to years, not days to weeks. Whereas these diseases appear from time to time throughout the Pacific and Caribbean islands, they are becoming increasingly rare as improved living conditions and medical services become more widespread.

Dangerous Terrestrial Animals

Here again, the fauna of tropical islands are relatively mild-mannered. There are no tigers in the jungles, only an occasional wild boar up in the hills. In the Pacific the Solomons have a couple of poisonous snakes under 3 feet in length; Fiji has only one species, a tiny burrowing snake that presents no threat to anyone. In the Caribbean the continental islands of Trinidad and Tobago and the Lesser Antilles islands of St. Lucia, Martinique, and Aruba have one species apiece of poisonous snakes that prefer plantations and damp forests. All the other islands of both oceans are either snake-free or at least poisonous snake-free. Centipedes can inject a toxin with their bites that produces a reaction reminiscent of a bad beesting, and some islands have small scorpions of one kind or another. If you are concerned about these animals you might wish to shake out your shoes before donning them in the morning. In the villages throughout Polynesia, particularly those of Tonga and Samoa, there may be large populations of "common-owned" dogs. These are essentially living by their wits, unmanaged and untrained, and dog bites are rather common injuries. In a single month on Tutuila there were forty-nine cases treated at the local hospital (and it's a pretty small island!) Fortunately rabies is rare in Oceania and the Caribbean, and there are strict quarantine regulations in most island groups to keep things that way. The average visitor or cruising sailor need not be concerned about such matters, but rabies is relatively common in Central and South America, and is found in Cuba, Grenada, Haiti, the Dominican Republic, Puerto Rico, and Trinidad, as well as the mainland United States (but not Hawaii). If you are planning to bushwack or hunt in the wilds of these areas you might consider taking the rabies pre-exposure injection series.

The only other dangerous animals you are likely to encounter will be human. The crime rates on tropical Atlantic and Pacific islands are almost ridiculously low, compared with anywhere in the continental United States, and the cultural outlook tends to be relaxed and easygoing. But people are people everywhere, and the inhabitants of the tropical islands can no more be universally prejudged as mild-mannered, jovial, and hospitable to strangers than all New Yorkers can be considered to be hyperactive, aggressive, and hostile to visitors. The crime rate wherever you live is likely to be ten times that of your destination, so you will not go wrong if you just refrain from doing anything while traveling that you would automatically avoid doing at home.

To summarize, while you are enjoying your tropical island retreat you should limit your exposure to the sun, wear cool, cotton clothes, treat all cuts and scratches promptly, follow the eight sanitation precautions listed, keep flies off your food and mosquitos off your body, shake out your shoes, beware of the dog, and not expect a land populated exclusively by angels.

Some additional precautionary measures can be taken before your departure to help insure your health and safety while you are traveling. In many respects these are just as important as watching your activities abroad, so I will devote a little time to them before closing this discussion. Plan your activities in light of any preexisting medical conditions, however slight. Individual problems such as diabetes, heart disease, asthma, kidney failure, and so forth are best reviewed with your doctor prior to your departure. These problems do not necessarily prevent your traveling throughout the world, as long as you plan your itinerary with an eye toward the availability of health facilities along the way (see the annotated tables throughout Chapter 9). If you are under a physician's care and taking regular medications, you should carry along enough pills to last you through your trip. This is important because medications differ from country to country in terms of name and availability. Any medications you do carry should be kept in the original prescription container so that Customs agents can easily identify them as legal drugs. You most certainly do not want to spend your time exploring the interiors of tropical prisons, and most island groups take an extremely dim view of possible trafficking in drugs.

For those of you who wear glasses, toting along a second pair is an absolute necessity. Having to spend a few weeks wearing your sunglasses indoors and out, or worse yet being hopelessly near- or far-sighted is not very enjoyable.

Allow yourself plenty of time to obtain all the required and/or recommended immunizations before leaving the country you are in. The standard shot record for travelers is titled the International Certificates of Vaccination, which is approved by the World Health Organization. It bears several pages containing blanks where your immunization history can be officially recorded. The key word here is *officially*, because to be valid and acceptable to a foreign health officer any required immunizations must be verified with the official stamp of the facility administering the shot, and the date must be entered in the internationally approved format, which is: 1/January/83. (Jan. 1, '83 or 1-1-83 simply will not suffice!) Immunizations can be divided into two categories, those designed to protect the country from the traveler and those that protect the traveler from the country. Only the former variety are required for admittance, and in today's world there aren't many diseases that a visitor can import that are not already there or that won't be controlled by sanitation. Yellow fever, cholera, and rabies (usually a problem for animal travelers, rather than human ones) are the only major diseases still being controlled by immunizations that may be required by a foreign country. The requirements of each of the major island groups is summarized in Table A–1.

There *are* several illnesses that the traveler might find new and potentially troublesome, and most of the modern inoculations are designed to protect visitors from the locally prevalent health hazards. Basically every traveler should obtain diptheria, tetanus, and oral polio immunizations. People who have never had measles should be immunized against it, and women of child-bearing age should have a rubella (German measles) shot as well. A gamma globulin shot for hepatitis A is also advisable for anyone anticipating a visit outside the reliable world of tourist centers. This shot must be given at least two weeks after immunizations for other diseases and is most effective if given just before you begin your trip. From personal experience, however, I would suggest you allow at least a day or two before your actual departure date or else risk a rather demoralizing tenderness in that portion of your anatomy facing the confines of your airline seat!

Most people are aware that smallpox has been eradicated, so vaccines are unnecessary. Nevertheless, your International Certificate booklet probably still retains a special page for recording smallpox inoculations. If you are traveling widely you might wish to obtain a notation attached to your record that verifies that the shot is no longer required by the World Health Organization. This sounds ridiculous, but believe me when I say that a health department official in an isolated island group is not likely to be up on current events. Trying to explain why blank "X" is not filled in appropriately can be frustrating, time-consuming, and even expensive.

Planning the basic series of typhoid, cholera, yellow fever, polio, measles, tetanus, diphtheria, and gamma globulin can be quite a scheduling nightmare. Therefore, I have included an inoculation schedule as Table A–2. This is the recommended schedule for a completely unimmunized person. If you have ever been immunized for

Table A-2: A suggested schedule for immunizations

Time Before Departure	Diptheria	Tetanus	Oral Polio	Measles and Rubella	Typhoid	Cholera	Gamma Globulin	Yellow Fever*
16 months	1st	1st	1st	one and only				
14 months	2nd	2nd	2nd					
5 months					1st			
4 months					2nd			
3 months	3d	3d	3d					
2 months								one and only
1 month						1st		
3 weeks						2nd		
1 week							one and only**	
Boosters?	every 10 years	every 10 years	every 10 years	probably never needed	every 3 years	every six months	every six months	one every 10 years

*available only at World Health Organization vaccine center
**dosage: 2 cc if trip will last less than 3 months; 5 cc if 3 to 6 months

one of these diseases, you will not need to repeat the entire series, and you will only need a booster shot if the elapsed time exceeds that indicated in the table. In a pinch, single doses of all could be given at once, with the exception of gamma globulin as noted above. Just keep in mind, before you procrastinate, that such a compression of the schedule is not without its problems. For example, typhoid and cholera shots produce systemic fevers for one to three days, and the diphtheria/tetanus shot produces a pronounced local swelling. If all three are taken at once, you will not find yourself in a very congenial frame of mind.

Finally, you should take a few items along with you so that you will be able to contend with everyday problems as they arise instead of only seeking assistance later. This will drastically reduce the chances that you will ever develop any unpleasant complications. If you are going to a modern tourist center such as Papeete, Tahiti, where there are full medical facilities available, your kit will still prove useful. Although the components might be available locally, the costs will be higher and you will have to take the time to go out and track them down when you could be doing something more amusing. At the very least, this medikit should include the items listed in Table A–3, which I have subdivided according to your planned destination. You should refer to the instructions accompanying the medications, and it would also help to refer to one of the references noted in the Additional Readings before using any of the more powerful drugs. If there is no improvement over the short term, a doctor should be consulted. In general you are always better off doing nothing rather than using drugs erratically or unwisely, so when in doubt seek advice from a reliable source. This packet of items should prepare you for even an extended visit anywhere in the tropical Atlantic or Pacific, with the exception of the New Hebrides (Vanuatu), the Solomon Islands, Haiti, and the Dominican Republic. Chloroquine comes in 500 mg pills (300 mg base). Take one pill each week beginning one week before your departure, continuing throughout your trip, and then for six weeks after you return home. Although you should consult your doctor first, if you are entering a high-risk area even pregnant women and children would usually be better off taking chloroquine (perhaps in smaller doses) than taking the risk of getting malaria.

Table A–3
A Portable Medical Kit for the Tropical Traveler

Basic medikit:*

sun screens

bandaid assortment

ice bag

baby powder or corn starch

ace bandage (wrap)

antacid (NP)

laxative (if needed at home)

aspirin or tylenol (NP)

cold tablets: with pseudo-ephedrine (NP)

cough syrup: with dextromethorphan (NP)

antibiotic ointment (NP)

antihistamine: benadryl (P)/chlortrimeton (NP)

Outside of heavily touristed areas, add:

betadine antiseptic soap

butterfly tapes for closing cuts

sterile gauze and adhesive tape

thermometer

birth control pills (if needed)

kwell shampoo or lotion (anti-lice)

anti-yeast medication (nystatin [P])

anti-fungal medication: tinactin (NP)/micatin (also anti-yeast) (P)

collapsible container and iodine drops

multiple vitamins with C and iron (NP)

pain relievers: aspirin or tylenol with codeine (P)

eye drops: sulfacetamide for pink-eye (P)

ear drops: corticosporin, for swimmer's ear (P)

salt pills with dextrose (NP)

antibiotics, oral: erythromycin, 250 mg (P)/ampicillin, 500 mg (P)

Selsun Blue shampoo (treats haole rot if rubbed on each night)

cortisone cream (0.5% NP; 1+% P)

acute nausea medication: dramamine (NP)/compazine (P)

anti-worm medication (vermox [P])

emergency diarrhea treatment: lomotil (P)

*P: prescription required; NP: nonprescription.

Glossary

aboral surface: the side of an echinoderm that does *not* have a mouth on it; the upper side in the case of urchins, starfish, and brittle stars

adaptation: alterations in the characteristics of a species in a response to a particular aspect of the environment

advection cell: a circulation pattern that develops when warm fluids are lighter than cool ones; examples in the text involve air, water, and molten rock

aft: a nautical term that refers to the rear or stern of a vessel, as opposed to the front or bow

algae: marine plants, single or many celled, lacking the sophisticated roots and various internal systems that are found in terrestrial plants; phytoplankton and seaweeds

amphibian: a vertebrate closely related to frogs, toads, or salamanders

annelid: a member of the worm phylum, *Annelida*

archipelago: an island group or chain

arthropods: members of the phylum *Arthropoda*, which includes insects, spiders, and crustaceans (along with many other forms); this is the largest animal phylum

atoll: a massive reef formation, often ring-shaped, built over a volcanic base that has subsided

bacteria: microscopic, single-celled organisms, many of which are involved with the decomposition of plant and animal remains and/or waste products

baleen: sheets of keratin fibers produced by the upper gums of certain whales, which are used to filter small animals from the surrounding waters

barometric pressure: the "weight" of the atmosphere over a particular spot as measured by a special instrument, called a barometer

barrier reef: a reef found off the coast of an island or continental land mass, but separated from it by a lagoon

caldera: a large crater that forms when a volcanic peak collapses in on itself after eruptions have ceased

carnivorous: a predator that preys on other animals

caudal: near or at the tail

cephalopods: active molluscs including the nautilus, octopus, cuttlefish, and squid

cetaceans: marine mammals, specifically the whales, porpoises, and dolphins

Chondrichthyes: a vertebrate class that includes the sharks, skates, rays, and rabbitfishes

Chordata: the animal phylum that includes the vertebrates

ciguatera: human poisoning that occurs after eating fish contaminated through the ingestion of poisonous algae

cilia: threadlike extensions of cells that are capable of coordinated movement

class: a term used to designate a collection of related families

coelenterates: members of the phylum *Coelenterata*, which includes hydrozoans, jellyfishes, corals, and anemones

condensation: an alteration in the arrangement of molecules to a more dense form, as in the change from gas to liquid, which releases stored energy

conductor (of heat): any material that transmits heat between two points; "good conductors" transmit heat for long distances, "poor conductors" only over short distances

continental drift: the movement of segments of the earth's crust across its surface

convergence: the evolution of similar characters in two separate groups of animals as a result of their adapting to similar environmental features

copepods: small, crustacean members of the zooplankton

corals: coelenterates with a reduction of the medusa-stage of the life cycle, and which usually are colonial and may produce a skeleton that can be fibrous or calcified

coriolis effect: the tendency for moving objects to turn to the right in the northern hemisphere, and to the left in the southern hemisphere

Cretaceous: a period of time from 65 million to 130 million years ago

crust (geological): the thin, solid, outermost layer of material that covers the surface of the earth

crustacea: arthropods of varied form, from copepods to crabs to barnacles, united by characteristic larval stages, internal features, and the possession of two pairs of antennae

cyclone: a powerful, potentially destructive storm in which the winds rotate around a central eye of low pressure; called a hurricane in the Caribbean, a typhoon in the northwestern Pacific

detritus: litter or debris composed of organic materials

dissection (geological): removal of surface materials by rainfall, producing a variegated landscape of valleys and sculptured ridge peaks

diurnal: active during daylight hours

doldrums: the region beneath the ITC where winds are light and rain showers common

dorsal: the upper surface of an animal; the aboral surface of a starfish, the oral disc of a polyp, or the area on a fish or other vertebrate that lies above the vertebral column

East Pacific Rise the active spreading center where new Pacific plate materials are forming

echinoderms: members of the phylum *Echinodermata*, which encompasses starfishes, sea urchins, brittle stars, sea cucumbers, and other less familiar creatures

echolocation: the use of reflected sound waves to provide information about objects in the environment

ectotherms: animals that rely on an external source of heat to bring their body temperatures to a desirable level

embayed (geological): a coastline that contains a number of bays created through the subsidence of the land and the drowning of valleys

emergence (geological): lifting of an island or portion of an island above the surface of the ocean as a result of activities in the underlying crust

endemics: species peculiar to a particular, relatively confined area that are found nowhere else and that presumably evolved from an isolated local population

endoderm(is): cells lining the digestive tract or chamber

endotherms: animals that utilize the heat produced by their internal metabolic activities to bring their body temperatures to a desirable level

epidermis: the layer of cells covering the body's external surfaces

evolution: change in species or the appearance of new species over time as a result of natural selection

family: a term used to denote a collection of related species

fault (geological): a crack or fissure in the earth's crust that is found within the body of a plate or that marks the boundary between the colliding continental margins of two plates, and which indicates that the two sides differ in direction or rate of movement

feral: an animal whose ancestors were domesticated but that has returned to the wild

flukes: broad, horizontal expanded finlike structures that lack skeletal supports and that are attached to the caudal (tail) vertebrae; the source of propulsion for sirens and cetaceans

fringing reef: a reef, found along the shores of a volcanic island or land mass, that does not enclose a lagoon

fumaroles: a vent or hole in the surface through which hot gases are released

gastroenteritis: a catchall medical term to denote a variety of illnesses characterized by symptoms of vomiting and diarrhea

gastropods: members of the phylum *Mollusca* who possess either a single shell or none at all, and who rely on hydraulic pressure and a muscular foot for locomotion

guyots: seamounts whose upper surfaces were truncated by wave action when they were subsiding or that represent atolls that have subsided below the depths tolerated by living corals

habitat: the restricted portion of the local environment occupied by an organism

herbivore: an animal that obtains energy solely through the consumption of plant materials

horse latitudes: the area of the earth's surface lying beneath the STC, characterized by light winds and clear skies

hydrozoans: coelenterates, usually having life cycles with both polyp and medusa stages, that lack pleats and folds in the walls of their digestive cavities

hydrozoan corals: colonial hydrozoans that secrete a calcified *outer* skeleton, as opposed to the inner skeleton of the true corals, and that possess powerful nematocyst toxins; fire or flame corals

insulator: a poor conductor of heat

Inter-Tropical Convergence (ITC): region within the tropical boundaries where solar energy is transferred from the earth's surface to the atmosphere at the greatest rate, and to which air from both hemispheres travels

invertebrates: all those animals lacking the characteristics of vertebrates

isostasy: the floating of the earth's solid crust on the more dense yet fluid mantle layers below

keratin: a nonliving, rugged, waterproof protein produced by the epidermal cells of vertebrates

krill: shrimplike crustaceans found in high-temperate and polar seas during the spring and summer months

lagoon: a body of water enclosed by a reef

larvae: young animals that differ greatly in form and habits from the adults

lateral line: a sense organ of fishes sensitive to underwater vibrations

lee: the downwind side; in the lee of "x" (i.e., sheltered by the mass of "x" from the forces of either wind or current)

leeward: the side of an island that does not face the prevailing winds

magma: molten rock; lava; materials of the mantle

mammal: a member of the class of vertebrates that includes all the hairy endotherms that suckle their young

mantle: a layer of molten rock lying between the solid crust of the earth and the more dense, metallic layers of the core.

medusa: the mobile, jellyfish stage in the life history of a coelenterate

Melanesian: dark-skinned descendant of the New Stone Age invasion of the Pacific, now native to the Solomons, New Hebrides Islands, New Caledonia, and Fiji

micro-carnivore: a predator that feeds on very small animals, such as those of the zooplankton

Micronesian: descendant of the Malay/Polynesian stock who invaded the western north Pacific and now are native to the northern Palau Islands, Guam, the Marianas, the Federated States of Micronesia, the Marshalls, and the Gilbert-Phoenix-Northern Line Islands region

Mollusca: the phylum that includes gastropods, bivalves, and cephalopods

natural selection: a term for the complex of interactions between an animal and its living and nonliving surroundings that determines its success at surviving and reproducing

nematocyst: a small, harpoonlike structure associated with a poison gland, found on the outer surfaces of most coelenterates, that can be used for offense or defense

neutral buoyancy: the ability to hover in the water at a particular depth without having to swim

nocturnal: an animal active at night

odontocetes: whales with teeth as opposed to baleen

pectoral: located at the chest; a fin or limb in the chest region

phylum(s)/phyla (pl.): a collection of related classes that form a distinct evolutionary line

phytoplankton: the microscopic plant members of the plankton

pinnipeds: marine mammals such as the sea lions, seals, or walruses

piscine: fishlike

plankton: animals and plants found near the surface of the ocean that are essentially unable to control their movements (other than relatively minor alterations in depth) and that drift from place to place at the mercy of the currents

planulae: planktonic larvae of reef-building corals

plate (geological): a discrete section of the earth's crust, whose boundaries are apparent in the form of trenches, volcanic ridges, or faults

pod: a herd of whales

Polynesian: descendant of sea-faring peoples who colonized the central and southern Pacific island groups including Hawaii

predator: an animal that obtains energy by preying on other animals

radiation (of heat): emission of heat in the form of energy packets that can be absorbed by other objects

rain-shadow: the dry area downwind of an obstacle of sufficient height that in ascending to pass over it most of the water vapor in the air is condensed and precipitated out over its windward slopes

reef: a massive structure representing the conglomerated skeletal remains of coral colonies, covered by the current generation of living colonies

rift (geological): a crack or fissure in the crust, not reflecting differential rates of motion

saturated (weather): air containing as much water vapor as it will hold at a given temperature

seamount: a volcanic mountain that does not protrude above the surface of the sea

seaward: facing the open ocean

seismic: earthquake-related

shield volcano: volcano formed over a mid-ocean hotspot and characterized by gentle slopes and distinctive lava

shoal: shallow area or bank

siltation: increase in nonorganic particles in the water as a result of wave action or runoff from the land

sirens: members of the Sirenian group of marine mammals; the dugongs and manatees

sonar: an abbreviation for *so*und *na*vigation *r*anging; a mechanism for mechanical or biological echolocation

speciation: the appearance of species

species: a term referring to a group of closely related organisms that may differ in appearance but that are still capable of successfully interbreeding

subaerial erosion: erosion by activities underway in the atmosphere, particularly rainfall

subduction: movement of one crustal plate beneath another, usually creating a trench in the process

subsidence: sinking of an island as a result of isostasy and crustal loading

Sub-Tropical Convergence (STC): an area of high pressure near the northern and southern limits of the tropics where cool, dry air descends from above as part of the atmospheric circulation pattern

surge: movement of water relatively close to the surface in oscillations toward and away from the shore caused by the arrival of large waves or swells in shallow waters

symbiosis: the intimate association of two unrelated organisms to mutual benefit

Tertiary: a period of time from 1.5 million to 65 million years ago

theca: a stony pocket secreted by a reef-building coral that forms part of the colonial skeleton

thermocline: a boundary between two water masses of differing temperatures

tradewinds: the strong surface winds that blow between the STCs and the ITC

transform faults: cracks in an oceanic plate that extend at right angles to a volcanic rise and indicate differing rates of eruption along the axis of the rise or different amounts of resistance to movement at the other end of the plate

trench: an area of relatively great depth formed by the subduction of oceanic plate materials

trophic levels: steps removed from the primary productivity of plants, with herbivores as T-II and carnivores as T-III and up

Tropic of Cancer: latitude 23½°N

Tropic of Capricorn: latitude 23½°S

upwelling: an area where cold, nutrient-rich waters rise to the surface

ventral: the opposite of dorsal, as in the oral surface of a starfish or the belly of a fish

vertebrate: a member of the phylum *Chordata* possessing a vertebral column and/or cranium, and including fishes, amphibians, reptiles, birds, and mammals

viruses: ultramicroscopic organisms that infect individual cells

weather: see windward

windward: facing the prevailing winds

zooplankton: any of the small animal members of the plankton

zooxanthellae: single-celled algae living within the endodermal cells of corals (and a few other marine invertebrates)

Additional Readings

CHAPTER 1

Friedrich, Hermann, *Marine Biology*. Seattle, WA: University of Washington Press, 1969. The opening chapters of this book give a nice overview of the historical aspects of the science and follows with a consideration of physical oceanography as it affects marine organisms. This book is a readable compromise that provides a wealth of technical information without drowning the reader in a deluge of jargon and dry data.

Scientific American Editorial Staff, *The Ocean*. San Francisco, CA: W.H. Freeman and Co., 1969.

Van Dorn, William G., *Oceanography and Seamanship*. New York, NY: Dodd, Mead and Co., 1974. This is an interesting, readable text for those interested in becoming involved with more technical aspects of oceanography. It is especially attractive to sailors because of an entire section devoted to practical seamanship that uses principles developed in the theoretical portions of the volume.

CHAPTER 2

Russell-Hunter, W.D., *The Biology of Lower Invertebrates*. London, England: The MacMillan Company, 1969. This is one of a pair of softcover volumes that I recommend to anyone interested in learning more about the invertebrate multitudes. The information is boiled down to a minimum, the specialized terms are well and clearly defined, and the diagrams and photographs are excellent.

Wiens, Herold J., *Atoll Environment and Ecology*. New Haven, CT: Yale University Press, 1962. This is one of the few books devoted to this topic, and it contains an enormous amount of information. I would not advise purchasing a copy without looking it over first, because it is intended more for specialists than laypersons.

CHAPTER 3

Beebe, William, and John Tee-Van, *Field Book of the Shore Fishes of Bermuda and the West Indies*. New York, NY: Dover Publications, Inc., 1970. Although there are some more recent volumes on this subject, I like the fact that this one is available in an extremely durable softcover version, which makes it easy to carry.

Carcasson, R.H., *A Field Guide to the Reef Fishes of Tropical Australia and the Indo-Pacific Region*. Sydney, AUS: Collins Publishers, 1977. If you are inclined to have one small, portable book to carry you throughout the Pacific, this is the one to get. The color plates are very nice, nice enough that you don't have to be a detail person to decide what you have seen, and both common and scientific names are included.

Marshall, N.B., *The Life of Fishes*. New York, NY: Universe Books, 1966. I think that anyone interested in fishes would enjoy having a copy of this book and the next one listed.

Norman, J.R., and P.H. Greenwood, *A History of Fishes*. London, England: Ernest Benn, Ltd., 1975. Both this and the previous listed book were written for the nonspecialist, and they are full of sketches, interesting anecdotes, and information. The layouts are enough alike, however, that having just one would probably suffice; this book has the advantage of being available in softcover, which makes it easy to pack.

CHAPTER 4

Baldridge, H. David, *Shark Attack*. Anderson, SC: Droke House/Hallux, Inc., 1974. If you are a person who is fascinated by the intimate details of attacks, you might as well get right to the point. This unusual volume is the result of years of work by the author in analyzing all recorded attacks in an effort to determine significant patterns. This is not a collection of fish stories, but a cool appraisal and evaluation of the events and details obtained at the scenes. My only reservation would be that reading about attacks for 263 pages will do very little for your sense of perspective.

Budker, Paul, *The Life of Sharks*. New York, NY: Columbia University Press, 1971. I have yet to find any work intended for the layperson that is quite as balanced in its approach to these fishes. All aspects of the biology of sharks are discussed at least briefly, and the horror stories are not overdone.

CHAPTER 5

Harrison, Richard J., and Judith E. King, *Marine Mammals*. London, England: Hutchinson University Library Series, Hutchinson and Company, Ltd., 1965. This is a handy, if brief, paperback that talks about all three groups of marine mammals considered in this book.

Slijper, E.J., *Whales* (2nd ed.). Ithaca, NY: Cornell University Press, 1979. The recent edition has been updated, and it is an excellent work. This is a volume filled with interesting stories, clear diagrams, and some remarkable photographs. If you are fascinated by cetaceans you ought to take a long look at this book, despite the rather hefty price.

CHAPTER 6

Levinton, J., *Marine Ecology*. (Englewood Cliffs, NJ: Prentice-Hall, Inc., 1982.

Russell-Hunter, W.D., *Aquatic Productivity*. New York, NY: The MacMillan Company, 1970. An interesting book that devotes considerable space to energy relationships and the physical and biological oceanography of the tropics as well as other marine and fresh-water environments.

Russell-Hunter, W.D., *The Biology of Higher Invertebrates*. London, England: The MacMillan Company, 1969. This is the companion volume to the one listed above, and the combination will guide you through more specifics on the invertebrates than we had space for in this volume.

CHAPTER 7

Chubb, Lawrence John, *Geology of the Marquesas Islands*. New York, NY: Kraus Reprint Company, 1971. This is a reprint of a Bishop Museum Publication (#68) first published in 1930 in Honolulu, HI. It is aimed at the geologist in the audience, but it does contain some of the best details available concerning these unusual islands.

Davis, William M., *The Coral Reef Problem*. Huntington, NY: Robert E. Krieger Publishing Company, 1976. This is a reprinting of the 1928 volume originally published by the American Geographical Society as Special Publication No. 9. If you are fascinated by the way islands are shaped by winds, waves, and rainfall you will find this book a delight. Davis visited most of the islands in the Pacific, and many in other oceans of the world in preparing this work. It was intended to settle the question of whether or not subsidence was occurring, and although he may not have managed to convince all the skeptics of his day, the book is impressive anyway. The islands of the tropical Atlantic are given relatively little space, but the patterns he establishes are useful in that area as well.

CHAPTER 8

Scientific American Editorial Staff, *Continents Adrift and Continents Aground*. San Francisco, CA: W.H. Freeman and Co., 1976. This is a collection of articles from *Scientific American* magazine, covering a number of aspects of the modern understanding of plate tectonics.

Tarling, Don, and Maureen Tarling, *Continental Drift: A Study of the Earth's Moving Surface*. New York, NY: Doubleday and Company, 1971. This little paperback contains an excellent summary of the theory and evidence for plate tectonics as of the late 1960s. It is intended for the layperson, and although a great deal of important information has been uncovered since the book was printed, you will still find it useful in describing the key aspects of the theory.

CHAPTER 9

Carter, John, ed., *Pacific Islands Yearbook and Who's Who*. Sydney, NSW Australia: Pacific Publishing Pty. Ltd., 1981.

Hart, Jerrems C., and William T. Stone, *A Cruising Guide to the Caribbean and the Bahamas*. New York, NY: Dodd, Mead, and Company, 1976. For the cruising sailor this volume has a great deal of useful information, and it is presented in a readable, informal fashion.

Ullman, James Ramsey, and Al Dinhofer, *Caribbean Here and Now*. New York, NY: The MacMillan Company, 1968. This book has a lot of useful data on the islands of the Caribbean, including tidbits on clothing, food, and night life.

APPENDIX

American Red Cross, *Standard First Aid and Personal Safety*. Garden City, NY: Doubleday and Company

Eastman, Peter F., *Advanced First Aid Afloat* (2nd ed.). Cambridge, MD: Cornell Maritime Press, 1974.

Halstead, Bruce, *Poisonous and Venomous Marine Animals*. Princeton, NJ: The Darwin Press, 1978. This is a volume to visit and admire, but it weighs in at over ten pounds, so it is not an ideal traveling companion. This is a reference to check if you would like additional details on marine organisms with venomous spines, stings, or other defenses as well as those poisonous to eat. It does not treat those that are dangerous for other reasons, for which I would suggest you refer to the next reference.

Halstead, Bruce, *Dangerous Marine Animals*. Cambridge, MD: Cornell Maritime Press, 1959. This is a more manageably sized work and will not tire your arms quite as much when you carry it around.

Martini, F., and R.M. Nilson, "Planning for Emergencies" in *The Best of Sail Cruising*. Boston, MA: Sail Books, 1977. This chapter deals with the preparation of a medical locker for offshore sailing.

The Merck Manual of Diagnosis and Therapy. Rahway, NJ: Merck, Sharp, and Dohme Research Labs, Division of Merck and Co., 1981. This volume is periodically updated and contains chapters covering the symptoms and treatment of a wide variety of medical problems. It is not oriented toward emergencies and does not deal with first aid at all, but it would be good to have in addition to the other references if you are planning to spend long periods of time removed from medical counsel.

Credits

Figures 1–1 and 6–8(c): Reprinted by permission of Macmillan Publishing Company, Inc. from *Aquatic Productivity* by W.D. Russell-Hunter. Copyright © 1970 by W.D. Russell-Hunter.

Figures 1–6, 7–3(a), 7–4, 7–5(c), 7–6(a), 7–7(a), 7–8, 7–9(a) (adapted), 7–10, 7–11 (adapted), 7–14(f). Island sketches redrawn from *The Coral Reef Problem* by William M. Davis. Copyright © 1928 by the American Geographical Society of New York. Reprinted by Robert E. Krieger Publishing Co., Melbourne, FL.

Figure 1–7: Reproduced courtesy of the State of Hawaii Department of Land and Natural Resources, Division of Water and Land Development from *Median Rainfall, State of Hawaii, 1959.*

Figure 1–9: Reprinted by permission of Dodd, Mead and Company, Inc., from *Oceanography and Seamanship* by William G. Van Dorn. Copyright © 1974 by William G. Van Dorn.

Figures 2–1 (c), (d), (e) and (f): reprinted with permission of Macmillan Publishing Co., Inc., from *A Biology of Lower Invertebrates* by W.D. Russell-Hunter. Copyright © 1968 by W.D. Russell-Hunter. (e) and (f) adapted from Vaughan, Thomas Wayland; and John West Wells (1943): Revision of the Suborders, Families, and Genera of the Scleractina; Special Papers No. 44, Geological Society of America.

Figure 2–2: Reprinted with permission of the American Geological Society of America from *A Revision of the Suborders, Families, and Genera of the Scleractinia* by Thomas W. Vaughn and John W. Wells.

Figures 2–3 and 2–4(b): Reprinted with permission of Yale University Press from *Atoll Environment and Ecology* by Herold J. Wiens. Copyright © 1962 by Yale University. Adapted from J.W. Wells, *Recent Corals of the Marshall Islands, Bikini, and Nearby Atolls, II, Oceanography (Biologic).* Reston, VA: U.S. Geologica Society Prof. Pap. 260-I, pp. 385–486. Figure 2–4(b) originally from J.I. Tracey, Jr., P.E. Cloud, and K.O. Emery, "Conspicuous Features of Organic Reef," *Atoll Research Bulletin*, no. 46 (15 August 1955).

Figure 2–7: Reprinted with permission of Dodd, Mead & Co. from *Oceanography and Seamanship*, © 1974 by William G. Van Dorn.

Figure 2–9: (a) Produced from portions of BA chart 2867 with the sanction of the Controller, HM Stationery Office, and the Hydrographer of the Navy.

Figure 3–1: Reprinted by permission of Chapman and Hall, Ltd. from J. Moy-Thomas and R.S. Miles, *Paleozoic Fishes* (New York: W.B. Saunders Company, 1971).

Figures 3–3, 3–4, 3–5, 3–6, and 3–7: Silhouettes adapted from P. Humphrey Greenwood, Donn E. Rosen, Stanley H. Weitzman, and George S. Myers, *Phyletic Studies of Teleostean Fishes, with a Provisional Classification of Living Forms.* Bulletin of the American Museum of Natural History, New York, NY, Volume 131, article 4 (1966). Courtesy of the American Museum of Natural History.

Figure 3–8: Reprinted with the permission of the University of Washington Press from Hermann Friedrich, *Marine Biology*, trans. Gwynne Vevers. Copyright © 1969 by the University of Washington Press. Copyright ©

1969 in this translation by Sidgwick and Jackson, Limited. This illustration was adapted from E.F. Abel (1962) "Freiwasserbeobachtungen an Fischen im Golf von Neapal als Beitrag zur Kenntnis ihrer Okologie und ihres Verhaltens" *Intern. Rev. qes. Hydrobiol.*, 47:219–290. With permission of Akademie-Velag.

Figure 4–2: (a) and (b) reprinted by permission of Columbia University Press from *The Life of Sharks* by Paul Budker. Copyright © 1971 by Paul Budker. English translation © 1971 by George Weidenfeld and Nicholson, Ltd. (c) and (d) reprinted by permission of The University of Chicago Press from Bernhard Peyer, *Comparative Odontology*, trans. R. Zangerl. Copyright © 1968 by The University of Chicago. After H.H. Landolt (1947) "Ueber den Zahnwechsel bei Selachiern," *Revue Suisse de Zool.* 54 (as referenced in Peyer, 1968). With permission of *Revue Suisse de Zool.*

Figure 4–3: (a) and (d) reprinted by permission of Columbia University Press from *The Life of Sharks* by Paul Budker. Copyright © 1971 by Paul Budker. English translation © 1971 George Weidenfeld and Nicholson.

Figure 4–5: Data extracted with the permission of the Mote Marine Laboratory from *Shark Attacks Against Man, A Program of Data Reduction and Analysis* by H. David Baldridge, Ph.D.

Figure 5–4: (c) reprinted by permission of Cornell University Press and Hutchinson Publishing Group, Ltd. from E.J. Slijper, *Whales*, 2nd English ed. published by Cornell University Press, 1979. English translation copyright © 1962 Hutchinson & Co., Ltd.

Figure 5–5: (a) and (b) reprinted by permission of Cornell University Press from E.J. Slijper, *Whales*, 2nd ed., trans. A.J. Pomerans. Copyright © 1962 Hutchinson & Co., Ltd.

Figure 5–6: (a) reprinted by permission of Cornell University Press from E.J. Slijper, *Whales*, 2nd ed., trans. A.J. Pomerans. Copyright © 1962 Hutchinson & Co., Ltd.

Figure 6–1(b): Reprinted with permission of Macmillan Publishing Co., Inc., from *A Biology of Lower Invertebrates* by W.D. Russell-Hunter. Copyright © 1968 by W.D. Russell-Hunter.

Figures 6–3: (a) to (e) and 6—7(e) reprinted with permission of Macmillan Publishing Company, Inc. from *A Biology of Higher Invertebrates* by W.D. Russell-Hunter. Copyright © 1969 by W.D. Russell-Hunter.

Figure 6–4: (b), (c), and (d) reprinted with permission of W.B. Saunders Company, CBS College Publishing, from *Invertebrate Zoology*, 3rd ed., by Robert D. Barnes. Copyright © 1974 by W.B. Saunders Company. (b) and (c) after P. Fauvel et al., "Embranchement des Annelides" in P. Grasse (ed.) *Traite de Zoologie*, Vol. 5, pt. 1, pp. 3–386. Reprinted by permission Masson, Editeur s.a. (e) reprinted from Henry Alleyne Nicholson *Manual of Zoology*, 2nd ed. ((New York: D. Appleton and Co., 1893).

Figure 6–5: (a), (b), (c) reprinted with permission of W.B. Saunders Company from *Invertebrate Zoology*, 2nd ed., by Robert D. Barnes. Copyright © 1968 by W.B. Saunders Company. (d), (e) reprinted from Henry Alleyne Nicholson *Manual of Zoology*, 2nd ed. (New York: D. Appleton and Co., 1893).

Figure 7–6: (c) reprinted by permission of the University Press of Hawaii from *Volcanoes in the Sea* by Gordon A. Macdonald and Agatin T. Abbott. Copyright © 1970 by University of Hawaii Press.

Index

Advanced First Aid Afloat (Eastman), 362
Advection cell, 6, 9, 23, 199
Ahe Atoll, 153
Ailinginae Island, 273
Aleutian island arc, 207
Aleutian trench, 203, 215
Algae, 139–40, 161
Ambergris, 122
American Red Cross, 362
Amphibians, 91, 100, 101
  air breathing system of, 98
  body fluids of, 97
  locomotion in, 97
  regulation of body temperature in, 94, 95
  reproduction in, 99
Ampullary system, 87
Anegada, 304
Anemenone fish, 160
Anemones, see Sea anemones
Angelfishes, 66, 161
Anglerfishes, 69
Anguilla, 208, 314–17
Annelids, 146–49
Antigua, 189, 314–17
Antilles, see Greater Antilles; Lesser Antilles
Arawak Indians, 224
Arthropods, 155–59
Aruba, 172, 186, 307, 380
Ascension Islands, 19, 210
Ata Island, 255
Athletes foot, 365
Atolls, 34–47, 181, 184, 189
Augers, 152
Austral Islands, 217–19, 249–51
Aunu'u, 172
Aves Island, 307
Azores, 122

Babelthuap Island, 282
Bacterial infections, 366–69
Bahamas, 38, 187, 189, 226, 285–86
Bahamas Banks, 209, 221
Baleen whales, 122–27, 135
  collision of ships with, 133, 134
  speed of, 129
Banaba Island, 261
Banks Islands, 207
Barbados, 172, 221, 307, 332–34
Barbuda, 314
Barnacles, 159, 162

Barracuda, 70
  attacks by, 347–49, 351
  poisoning from eating, 359
Barrier reefs, 45, 181, 182, 184
Basking shark, 80
Basse-Terre, 311
Bays, formation of, 177
Beaked whales, 117
Benguela Current, 19, 31
Bermuda, 19, 187, 210, 226, 372
Bikini Atoll, 218, 273
Bivalve molluscs, 153, 162
Blenny, 68
Bligh, Captain, 225
Blue whales, 124, 125
  growth rate of young, 129
  lifespan of, 129
Bonaire, 186
Bonin Islands, 207
Bony fishes, 48–50, 58
Bottlenose dolphin, 117–18
  intelligence of, 131–32
  sonar system of, 130
  speed of, 129
Bougainville, Captain, 225
Bougainville Islands, 270
Bounty (ship), 237
Boxfish, 74, 356
Break-bone fever, 379
Brittle stars, 143, 145, 162
Brown algae, 139
Budding, 27
Bulca Islands, 270
Butterfly fishes, 66, 163

Caicos Islands, 287–89
Caldera, 171
Candidiasis, 366
Canton Island, 261
Carapace, 155
Cardinalfish, 72, 162
Carib Indians, 224–25
Carolines, 219, 220, 276–78
Carriacou, 329
Cartilaginous fishes, 48, 78
Catastrophic theory, 195
Cayman Brac Island, 292
Cayman Islands, 209, 292–94
Centipedes, 380
Cephalopods, 153–55, 163, 345–46, 348, 349

Cetaceans, *see* Whales
Chambered nautilus, 154
Charles Darwin Research Station, 230
Chlorophyll, 137, 138
Cholera, 371, 373, 382, 383
Chondrichthyes, 48
  dangerous, 346
Chordates, 48
Christmas Island, 45, 46, 243
Ciguatoxin (CTX), 358–60
Cilia, 25
Clams, 153
Cliff formation, 172–74
Climate, cyclical changes in, 186
Cobras, 106
Coconut crabs, 157
Coelenteratas, 24, 142–43, 342–44, 350
  symbiosis of fish and, 160
Cold-blooded animals, *see* Ectotherms
Columbus, Christopher, 285, 290, 292, 295,
    299, 303, 304, 311, 314
Conch, 150
Cone shells, 150, 345, 350, 351
Contaminated seafood, 357–61
Continental drift, 195–96
Cook, Captain, 225
Cook Islands, 217, 218, 249–51
Copepods, 159–61, 164
Copernicus, 197
Coral reefs, 24–47
  anatomy of polyps, 25–27
  atolls, 34–47
  bacterial activity of, 22
  biological activity around, 31–33
  climatic cycles and, 186–87
  destruction of, 166–68
  energy relationships among inhabitants
    of, 160–66
  fishes of, 51–76
  formation of, 176, 178–85
  invertebrates of, 140–59
  ocean currents and, 18–19
  plants of, 136–40
  reproduction of, 27–28
  shapes of, 33–34
  sharks of, 87, 90
Coral Reefs (Darwin), 181
Coralline algae, 38, 139–40
Corals, 142, 162
  dangerous, 342–44, 351
Coriolis effect, 9, 18, 20
Crabs, 157, 163, 357
Crime rates, 380–81
Crinoids, 144, 146
Crocodiles, 101, 103, 104, 107, 108, 348
Crown-of-thorns starfish, 144, 150, 345,
    349, 351, 354

Crustaceans, 155–59
Cuba, 209, 285, 290, 292, 295
  geology of, 176
  rabies in, 380
Cubomedusae, 343
Curacao, 186
Cuttlefish, 154
Cyclones, 15, 16

Damselfish, 67, 161, 162, 164
Dangerous Archipelago, 217, 237
Dangerous organisms, 342–54
  avoiding incidents with, 348–51
  treating injuries from, 351–54
Darwin, Charles, 181, 197
Dengue fever, 375, 379
Denticles, 80, 82
Desirade, 311
Detritus, 162
Dinosaurs, 95, 96, 103
Diptheria, 382, 383
"Doldrums," 9
Dolphins, 117–19, 130, 135, 360
  intelligence of, 131–32
  leaping by, 129
  lifespan of, 129
  ornery behavior in, 133
  sharks and, 92, 130–31
  speed of, 129
  training of, 132–33
Dominica, 311, 320–21, 325
Dominican Republic, 295–98, 380, 384
Dugongs, 113–15, 135

Earthquakes, 199
East Pacific Barrier, 206
East Pacific Rise (EPR), 202–5, 208, 213, 218
Easter Island, 15, 210, 223, 236
Eastman, Peter, 362
Echnioderms, 143–47, 344–45
Echolocation, 110, 117, 118, 121, 134
Ectodermis, 27
Ectotherms, 94–97
Eel grasses, 138–39
Eels, 67
  dangerous, *see* Moray eels
Efate Island, 267
Elephantitis, 379
Elephants, 112
Ellice Island, 218, 243, 261–63
Encephalitis, 375, 379
Endemic species, 58
Endodermis, 27
Endotherms, 95, 96
Enewitok Atoll, 273
Enzymes, 94
Epidermis, 27

Erosion, 172
Espiritu Santo Island, 267
Essex (ship), 133
Estuarine crocodiles, *see* Crocodiles
Eua, 189

Falcon Island, 189
Fatu Hiva, 220
Featherduster worm, 149, 162
Featherstars, 146
Fiji, 207, 223, 258–60
  crocodiles of, 103
  dangerous marine organisms of, 345
  reefs of, 181, 185, 189
  snakes of, 106, 380
Filariasis, 375, 379
Filefishes, 74, 356
Finback whales, 124, 125
  speed of, 129
Fire corals, 343
Fishes, 48–76
  advertisers, 72–74
  commandos, 69–70
  energy accounts of, 53–55
  evolution of, 48–50, 58
  evolution of land animals from, 93–94,
    97, 99
  generalists, 60–62
  grazers, 70–72
  maneuverers, 64–67
  mechanism for change in species of,
    55–58
  natural selection and, 52–53
  specialization of, 59–60
  speeders, 62–64
  wrigglers, 67–68
Florida Bank, 221
Flutefish, 70
Fonuafoo Island, 189
Food poisoning, 371, 373–75
French Oceania, 237, 240
Fringing reefs, 45, 178, 181, 182, 184
Fringing/barrier reef intergrades, 184
Frogs, 95
Fugu, 355
Funafuti Atoll, 218, 261
Fungal rashes, 365

Galapagos, 19, 119, 174, 218, 226, 230–32,
  347
  iguanas of, 101–2
  sea lions of, 110
  whales of, 121, 122
Gambier Islands, 217
Gamma globulin, 382, 383
Garbage dumping, 167
Gastrodermis, 27

Gastroenteritis, 371–75
Gastropods, 150–53
Geology:
  changing theories in, 195, 197
  of islands, 171–72
German measles, 382
Giant clams, 153
Gilbert Islands, 218, 243, 261–63
Gizo Island, 270
Glacial periods, 186
Glasses, 391
Goatfish, 72
Grand Cayman Island, 292
Grand-Terre, 311
Great white shark, 88–89
  whales and, 130
Greater Antilles, 209, 224, 290–306
Green algae, 139
Green flies, 375
Green turtles, 105
Grenada, 208, 329-31, 380
Grenadines, 329–31
Grey sharks, 90
Grey whales, 124, 125
Groupers, 62, 163, 164
Grunts, 72
Guadalcanal Island, 270
Guadeloupe, 311–13
Guam, 225, 279–81, 372
Gulf Stream, 19
Guyouts, 174

Ha'apai Islands, 255
Haiti, 295–98, 380, 384
Haole rot, 365
Harp seals, 112
Hawaiian Islands, 13, 15–16, 205, 213–18,
    224–26, 246–48, 347, 372
  ciguatera poisoning in, 358
  dangerous marine organisms of, 343
  dolphins of, 118
  fishes of, 58
  geology of, 171, 172, 176, 190
  reefs of, 28, 38, 167, 181, 187
  sea snakes of, 106
  seals of, 112
  shark attacks in, 90–91
  shellfish of, 150
  squids of, 154
  whales of, 126
Hawksbill turtles, 105, 106
Heat prostration, 369–70
Heat stroke, 370–71
Helmets, 152
Hepatitis A, 382
Hermit crabs, 157, 160

Hispaniola, 209, 285, 290, 295–98
geology of, 176
malaria in, 375
Histamine, 357, 358
Holoplankton, 159
"Horse latitudes," 9
Hotspots, 209–20
Humidity, medical problems related to, 364–66
Humpback whales, 124–28
leaping by, 129
songs of, 126–27
Hurricanes, 16
Hydrozoans, 142–43, 343
Hypothermia, 109, 134

Iguanas, marine, 101–2, 107, 108, 110
Iles des Santes, 311
Immunizations, 381–83
Indonesia, 29, 103
Infectious diseases, 373, 374, 379–80
Insects, 93
diseases carried by, 375, 379
International Certificate of Vaccination, 381, 382
Intertropical convergence (ITC), 9, 15, 18
Island arcs, 206–9
Island chains, 209–20
Islas Testigos, 307
Isle Ouen, 264
Isle of Pines, 264
Isostasy, 195

Jacks, 64
Jamaica, 177, 209, 290–94
Japan, islands of, 207
Japan trench, 203
Japanese-B encephalitis, 379
Jellyfish, 142–43, 162, 163, 342–44, 351
Johnston Island, 59, 243

Kahoolawe, 190, 246
Kauai, 215, 246
Keratin, 97
Kicker Rock, 174
Killer whales, 117, 119, 135, 163, 348
intelligence of, 132
sharks and, 130
Kingman Reef, 218
Kiribati Republic, 243, 261–63
Koko Seamount, 215
Kona storms, 16
Krill, 122, 124, 125, 164
Kurile Islands, 207
Kurile trench, 203
Kuroshio Current, 18

Kusaie Island, 219
Kwajalein Atoll, 273

Lagoons, 38–41, 47
Lanai, 190, 246
Lau Islands, 207
Leatherback turtles, 106, 107
Leeward Islands, 209, 213, 215, 246, 307, 308–24
Leprosy, 379–80
Lesser Antilles, 224, 307–41, 380
Limpets, 150, 161
Line Island, 45, 118, 218, 243-45, 358
Lionfish, 74, 347
Little Cayman Island, 292
Lizardfishes, 69
Lizards:
marine, 101
body temperature of, 95
Lobster, 357
Loggerhead turtles, 106

MacDonald Seamount, 217
Mackerel, 63, 64, 356
Mackerel sharks, 89–90
Magellan, Ferdinand, 225, 287
Magma, 198
Mahi-mahi fish, 360
Mako shark, 89
Malaria, 375, 384
Malaysia, 103, 106
Mammals, 93–101
air breathing system of, 98
body fluids of, 97
dangerous, 348
food location of, 98
locomotion in, 97
marine, 108–35
regulation of body temperature in, 94–97
reproduction in, 99
Manatees, 113, 135
Mangaia Island, 218
Mangereva, 217
Mangroves, 138–39, 167–68
Marianas Islands, 207, 219, 224
Marianas trench, 203
Marie Galante, 189, 311
Marine iguanas, 101–2, 107, 108, 110
Marlin, 360
Marquesas Islands, 15, 19, 102, 119, 187, 189, 190, 205, 220, 225, 233–35, 347
coral reefs of, 29, 178
dolphins of, 118
insects of, 375
sea snakes of, 106

Marshall Islands, 15, 218, 219, 224, 273–75, 358
Martinique, 173, 322, 325, 380
Maui, 215
Mauke Island, 218
Measles, 382
Medical problems and precautions, 361–85
Medications, 381
Medusae, 142, 143
Meiji Seamount, 215
Melanesia, 113, 114
Melanesians, 223, 226
Melon, 117, 121
Melville, Herman, 133, 233
Meroplankton, 159
Microcarnivores, 162
Micronesia, 103, 113
Micronesia, Federated States of, 219, 276–79
Micronesians, 224, 226
Mid-Atlantic Ridge (MAR), 210
Midwater shark, 88
Minke, 135
Mitres, 152
Moby Dick (Melville), 133
Molokai, 172, 190
Molluscs, 149–55, 345–46
Moniliasis, 366
Monk seals, 112, 135, 360
Montserrat, 318–19
Moonsnails, 152
Moorea, 217
Moray eels, 347, 349, 351, 359
Mosquitos, 375, 379
Murexes, 152
Mysticete whales, 123, 124

Natural selection, 52–53 55, 94, 115, 206
Nauru Island, 261
Navassa, 189
Needlefish, 70
Nemotocysts, 25, 162, 342, 344
Netherlands Antilles, 209, 226
    northern sector, 308–10
    southern sector, 338–40
Neuromasts, 83, 87
Nevis, 314
New Caledonia, 114, 166–67, 220, 223, 264–66
New Guinea, 270
New Hebrides, 103, 207, 220, 223, 267–69, 384
New Providence Island, 286
New Stone Age, 223
New Zealand, 224
Ngulu Islands, 219

Niihau, 246
Niuafoo Island, 255
Niuatobutabu Island, 255
Niue Island, 255
"No-no" flies, 375
North Marianas, Commonwealth of, 279–81
Nuclear weapons testing, 167
Nuku Hiva, 189–91, 220, 233

Oahu, 187, 190
Ocean currents, 16–20
    and coral, 28–29
Ocean Island, 261
Octopus, 155, 345, 351, 357
Odontocetes, 117–22, 134
Old Stone Age, 223
Omoo (Melville), 233
Oolites, 221
Osteichthyes, 48
    dangerous, 346–47
Otitis externa, 365–66

Painted turtles, 107
Palau Islands, 219, 226, 279, 282–84
Palmerston atoll, 218
Pangaea, 195, 203–5, 210
Papua, 270
Paralytic shellfish poisoning (PSP), 359–60
Parasites, 371, 373, 374
Parrotfish, 70–71, 161, 163
Patch reefs, 39
Peru Current, 19, 21, 29, 101, 102, 122, 187, 218, 230
Peysonnel (naturalist), 24
Philippines, 28, 106, 225
Phoenix Islands, 189, 261
Photosynthesis, 137, 140
Phytoplakton, 139, 157, 158, 160–62, 164
Pinnipeds, 108, 111, 112
Pipefish, 69–70
Pitcairn Island, 217, 237
Planation, 175
Plankton blooms, 22
Plants, 136–40
Planulae, 28
Plate techtonics, 197–206
Polio, 382
Pollution, 23, 109
Polynesians, 223–24, 226
Polyps, 142–43
Ponape Island, 276
Porbeagle shark, 89
Porcupine fish, 73
Porifera, 140

Porpoises, 118, 130, 135
  lifespan of, 129
Portuguese man-o-war, 160, 343
Prickly heat, 365
Protein intake, 368
Puerto Rico, 113, 209, 292, 299–301
  rabies in, 380
  sanitation standards in, 372
  whales of, 126
Puffers, 161, 163, 355

Queen conch, 150

Rabbitfishes, 48
Rabies, 380, 382
Radula, 150
Rapa, 217
Raraka Atoll, 153
Raroia Atoll, 41
Rarotonga, 249
Rashes:
  from allergic reaction to sunlight, 363–64
  humidity and, 364–65
Rays, 48, 346
Red algae, 139
Red tide, 359
Redonda, 314
Remoras, 129
Reptiles, 93–108
  air breathing system of, 98
  body fluids of, 97
  dangerous, 348
  locomotion in, 97
  marine, 101–8, 135
  regulation of body temperature in, 94–97
  reproduction in, 99
Right whales, 124
"Ring of Fire," 208
Ringworm, 365
Rocas Islands, 38
Rognelap Island, 273
Rongerik Atoll, 273
Rorquals, 124–25
Rose Island, 252
Rostrum, 117
Rubella, 382
Ruruta, 218

Saba, 308
Saipan Island, 279
St. Barthelamy, 311
St. Croix, 302
St. Eustatius, 308
St. Helena, 210
St. John, 302
St. Kitts, 314

St. Lucia, 326–27, 380
St. Maarten, 308
St. Martin, 311
St. Paul's Rocks, 174
St. Thomas, 302
St. Vincent, 326–27, 329
Salamanders, 95, 97
Sala-Y-Gomez, 210
Salt water crocodiles, 101, 103, 104, 107, 108
Samoa, 146, 219, 220, 252-54
  changes in reefs of, 167
  cliffs of, 172
  dogs of, 380
  sea snakes of, 106
San Crostobal Island, 270
Santa Cruz Islands, 207
Savai'i Island, 219
Scales of fishes, 50
Scomberotoxin, 356, 357
Scorpionfishes, 69, 347, 349, 351
Scorpions, 380
Scrimshaw, 122
Sea anemones, 24, 25, 142, 160, 163
  dangerous, 342–44
  poisoning from eating, 356
Sea cows, 101, 112–15
  food sources of, 139
Sea cucumbers, 143–46, 162
Sea lions, 101, 108–12, 134, 135, 348
Sea snakes, 101, 103, 104, 106–8, 135, 348, 351, 353
Sea turtles, 101, 103–8, 134
  food sources of, 139
  poisoning from eating, 356
Sea urchins, 143, 145, 161, 344–45, 349–51, 356
Sea wasps, 343, 353
Seafood poisoning, 354–61
Seals, 101, 108–12, 135
Sei whales, 124
Sexual robots, 149
Shagreen, 80
Sharks, 48, 77–92, 163
  anatomy of, 78–80
  attacks by, 77–78, 90–92, 342, 347–49, 351
  poisoning from eating, 356
  reproduction of, 80
  sensory system of, 83–88
  teeth of, 82–83
  whales and, 130–31
Shellfish, 149–55, 345–46
  poisoning from eating, 357, 359–60
Shipworm, 153
Shrimp, 157, 160
Sirenians, 112–16, 134, 135
Skates, 48, 346

Snails, 150
Snakes:
  terrestrial, 380
  See also Sea snakes
Snappers, 62, 163, 164, 359
Snapping shrimp, 157, 163
Snapping turtles, 107
Society Islands, 217, 240–42
  reefs of, 181
  sea snakes of, 106
Solar energy, 136–37
Solomon Islands, 103, 204, 207, 223, 270–72, 384
  malaria in, 375
  reefs of, 189
  snakes of, 380
Sombrero, 189, 314
Sperm whales, 117, 119–22, 135
  lifespan of, 129
  sharks and, 130
  vessels attacked by, 133
Spermaceti, 121
Spice Islands, *see* Philippines
Spinners, 118
Spiny lobsters, 155–57
Sponges, 140–42, 162, 356
Spotted dolphins, 118
Squids, 121, 154–55
Squirrelfish, 62, 163
Standard First Aid and Personal Safety (American Red Cross), 362
Staph bacteria, 366–68
Starfishes, 143, 144, 163, 344–45, 349, 351
Sting-rays, 346, 349
Stone age, 223
Stonefishes, 69, 74, 347, 354
Subtropical convergences (STCs), 9–10, 15, 18
Subduction, 199, 201
Sunlight:
  overexposure to, 363–64
  plants and, 136–40
Surgeonfish, 72, 73, 161
  injuries from, 346–47, 349, 351
  poisoning from eating, 359
Swim bladder, 50, 51, 94
Swimmer's ear, 365–66
Symbiosis, 160

Tafahi Island, 255
Tahiti, 217, 240
  changes in reefs of, 167
  medical facilities of, 384
  sanitation standards in, 372
Tahiti'iti, 217
Taievavae, 217
Tarawa Atoll, 261

Temperature, medical problems related to, 369–71
Terrestrial animals, dangerous, 380–81
Tetanus, 382, 383
Tetrodotoxon (TTX), 355, 357
Thecae, 27
Thermoclines, 4, 5, 20–22, 125
Tidal cycles, 47
Tiger sharks, 90, 130
Tobago, 220, 307, 355–57, 380
Tongan Islands, 204, 206–7, 255–57
  dogs of, 380
  reefs of, 189
  sea snakes of, 106
Tongatapu Island, 255
Toothed whales, 117–22
Tortoal, 304
Trachoma, 379–80
Tradewinds, 15–16, 18, 172
Triggerfish, 74, 161, 356
Trinidad, 220, 307, 335–37, 380
Triton's trumpet, 150, 163
Tropical ulcer, 368
Truk Island, 219, 276
Trumpetfish, 69–70
Tubae, 218
Tubai Island, 249
Tuberculosis, 379–80
Tubeworms, 162
Tuna, 63, 64, 360
  dolphins and, 119
  poisoning from eating, 356
Triomotus Islands, 153, 217, 218, 237–39
  nuclear weapons testing in, 167
Turks Islands, 287–89
Turtles, sea, 101, 103–8, 134
Tutuila Island, 13, 219, 252, 381
  geography of, 172, 187–89
Tuvalu Islands, 261–63
Typee (Melville), 233
Typhoid, 371, 382, 383

Upolu Island, 252
Upwellings, 20, 21
Urchins, *see* Sea urchins
Utirik Island, 273

Vanua Levu Island, 258
Vanuata, Republic of, 267–69, 384
Vava'u Island, 255
Vegetarians, 368
Virgin Gorda, 304
Virgin Islands, 209, 292–306
Viruses, 379
Vitamin A, 356
Vitamin C, 368
Viti Levu Island, 258

Volcanic islands, 171–76
    continental drift and, 197
    reef formation and, 176, 178–85, 189
Volcano Islands, 207

Wake Island, 273
Walruses, 108, 112
Wegener, Alfred, 195, 197
Whale shark, 88
Whales, 101, 115–36
    baleen, 122–27
    growth rate of young, 129
    intelligence of, 131–32
    leaping by, 129
    lifespan of, 129

sharks and, 130–31
speed of, 129
toothed, 117–22
vessels attacked by, 133–34
Windward Islands, 208, 307, 325–31
World Health Organization, 381, 382
Worms, annelid, 146–49, 162, 163
Wrasses, 70–72, 162

Yap Islands, 219, 276
Yeast-related rashes, 365
Yellow fever, 382

Zooplankton, 157–62
Zooxanthellae, 31–33, 37